KU-504-333

Beautiful Boy

Praise for *Beautiful Boy*:

'A brilliant, harrowing, heartbreaking, fascinating story, full of beautiful moments and hard-won wisdom. This book will save a lot of lives and heal a lot of hearts.'   —Anne Lamott

'Those of us who love an addict – or are addicts ourselves – will find *Beautiful Boy* a revelation. David Sheff knows all too well what must be endured with faith, and his extraordinary book describes it better than anything else I've read. While painfully candid, *Beautiful Boy* is equally optimistic and powerful.'

—Martin Sheen, actor

'Both takes on this story are riveting, brilliantly written, thoughtful, searingly honest and equally essential. They should be mandatory reading for every teenager and every parent of one.' —*Daily Mail*

'My generation experimented with drugs and, now that we are parents, we're caught off guard: we never contemplated having to face what David Sheff has faced. He writes with candour, courage and grace of his family's harrowing – and sadly not atypical – story. *Beautiful Boy* is an important book. It is moving, timely and startlingly beautiful.'

—Sir Richard Branson, chairman, Virgin Group

'Moving, painfully honest, very revealing, it tells a story which just never gets told and which is extraordinarily important.'

—Rosie Boycott

'An extraordinary story of pain, perseverance, and hope.'
—William C. Moyers, author of *Broken*

'Here are the mysteries of love and grief, fear and faith, power and surrender. Here is a perilous, redemptive read: a text for any father, any parent, anyone who has ever wrestled with holding on and letting go.'

—Thomas Lynch, author of *The Undertaking and Bodies in Motion and at Rest*

'*Beautiful Boy* is so beautifully written that it will come as a welcome balm to millions of parents and loved ones who thought they were making this journey alone.'

—Armistead Maupin, author of *Michael Tolliver Lives* and *The Night Listener*

'An honest, hopeful book, coming at a propitious moment in the meth epidemic.'   —*Publishers Weekly*

'An excellent book that all parents can relate to whatever their children's situation.'   —*Library Journal*, starred review

'A clear picture of what meth addiction does to a user and those who love him that may help other families better cope with this growing problem.'   —*Kirkus Reviews*

Beautiful Boy

David Sheff

A Father's Journey Through
His Son's Meth Addiction

SCRIBNER

LONDON NEW YORK TORONTO SYDNEY NEW DELHI

First published in Great Britain by Simon & Schuster UK Ltd, 2008
This edition published by Scribner, an imprint of Simon & Schuster UK Ltd, 2018
A CBS COMPANY

Copyright © David Sheff, 2008
Afterword © David Sheff, 2018

SCRIBNER and design are registered trademarks of The Gale Group, Inc.,
used under licence by Simon & Schuster Inc.

The right of David Sheff to be identified as the author of this work has been asserted
in accordance with the Copyright, Designs and Patents Act, 1988.

5 7 9 10 8 6

Simon & Schuster UK Ltd
1st Floor
222 Gray's Inn Road
London WC1X 8HB

www.simonandschuster.co.uk
www.simonandschuster.com.au
www.simonandschuster.co.in

Simon & Schuster Australia, Sydney
Simon & Schuster India, New Delhi

The author and publishers have made all reasonable efforts to contact
copyright-holders for permission, and apologise for any omissions or errors in
the form of credits given. Corrections may be made to future printings.

A CIP catalogue for this book is
available from the British Library.

Paperback ISBN: 978-1-4711-8220-4
Film tie-in ISBN: 978-1-4711-7793-4
eBook ISBN: 978-1-4711-7396-7

Typeset in Fournier by M Rules
Printed and bound by CPI Group (UK) Ltd, Croydon, CR0 4YY

Simon & Schuster UK Ltd are committed to sourcing paper
that is made from wood grown in sustainable forests and support the Forest
Stewardship Council, the leading international forest certification organisation.
Our books displaying the FSC logo are printed on FSC certified paper.

This book is dedicated to the women and men who devote their lives to understanding and combating addiction at rehabs, hospitals, research centers, sober-living and halfway houses, organizations dedicated to education about drug abuse, and so on, as well as the anonymous — brave and devoted, the ones who keep coming back — at countless twelve-step meetings every day and night in every large city and small town in the United States and throughout the world — to them and their families: the people who understand my family's story because they have lived and are living it, the families of the addicted — their children, brothers and sisters, friends, partners, husbands and wives, and parents like me. "It's just that you can't help them and it's all so discouraging," wrote F. Scott Fitzgerald. But the truth is, you do help them and you help one another. You helped me. Along with them, this book is dedicated to my wife, Karen Barbour, and my children, Nic, Jasper, and Daisy Sheff.

Contents

When you cross the street,
Take my hand.

—JOHN LENNON,
"Beautiful Boy (Darling Boy)"

Introduction

It hurts so bad that I cannot save him, protect
him, keep him out of harm's way, shield him
from pain. What good are fathers if not for
these things?

—THOMAS LYNCH, "The Way We Are"

"*Howdy Pop, God, I miss you guys so much. I can't wait to see
you all. Only one more day!!! Woo-hoo.*"

Nic is emailing from college on the evening before he arrives
home for summer vacation. Jasper and Daisy, our eight- and five-
year-olds, are sitting at the kitchen table cutting, pasting, and
coloring notes and welcome-home banners for his homecoming.
They have not seen their big brother in six months.

In the morning, when it's time to leave for the airport, I go
outside to round them up. Daisy, wet and muddy, is perched on a
branch high up in a maple tree. Jasper stands below her. "You give
me that back or else!" he warns.

"No," she responds. "It's *mine*." There is bold defiance in her
eyes, but then, when he starts to climb up the tree, she throws
down the Gandalf doll he's after.

"It's time to go get Nic," I say, and they dash past me into the
house, chanting, "Nicky Nicky Nicky."

We drive the hour and a half to the airport. When we reach the terminal, Jasper yells, "There's Nic." He points. "*There!*"

Nic, an army green duffel bag slung over his shoulder, leans against a NO PARKING sign on the curb outside United baggage claim. Lanky thin in a faded red T-shirt and his girlfriend's cardigan, sagging jeans that ride below his bony hips, and red Converse All-Stars, when he sees us, his face brightens and he waves.

The kids both want to sit next to him and so, after throwing his bags into the way back, he climbs over Jasper and buckles in between them. In turn he clasps each of their heads between the palms of his hands and kisses their cheeks. "It's so good to see you," he says. "I missed you little boinkers. Like crazy." To us up front, he adds, "You, too, Pops and Mama."

As I drive away from the airport, Nic describes his flight. "It was the worst," he says. "I was stuck next to a lady who wouldn't stop talking. She had platinum hair with peaks like on lemon meringue pie. Cruella De Vil horn-rimmed eyeglasses and prune lips and thick pink face powder."

"Cruella De Vil?" Jasper asks. He is wide-eyed.

Nic nods. "Just like her. Her eyelashes were long and false—purple, and she wore this perfume: Eau de Stinky." He holds his nose. "Yech." The kids are rapt.

We drive across the Golden Gate Bridge. A river of thick fog pours below us and wraps around the Marin Headlands. Jasper asks, "Nic, are you coming to Step-Up?" referring to his and Daisy's upcoming graduation celebration. The kids are stepping up from second grade to third and kindergarten to first grade.

"Wouldn't miss it for all the tea in China," Nic responds.

Daisy asks, "Nic, do you remember that girl Daniela? She fell off the climbing structure and broke her toe."

"Ouch."

"She has a cast," Jasper adds.

"A cast on her toe?" Nic asks. "It must be teeny."

Jasper gravely reports, "They will cut it off with a hacksaw."

"Her toe?"

They all giggle.

After a while, Nic tells them, "I have something for you kiddos. In my suitcase."

"Presents!"

"When we get home," he responds.

They beg him to tell them what, but he shakes his head. "No way, José. It's a surprise."

I can see the three of them in the rearview mirror. Jasper and Daisy have smooth olive complexions. Nic's was, too, but now it's gaunt and rice-papery. Their eyes are brown and clear, whereas his are dark globes. Their hair is dark brown, but Nic's, long and blond when he was a child, is faded like a field in late summer with smashed-down sienna patches and sticking-up yellowed clumps—a result of his unfortunate attempt to bleach it with Clorox.

"Nic, will you tell us a PJ story?" Jasper begs. For years Nic has entertained the kids with The Adventures of PJ Fumblebumble, a British detective of his invention.

"Later, mister, I promise."

We head north on the freeway, exiting and turning west, meandering through a series of small towns, a wooded state park, and then hilly pastureland. We stop in Point Reyes Station to retrieve the mail. It's impossible to be in town without running into a dozen friends, all of whom are pleased to see Nic, bombarding him with questions about school and his summer plans. Finally we drive off and follow the road along Papermill Creek to our left turn, where I head up the hill and pull into our driveway.

"We have a surprise, too, Nicky," says Daisy.

Jasper looks sternly at her. "Don't you tell him!"

"It's signs. We made them."

"Dai-sy . . ."

Lugging his bags, Nic follows the kids into the house. The dogs charge him, barking and howling. At the top of the stairs, Nic is greeted by the kids' banners and drawings, including a hedgehog, captioned, "I miss Nic, boo hoo," drawn by Jasper. Nic praises their artistry and then trudges into his bedroom to unpack. Since he left for college, his room, a Pompeian red chamber at the far end of the house, has become an adjunct playroom with a display of Jasper's Lego creations, including a maharaja's castle and motorized R2-D2. Preparing for his return, Karen cleared off Daisy's menagerie of stuffed animals and made up the bed with a comforter and fresh pillows.

When Nic emerges, his arms are loaded with gifts. For Daisy, there are Josefina and Kirsten, American Girl dolls, hand-me-downs from his girlfriend. They are prettily dressed in, respectively, an embroidered peasant blouse and serape and a green velvet jumper. Jasper gets a pair of cannon-sized Super Soakers.

"After dinner," Nic warns Jasper, "you will be so wet that you will have to swim back into the house."

"You'll be so wet you'll need a boat."

"You'll be wetter than a wet noodle."

"You'll be so wet that you won't need a shower for a year."

Nic laughs. "That's fine with me," he says. "It'll save me a lot of time."

We eat and then the boys fill up the squirt guns and hasten outside into the windy evening, running in opposite directions. Karen and I watch from the living room. Stalking each other, the boys lurk among the Italian cypress and oaks, duck under garden furniture, and creep behind hedges. When there's a clean shot, they squirt each other with thin streams of water. Hidden behind some potted hydrangeas, Daisy watches from near the house. When the boys race past her, she twirls a spigot she's grasping with one hand and takes aim with a garden hose she's holding in the other. She drenches them.

I stop the boys just as they're about to catch her. "You don't deserve to be rescued," I tell her, "but it's bedtime."

Jasper and Daisy take baths and put on their pajamas and then ask Nic to read to them.

He sits on a miniature couch between their twin beds, his long legs stretched out on the floor. He reads from *The Witches*, by Roald Dahl. We hear his voice — voices — from the next room: the boy narrator, all wonder and earnestness; wry and creaky Grandma; and the shrieking, haggy Grand High Witch.

"Children are foul and filthy!... Children are dirty and stinky!... Children are smelling of dogs' drrrroppings!... They are vurse than dogs' drrroppings! Dogs' drrroppings is smelling like violets and prrrimroses compared with children!"

Nic's performance is irresistible, and the children, as always, are riveted by him.

At midnight, the storm that has been building finally hits. There's a hard rain, and intermittent volleys of hailstones pelt down like machine-gun fire on the copper roof tiles. We rarely have electrical storms, but tonight the sky lights up like popping flashbulbs.

Between thunderclaps, I hear the creaking of tree branches. I also hear Nic padding along the hallway, making tea in the kitchen, quietly strumming his guitar and playing Björk, Bollywood soundtracks, and Tom Waits, who sings his sensible advice: "Never drive a car when you're dead." I worry about Nic's insomnia but push away my suspicions, reminding myself how far he has come since the previous school year, when he dropped out of Berkeley. This time, he went east to college and completed his freshman year. Given what we have been through, this feels miraculous. By my count, he is coming up on his one hundred and fiftieth day without methamphetamine.

In the morning the storm has passed, and the sun shimmers on the wet maple leaves. I dress and join Karen and the little kids in the kitchen. Nic, wearing flannel pajama bottoms, a fraying wool sweater, and x-ray specs, shuffles in. He hovers over the kitchen counter, fussing with the espresso maker, filling it with water and coffee and setting it on a flame, and then sits down to a bowl of cereal with Jasper and Daisy.

"Daisy," he says. "Your hose attack was brilliant, but I'm going to have to repay you for it. Watch your back."

She cranes her neck. "I can't see it."

Nic says, "I love you, you wacko."

Soon after Daisy and Jasper leave for school, a half-dozen women arrive to help Karen make a going-away gift for a beloved teacher. They bejewel a concrete birdbath with seashells, polished stones, and handmade (by students) tiles. As they work, they chat and sip tea.

I hide in my office.

The women are taking a lunch break in the open kitchen. One of the mothers has brought Chinese chicken salad. Nic, who had gone back to sleep, emerges from his bedroom, shaking off his grogginess and greeting the women. He politely answers their questions — once again, about college and his summer plans — and then excuses himself, saying that he's off to a job interview.

After he leaves, I hear the mothers talking about him.

"What a lovely boy."

"He's delightful."

One comments on his good manners. "You're very lucky," she

tells Karen. "Our teenage son sort of grunts. Otherwise he never gives us the time of day."

In a couple hours, Nic returns to a quiet house — the mosaicing mothers have gone home. He got the job. Tomorrow he goes in for training as a waiter at an Italian restaurant. Though he is aghast at the required uniform, including stiff black shoes and a burgundy vest, he was told that he will make piles of money in tips.

The following afternoon, after the training session, Nic practices on us, drawing his character from the waiter in one of his memorized videos, *Lady and the Tramp*. We are sitting down for dinner. With one hand aloft, balancing an imaginary tray, he enters, singing in a lilting Italian accent, "Oh, this is the night, it's a beautiful night, and we call it *bella notte*."

After dinner, Nic asks if he can borrow the car to go to an AA meeting. After missed curfews and assorted other infractions, including banging up both of our cars (efficiently doing it in one accident, driving one into the other), by last summer he had lost driving privileges, but this request seems reasonable — AA meetings are an essential component of his continued recovery — and so we agree. He heads out in the station wagon, still dented from the earlier mishap. Then he dutifully returns home after the meeting, telling us that he asked someone he met to be his sponsor while he's in town.

The next day he requests the car again, this time so that he can meet the sponsor for lunch. Of course I let him. I am impressed by his assiduousness and his adherence to the rules we have set down. He lets us know where he's going and when he will be home. He arrives when he promises he will. Once again, he is gone for a brief couple hours.

The following late afternoon a fire burns in the living room. Sitting on the twin couches, Karen, Nic, and I read while nearby, on the faded rug, Jasper and Daisy play with Lego people. Looking up from a gnome, Daisy tells Nic about a "meany potatohead" boy who pushed her friend Alana. Nic says that he will come to school and make him a "mashed meany potatohead."

I am surprised to hear Nic quietly snoring a while later, but at a quarter to seven, he awakens with a start. Checking his watch, he jumps up and says, "I almost missed the meeting," and once again asks if he can borrow the car.

I am pleased that though he is exhausted and would have been content to sleep for the night, he is committed to the work of recovery, committed enough to rouse himself, splash his face with water in the bathroom sink, brush his hair out of his eyes with his fingers, throw on a clean T-shirt, and race out of the house so that he will be on time.

It's after eleven and Nic isn't home. I had been so tired, but now I'm wide awake in bed, feeling more and more uneasy. There are a million harmless explanations. Oftentimes, groups of people at AA meetings go out afterward for coffee. Or he could be talking with his new sponsor. I contend with two simultaneous, opposing monologues, one reassuring me that I'm foolish and paranoid, the other certain that something is dreadfully wrong. By now I know that worry is useless, but it shoots in and takes over my body at the touch of a hair trigger. I don't want to assume the worst, but some of the times Nic ignored his curfew, it presaged disaster.

I stare into the dark, my anxiety mounting. It is a pathetically familiar state. I have been waiting for Nic for years. At night, past his curfew, I would wait for the car's grinding engine, when it pulled into the driveway and then went silent. At last—Nic. The shutting car door, footsteps, the front door opening with a click. Despite Nic's attempt at stealth, Brutus, the chocolate Lab, usually yelped a half-hearted bark. Or I would wait for the telephone to ring, never certain if it would be him ("Hey, Pop, how're ya doin'?") or the police ("Mr. Sheff, we have your son"). Whenever he was late or failed to call, I assumed catastrophe. He was dead. Always dead.

But then Nic would arrive home, creeping up the hallway stairs, his hand sliding along the banister. Or the telephone would ring. "Sorry, Pop, I'm at Richard's house. I fell asleep. I think I'll just crash here rather than drive at this hour. I'll see you in the morning. I love you." I would be furious and relieved, both, because I had already buried him.

Late this night, with no sign of him, I finally fall into a miserable half-sleep. Just after one, Karen wakes me. She hears him sneaking in. A garden light, equipped with a motion detector, flashes on, casting its white light across the backyard. Clad in my pajamas, I slip on a pair of shoes and go out the back door to catch him.

The night air is chilly. I hear crunching brush.

I turn the corner and come head-to-head with an enormous startled buck, who quickly lopes away up into the garden, effortlessly leaping over the deer fence.

Back in bed, Karen and I are wide awake.

It's one-thirty. Now two. I double check his room.

It is two-thirty.

Finally, the sound of the car.

I confront Nic in the kitchen and he mumbles an excuse. I tell him that he can no longer use the car.

"Whatever."

"Are you high? Tell me."

"*Jesus. No.*"

"Nic, we had an agreement. Where were you?"

"What the fuck?" He looks down. "A bunch of people at the meeting went back to a girl's house to talk and then we watched a video."

"There was no phone?"

"I know," he says, his anger flaring. "I said I'm sorry."

I snap back, "We'll talk about this in the morning," as he escapes into his room, shutting his door and locking it.

At breakfast, I stare hard at Nic. The giveaway is his body, vibrating like an idling car. His jaw gyrates and his eyes are darting opals. He makes plans with Jasper and Daisy for after school and gives them gentle hugs, but his voice has a prickly edge.

When Karen and the kids are gone, I say, "Nic, we have to talk."

He eyes me warily. "About?"

"I know you're using again. I can tell."

He glares at me. "What are you talking about? I'm not." His eyes lock onto the floor.

"Then you won't mind being drug-tested."

"Whatever. Fine."

"OK. I want to do it now."

"All *right!*"

"Get dressed."

"I know I should have called. I'm *not* using." He almost growls it.

"Let's go."

He hurries to his bedroom. Closes the door. He comes out wearing a Sonic Youth T-shirt and black jeans. One hand is thrust in his pocket, his head is down, his backpack is slung on one shoulder. In his other hand he holds his electric guitar by the neck. "You're right," he says. He pushes past me. "I've been using since I came home. I was using the whole semester." He leaves the house, slamming the door behind him.

I run outside and call after him, but he is gone. After a few stunned moments, I go inside again and enter his bedroom, sitting on his unmade bed. I retrieve a crumpled-up piece of paper under the desk. Nic wrote:

*I'm so thin and frail
Don't care, want another rail.*

Late that afternoon, Jasper and Daisy burst in, dashing from room
to room, before finally stopping and, looking up at me, asking,
"Where's Nic?"

I tried everything I could to prevent my son's fall into meth addiction. It would have been no easier to have seen him strung out on
heroin or cocaine, but as every parent of a meth addict comes to
learn, this drug has a unique, horrific quality. In an interview,
Stephan Jenkins, the singer in Third Eye Blind, said that meth
makes you feel "bright and shiny." It also makes you paranoid,
delusional, destructive, and *self*-destructive. Then you will do
unconscionable things in order to feel bright and shiny again. Nic
had been a sensitive, sagacious, exceptionally smart and joyful
child, but on meth he became unrecognizable.

Nic always was on the cutting edge of popular trends — in their
time, Care Bears, Pound Puppies, My Little Pony, Micro Machines,
Transformers, He-Man and She-ra, Teenage Mutant Ninja Turtles,
Star Wars, Nintendo, Guns N' Roses, grunge, Beck, and many
others. He was a trailblazer with meth, too, addicted years before
politicians denounced the drug as the worst yet to hit the nation.
In the United States, at least twelve million people have tried meth,
and it is estimated that more than one and a half million are addicted
to it. Worldwide, there are more than thirty-five million users; it
is the most abused hard drug, more than heroin and cocaine combined. Nic claimed that he was searching for meth his entire life.
"When I tried it for the first time," he said, "that was that."

Our family's story is unique of course, but it is universal, too,
in the way that every tale of addiction resonates with every other
one. I learned how similar we all are when I first went to Al-Anon

meetings. I resisted going for a long time, but these gatherings, though they often made me weep, strengthened me and assuaged my sense of isolation. I felt slightly less beleaguered. In addition, others' stories prepared me for challenges that would have otherwise blindsided me. They were no panacea, but I was grateful for even the most modest relief and any guidance whatsoever.

I was frantic to try to help Nic, to stop his descent, to save my son. This, mixed with my guilt and worry, consumed me. Since I am a writer, it's probably no surprise that I wrote to try to make some sense of what was happening to me and to Nic, and also to discover a solution, a cure that had eluded me. I obsessively researched this drug, addiction, and treatments. I am not the first writer for whom this work became a bludgeon with which to battle a terrible enemy, as well as an expurgation, a grasping for something (anything) fathomable amid calamity, and an agonizing process by which the brain organizes and regulates experience and emotion that overwhelms it. In the end, my efforts could not rescue Nic. Nor could writing heal me, though it helped.

Other writers' work helped, too. Whenever I pulled it off the shelf, Thomas Lynch's book *Bodies in Motion and at Rest: On Metaphor and Mortality* opened by itself to page 95, the essay "The Way We Are." I read it dozens of times, each time crying a little. With his child passed out on the couch, after arrests and drunk tanks and hospitalizations, Lynch, the undertaker and poet and essayist, looked at his dear addicted son with sad but lucid resignation, and he wrote: "I want to remember him the way he was, that bright and beaming boy with the blue eyes and the freckles in the photos, holding the walleye on his grandfather's dock, or dressed in his first suit for his sister's grade-school graduation, or sucking his thumb while drawing at the kitchen counter, or playing his first guitar, or posing with the brothers from down the block on his first day of school."

Why does it help to read others' stories? It's not only that misery loves company, because (I learned) misery is too self-absorbed to want much company. Others' experiences did help with my emotional struggle; reading, I felt a little less crazy. And, like the stories I heard at Al-Anon meetings, others' writing served as guides in uncharted waters. Thomas Lynch showed me that it is possible to love a child who is lost, possibly forever.

My writing culminated in an article about our family's experience that I submitted to the *New York Times Magazine*. I was terrified to invite people into our nightmare, but was compelled to do so. I felt that telling our story would be worthwhile if I could help anyone in the way that Lynch and other writers helped me. I discussed it with Nic and the rest of our family. Though encouraged by them, I was nonetheless nervous about exposing our family to public scrutiny and judgment. But the reaction to the article heartened me and, according to Nic, emboldened him. A book editor contacted him and asked if he was interested in writing a memoir about his experience, one that might inspire other young people struggling with addiction. Nic was eager to tell his story. More significantly, he said that he walked into A A meetings and when friends — or even strangers — made the connection between him and the boy in the article, they offered warm embraces and told him how proud they were of him. He said that it was a powerful affirmation of his hard work in recovery.

I also heard from addicts and their families — their brothers and sisters, children, and other relatives, and, most of all, parents — hundreds of them. A few respondents were critical. One accused me of exploiting Nic for my own purposes. Another, outraged at my description of a period when Nic briefly wore his clothes backward, attacked, "You let him wear backward clothes? No wonder he became an addict." But the great majority of letters were outpourings of compassion, consolation, counsel, and, most of all, shared grief. Many people seemed to feel that finally someone understood what they were going through. This is the way that misery does love company: People are relieved to learn that they are not alone in their suffering, that we are part of something larger, in this case, a societal plague—an epidemic of children, an epidemic of families. For whatever reason, a stranger's story seemed to give them permission to tell theirs. They felt that I would understand, and I did.

"I am sitting here crying with shaking hands," a man wrote. "Your article was handed to me yesterday at my weekly breakfast of fathers who have lost their children. The man who handed it to me lost his sixteen-year-old son to drugs three years ago."

"Our story is your story," wrote another father. "Different drugs, different cities, different rehabs, but the same story."

And another: "At first, I was simply startled that someone had written my story about my child without my permission. Halfway through the emotional text of very familiar events and manifest conclusions, I realized that the dates of significant incidents were wrong, and thereby had to conclude that other parents may be experiencing the same inconceivable tragedies and loss that I have . . .

"Insight acquired over a quarter of a century forces me to rewrite the last paragraph: Escaping from his latest drug rehab, my son overdosed and nearly died. Sent to a very special program in another city, he stayed sober for almost two years, then began disappearing again, sometimes for months, sometimes years. Having been one of the most brilliant students in the country's highest ranking high school, it took him twenty years to graduate from a mediocre college. And it has taken me just as long to discard my veil of impossible hope and admit that my son either cannot or will not ever stop using drugs. He is now forty years old, on welfare, and resides in a home for adult addicts."

There were so many more, many with unfathomably tragic conclusions. "But the ending of my story is different. My son died last year of an overdose. He was seventeen." Another: "My beautiful daughter is dead. She was fifteen when she overdosed." Another: "My daughter died." Another: "My son is dead." Letters and emails still interrupt my days with haunting reminders of the toll of addiction. My heart tears anew with each of them.

I kept writing and, through the painstaking process, had some success viewing our experience in a way that made sense to me—as much sense as is possible to make of addiction. It led to this book. When I transformed my random and raw words into sentences, sentences into paragraphs, and paragraphs into chapters, a semblance of order and sanity appeared where there had been only chaos and insanity. As with the *Times* article, it scares me to publish our story. But with the continued encouragement of the principals, I go forward. There's no shortage of compelling memoirs by addicts, and the best of them offer revelations for anybody who loves one. I hope Nic's book will become a compelling addition. And yet—with rare exceptions, such as Lynch's essay—we have not heard from those who love them. Anyone who has lived through it, or those who are now living through it, knows that caring about an addict is as complex and fraught and debilitating as addiction itself. At my worst, I even resented Nic because an addict, at least when high, has a momentary respite from his suffering. There is no similar relief for parents or children or husbands or wives or others who love them.

Nic used drugs on and off for more than a decade, and in that time I think that I have felt and thought and done almost everything an addict's parent can feel and think and do. Even now, I know that there's no single right answer, nor even a clear road map, for families of the addicted. However, in our story, I hope that there may be some solace, some guidance, and, if nothing else, yes, some company. I also hope that people can catch a glimpse of something that seems impossible during many stages of a loved one's addiction. Nietzsche is often quoted for having said, "That which does not kill us makes us stronger." This is absolutely true for family members of an addict. Not only am I still standing, but I know more and feel more than I once thought was possible.

In telling our story, I resisted the temptation to foreshadow, because it would be disingenuous — and a disservice to anyone going through this — to suggest that one can anticipate how things will unfold. I never knew what the next day would bring.

I've strived to honestly include the major events that shaped Nic and our family — the good and the appalling. Much of it makes me cringe. I am aghast by so much of what I did and, equally, what I did not do. Even as all the experts kindly tell the parents of addicts, "You didn't cause it," I have not let myself off the hook. I often feel as if I completely failed my son. In admitting this, I am not looking for sympathy or absolution, but instead stating a truth that will be recognized by most parents who have been through this.

Someone who heard my story expressed bafflement that Nic would become addicted, saying, "But your family doesn't seem dysfunctional." We are dysfunctional — as dysfunctional as every other family I know. Sometimes more so, sometimes less so. I'm not sure if I know any "functional" families, if functional means a family without difficult times and members who don't have a full range of problems. Like addicts themselves, the families of addicts are everything you would expect and everything you wouldn't. Addicts come from broken and intact homes. They are longtime losers and great successes. We often heard in lectures or Al-Anon meetings or AA meetings of the intelligent and charming men and women who bewilder those around them when they wind up in the gutter. "You're too good a man to do this to yourself," a doctor tells an alcoholic in a Fitzgerald story. Many, many people who have known Nic well have expressed similar sentiments. One said, "He is the last person I could imagine this happening to. Not Nic. He is too solid and too smart."

I also know that parents have discretionary recall, blocking out everything that contradicts our carefully edited recollections—an understandable attempt to dodge blame. Conversely, children often fixate on the indelibly painful memories, because they have made stronger impressions. I hope that I am not indulging in parental revisionism when I say that in spite of my divorce from Nic's mother; in spite of our draconian long-distance custody arrangement; and in spite of all of my shortcomings and mistakes, much of Nic's early years was charmed. Nic confirms this, but maybe he is just being kind.

This rehashing in order to make sense of something that cannot be made sense of is common in the families of addicts, but it's not all we do. We deny the severity of our loved one's problem not because we are naive, but because we can't know. Even for those who, unlike me, never used drugs, it's an incontrovertible fact that many—more than half of all children—will try them. (Six thousand children try them in the US for the first time every day.) For some of those, they will have no major negative impact on their lives. For others, however, the outcome will be catastrophic. We parents wrack our brains and do everything we can and consult every expert and sometimes it's not enough. Only after the fact do we know that we didn't do enough or what we did do was wrong. Addicts are in denial and their families are in it with them because often the truth is too unimaginable, too painful, and too terrifying. But denial, however common, is dangerous. I wish someone had shaken me and said, "Intervene while you can before it's too late." It may not have made a difference, but I don't know. No one shook me and said it. Even if they had, I may not have been able to hear them. Maybe I had to learn the hard way.

*

Like many in my straits, I became addicted to my child's addiction. When it preoccupied me, even at the expense of my responsibilities to my wife and other children, I justified it. I thought, How can a parent not be consumed by his child's life-or-death struggle? But I learned that my preoccupation with Nic didn't help him and may have harmed him. Or maybe it was irrelevant to him. However, it surely harmed the rest of my family — and me. Along with this, I learned another lesson, a startling one: our children live or die with or without us. No matter what we do, no matter how we agonize or obsess, we cannot choose for our children whether they live or die. It is a devastating realization, but also liberating. I finally chose life for myself. I chose the perilous but essential path that allows me to accept that Nic will decide for himself how — and whether — he will live his life.

As I said, I don't absolve myself, and meanwhile, I still struggle with how much I can absolve Nic. He is brilliant and wonderful and charismatic and loving when he's not using, but like every addict I have ever heard of, he becomes a stranger when he is, distant and foolish and self-destructive and broken and dangerous. I have struggled to reconcile these two people. Whatever the cause — a genetic predisposition, the divorce, my drug history, my overprotectiveness, my failure to protect him, my leniency, my harshness, my immaturity, all of these — Nic's addiction seemed to have had a life of its own. I have tried to reveal how insidiously addiction creeps into a family and takes over. So many times in the last decade I made mistakes out of ignorance, hope, or fear. I've tried to recount them all as and when they happened, in the hope that readers will recognize a wrong path before they take it. When they don't, however, I hope that they may realize that it is a path they can't blame themselves for having taken.

*

When my child was born, it was impossible to imagine that he would suffer in the ways that Nic has suffered. Parents want only good things for their children. I was a typical parent who felt that this could not happen to us — not to my son. But though Nic is unique, he is every child. He could be yours.

Finally, the reader should know that I have changed a few names and details in the book to obscure the identities of some of the people herein. I begin when Nic was born. The birth of a child is, for many if not every family, a transformative event of joy and optimism. It was for us.

PART I

STAY UP LATE

I have a daughter who reminds me too
much of what I used to be, full of love and
joy, kissing every person she meets because
everyone is good and will do her no harm.
And that terrifies me to the point to where
I can barely function.

—KURT COBAIN,
in his suicide note

I

M y wife, Vicki, and I live in Berkeley in a whitewashed clap-board bungalow built in the 1920s, hidden from the street behind a wall of black bamboo. It is 1982, a summer of waiting. Everything else—work, social engagements—are all biding time. Our baby is due in July.

An ultrasound identifies him as a him. We prepare for his arrival. We paint and decorate a nursery, furnishing it with a white crib, light-blue dresser, bookshelves stocked with Maurice Sendak and Dr. Seuss, and, sitting sentinel on either side of the doorway, a pair of enormous stuffed panda bears, early baby gifts from a friend. Another friend has loaned us a family heirloom, a buttery yellow cradle in the shape of a new moon. It hangs from a chain in the corner of the living room, appearing to float above San Francisco, which glitters in the distance.

Vicki's contractions begin after midnight on the morning of July 20. As we have been instructed to do in our Lamaze class, we clock the intervals between them. It is time. We drive to the hospital.

Nic is born at dawn—our beautiful boy.

We are enraptured by our child. We willingly forsake sleep. We soothe his crying. We sing him lullabies. We fall into a languorous altered state, a dreamy contentment that would have appalled us had it befallen any of our friends. (Indeed, many of our friends *are* appalled.) Life is accompanied by a soundtrack of Pete Seeger, the

Limelighters, and Raffi, whose songs, played over and over and over and over and over and over and over, would crack any criminal into confessing after other forms of torture fail. Sometimes we just stare at the baby's tiny grasping hands and luminous, exuberant eyes.

We are among the first generation of self-conscious parents. Before us, people had kids. We parent. We seek out the best for our children—the best stroller and car seat recommended by *Consumer Reports*—and fret over every decision about their toys, diapers, clothes, meals, medicine, teething rings, inoculations, and just about everything else.

Before long the crib is replaced by a single bed with zebra sheets. We take walks in the stroller and a Snugli, play in Berkeley parks and baby gyms, and visit the San Francisco Zoo. His library overflows. *Goodnight Moon, Pat the Bunny, Where the Wild Things Are, A Hole Is to Dig.* I read them so often I know them by heart.

"Milk, Milk, Milk for the Morning Cake."

"From here to there and there to here, funny things are everywhere."

"Dogs are to kiss people. Snow is to roll in. Buttons are to keep people warm. Boodly boodly boodly."

At three, Nic spends a few mornings a week at a pastel-colored preschool a short walk from home. His day includes circle time; games like duck, duck, goose; painting and clay; and songs. "Pulling weeds, picking stones," Nic sings, "we are made of dreams and bones." There is outside time on the climbing structure and swingset. He ventures out on his first play dates, formerly known as going over to some kid's house. Sometimes we meet other families at a park with a concrete slide that follows a hillside down under a canopy of oaks. Nic spins on a whirling merry-go-round.

Nic is a natural architect and builder, constructing sprawling block, Duplo, and Lego Lilliputs. He loves Teddy Ruxpin, Pound Puppies, and the twin pandas. He scoots around the house on a big-wheeled tricycle and, on the red-brick front patio, in a plastic sky-blue convertible, a gift from my parents, which he powers like a Flintstones car with high-top-sneakered feet.

We visit Train Town in nearby Sonoma, where Nic conducts a steam locomotive past miniature barns and windmills. We travel to Yosemite National Park—in spring, with wildflowers abloom, we hike to the waterfalls; in wintertime, we play in the snow in the valley watched over by Half Dome—and the Monterey Bay Aquarium, where Nic is mesmerized by fluorescent jellies and circling sharks.

There are puppet shows and board games and singing along with the bashing of a tambourine. Wearing a kimono and flannel pajama bottoms and holding a plastic guitar, Nic sings at the top of his lungs:

> *Tingalayo, run my little donkey run*
> *Tingalayo, run my little donkey run*
> *Me donkey walk, me donkey talk*
> *Me donkey eat with a knife and fork*
> *Me donkey walk, me donkey talk*
> *Me donkey eat with a knife and fork*

Then he peels off the kimono and he's in his clown pajama top with polka dots, lime-green and sky-blue and cherry-red. He's wearing fluorescent, swirly blue-green-pink rain boots.

We walk down the sidewalk, him shuffling in the too-large boots, my big hand enveloping his tiny one, his plastic guitar slung over his shoulder. He stomps in every puddle.

His eyes are thoughtful and the bronze sometimes melts into greenness, alive like the sea.

He dances a funny little dance as he walks along, holding a yellow umbrella over his head.

"Tut, tut, it looks like rain."

This apparent idyll distracts us from a looming catastrophe. Vicki and I have spent Nic's first three years in the tired but blissful half-sleep of new parenthood and then wake up in harsh light and an oppressive chill of a shattering marriage. I maturely address our disagreements by falling in love with a family friend. Her son and Nic are playmates.

Vicki and I share a devotion to Nic, but I am ill-equipped to deal with our escalating problems. When we visit a couples' therapist, I announce that it is too late. My marriage is over. Vicki is caught off-guard. It is not the first relationship that I have sabotaged, but now there is a child.

Nic.

At home when his mother and I argue, Nic finds refuge in the laps of the pandas.

No child benefits from the bitterness and savagery of a divorce like ours. Like fallout from a dirty bomb, the collateral damage is widespread and enduring. Nick is hit hard.

We divide the china and the art and our young son. It seems obvious that joint custody is the best approach; Vicki and I both want him with us and have no reason to doubt the prevailing wisdom, that it will be best for him to continue to be raised by both parents. Soon Nic has two homes. On the days I drop him off at his mother's, we hug and I say goodbye at the white picket gate and watch him march inside.

Vicki moves to Los Angeles, where she remarries. We still both want Nic with us, but now that five hundred miles separate us, the informal yo-yo joint-custody arrangement is no longer tenable. Each of us believes with sincerity and vengeance that it is in Nic's best interest to be with us, *not* his other parent, and so we hire divorce lawyers.

Some attorneys successfully mediate agreements, but many custody battles wind up in court. Usually it's traumatic and expensive. Our lawyers charge more than two hundred dollars an hour and require five-to-ten-thousand-dollar retainers. When we learn that judges often follow the arrangement recommended by a court-appointed child psychologist after he or she conducts a thorough assessment, our wiser selves and drained bank accounts prevail. Nic has been seeing a therapist since soon after we separated, and we hire her to conduct an evaluation. We agree to abide by her decision.

The doctor launches a three-month investigation that feels like an inquisition. She interviews us, our friends, and our families, visits our respective homes in San Francisco and Los Angeles, and spends long therapy sessions in her office playing checkers, cards, and blocks with Nic. He calls her his worry doctor. One day, while playing with a dollhouse in her office, he shows her the mother's room on one side and the father's room on the other. When she asks him about the little boy's room, he says, "He doesn't know where he will sleep."

We meet in her office among the toys and modern furniture and framed prints of paintings by Gottlieb and Rothko and she hands down her verdict. Vicki and I sit in matching leather armchairs facing the doctor, an imposing woman in a flowered dress, iron-black curls, and penetrating eyes behind bottle-thick glasses. She folds her hands on her lap and speaks.

"You are both loving parents who want the best for your son. Here are some of the things I have learned about Nic over the course of this evaluation. I don't have to tell you that he is an exceptional child. He is resourceful, sensitive, expressive, and highly intelligent. I think you also know that he is suffering from the divorce and the uncertainty about his future. In coming to my very difficult decision, I have attempted to weigh every factor and devise a plan that is the best for Nic—the best in a situation where there is no ideal choice. We want to minimize the stress in Nic's life and to keep things as consistent as possible."

She looks at each of us in turn and then shuffles through a sheaf of papers. She exhales heavily and says that Nic will spend the school year with me in San Francisco and holidays and summers with Vicki in Southern California.

I try to comprehend exactly what she has said. I won. No, I lost. So did Vicki. I will have him with me for the day-to-day of the school year, but what will Christmas be without him? Thanksgiving? Summertime? The doctor hands us copies of the document that outlines her decision. Using her desk to write on, we sign them. Inconceivably, in an instant marked by the scratching of a pen on coarse paper, I sign away half of my son's childhood.

As bad as it is for Vicki and me, it is worse for Nic. Preparing for the handoffs, he packs his toys and clothes in a Hello Kitty suitcase with a pretend lock and key. I drive him to the airport. He says that he has a pit in his stomach, not because he doesn't want to see his mother and stepfather—he does—but because he doesn't want to leave.

At first one of us always flies with him, but at five, he begins traveling on his own. He graduates from the tiny suitcase to a canvas backpack filled with a revolving arsenal of essential stuff (books and journals, *Star Trek*, Micro Machines, plastic vampire teeth, a Discman and CDs, a stuffed crab). A flight attendant leads him onto the plane. We say "everything" to each other. It is our way of saying I love you, I will miss you so much, I am sorry—the jumble of feelings when he comes and goes.

The flights between San Francisco and Los Angeles are the only times a parent isn't lording over him, so he orders Coca-Cola, verboten at home; flight attendants don't care about cavities. But such benefits are insignificant when contrasted with his fear of a plane crash.

At five, Nic begins kindergarten at a progressive San Francisco school in a hundred-year-old redwood-shingled building, where you can wander in at snack time and parents are, for example, grilling quesadillas with the children. The school has stone steps and old barnlike doors that open onto a play yard with a bouncy, rubberized ground made from shredded recycled tires. There is tetherball, a redwood climbing structure, and basketball. The school is staffed by teachers dedicated to "the whole child," so the three Rs are integrated with an impressive music program; plays that the children write (during his first of many annual follies performances, Nic, cast as a mosquito, falls asleep on stage); art; noncompetitive sports such as freeze tag and broom hockey; inventive spelling; and the celebration of secular and religious holidays, including Christmas, Hanukkah, Chinese New Year, and Kwanza. It seems ideal for Nic, who, in kindergarten, displays his creativity in clay, finger-paint, and an inimitable wardrobe. A typical costume is a huge out-of-shape cowboy hat pulled so low that only his owl eyes can be seen peering out from beneath, a Keith Haring T-shirt under a fringed leather vest, blue tights under a pair of underpants, and sneakers with Velcro fasteners in the shape of elephants' ears. When the other children tease him — "Only girls wear tights" — Nic responds, "Uh, uh. Superman wears tights."

I am proud of his confidence and individuality.

Nic has an eclectic group of friends. He plays regularly in Golden Gate Park with a boy who has secret-agent aspirations. He and Nic slink soundlessly on their bellies, sneaking up on unsuspecting parents gossiping on park benches. They also play tag in the labyrinthine play structure, a series of interconnecting passageways inside geodesic domes. With another close friend, a boy with a rooster's crown of dark hair and piercing emerald eyes, Nic builds Lego cities and wood-block tracks on which they race Hot Wheels.

Nic loves movies. Impressed and amused by Nic's taste in them, a friend who edits a regional magazine asks Nic to write an article titled "Nic Picks Flicks." Nic dictates his comments. "Sometimes kids have to choose a video, you know, and can't make up their mind which one to get but they have to make up their mind fast because the grown-ups have to go to the barbershop in ten minutes," he begins. He reviews *Lady and the Tramp* and *Winnie the Pooh*. "*Dumbo* is great," he says. "Great songs. Great crows." Of *The Neverending Story*, he says, "The story really does end."

When I turned six, my mother baked a coconut-and-white-frosted giraffe-shaped cake, and my friends and I played pin the tail on the donkey. Nic goes to birthday parties at stables, Great America, Raging Waters, and the Exploratorium, a hands-on science museum. Tea sandwiches or sushi, unfiltered apple juice, and wheat-free cupcakes are served.

One afternoon, Nic announces that he wants to make a donation to the school's Toys for Tots Christmas program, and so he goes through his bedroom, weeding out most of his stuffed animals, games like Candyland and Chutes and Ladders, his trolls, and over-the-hill action figures. The bookshelves are stripped of many of the picture books to make way for the Narnia and Redwall series and E. B. White. Nic is trying hard to grow up, although selectively. He keeps the pandas and Sebastian, the stuffed *The Little Mermaid* crab.

Nic has antennae that detect, before most kids, upcoming waves of popular culture, ranging from My Little Pony to Masters of the

Universe. Disney — *101 Dalmatians* and *Mary Poppins* — makes way for *Star Wars*. Nic and his friends discover Nintendo and begin speaking its impenetrable (for adults) language about minibosses, warp zones, secret levels, and pumpkins that give one-ups. One Halloween Nic is a Teenage Mutant Ninja Turtle (Michelangelo to his friend's Donatello). Another time he is Indiana Jones.

Nic gets in mild trouble on occasion. When he spends the night at a friend's house, the two are caught making prank calls they learned about while watching *The Simpsons*. They call bars listed in the yellow pages.

"Hello, may I please speak to Mr. Kaholic, first name Al?"

"Sure, kid." To the crowd: "Is there an Al Kaholic here?"

They break up laughing and slam down the phone.

Next they dial random numbers from the telephone book.

"Is there a John there?"

After a beat: "No? Then where do you go to the bathroom?"

Mostly, though, Nic is well behaved. One time in the comments section of his report card, a teacher writes that Nic sometimes seems a little depressed, which I share with his new therapist, with whom he meets one afternoon each week. "But," she continues, "he pulls himself out of it and is energetic, involved, fun — a leader in class." Other comments from his teachers are effusive praise of his creativity, sense of humor, compassion, participation, and stellar work.

I keep a box in which I store his artwork and writings, like his response to an assignment in which he has been asked if you should always try your best. "I don't think you should always try your best all the time," he writes, "because, let's say a drug atick asks you for drugs you should not try your best to find him some drugs."

Another assignment that goes into the box is a persuasive letter he writes to me when the students are asked to argue for or against

---

whatever they choose. The note ends, "So in conclusion, I think I should be allowed to eat more snacks."

Occasionally Nic has nightmares. In one, he arrives at school and he and his classmates have to submit to vampire checks. They are similar to the lice checks they have during an infestation. For lice checks, teachers, their hands protected in surgical gloves, move their fingers through each student's hair like a mother monkey, inspecting each follicle. With the discovery of a single nit, the infected child is sent home for delousing with Kwell and a meticulous raking with a fine-toothed comb. It hurts, bringing on the type of screams that can cause well-meaning neighbors to call Child Protective Services.

In Nic's dream, he and his friends line up for the morning vampire check. Gloved teachers lift the sides of their lips to see if fangs have replaced their eyeteeth. The children who are vampires are instantly struck dead with a stake through the heart. Nic, recounting the dream in the car one morning, says it is unfair to the vampires, because they can't help themselves.

I don't know if it is our constant watchfulness, the faces of missing children on milk cartons, or terrifying stories they overhear, but Nic and his friends seem unduly afraid. There is a small yard behind our apartment, but they won't play outside unless I come along. I hear other parents fret that their children are scared of the dark, cry at night, will not sleep alone, or fear sleeping over at friends' houses. After a story, before Nic goes to sleep, he asks me to check on him every fifteen minutes.

I sing to him.

> *Close your eyes*
> *Have no fears*
> *The monster's gone*
> *He's on the run and your daddy's here*

2

Waaaake up!
Wake up! Wake up! Wake up!
Up ya wake! Up ya wake! Up ya wake!
This is Mister Señor Love Daddy.
Your voice of choice. The world's
only twelve-hour strongman, here on
WE LOVE radio, 108 FM. The last on
your dial, but the first in ya
hearts. And that's the truth, Ruth.

The crisp fall morning begins with Nic's recitation of the opening soliloquy from *Do the Right Thing*, one of his favorite movies. We dress and go for a walk in Golden Gate Park. "Look at those orangies," Nic says as we walk by the conservatory of flowers. "And, oh, the greenies and reddies and goldies! It's like last night the world was finger-painted by giants." Back home, Nic helps make pancake batter. He does everything but crack the eggs—he doesn't want to get "gunky" stuff on his hands. He says that the pancakes should be Uncle Buck–sized. In the movie of the same name, they are so large that Uncle Buck uses a snow shovel in place of a spatula.

Our apartment is a child's domain, no matter how much I

try to isolate Nic's influence to his room. The place may have been cleaned the day before, but kid-sized clothes are scattered everywhere. There are board games (he trounced me last night in Stratego) and video games (we are on the penultimate level of the Legend of Zelda) and a multicolored sea of Lego in the center of the living room. In fact, Legos are everywhere—in the silverware drawer, under couch cushions, hidden among the roots of potted plants. Once, when my printer didn't work, a serviceman determined that the problem was a Lego cog jammed behind the daisy wheel.

Awaiting the pancakes under a gallery of his paintings taped onto the walls, Nic sits at the breakfast table, where he writes on lined paper with a fat red pencil. "We got to make our own pizza at school yesterday," he says. "We could choose cheddar cheese or modern jack. Hey, do you know how to spell the *ooo* word? They said that Jake kissed Elena and all the kids said, 'Oooooo.' Did you know that owls can turn their heads all the way around?"

I place a pancake, disappointingly average-sized, in front of him. He pours on maple syrup, making sound effects—"eeeyaaa! hot lava!"—as I fix him a bag lunch of a peanut butter and jelly sandwich, carrot sticks, an apple, a cookie, and a juice box.

He dresses for school. While tying his shoes, he hums "Eensy Weensy Spider." We'll be late, so I hurry him along, and he's soon in the backseat of the car, spitting on his Papa Bear doll.

"What are you doing?"

"He's in the slime pit. Would you tickle my knee?"

I reach back and dig my fingers into the sides of his knee, which causes hysterics.

"OK, OK, stop. I just wanted to remember what it feels like when you're tickled."

Changing the subject, Nic asks if he can take Klingon instead of Spanish in school.

"Why Klingon?"

"So I won't have to read the subtitles in *Star Trek* movies."

When I park in front of the school, there are still a few minutes to go before the cowbell will be rung. My greatest accomplishment of any day is getting him to school on time, but today something is wrong. Where are the other cars, the busy crowd of arriving children and the teacher who greets them? It dawns on me. It is Saturday.

I do not subscribe to the concept of karma, but I have come to believe in instant karma, as it was defined by John Lennon in his song of that name. It means, in essence, that we reap what we sow in *this* lifetime — and explains my comeuppance when my girlfriend does to me what I did to my wife. (It actually isn't quite as reprehensible; when she runs off to South America, it is with a relative stranger.) Of course I am distraught, and Nic not only has to contend with my despair, but, upon my recovery after many pathetic months, subsequent girlfriends, gifted at some things but not substitute motherhood. It is like *The Courtship of Eddie's Father,* but Eddie never went in for breakfast to encounter a lady in a kimono eating his Lucky Charms.

"Who are you?" Nic asks. He shambles over to the table in the kitchen, a jarringly lit room with a black-and-white-checked linoleum floor. He is clad in his pajamas and Oscar the Grouch slippers. The object of the question is a woman with a volcano of dreadlocked hair. An artist, her recent exhibition included hand-tinted photocopies of intimate parts of her body.

The woman introduces herself and says, "I know who you are. You're Nic. I have heard a lot about you."

"I haven't heard about you," Nic responds.

One evening, Nic and I have dinner at a Chestnut Street Italian restaurant with another woman, this one with blond curls and bottle-green eyes. Our dates so far have included Frisbee with Nic on the Marina green, and, one Sunday, a San Francisco Giants game, where Nic snagged a foul ball. Back at the flat after dinner, the three of us watch *The 5,000 Fingers of Dr. T.* She flips through magazines in the living room while I read to Nic in his bedroom until he falls asleep.

Usually, I am careful to lock the door to my bedroom, but this time I forget. In the morning, Nic crawls into my bed. When he notices the girl, who awakens, meeting his eyes, he asks, "What are you doing here?"

She responds brilliantly. "I spent the night."

"Oh," Nic says.

"Like a sleepover."

"Oh," Nic says again.

I send Nic to his room to get dressed.

Later I try to explain it to him, but I know I have made a ghastly mistake.

It doesn't take much longer for me to realize that my bachelor-father lifestyle probably isn't great for Nic, and so I take a break from dating. Determined to stop repeating the embarrassing and enormously painful mistakes that led to my divorce and other failed relationships, I enter a period of singlehood, self-reflection, and therapy.

Our lives are quieter.

On weekends, we take walks around the Embarcadero and up Telegraph Hill to Coit Tower; ride the cable car to Chinatown for dim sum and firecrackers; with our neighbors, Nic's unofficial godfathers, go to movies at the Castro Theatre, where an organist plays "Whistle While You Work" and "San Francisco" on a gilded Wurlitzer before the shows. We ride BART to Berkeley and walk down Telegraph Avenue, watching out for such regulars as the woman with dozens of slices of toast pinned onto her clothing and the Sensitive Naked Man who nonchalantly strolls by.

On weekday evenings, after Nic does his homework, we play games. We often cook together. And read. Nic loves books: *A Wrinkle in Time*, Roald Dahl, *The Outsiders*, *The Hobbit*. One night, on the occasion of one of Nic's many unbirthday parties—these are popular after we read *Alice in Wonderland* and *Through the Looking Glass*—we set the table formally, placing stuffed animals at each setting. We dine with the stuffed animals, sitting like sultans on pillows.

One summer evening, in 1989, I am at a friend's dinner party seated opposite a woman from Manhattan who is visiting her parents in Marin County. Karen, with dark brown hair and wearing a plain black dress, is a painter. She also writes and illustrates children's books. Karen says that she is flying back to New York tomorrow, and I mention that I am going there next week to conduct an interview. There is awkward silence. My friend sitting near me hands me a slip of paper and a pen, whispering in my ear, "Get her phone number."

I do.

The next day I call her at her parents' house. I hear her tell her mother to say that she isn't home, but her mother ignores her, handing over the telephone.

Yes, she says, she will meet me when I come to New York.

Our first cautious date is at a friend's party on the Upper East Side. The Fine Young Cannibals play on the music system, waiters circulate with trays of Champagne and canapés, and then, though it is a sweltering night, I walk her the length of Manhattan to her downtown loft. It takes a couple hours, during which time we do not stop talking. Whenever we come upon an all-night grocery, we get Popsicles. It's dawn when we say good night at her front door.

Karen and I keep in touch by telephone and letters. We see each other when she comes out to visit her parents and when I travel to New York on business. After six or so months, during one of her trips to San Francisco, I introduce Karen to Nic. She shows him her art books and they spend hours drawing cartoons. They work for days on long strips of butcher paper, creating an elaborately decorated scene of a park populated by Mr. Grouch, a rotund man sitting on a bench eating a tuna-fish sandwich; skinny Mr. Noodle and his noodle baby; Mr. Fake Hair; and Mr. and Mrs. No Body. (They have no bodies.)

After living on the fifth floor of a walk-up in the shadow of the World Trade Center for six years, Karen moves in with us in San Francisco. Maybe Nic is just trying to ingratiate himself with this new force in his life, now that it is clear that she is sticking around, but he writes a report about her for school, in which he explains, "She lived in a big loft on top of a restaurant called Ham Heaven. Her loft was a cool place and you could light firecrackers on the roof . . . She decided to come back to San Francisco to be with her new family, which is my dad and me and her."

Soon after, we rent a house across the bridge in Sausalito so that we can have a backyard. Our home is reputed to be one of the oldest in town. A rickety, leaky Victorian, it is slightly warmer inside than out but not much. To compensate, fires roar in the fireplace and at night we pile on heavy quilts. Bundled up in down jackets, the three of us go tide pooling along the seashore and ride the ferry across the bay past Alcatraz Island to San Francisco. We carpool with another family to Nic's school in the city. Nic, who is now a fourth grader, plays on the local Little League team. Karen and I cheer him on. In his green Braves baseball jersey and ball cap, he is a focused and poised second baseman. The other boys joke around, but Nic is solemn. His coach tells us that Nic is a leader among his teammates; the other children look to him for guidance.

Parents often gush about their children, but ask anyone who knows Nic and they will describe his humor, creativity, and infectious joie de vivre. Nic is often the unwitting center of attention, whether in school plays or at dinner parties. One day a casting director comes to his school and watches the children on the playground and then interviews some of them. In the evening, she calls our house to ask if I will consider allowing Nic to be in a television commercial. I discuss it with him and Nic says it sounds fun, so I agree. He gets to spend ten dollars, but with the rest of the hundred-dollar fee, we open a college account in his name.

The commercial, for a car company, opens with a group of children sitting in a semicircle on the floor of a kindergarten classroom. Their teacher, seated in a child's chair, reads to them and then closes the book, setting it on her lap.

"So, class," she says, "what does the *Dick and Jane* story mean to you?"

A little girl with plaited hair and large blue eyes says, "The house is the mother."

After a series of similar comments, a serious, dark-haired boy asks, "But what about Spot?"

Nic raises his hand and the teacher calls on him.

"Nicolas?"

"Spot's the id, the animal force, searching for release."

A girl with big, brown eyes, her hair in a bouncy ponytail, rolls her eyes and shrugs. "Leave it to Nicolas to invoke Freud," she says, grumpily placing her chin on her fist.

The final scene shows the kids at the end of the school day at dismissal. They run out of the building to their parents' cars, lined up out front. Nic leaps into the backseat of a Honda and his mother asks, "What did you do at school today, Nicolas?"

He answers, "Oh, same old stuff."

A month or two after the commercial begins airing, we are at the movies. A man wearing a studded leather jacket and pants and black motorcycle boots recognizes Nic. "Oh, my God," he squeals, pointing. "It's Nicolas!"

In May, Karen and I are married under roses and bougainvillea on the deck of her parents' house. With his skinny arms and neck jutting out of a short-sleeved oxford shirt, Nic, now nine, is nervous, though we try to reassure him. In the morning, however, he seems hugely relieved. "Everything's the same," he says, looking from me to Karen, around the house, and back to me again. "That's so weird."

"Miss Amy, she was a mean old bitch. Stepmothers always were." Truman Capote summed up the popular view of stepmotherhood. It's not a new sentiment. Euripides wrote, "Better a servant than a stepmother." And yet Karen and Nic grow closer. Am I seeing only what I want to see? I hope not; I don't think so. They continue to paint and draw together. They are always doing "together drawings," where one adds something and then the other, back and forth. They look at art books and discuss artists. Karen takes him to museums, where Nic sits on gallery floors with his pad on his lap. He makes feverish notes and sketches inspired by Picasso, Elmer Bischoff, and Sigmar Polke.

She teaches him French — grilling him on his vocabulary as they drive in the car — and they are very funny carrying on conversations about their shared favorite books, the kids in his class, and movies, especially ones starring Peter Sellers and Leslie Nielsen, the Inspector Clouseau movies, *Airplane, Naked Gun,* and its sequels. For some reason, for four consecutive evenings they watch *Pollyanna,* trying to get through it, but each time they get too sleepy and shut it off. On the fifth night, however, they finish it. After that, the movie is a shared language they speak together.

"Karen, you have a stuffy little nose," Nic will say, imitating Agnes Moorehead.

Nic tries to get me to play a video game called Streetfighter 2, but I quickly tire of the bashing, head-butting, and biting. Karen, however, not only enjoys it but is good at it, beating Nic. She also loves Nic's music and, unlike me, never tells him to turn it down.

Karen and Nic tease each other. Relentlessly. Sometimes she teases him too much and he gets mad. When we go out to eat, they always order milkshakes. He slowly savors his, but Karen drinks hers down quickly and then tries to steal Nic's.

They play a word game and laugh their heads off.

Karen says "Dave."

Nic says "has."

Karen says "a."

Nic: monkey

Karen: butt.

I look up from my magazine. "Very funny," I say.

Nic says, "Sorry. There."

Karen: was

Nic: a

Karen: man

Nic: who

Karen: said

Nic: that

Karen: Dave

Nic: has

Karen: a

Nic: monkey

Karen: butt.

They play it, and variations, over and over. I roll my eyes.

Karen works a lot and resists doing motherly duties, but she starts driving carpool sometimes and, one evening, makes a meatloaf for dinner. It's terrible and Nic refuses to eat it. Karen starts telling Nic to put his napkin on his lap, which makes him furious. She enlists him to help around the house, hiring him to kill slugs in the garden. He's paid ten cents a slug. Nic puts them on a shovel and flings them over the fence into the woods.

Karen, whom Nic calls Mama or Mamacita or KB (she calls him Sputnik), admits that it is not a natural relationship for her. Once, in the car with Nic and Nancy, Karen's mother, Nic, tired and frustrated over nothing in particular, starts crying. Karen is amazed and asks Nancy, "What's wrong with him?" She responds, "He's a little boy. Little boys cry." Another evening, they are together at her parents', and Karen notices that as they sit around the television, Nancy pulls Nic close to her and rubs his back. He seems completely contented. Karen tells me about it as if it's a revelation. She says that at first Nic seemed foreign to her; she had not been around children since she was one. "I never expected this," she says. "I had no idea. I didn't know what I was missing."

She doesn't always feel this way. On occasion Nic is churlish — toward me, too, for that matter — but the larger problem is inherent to the position of stepparent. Sometimes Karen says that she wishes that she were Nic's real mother, but she is realistic about the fact that she isn't. He has a mother whom he adores and to whom he is devoted. Karen is frequently reminded that a stepmother is not a mother. She has much of the responsibility but not the authority of a parent. Sometimes I'm quiet when she gets on his case about his elbows on the table, but though I always encourage her to say what is on her mind, I often rescue him. "His manners are fine," I insist before I realize that I have undermined her again. The worst for Nic may be that he feels guilty about a close relationship with someone who is not his mother, which is typical, according to one of the many how-to-stepparent books Karen keeps on her bedside table.

Sometimes we all acutely feel Vicki's absence. When Nic misses her, the telephone helps, though after hearing her voice he can be sadder. We encourage him to visit her whenever possible and to call her as often as he wants. We try to get him to talk about it. It's all we know to do.

I sense that Nic is undergoing a fitful transformation, as if a tug of war is being waged inside him. He holds onto his stuffed crab and the pandas, but he has taped a Nirvana poster on his bedroom wall. Though he still often rebels against conventional habit and taste, more and more he succumbs to peer pressure. He is trying on an awkward preteen skulk and he often wears grungy flannel and shuffles around in a pair of clunky Doc Martens. His bangs hang Cobainlike over his eyes, and he hennas his hair. I allow it, but not without considering whether I should, and meanwhile I force haircuts, even though he becomes furious with me. In choosing my battles, I weigh the relevant factors. Nic is occasionally moody, but not more than other children we know. There are minor reprimands—for writing "Sofia sucks" on a notebook, for example. (Sofia is a headstrong girl in his class.) Once he has to write a note of apology for interrupting Spanish class. For the most part, however, Nic continues to do well in school. In a report card, a teacher writes about his "burgeoning sense of kindness and generosity" and concludes, "I wonder at the gifts he will undoubtedly bring to the world."

3

W hat is now the town of Inverness on the Point Reyes Peninsula, an hour north of the Golden Gate Bridge, was, a few million years ago, in Southern California. The arrow-shaped landmass still creeps northward at the unhurried pace of an inch or so a year. Inverness and the surrounding ridges, hillsides, and valleys, and miles of ranchland and shoreline, will, in another million years, be an island floating off the coast of Washington.

Inverness is separated from the rest of the continent by the twelve-mile-long Tomales Bay, which cuts a jagged line to the ocean directly over the San Andreas Fault. The submerged border may account for the looming sense of transience and fragility—and an ethereal grace.

The town of Point Reyes Station is on the mainland side. It has a grocery store, an automobile repair shop, two bookstores, and restaurants that specialize in local foods—organic, free-range, and grass-fed. At Cowgirl Creamery, rounds of cheese are made from milk from the nearby Straus Family Dairy. Toby's Feed Barn carries a range of goods that sum up the local community: hay, lavender bath salts, fresh-pressed olive oil, dried pigs' ears, the Strauses' crème fraîche, and puppy dewormer. Down the street, there's a barbershop, a deli, real-estate offices, a hardware store, and a post office.

The area has a diverse population. There are many first- and second-generation immigrant families who hail from Latin America and Mexico; Hollywood refugees; fine craftsmen, homebuilders, cabinetmakers, and stonemasons; fishermen and oystermen; and aged hippies (the town supports a tie-dye shop). There are former high-tech executives; teachers; artists; ranchers and farmhands; summer people; weekenders; horse people; masseuses; therapists of every persuasion; environmentalists; and a medical clinic that does not turn anyone away. There are a few old curmudgeons and a new generation of them. Indeed, some of the locals embrace differences but will avoid you after you show up at a community potluck barbecue with Ball Park, not tofu, hot dogs. On one hand, there is an ardent social conscience — women who strip for peace. On the other, some locals will verbally assault you if you tread on a blackberry patch they have claimed as their own. Still, Point Reyes is mostly a place overflowing with generosity and magnanimity.

Karen has a small cabin in a garden in Inverness, not far from town. We spend as much time as possible there these days and the more time we spend, the more we appreciate the anachronistic sense of community and spectacular natural beauty. We regularly drag our old canoe down to Papermill Creek, draped over pastureland like a silver ribbon. We paddle among river otters and, at high tide, set a course for a secluded inlet up the bay, where we go ashore for a picnic and uncover Miwok arrowheads on the rocky beach. We hike trails that crisscross national seashore and state parkland, where a billion wildflowers blossom in spring. The fields are parched gold by midsummer, when the blackberries ripen and blue irises come into breathtaking bloom. In winter, drenched, we bundle up and hike through the state park or along North and South Beach, where the Pacific Ocean waves reach more than twenty feet high, and watch the migrating gray whales.

Indeed, the peninsula is surrounded on three sides by some of the wildest, most magnificent coastline anywhere. Until now, Nic rarely chose to go to the beach — he didn't like getting sandy— but soon he spends every possible moment near and in the water. We drive out to McClure's Beach, past sweeping arcs of yellow mustard flowers, to catch a minus tide. We walk along the shore to the outcroppings and balance on slippery rock, watching the crashing waves, while searching tide pools for mussels, sea star, anemone, and octopi. Nic watches Karen dive into the cold ocean in the middle of December at Limantour Beach. He jumps in, too. They whip each other with long strands of seaweed. When he gets out, he can't stop shivering. The Tomales Bay is warmer. When they swim there, Karen and Nic play a game in which she tries to buck him off her back. On the sandy beaches at Drakes, Stinson, and Bolinas, Nic skim boards. He tries boogie boarding and then surfing. He is natural and elegant on a board. The better he gets at surfing, the more that is all he wants to do. We spend sublime hours together in the ocean. We pore over buoy and weather reports and head to the beach when the swell is up and the wind is offshore. Waxing his board on the beach, Nic is slender and strong, bronzed from the sun. He wears orange beads around his neck. He has long bending limbs, brown hands with dirty fingernails, and narrow brown feet. His light eyes with coarse black eyelashes slant down. When he pulls on his four-mm-thick black wetsuit, he has the skin of a seal.

Enticed by West Marin, we build a home and painting studio in the Inverness hillside garden, moving in before fall, when Nic begins sixth grade at a new school—with trepidation.

After his first day, we sit in the high-backed dining chairs around a square purple table. Nic tells us that he thinks he is going to like this school after all. "My teacher asked, 'How many of you hate math?'" Nic says. "Almost everyone raised their hands. I did. She said, 'I hated math, too.' Then she gave this smile and said, 'You won't hate it when I'm finished with you.'"

He goes on to say that lots of the kids seem nice. He reports that after we dropped him off, he was walking through the corridor when he heard a boy call out to him: "Nic!"

He looks up.

"I was pretty excited, but then I thought maybe he was yelling to someone else and I was acting like a complete idiot, waving at him. But no, it was me. He remembered me from when I visited the school."

After the second day, Nic reports that another boy called him his friend. "This red-haired boy handed me a hockey stick in PE, and when this other kid said, 'No, that's my stick, I had it first,' the red-haired kid said, 'It's for my friend Nic.'"

Nic looks cool these days in pants that ride low on his hips, a Primus or Nirvana T-shirt, a slumped adolescent posture, and his now-red-orange-tinged hair. And yet he has essentially one ambition: coming home and being able to say, "Dad, I made two new friends today."

On a Friday, some of the children come over for a party. We drive to Stinson Beach, where they play sand tag and kickball and Nic teaches them to skim board. Their preteen awkwardness dissolves as they play like much younger children, laughing without self-consciousness, tumbling and wrestling in the sand. Before dark, we drive back home, where they play Twister and Truth or Dare, with risqué questions like, "Do you think Skye is cute?" (Nic does: She's the big-eyed, brown-haired girl whose name, when he mentions it, makes him blush. He talks to her on the phone at night, sometimes for an hour or more at a time.) And, "In a fight to the death between Batman and the Hulk, who would win?" Dares include biting into a jalapeño pepper and kissing a Barbie doll. They eat pizza and popcorn and then their parents pick them up at ten.

Karen and I attend the school's art shows and plays. Nic is

Viola in a production of *Twelfth Night* and George Gibbs in *Our Town*. Parents are invited to hear their oral reports on foreign countries. Nic, assigned Bolivia, after showing the country on a homemade poster-board map and describing its history, topography, agriculture, and gross national product, performs a song he wrote. "Olivia, oh, Olivia," he sings, "down in La Paz, Bolivia. My Olivia." He accompanies himself on guitar.

He cartoons a series of panels featuring a character called Super Cow the Avenger, who imparts lessons about nutrition. For a science assignment, he rigs our bathtub and shower stalls with buckets and rulers, measuring the amount of water used in each. (Showers are far more ecofriendly.) For another science project, Nic tests household cleaners and solvents on oil-drenched feathers to see what would work best to clean birds after an oil spill. Dove, the dishwashing liquid, wins. He bakes an apple in the oven and through the oven window tracks its disintegration, reporting the result in a paper written from the perspective of the apple. "I am becoming dehydrated. I sigh, 'Hello? Out there? Can anyone hear me? It's getting hot in here ...'"

Every morning and afternoon there are carpools between school and Point Reyes Station. When I drive, I sometimes educate Nic and his friends in the oeuvre of Van Morrison and the Kinks and guitar solos by Jorma Kaukonen, Jimmy Page, Jeff Beck, Robin Trower, Duane Allman, and Ronnie Van Zant. (Air guitar is encouraged.) Nic and his friends often play the complaining game, Karen's invention. Nic, imitating the *Newlywed Game*'s Bob Eubanks, is the announcer, explicating the rules. Contestants are awarded points on a scale of one to ten for unburdening themselves. The kids generally rail about their annoying siblings, jerks at school, unsympathetic teachers, and ogreish parents. Prosaic complaints receive middling scores. Admitting that you have had nightmares ever since you watched a horror movie in which teenage girls were stabbed and a man was buried alive wins eight points. When a girl tells about the time she was kidnapped by her father, she is applauded and awarded a ten. A boy also receives a ten for a fuming denunciation of his mother, who, he says, has dragged him to eight cities with four successive husbands. After months of hearing stories such as these, one girl uses her turn to complain, "I'm too normal. My parents have never been divorced and I have always lived in the same house." The other children sympathetically award her a ten.

Looking for a puppy at the Humane Society, Karen falls in love with a smelly, sad-eyed, near-starved hound sitting with its paws crossed on the cement floor of a kennel. She brings Moondog home, and also a ball of fur, a chocolate Labrador puppy we call Brutus. Moondog, who had never been inside a home before, lifts his leg on the floor and chews the wooden furniture. He tears through the house, baying and barking whenever a car drives by or when someone comes to the front door. He howls at the vacuum cleaner. Brutus hops in the grass like a bunny.

Every Wednesday we take the dogs and ourselves over to dinner at Karen's parents' house. Nancy and Don live in a barnlike board-and-batten home tucked into the side of a wooded canyon a half-hour from Inverness. The main room is cavernous and airy, with a twenty-four-foot-high single-pane plate glass door that slides open. Floor-to-ceiling shelves, lining two walls, are filled with books about shells and rocks and trees and birds. There are also portraits of their three children (Karen, at five or so, has large brown eyes and pinned-back dark hair) and sand dollars and pewter plates and a painting of a marmot.

Karen's father, Don, is a retired doctor. Karen grew up waiting in the car while he made house calls. Don grows tomatoes and squash in a terraced garden, but he spends most of his time in his second-story office doing his current job, evaluating studies designed to assess the effectiveness of new medicines.

Nancy, his wife of more than fifty years, works every day in the garden. She has gray eyes and silver hair cut in a pageboy. She is vivacious, handsome, gentle, and imposing.

None of Nancy and Don's children lives farther than San Francisco, and on any given afternoon it's not uncommon to find one or more or all of them sitting at the kitchen table in front of cups of reheated coffee and a plate of cookies, chatting with their mother.

The weekly Wednesday night dinners are raucous and memorable evenings with Nancy and Don and their three children and their families, plus occasional guests and always a revolving pack of our various unmannered dogs, which hog the best couches and steal unguarded food off the dining table.

At these dinners, Nancy recounts every newspaper or TV news story of toxic mattresses, molested children, teen suicide, poisoning, shopping-cart handles infected with bacteria, shark attack, car crash, electrocution — mostly endless tales about the hideous deaths of children. She tells us about a swimmer who drowned because she held her breath too long. She says that someone was killed in Mill Valley when a tree fell on his car, completely squishing him. She reports news about skyrocketing rates of childhood depression, eating disorders, and drug abuse. "A girl drowned after getting her hair caught in a hot-tub drain," she says one day. "I just want you to know so you'll be careful."

These warnings are meant to increase our vigilance, but it's impossible to prepare for every possible calamity. It's one thing to be safe, but panic is useless and too much caution can be stifling. No matter. The bad news pours forth along with the rosemary au jus.

On a Wednesday dinner in October of 1993, Karen, who is seven months pregnant, and I are sitting around the kitchen table with her parents and brother and sister. Nic plays outside with Brutus when Nancy imparts the latest gruesome news. The setting is Petaluma, a half-hour drive east of Inverness. A twelve-year-old girl was abducted from her bedroom. She was having a slumber party. Her mother was home.

Within a day, pictures of Polly Klaas with her long brown hair and gentle eyes are plastered on every store window and telephone pole in town. Soon a psychopath is arrested; he leads police to Polly's body. Every parent I know mourns Polly's death, and we hold tighter to our children.

Kids in Nic's carpool are obsessed with the murder. One girl says that she would have screamed and run. Another says there is no way she could have. "The guy was a giant, over seven feet." Nic is silent for a while and then says, "You have to scream and run anyway. You have to try to get away." A boy says there was an accomplice. "The guy who kidnapped her stole her for a child prostitute ring." Then no one talks until Nic asks if the killer was really seven feet tall. The girl says, "Seven feet eight."

We parents talk about our children's fitful sleep and nightmares and the kids respond with jokes they overhear at school. The ones they repeat in carpool aren't always about Polly Klaas, but other grisly news stories, too.

"What did Jeffrey Dahmer say to Lorena Bobbitt?"

After a pause and smirk: "You gonna eat that?"

"Jeffrey Dahmer's mother says, 'Jeffrey, I really don't like your friends,' and so he tells her, 'That's okay. Just eat the vegetables.'"

Nic never reads newspapers or watches the news, but there is no filtering out these disturbing events, because the kids—in carpool, on the playground—become preoccupied by them.

Jasper is born in early December.

Nancy and Don bring Nic to the hospital to see the baby when he is a few hours old. Jasper has swollen eyes because of some drops they put in them. Nic, sitting in a pink upholstered chair next to Karen's hospital bed, holds the baby, who is wrapped in a blanket like a burrito. He stares for a long time.

One can easily forget how tiny and delicate they are when they are just born. Back home in Inverness, when Jasper is sleeping, we check him to make certain that he is breathing. His presence with us seems tentative, and we worry that he could slip away.

We try our best to make the transition easy for Nic, who seems to like playing with Jasper, seems enchanted by him. Am I sugarcoating it? Maybe. I do know that it is complicated for him. In the best circumstances, second families must always be at least a little bit terrifying for the children from an earlier marriage. We reassure Nic, but he must wonder exactly where this new baby fits into our lives.

Karen and I are more tired. Jasper fights sleeping but passes out whenever he is in the car, so we drive him for long meandering rides to induce naps. Otherwise, not much has changed. Nic and I, often with his friends, surf whenever we can find the time. We play guitars together and listen to music. For New Year's Eve 1993, when I score tickets for the Nirvana concert at the Oakland Coliseum, I arrange for Nic to fly up from LA. It's an unforgettable evening. Kurt Cobain's performance is riveting, brilliant, and haunted. He sings:

> *I'm not like them*
> *But I can pretend*
> *The sun is gone*
> *But I have a light*
> *The day is done*
> *But I'm having fun*
> *My heart is broke*

But I have some glue
Help me inhale
And mend it with you
We'll float around
And hang out on clouds
Then we'll come down
And I'll have a hangover

Three months later, Nic, Karen, and I are sitting in the living room, with its cerulean wall panels framed in oiled redwood. The room is furnished sparsely with twin couches covered with strips of red silk fabric from China that Karen found at a thrift store and mismatched thrift store throw pillows. We watch Jasper, who is on a baby blanket. He starts to roll over onto his back and tries to crawl but doesn't go anywhere. Eventually, Jas gets in the right position, on all fours, and he huffs and puffs, rocks forward, and then begins crying. When he finally starts crawling, he goes sideways like a crab.

In the morning, Nic goes off to school as usual. But when he comes home, from his face I can tell that he is distressed. He drops his backpack on the floor, looks up, and tells me that Kurt Cobain shot himself in the head. From Nic's room I hear Cobain's voice.

I found it hard, it was hard to find.
Oh well, whatever, nevermind.

After summer, Nic begins seventh grade. Anne Lamott wrote, "The seventh and eighth grade were for me, and for every single good and interesting person I have ever known, what the writers of the Bible meant when they used the words *hell* and *the pit* . . . It was all over for any small feeling that one was essentially all right. One wasn't. One was suddenly a Diane Arbus character. It was

springtime, for Hitler, in Germany." These days there are reasons
more troubling than preteen awkwardness and cruelty for parents
to worry. A junior high school principal I know tells me that she
doesn't understand what it is, but things are worse for her students
than ever before. "I can't believe the things they do to themselves
and to each other," she says. In a survey of public-school teachers
in 1940, the top disciplinary problems listed included talking out
of turn, chewing gum, running in the halls, dress-code violations,
and littering. More than fifty years later, they are drug and alcohol
abuse, pregnancy, suicide, rape, robbery, and assault.

When Nic enters seventh grade, he still seems to enjoy playing
with Jasper, whose first word is *duck,* followed by *up, banana,
doggie,* and *Nicky.* Nic meanwhile has discovered an unanticipated
benefit of a baby in the family. The girls in his grade flock to
Jasper. They come over to play with him — to bounce him around
and dress him up. Nic is delighted with his expanding harem.

But Nic is also increasingly less interested in the carpool kids
and instead spends most of his free time with a group of boys with
buzzed hair who skateboard, talk about, but do nothing about,
girls, and listen to music: Guns N' Roses, Metallica, Primus,
and Jimi Hendrix. As always, Nic has eclectic and hip — and
often fickle — taste. He does not seem to tire of some discover-
ies — Björk, Tom Waits, Bowie — but otherwise he is into the
edgiest music and then grows bored with it. By the time an artist,
from Weezer to Blind Melon to Offspring to Cake to Green Day,
has a hit record, he has discarded them in favor of the retro, the
obscure, the ultracontemporary, or the plain bizarre, a list that
includes Coltrane, polka collections, the soundtrack from *The
Umbrellas of Cherbourg,* John Zorn, M. C. Solar, Jacques Brel,
or, these days, samba, to which he cha-chas through the living
room. He discovers Pearl Jam, a song called "Jeremy" about a
teenage boy in Texas who shot himself in front of his English class.

Jeremy's teacher asked him to go to the office to get a late slip. He returned and told her, "Miss, this is what I actually went for," before turning the gun on himself. But most of all Nic listens to Nirvana. The music blasts like mortar fire from his room.

> *I feel stupid and contagious*
> *Here we are now entertain us*

In early May, I pick Nic up after school one day to drive him to a dinner at Nancy and Don's. When he climbs into the car I smell cigarette smoke. At first, he denies that he has smoked. He says that he was hanging out with some kids who were smoking. When I press him, however, he admits that he had a few puffs with a group of boys who were smoking behind the gymnasium. I lecture him and he promises not to do it again.

The next Friday after school, he and a friend, with whom Nic is spending the night, are tossing a football in the garden in Inverness. I am packing an overnight bag for him and look for a sweater in his backpack. I do not find the sweater, but instead discover a small bag of marijuana.

4

When I was a young child, my family lived near Walden Pond, in Lexington, Massachusetts. Our home was next to a farm with apple trees, corn and tomatoes, and a row of stacked beehives. My father was a chemical engineer. He watched a television commercial that said to take your sinuses to Arizona. He had hay fever, so he did. He secured a job at a semiconductor plant in Phoenix. We drove west in our pea-green Studebaker, staying overnight along the way at Motel 6s and eating at Denny's and Sambo's.

We settled in Scottsdale, living in a motel until our tract home was built. My father's new job at Motorola was to grow, slice, and etch silicon wafers for transistors and microprocessors. My mother wrote a column about our school and neighborhood — science fair winners and little league results — for the *Scottsdale Daily Progress*.

My friends and I often reminisce about our childhoods, when things were different. It was a far more innocent world and a safer one. My sister, brother, and I, along with the rest of the kids on our block, played on the street until twilight, when our mothers called us in for dinner. We played ring and run, tag, and boys chase the girls. TV dinners — fried chicken, mashed potatoes with a pat of butter, apple cobbler, each isolated in its own compartment — set on folding trays, we watched *Bonanza*, *Wonderful World of Disney*, and *The Man from U.N.C.L.E.* We were Cub Scouts and Brownies. We had barbecues, built go-carts, made cakes in my sister's Easy-Bake Oven, and rode inner tubes down the Salt and Verde rivers.

But I'm not certain if the wistful recollections of those times are justified. The news in our neighborhood traveled by way of our mothers' hushed voices. Charles Manson and 50-percent-off sales and fad diets were favorite topics on the sidewalk in front yards, at Tupperware parties and mahjong games, and in the beauty shop where my mother got her hair frosted. They whispered when a ten-year-old child who lived on our block hung himself. Then a girl who lived two doors down was killed in a car accident. The driver, an older boy, was high on drugs.

The proximity to Mexico meant that drugs were abundant and cheap. Geography, however, probably didn't make a lot of difference. A smorgasbord of previously unknown or unavailable drugs flooded our school and our neighborhood like they have flooded America since the mid-60s.

Marijuana was most prevalent. Kids hung out by the bike rack after school offering single joints for fifty cents and ounce bags for ten dollars. They offered hits of their joints in the bathroom and walking to and from our high school. One of my friends sought it out and, after smoking it, told a group of us about it. He said that he asked a boy we all knew was a stoner for marijuana and smoked the joint in the backyard of his parents' house, coughed a lot, felt nothing, and then went inside and ate a box of Chips Ahoy cookies. He began smoking almost every day.

A year or so later a boy on our block asked if I wanted to smoke a joint. It was 1968 and I was a high school freshman. It didn't do much for me, but neither did it cause me to hallucinate or to try to fly off the roof of our house like Art Linkletter's daughter supposedly did when she tried LSD. That is, it seemed harmless, and so I didn't think twice about trying it again when I walked into another boy's house and his older brother passed me a glowing roach held by an alligator clip.

Of course it wasn't articulated, but pot, with its outlaw cachet, was a passkey into a loosely defined social circle. To be inside was a relief after my lonely geekiness in junior high. I laughed easier and felt funnier with a stoned—that is, less discerning—audience. Here was a palliative for raging insecurity. I experienced everything—music, nature—in a heightened, far more intense way, and was less shy around girls, a benefit that cannot be overstated for a boy of fourteen or fifteen. The world seemed at once obscured and more vivid. But even these probably weren't the main reasons I continued smoking. On top of the continuous peer pressure and the high, plus the sense of rebellion in lighting a joint, plus the camaraderie, and besides the ways that pot helped assuage my awkwardness and insecurity ... besides all this, marijuana helped me feel something when I felt almost nothing and block out feelings when I felt too much. In precisely the way that pot made things both blurrier and more vibrant, it allowed me to feel more and to feel less.

Nowadays people of my age often say that drugs were different then—less potent pot and purer psychedelics. This is true. Tests of marijuana have shown that there is twice as much THC, the active ingredient, in the average joint or pipeful today than in the weed of a decade ago, which itself was stronger than in the 1960s and 70s. There are frequent reports that psychedelics and ecstasy are laced with or even substituted by meth and other drugs or impurities, though back then we heard of kids snorting Drano in place of cocaine. One thing is undeniably different. A body of research unequivocally proves a wide range of dangerous physical and psychological effects of drugs, including marijuana. We thought they were safe. They weren't. I know that some people look back on what they consider the good old days of "harmless" drug use. They survived intact, but many people did not. There were accidents, suicides, and overdoses. I still run into a shocking number of drug casualties from the 1960s and 70s who wander the streets, some of them homeless. Some rant about conspiracies. Apparently it's a trait common in drug addicts and alcoholics. "Whenever his liquor began to work he most always went for the government," said Huck Finn about his drunkard father.

And so throughout Nic's childhood, ever since he was seven or eight, I talked to him about drugs. We spoke about them "early and often" in ways prescribed by the Partnership for a Drug-Free America. I told him about people who were harmed or killed. I told him about my mistakes. I watched for the early warning signs of teenage alcoholism and drug abuse. (Number fifteen on one organization's list: "Is your child suddenly volunteering to clean up after cocktail parties, but forgetting his other chores?")

When I was a child, my parents implored me to stay away from drugs. I dismissed them, because they didn't know what they were talking about. They were — still are — teetotalers. I, however, knew about drugs from first-hand experience. So when I warned Nic, I thought I might have some credibility.

Many drug counselors tell parents of my generation to lie to our children about our past drug use. It's the same reason that it may backfire when famous athletes show up at school assemblies or on television and tell kids, "Man, don't do this shit, I almost died," and yet there they stand, diamonds, gold, multimillion-dollar salaries and cereal-box fame. The words: I barely survived. The message: I survived, thrived, and you can, too. Kids see that their parents turned out all right in spite of the drugs. So maybe I should have lied to Nic, and kept my drug use hidden, but I didn't. He knew the truth. Meanwhile, our close relationship made me certain that I would know if he were exposed to them. I naively believed that if Nic were tempted to try them, he would tell me. I was wrong.

*

We are still nearer the winter edge of spring on this cool and misty May afternoon, the scent of wood smoke in the air—a remnant of the afternoon fire. This time of year the sun falls early behind the ridge and poplars, and so though it is only four o'clock, the yard is shrouded in shadow. Fog swirls at the boys' feet as they toss the ball back and forth. It is a desultory game; they appear to be more interested in their conversation, maybe about girls or bands or the rancher who shot a rabid dog in Point Reyes Station yesterday.

The boy with Nic is muscular, a weightlifter who shows off his pumped-up chest and biceps in a tight T-shirt. Nic wears an overlarge gray cardigan—mine. With his stringy hair and world-weary visage and languor, anyone else would guess he'd go on to smoke pot, at least. Yet in spite of his costume, and in spite of his variable moods—his increasing ennui and hunched surliness—and in spite of his new crowd that includes the school's tough, phlegmatic boys, when I look at Nic I see youthfulness and vitality, playfulness and innocence. A child. And so I am utterly bewildered by the tightly wound green buds of marijuana that I hold in my hand.

Karen sits on the living room couch, bent over her journal, drawing with India ink. Jasper is asleep near her on the couch, lying on his back with his hands clenched in tiny fists.

When I approach her, Karen looks up.

I show her the marijuana.

"What is that? Where did you . . . ?"

And then: "What? Is it Nic's?" It is half a question. She knows.

As usual, I manage my panic by trying to forestall hers. "It will be all right. It was bound to happen at some point. We'll deal with it."

Standing on the deck, I call to the boys. They come over, Nic palming the ball, breathing hard.

"I have to talk to you."

They look at my outstretched hand holding the marijuana.

"Oh," Nic says. He stiffens a little, waiting, docile. Moondog comes up to Nic and nuzzles his leg. Nic is not one to fight back in the face of hard evidence. He tentatively glances up at me, his scared eyes large, trying to evaluate how much trouble he is in.

"Come inside."

Karen and I stand facing the boys. I look to her for guidance, but she is as uncertain as I am. I am shaken not only by the discovery that Nic is smoking pot, but by the even more perplexing fact that I had no idea.

"How long have you been smoking this stuff?"

The cornered boys look at each other. "It's the first time we bought it," Nic says. "We tried it one other time."

I think: Do I trust him? This too is a radically confounding proposition, one that has never crossed my mind. Of course I trust him. He would not lie to me. Would he lie? I know parents whose children are in constant trouble at school and at home. The most disconcerting part is the dishonesty.

"Tell me exactly what happened."

I look at his friend, who hasn't said a word. He stares at the floor. Nic answers for them both: "Everyone does it."

"Everyone?"

"Almost everyone."

Nic's eyes aim at the long fingers of his boyish hands, which are spread out wide on the table. He closes them and stuffs his fists into his pockets.

"Where did you get it?"

"Just somebody. Some kid."

"Who?"

"It's not important."

"Yes, it is."

They tell us the boy's name. "We just wanted to see what it was like," Nic says.

"And?"

"It's no big deal."

Nic's friend asks if I am going to call his parents. When I say yes, he begs me not to. "I'm sorry, but they need to know. I am going to call them and then I'll take you home."

Nic asks, "What about the sleepover?"

I glare at him. "We'll take him home and then you and I will talk."

He is still looking down.

The boy's father, when I call, thanks me for letting him know. He says that he is concerned but isn't entirely surprised. "We have gone through this with our older kids," he says. "I guess they all go through it. We'll talk to him." He resignedly adds, "We are so busy. We can't monitor him."

When I call the mother of the boy who sold them the pot, she is livid, adamant that her son wasn't involved. She charges that Nic and the other boy are trying to get her son in trouble.

When Nic and I are alone, he is contrite. He nods when I tell him that Karen and I have decided to ground him. "Yeah, I understand."

Our thinking went like this. We don't want to overreact, but even more, we don't want to underreact. We issue a punishment to show how seriously we take the breach of the rules of our household as well as our relationship. There are consequences for one's actions, and we hope that these are appropriately onerous. In addition, I am wary of his new crowd of friends. I understand that I can't choose his friends for him, and forbidding friends might only make them more attractive, but at least I can minimize the time he spends with them. The other part is simply that I want to watch him. To look at him. To try to fathom what is going on.

"How long am I grounded?"

"Let's see how things go over the next couple weeks."

We sit down on facing couches. Nic appears genuinely chastened. I ask, "What made you want to try pot? It wasn't very long ago that the idea of smoking anything — a cigarette, never mind marijuana — repulsed you. You and Thomas" — I mention one of his city friends — "used to get in trouble for throwing away his mother's cigarettes."

"I don't know."

Using the red pen that is lying on the coffee table, he begins to scribble crosshatched lines on the day's newspaper.

"I guess I was curious." In a minute, he says: "I didn't like it anyway. It made me feel. I don't know. Weird." Then he adds, "You don't have to worry. I won't ever try it again."

"What about other drugs? Have you tried any?"

His incredulous look convinces me that he is telling the truth. "I know this was stupid," he says, "but I'm not that stupid."

"How about alcohol? Have you been drinking?"

He waits before answering. "We got drunk. Once. Me and Philip. It was on the ski trip."

"The ski trip? To Lake Tahoe?"

He nods.

I recall the midwinter long weekend before Jasper was born, when we rented a cabin at Alpine Meadows. We let Nic bring along Philip, a friend we like, a soft-spoken, easy-to-be-with boy. He is small with hair combed down over his forehead. We are friends with his parents.

We arrived in the mountains at night, just before a blizzard shut down the roads. In the morning, the pine trees were dusted white. Nic had skied before, but this time he and Philip decided to try snowboarding. As a surfer, Nic thought it would be easy to switch over. "You're carving snow instead of water," he had said. "They are both about balance and gravity." Maybe, but he spent most of the trip tumbling down the mountainside before he finally got it.

Now I ask, "When did you have an opportunity to drink? Where did you get liquor?"

His body rocks back and forth on the couch. "One night you and Karen went to sleep early," he says. "We were hanging out by the fire watching TV. We got bored and wanted to play cards, but I couldn't find any. I went around looking and found the liquor cabinet. We got glasses and poured in some of everything—only a little of each so that no one would be able to tell. Rum, bourbon, gin, sake, tequila, vermouth, Scotch, some weird-ass green shit, crème de something." He pauses and says, "We drank it all. It was gross, but we wanted to see what it was like to get good and drunk."

I remember the night. Karen and I had been awakened by the sounds of the two of them throwing up. Simultaneously in the two downstairs bathrooms. We went to check on them. They were sick throughout the night. We thought they had the flu.

In the morning, we called Philip's mother. "Yes, the flu is going around," she agreed. The boys were ill the next day on the long, windy drive home down from the Sierra. One time we couldn't make it to the shoulder of the road quickly enough, and Philip threw up out the car window.

"That was the only time. I haven't touched anything since. It makes me sick to think about it."

His reasonableness is disarming, but I take in this information like a punch in the gut, reeling as much from the deception as the drunkenness. And yet at the same time I appreciate Nic's candor. I think, At least he's coming clean.

Then he says: "If it's any comfort to you, I hate all this. I'm not making an excuse, but" —after a moment—"it's hard."

"What's hard?"

"It's hard. I don't know. Everybody drinks. Everybody smokes." I think about his beloved Salinger, from the mouth of Franny: "I'm sick of not having the courage to be an absolute nobody."

On Monday, I call his teacher and tell him what happened. He sets up a conference with Karen and me for after school. We meet with him in his vacated classroom, the three of us sitting at students' desks.

The teacher has given me one of Nic's binders of work — mathematics, geography, literature. Nic has covered a page with ballpoint graffiti, a buxom, big-eyed girl, hollow-eyed men, and blocky initials. In style and content, these drawings contrast sharply with the chalk mural of a scene from the Middle Ages meticulously shaded over the entire green board along the front of the classroom. The students' expressive self-portraits are pinned up on another wall. I easily pick out Nic's: harshly drawn, more of a cartoon, it is a boy with a wild smile and big, wide-open eyes.

The teacher is built like Ichabod Crane, with receding, flyaway auburn hair and a crooked nose. Bending forward on the small chair, he pages through Nic's folder in front of him. "He's doing fine in his schoolwork," he says. "He's doing *quite* well. I'm sure you know. He's a leader in the class. He gets other kids — some who wouldn't necessarily be engaged — he gets them excited about contributing to the discussion."

"But what about the marijuana?" Karen asks.

The teacher, way too large for the student's chair into which he is folded, leans uncomfortably on his elbows. "I have noticed that Nic is being pulled by the students who the others see as cool," he says. "They are the ones who sneak cigarettes and — I'm only guessing — probably smoke pot. They may. But I don't think you have to be overly concerned. It's normal. Most kids try it."

"But," I say, "Nic is only twelve."

"Yes." The teacher sighs. "That's when they try it. There's only so much that we can do. It's a force out there. The children have to figure it out sooner or later. Often sooner."

When we ask for his advice, he says: "Talk to him about it. I will, too. If it's all right with you, we'll talk about it in class. We won't mention any names." Whether out of guilt or resignation, he repeats, "There's only so much we can do. If we work together —the school, the families—then maybe."

"Would you forbid him from playing with . . .?" I name the boys. "They don't seem to be a very good influence."

The leaves of a tree outside the window flicker in the afternoon sun as the teacher mulls the question. "I would encourage healthier friendships, yes," he says, "but I'm not sure how far you'll get by forbidding him. From what I've seen in the past, when you forbid children, they usually sneak what they want. Steering them works better than forcing them. You can try."

He recommends a book about teenagers and he promises to keep in close touch.

It is breezy outside. The schoolyard is abandoned except for Nic, who is waiting for us. He sits on a tiny swing in the kinder-garteners' playground, his long legs bent underneath him.

Alone in our bedroom, Karen and I talk it over, sorting out our puzzlement and worry. What am I worried about? I know that marijuana can become a habit and Nic could be sidetracked from his schoolwork. I worry that he could go on to try other drugs. I warn Nic about pot. "It really can—often does lead to hard drugs," I say. He probably doesn't believe me, just like I didn't believe the adults who said it when I was young. But in spite of a myth perpetrated by my generation, the first to use drugs en masse, marijuana *is* the gateway drug. Almost every-one I know who smoked pot in high school tried other drugs.

Conversely, I never met anyone who used hard drugs who didn't start with pot.

I begin to second-guess each of my past decisions, including our move to the country. I have never fantasized that any American suburb or exurb or country town, no matter how remote, is far enough away to be untouched by the perils most often associated with inner cities, but I thought that towns like Inverness must be safer than the Tenderloin. Now I'm not sure. I wonder if we should ever have moved out of San Francisco. Moving probably was irrelevant; this would have happened wherever we lived.

I blame my hypocrisy. It makes me wince. How can I tell him not to use drugs when he knows that I have? "Do as I say, not as I did." I tell him that I wish I hadn't used them. I tell him about friends whose lives were ruined by them. And meanwhile, in my mind, as always I blame the divorce. I tell myself that many children of divorce do all right and many children in intact families don't. Regardless, there is no way to undo what I know to be the most traumatic event of Nic's life.

The next few days, I continue to talk to Nic about drugs, about peer pressure, and about what cool really is. "It may not seem like it, but it is far cooler to be engaged, to study and learn," I say. "Looking back, I now think the coolest kids were the ones who stayed away from drugs."

I know how lame I sound and how I would have responded at Nic's age: "Yeah, right." Even so, I try to convince him that I know what I am talking about, that I understand the ubiquity and the persistent pressure to do drugs, that I understand their seductiveness.

Nic seems to listen intently, though I am unsure if or how he is taking it in. Indeed, I sense that my close relationship with Nic has changed. Now I am the occasional target of his exasperation. We sometimes argue over sloppy homework or half-done chores. But it's confusing, because it all seems within the realm of acceptable and expectable adolescent rebellion.

Three weeks later, I'm driving Nic to a doctor's appointment for a checkup. I turn down the music on the tape player and start in again. I know that there is no point in haranguing him because he will just shut down, but I want to cover every angle. In the conversation that has been going on now for weeks, my tone has ranged from warning to pleading. Today is less strained. I inform him that Karen and I have decided that he is no longer grounded. He nods and says, "Thanks."

I continue to watch him over the next few weeks. Nic's somberness seems to have diminished. I file away the marijuana bust as an aberration, maybe even a useful one because it has taught him a salient lesson.

I think it did. Nic is in the eighth grade. And things seem much better.

He rarely hangs out with the boy who had been (I'm convinced) the worst influence on him — the one who, according to Nic, sold him the pot. (About this, I believe Nic, not the boy's mother.) Instead, he spends a lot of his free time surfing with his West Marin friends. We surf together, too, driving up and down the coast, chasing waves from Santa Cruz to Point Arena. On these outings, there's time to talk, and Nic seems open and optimistic. He's motivated in school, too. He wants to do well, in part to increase his chances of being accepted at one of the local private high schools.

Nic continues to devour books. He reads and rereads *Franny and Zooey* and *Catcher in the Rye*. After reading *To Kill a Mockingbird*, he turns in a book report in the form of a tape from Atticus Finch's answering machine with messages for Scout and Jem from Dill and anonymous, threatening phone calls to Atticus for defending

Tom Robinson. He reads *Streetcar Named Desire* and then tapes a radio interview with Blanche DuBois. For an assignment about *Death of a Salesman*, he draws a cartoon bemoaning the Lomans' family values. Next is a biography project for which Nic, dressed in a white wig, white mustache, and white suit, walks onstage and recites, in a lilting southern accent, the life story of Samuel Clemens. "My pen name is Mark Twain. Sit back and let me tell you my story." There have been no more indications that he is smoking anything—neither marijuana nor cigarettes. In fact, he has seemed happier and guardedly excited about his upcoming eighth-grade graduation.

It is a warm, windless weekend. Nic is thirteen. After a quiet day around the house and with the promise of a mounting south swell, he and I strap our surfboards onto the roof of the station wagon and drive on the winding road that leads to a beach south of Point Reyes. The surf break is reached only after an hour-long hike on a grassy path through sand dunes.

Lugging our boards under our arms, Nic and I trudge to the mouth of an estuary, reputed to be a breeding ground for great white sharks. Rabbits skitter past us and a V formation of pelicans flies overhead. The sun hangs low; its rays seem painted on with a watery apricot wash. As dusk settles in, the fog pours like pancake batter onto the hilly ranchland and, from there, spills over the bay. We have never seen better surf here. Six- to eight-foot-high waves roll in, breaking in long, peeling, silky lines. We quickly change into our wetsuits and gallop into the water, leaping atop our boards. The disappearing sun projects a stunning array of ruby-red stripes along the western horizon. Opposite, the moon, fat and yellow, dangles low. Two other surfers are in the water, but they soon leave, so Nic and I have the place to ourselves. It is thrilling surfing, as good as it gets.

Paddling out, there is no sound other than the smooth *whoosh* of the surfboard cleaving the water and then, at regular intervals, the rumble of a breaking wave. We ride one, paddle out, and then ride another. Once I look up and see Nic crouched low on his board inside a barrel, the wave's waterfall encasing him.

It gets darker. Fog obscures the moon and envelops us. I realize that Nic and I are in two different currents that are pushing us to opposite sides of the channel. We are separated by a hundred yards. I begin to panic, because the thickening fog and growing dimness prevent us from seeing each other well.

I paddle blindly toward Nic, frantically seeking him until my arms are exhausted from fighting the current. Finally, after what seems like a half-hour of nonstop paddling, a gust of wind wipes clean a section of fog and I see him. Tall and magnificent, Nic, standing atop a sliver of ivory, carves up and down a dazzling, glassy wall of water, white spray sparking off the edge of his board, a brilliant smile on his face. When he sees me, he waves.

Exhausted, famished, wind-burned, and waterlogged after a long session, we peel off our wetsuits, load up our backpacks, and walk back to the car.

On our way home, we stop at a taqueria. We eat burritos the size of pot-bellied pigs and sip lime soda. Nic is reflective, talking about the future—about high school. "I still can't believe I got in," he says.

I don't know if I had ever seen him as excited as he was after he spent a day visiting the school. "Everyone seemed so . . ." He paused to find the right word. "Passionate. About everything. Art, music, history, writing, journalism, politics. And the teachers . . ." He stopped again to catch his breath. "The teachers are *amazing*. I sat in on a poetry class. I didn't want to leave." Then, quieter, he said, "I'll never get in." The competition for slots at this school is intense.

He did get in, and now, in the euphoric moment, he concludes: "Everything seems pretty great."

The graduation ceremony is planned for an early June afternoon. A church auditorium has been booked and parents have been enlisted to set up chairs, a podium, decorations, and refreshment tables. On the day of the event, I come early to help prepare.

A couple hours later, the teachers and family members arrive and are seated in rows of folding chairs. Next come the graduates. They are awkward in their fancy clothes. Many of the girls wear new or borrowed dresses. Most can barely walk in their high heels; they wobble as if they're tipsy. The boys appear surly in their stiff collars, fidgeting with their neckties and tugging morosely on their shirttails, which somehow manage to untuck a half-inch at a time until almost all of them hang out over their dress pants.

The children may be miserably costumed, but their moods rise to the occasion. Somehow their decency does, too. One by one, the graduates' names are called by the school principal. Some more steady than others, they march up a small flight of stairs and walk across the low stage to accept their diplomas. Their classmates cheer wildly. For that day and only for that day, they root for one another with unbridled and generous enthusiasm. For each girl and each boy. With equal vigor, they hoot and holler. They applaud the nerds and foxes and dweebs and queen-bees and hoods; the meek, the jocks, the hip, the outcasts.

I never anticipated being moved by an eighth-grade graduation, but I am. We have come to know these children well after three years of driving them in various carpools and to field trips; of having them at our house for parties; of attending their speeches, plays, music recitals, and sporting tournaments; of commiserating with their parents; and of hearing from one another and mostly from Nic about their every success, crisis, crush, and hurt feeling.

The boys and girls, still children but testing the waters of adulthood, march forward. The boy whose mother denied that her son had sold Nic the marijuana. The one with whom he got drunk. A surfing friend. The buzz-headed skateboarders. The girl with whom Nic used to speak for hours on the phone at night until I made him hang up. The carpool kids. All the children, gawky and uncertain, diplomas fluttering in their hands, walk unsteadily down from the dais, now middle-school graduates, heading to the snake pit of high school.

It is the weekend after graduation and some families are gathered at Heart's Desire Beach on this sultry June afternoon. The bay is still. We eat a potluck dinner of chips and salsa, a whole roasted salmon, grilled hamburgers, soda. The shimmering bay is warm and the kids swim and kayak and canoe, inevitably capsizing. On shore in sweatshirts, their hair still wet, Nic's friends talk excitedly about their summer plans together—the beach, camps—but not Nic. It never gets any easier when he prepares to leave.

The fog rolls in and the party adjourns. Back home, we sit by the fire and Nic reads us the yearbook entries from his friends. "You'll have a million girlfriends in high school." "Have fun surfing." "I'm not going to be living here next year so I'll probably see you in like ten years. Keep in touch." "I love you funny bunny baby. I've loved you as long as I've known you." "I'm dying to see the new baby whatever I should call her. I hope Jasper likes her." "Good luck with high school and the new little fart." "I didn't know you that well but have a fun summer." "Have fun this summer you stupid dickhead. Just kidding." "Dedicate a book to me sometime. I'll thank you when I get the Oscar. Toodles . . ." His teacher wrote: "Wherever you be, wherever you may, seek the truth, strive for the beautiful, achieve the good."

We are beginning another summer made bittersweet by the knowledge that Nic is going to Los Angeles, though he has arranged with Vicki to wait until the baby is born.

On the morning of June 7, Karen, Nic, Jasper, and I get into the car. The baby is breach and so will be delivered by C-section. Karen chose her mother's birthday. The appointment is for six. Karen's sister has given us soothing music by Enya, but Karen asks for Nirvana. She turns "Nevermind" up loud.

> *Gotta find a way*
> *A better way*
> *I better wait*
> *I better wait*

I drive through the forest and then stop at Nancy and Don's, dropping off Nic and Jasper, who wait with their grandparents for a call from the hospital.

Our daughter is born at seven in the morning. Her hair is curly and black and her eyes are luminous. We name her Marguerite but call her Daisy.

Nancy arrives at the hospital with Nic and Jasper, who are escorted into the dimly lit room, where Karen holds Daisy. A nurse asks Nancy and Nic if they would like to give the baby her first bath. Jasper sits near Karen, while Nancy and Nic, guided by the nurse, wheel Daisy in her bassinet to the nursery, where they help weigh, bathe, and dress her in a soft white nightgown with little pink elephants and doll-sized booties. She is eight pounds, twenty-one inches long. Staring at the baby, Nic tells Nancy, "I never thought I would have a family like this."

We drive home the following day. Alongside Nic in the backseat, there are now two car seats.

I wake up early the next morning and find the two boys, both in flannel pajamas, sitting on the couch with cups of hot chocolate. Nic reads *Frog and Toad Are Friends*. Jasper cuddles close to him. A small fire burns in the fireplace. Nic closes the book and gets up to cook breakfast for all, and while he stands over the stove he sings in his best Tom Waits growl, "Well, the eggs chase the bacon round the fryin' pan."

We eat and then the boys and I go for a walk at a nearby beach, stopping afterward to pick blackberries for a pie. It takes longer than it should, because Nic and Jasper, blue-fingered and blue-mouthed, place one berry in the basket for every dozen that wind up in their mouths.

Back home, after an early dinner and the pie, Nic and Jasper play in the grass. Like a lion cub, Jasper climbs onto Nic's head, and they roll around on a big red ball. Karen is holding Daisy, who is looking around with her wide eyes. Brutus, lumbering over like a sleepy brown bear, sprawls on the grass near the kids. With Jasper hanging onto his neck, Nic rolls over and, holding the dog by the jowls and staring into his eyes, sings, "Give me a kiss to build a dream on." He plants a big kiss on Brutus's nose. Brutus yawns, Nic playfully tosses Jasper into the air, and Daisy drifts into a soft sleep.

I look at the three of them and recall a bewildering emotion that I recognized for the first time back when Nic was born. Along with the joy of parenthood, with every child comes a piercing vulnerability. It is at once sublime and terrifying.

In the newspaper a few days ago, I read about a school-bus explosion in Israel and an update on some of the families of the children killed over a year ago in the Oklahoma City bombing; stray bullets hitting children in a refugee camp in Bosnia; and a story from China, where a convicted armed robber, on his way to the gallows, screamed out to his brother, "Take care of my son."

I felt a new quality of anguish. Maybe parents feel for every child. Maybe we feel more and more than we ever knew possible. As I look at my three children, in the diffused gold light that shines unsteadily through the poplar leaves, I feel overfull with the knowledge that for this moment they are safe and happy, which is ultimately all we parents want. If only it could be like this always—the children nearby, getting along, happy, and safe.

5

Y our psycho husband is torturing my little brother."

Nic, addressing Karen, who has just entered the room, is standing near me with his arms on his hips. It is a rainy morning on the day he heads to Los Angeles. I am brushing out a matted tangle in Jasper's hair and Jas is shrieking as if I am pulling out his fingernails with pliers. Nic, who after a shower is wrapped in a blue towel, dons an orange parka, steps into a large pair of green garden boots by the front door, and snaps on a pair of the little kids' dress-up driving goggles. He brandishes a wooden spoon.

"Unhand that knave," he says to me. To Jasper, he says, "Oh, the wretched, wretched sorrow of your plight, my lovely brother. Oh, the unfairness. The cruelty."

Into the spoon he then sings, "My Gallant Crew, Good Morning," from *HMS Pinafore*, further distracting Jasper, who allows me to finish brushing his hair.

Nic, who has already packed, says his goodbyes. Jasper and Nic do their secret handshake, a complicated ritual: a normal shake, their hands skimming off each other and clasping together, Nic's fist tapping the top of Jasper's, and then the reverse, another clasping shake from which the two hands slide slowly apart and ending with their forefingers pointing toward each other while in unison they say, "You!"

Jasper cries. "No, Nicky, I don't want you to go." They hug and then Nic kisses baby Daisy on the forehead. He and Karen hug again.

"Sputnik, old buddy, have a great summer," she says.

"I'll miss you, KB."

"Write me."

"Write back."

Driving to the airport, I take the scenic route along Ocean Beach rather than drive through the city. Nic stares at the rough sea. At the United terminal, I park the car in the garage and walk with Nic to the counter, where he checks his suitcase. We say our goodbyes at the gate.

Nic says, "Everything."

I respond, "Everything."

Saying goodbye at the airport cuts a new slice into my heart each time, but I put up a good show because I don't want him to feel worse than he already does.

After he boards, I watch through the glass wall as the massive metal shell containing him pulls away from the gate and takes off.

Though it may be the best we can do, I loathe joint custody. It presupposes that children can do just as well when they are divided between two homes, each defined by a different parent and different step-parents and sometimes step-siblings and a jumble of expectations, discipline, and values that often contradict one another. "Home is a holy thing," Emily Dickinson said. But *homes* is an antilogy. How many adults can imagine having two primary homes? For children, home is even more important, the psychological as well as physical cradle of development, the brick-and-mortar incarnation of all that their parents represent: stability, safety, and the rules of life.

The week after Nic leaves, I interview a renowned child psychologist named Judith Wallerstein, who founded the Judith Wallerstein Center for the Family in Transition in Marin County, not far from Inverness, for a magazine article. She gained international attention when she brought sobering news to divorce-happy post-60s America. Before that time, divorce was difficult, stigmatized, and rarer, but changing mores and no-fault splitups made it easy and common. It was a liberating change for many adults — societal conventions no longer confined people to bad marriages. The general assumption, mostly based on wishful thinking, was that children would be happier if their parents were. But Dr. Wallerstein discovered that in many cases, they were traumatized.

She began her interviews with two- to seventeen-year-olds whose parents had divorced in the early 1970s. She found that the children were having a difficult time coping with the breakups, but she assumed that the strains would be short-lived. She met these children for a second interview more than a year later. Not only had they not recovered, but they were doing worse.

Wallerstein followed the children every few years for the next twenty-five years. In her series of books, she reports her findings — that more than one-third of these kids experienced moderate to severe depression and a significant number were troubled and underachieving. Many struggled to establish and maintain relationships.

No one wanted to hear the message, and the messenger was attacked. Feminists said that Wallerstein was part of the backlash against women, in effect telling them to go back home, stay married, and take care of their children. Her work was appropriated by various special interest groups, including the conservative new right, who used it to "prove" their arguments about traditional family values — and to attack single parents and nontraditional families. Men's rights groups praised her for emphasizing the importance of fathers in children's lives and attacked her when she said that some forms of joint custody seemed to be harming children. But her work reverberated throughout the country, influencing courts, legislatures, therapists, and parents. Her books were bestsellers, and they are still used as a bible by many judges and therapists. Some judges assign Wallerstein's books to divorcing parents.

I meet Dr. Wallerstein at her wood-shingle house in Belvedere, overlooking the bay and Sam's Grill on the Tiburon waterfront. She is diminutive with silver hair, gentle crystal-blue eyes, precisely dressed. When I ask her about joint custody, particularly long-distance joint custody like Nic's, she tells me that she has observed young boys and girls who, upon returning from one home to the other, wander from object to object — table to bed to sofa — touching them to affirm that they are still there. The absent parent may well seem even more elusive than the furniture. As children grow older, though they no longer require tactile proof, they may incorporate a sense that both of their homes are illusory and impermanent. Also, while young children may suffer when joint custody keeps them apart from a parent for too long, frequent transitions, especially when parents live far apart, may harm older ones. Dr. Wallerstein explains, "Going back and forth made it impossible for children to enjoy activities with other children . . .Teenagers complained bitterly about having to spend their summers with parents instead of with friends." She concludes: "You'd like to think that these kids could simply integrate their lives between their two homes, have two sets of peers, and easily adjust to being with each parent, but most children do not have the flexibility. They begin to feel as if it's a flaw in their character when it is simply impossible for many people to conduct parallel lives."

For many families, summer vacation is a respite from the stresses of the school year, devoted to time together. I just want to get through it as fast as possible. Nic and I speak regularly on the telephone. He tells me about the movies he sees, the ball games he plays, a bully on a playground, a new friend, the books he reads. It is quieter when he is in LA, but even the fun of the new baby is tempered by a low-grade melancholia. We never get used to him being gone.

We make the best of the times we have with him. He comes up for two weeks and we cram in as much surfing, swimming, kayaking, and other fun as possible. We go to San Francisco to hang out with our friends. In the evenings, Nic plays with the little kids or we talk. His reenactments of movies have long been regular evening entertainment. Nic's impressions are precise. De Niro: "You talkin' to me?" Not only the line, but the entire *Taxi Driver* scene. And Tom Cruise—"Show me the money"—and Mr. T—"I pity da fool . . ." He does Jack Nicholson in *The Shining,* "He-e-e- e-re's Johnny," and, impeccably, Dustin Hoffman's *Rain Man.* And Schwarzenegger: "Hasta la vista, Baby"; "Chill out, dickwad"; "I'll be back"; "Come with me if you want to live." Possibly his best is Clint Eastwood: "You've got to ask yourself one question: 'Do I feel lucky?' Well, do ya, punk?"

We also visit Nic in Los Angeles on our predetermined weekends, picking him up and driving north to Santa Barbara or south to San Diego. Once we rent bicycles on Coronado Island and, on an orange full-moon night, walk the broad beach, where we are startled by the spectacle of tens of thousands of shimmering grunion, brought onto the sand by a wave and left behind for their transfixing mating ritual. The female fish wriggle into the sand, depositing their eggs. The males wrap their eellike bodies around them, fertilizing them. Within a half-hour, the rising waves sweep the fish back into the sea. It seems as if they have never been there, as if we'd imagined them.

After these weekends, we drop him back at his mother and stepfather's house in Pacific Palisades, hug him, and he vanishes.

*

Summer is over. Finally. Karen, Daisy, Jasper, and I go to the airport. We wait at the gate for the joint-custody shuttle to arrive. A long line of commuters and families pass by and then, trailing them, come the unaccompanied minors, wearing pink paper badges with their names written in Magic Marker. The littler children also have pilot's wings pinned to the lapels of their jackets. And there is Nic. He has a short haircut and a new light-blue button-down cardigan that he wears open over a T-shirt. We take turns hugging. "Everything." Then we claim his suitcase filled with his summer things.

As we drive home to Inverness, Nic tells us about his seatmate on this flight. "So she pulls out these red earmuff-style headphones," he says of a woman who had zeroed in on him when she realized that he was alone. "And she flips on a Walkman and starts rocking and moving her head, her eyes closed, mouthing the lyrics, singing them in this warbling voice: 'Ooooo, baby. I lo-v-v-e you my rock and my redeemer . . . Ooooo, baby, it's you, my Lord, you send me, it's you-u-u who sends me.'"

Nic surveys his audience—us. "When she gets to the place on the tape she is looking for, she pulls off the headphones and puts them on me," he says. "'Listen,' she says to me. 'You gotta hear this.' She just puts them on me and cranks up the volume all the way. Doesn't ask if I want to hear or anything. The song goes: 'I rock to Jesus. Whoa-o-o. Jesus rocks me. Yeah. Jesus—you blow my mind.' Practically blows my head off it's so loud, but I am smiling pleasantly and I take off the headphones and hand them to her and tell her what a good song it is and she says, now sort of steely, 'No, the next one is best,' and she jams them back on me and now I'm listening to a . . . It's a rap song: 'Oh the devil wants to tempt me, yo, and I ain't gonna listen, no . . .' and I'm still smiling and nodding and finally I take off the headphones and hand it back to her. She says, 'The tape's for you, son,' and she removes it from the player. 'No, thank you, it's very kind of you,' but her eyes are scary now, so I say, 'Well, if you're sure you can spare it, I'd love the tape, thank you.' "

Nic produces the tape from his pants pocket. "Wanna listen?"

We play it as we drive on. Nic holds Jasper's hands in his, moving them to the beat and singing along with the "woo woo" chorus.

The noise level at our house has escalated. What with three children and Nic's assorted friends and numerous amplified and percussion instruments and the two dogs, our house is a cacophony of singing, wailing, barking, laughing, yelping, Raffi, pounding, screeching, Axl Rose, thumping, crashing, and howling. My agent one day is speaking to a friend of mine. She says, "I don't know if he lives in a daycare center or dog kennel."

We need a new car. With our horde of beasts and children the obvious way to go is a minivan. We visit car dealers and test drive some. I compare minivans, examining their safety features. We are not fooled by the Honda Odyssey ads about it being a minivan for people who hate minivans, but we buy one. As a feeble gasp of dissent, we add surf racks on top.

There are far more beautiful and less trampled beaches along this coastline than Bolinas, which throughout summer is overrun by dogs and teenagers. However, on the day before Nic's freshman orientation, we take to the beach on a dazzlingly bright afternoon. Karen, Jasper, and Daisy are on the sand, where Jasper ties Daisy up in seaweed, and together the little kids stack shells and eat sand and roll in the waves at the edge of the lagoon. Brutus and Moondog run amok with a motley pack of local dogs. Brutus at one point steals a picnicker's baguette.

Nic and I paddle out into the lineup of surfers, where we sit up on our surfboards. Waiting for a set of waves, Nic tells me more about his summer of baseball and movies, plus an update about the bully who taunted him at a local park and then chased him home on his bike. When we begin discussing the following day's freshman orientation, he admits that he is nervous about high school, but says he is excited, too.

The best set of the day comes rolling in and we catch one more wave apiece and ride in to the beach, where Nic joins Jasper in the building of a sand-and-driftwood Hobbit Shire decorated with kelp and seashells.

As they work, Jasper asks Nic, "What's LA like?"

"It's a big city, but I stay in a nice town on the edge," he says. "There are parks and beaches. It's kind of like here, but no you. I miss you when I'm there."

"I miss you, too," says Jasper, and then he asks, "Why doesn't your mom move here and we can all live in the same house and you would never have to go away?"

"What a nice idea," Nic says, "but somehow I can't see it."

On the way home from Bolinas, we talk more about the ceaseless back and forth between here and LA. Nic complains about it. Though he would never want to choose between his parents, neither would he choose joint custody. This is my conclusion about it: yes, it has contributed to his character. He is a remarkable child, more responsible, sensitive, worldly, introspective, and sagacious than he might have been otherwise. But the toll has been such that, given the geographic and emotional chasms that came with our divorce—that probably come with almost every divorce—at the least Nic should not have been forced to do the traveling. We should have. Though the visits would be far more inconvenient, I am convinced that Nic's childhood would be easier for him. Instead, he is left with a meager consolation prize for all his commuting between parents: he has more frequent-flier miles than most adults.

6

"Mark, is eighth grade better than seventh?" Dawn asks her older brother in Todd Solontz's *Welcome to the Dollhouse*. "Not really."

"What about ninth?"

"All of junior high school sucks. High school's better. It's closer to college. They'll call you names, but not as much to your face."

I hated high school, a Darwinian laboratory of cliques and random acts of cruelty and violence. My grades were unaccountably decent and I didn't get into any trouble, but other than one writing course school was a waste of time. I learned nothing, and no one noticed. But Nic's high school has more in common with a small liberal arts college. It has vibrant programs in the arts, science, mathematics, English, foreign language, journalism, and so on, as well as courses in justice in America, Langston Hughes, and religion and politics, all taught by devoted teachers. The tuition is expensive. Vicki and I strain to pay it. We rationalize that nothing is more important than our child's education. Even so, I sometimes wonder how much it will matter. Kids in my hometown went to private schools. From the stories that have filtered back, they didn't fare any better or worse than those of us at my public school. Maybe we delude ourselves that we can purchase a better, at least easier, life for our children.

Nic's school is located on the 115-year-old campus of a former military academy. The classrooms are open and airy. There is an outdoor pool and green playing fields and impressive science labs, art studios, and a theater. Within the first month, Nic is playing on the freshman basketball team and has gotten a role in a play. We meet Nic's new friends on campus and at a Friday evening get-together at our house. They seem like good kids, busy with student council, local politics, sports, painting, acting, writing plays, and performing jazz and classical music. Nic adores his teachers. It is an auspicious beginning.

Nic continues to devour movies, an obsession ever since he could push PLAY on a VCR. As a young child, he once asked me if FBI meant Disney, because he associated the stern antipiracy warnings at the start of home videos with the promise of adventure, romance, drama, and comedy. Along with *Pink Panther, Thin Man,* and Monty Python movies, educated by Karen, he is now obsessed with Godard, Bergman, and Kurosawa.

After school and before movies, and between sports and plays and hanging out with his friends, Nic makes time for Daisy and Jasper. Daisy was just getting the hang of English but for some reason switched to animal languages — she oinks, brays, and meows. She and Jasper, whom we call Boppy after Hale-Bopp, the comet that is buzzing around earth — a mop of brown hair over serene, wise eyes — are enamored of their big brother, and Nic seems to adore them back.

The school year sails along smoothly. Nic does his homework swiftly and conscientiously. Karen quizzes him on the week's French vocabulary. I help him proofread his writing assignments. The notes from Nic's teachers in his report cards are glowing.

Then, on an afternoon in May, Nic, Jasper, and Daisy are in the yard with Karen. The telephone rings. It is the freshman dean, who tells me that Karen and I have to come in for a meeting to discuss Nic's suspension for buying marijuana on campus.

"His *what?*"

"You mean you don't know?"

Nic had not told us.

Even after discovering the marijuana two years ago, I am stunned. "I'm sorry, but this must be some sort of a mistake."

It's no mistake.

My rationalizing begins immediately. He is experimenting again, I think, and many kids experiment. I tell myself that Nic isn't a typical druggie, not like the boys who hang out on the main street of town, unsupervised, cigarette-smoking, aimless, or the teenage son of an acquaintance back east who, high on heroin, was in a car wreck. I recently heard about a girl Nic's age who is in a psychiatric hospital after she slit her wrists. She was on heroin, too. Nic is not like those children. Nic is open and loving and diligent.

My parents never found out about my drug use. Even today they will tell you that I am making it up or at least exaggerating it. I'm not. In high school, I earned money for pot from my small allowance and a newspaper route. I was like many children who grew up in the late 1960s and 1970s who encountered not only copious marijuana but a range of drugs unknown to any previous generation. Before us, kids snuck beer, but drug users were exotic opium smokers in Chinese dens or heroin-addicted jazz musicians. In our middle-America neighborhood, where the television had three channels and telephones had dials, one of our neighbors grew marijuana under grow lights in his attic and another neighbor sold LSD. Random people from many crowds at school, not only stoners but jocks and bookish girls, including one I lusted after for most of my time in high school, seemed always to have pot and a variety of pills.

In the evenings, with my new friends, united by marijuana and rock and roll, I got stoned and hung out on the street, or we went to someone's home. Usually we snuck in undetected, but sometimes we were cornered and forced to eat dinner with our parents.

One time my mother said, "You two are in an awfully good mood tonight, aren't you?"

After dinner, we went to my black-lit bedroom, a poster of Jefferson Airplane on my wall, and listened to music on my eight-track turntable combo stereo system. The Beatles, solo Lennon, the Kinks, and Dylan: "Although the masters make the rules, for the wise men and the fools, I got nothing, Ma, to live up to."

Brian Jones, Janis Joplin, Jimi Hendrix, Jim Morrison, Keith Moon—rock stars we revered—died. These tragedies did not slow down our drug use a bit. Their deaths didn't seem to apply to us, maybe because their deaths, like their lives, were exercises in excess. In some ways they were simply living out the music. "I'm wasted," sang the Who. "I hope I die before I get old." And "Why don't you all just f-f-f-f-fade away."

We dismissed what we viewed as hysterical "speed kills" warnings and many other antidrug public-service announcements. "They" — the government, parents — were trying to scare us. Why? On drugs we saw through them and we were no longer afraid of them. But they could not control us.

My parents were relatively hip. They listened to Herb Alpert and the Tijuana Brass. They had occasional Saturday night parties with their friends, a mod assemblage of amateur musicians who gathered in our living room for cheese fondue and jam sessions. My father played like Al Hirt on a banged-up trumpet, and my mother, who wore miniskirts and, for a brief period in the late 1960s, orange and purple paisley paper dresses, pumped a wheezy accordion, playing "The Girl from Ipanema" and the theme from *A Man and a Woman*. But my parents' modishness stopped at drug use. Indeed, their parties didn't even include alcohol. Beverage choices ranged from Fresca to Sanka.

Arizona summers were so hot that a reporter famously fried an egg on the hood of his car. Whenever we opened the front door, my dad would yell: "In or out, in or out. What are you trying to do, air-condition the desert?"

In the evenings, I rode my bike with a friend, a tanned kid with a regular boy's haircut, past homes like ours, trying to escape the claustrophobia of our grid, down to the Indian reservation and endless desert.

One stifling summer night, we rode like always to the reservation and, ignoring the NO TRESPASSING and DANGER signs, climbed up onto the side of one of the cement canals that cut through the desert floor. As we leaned back on our elbows, watching the stars, my friend pulled out a small piece of aluminum foil. He unwrapped it and handed me a tiny square of paper stamped with a lion's face. "It's LSD," he said.

Nervously, I placed the lion on my tongue, where I felt it dissolve.

I was nauseated and immobile at first, but soon pleasurable waves began to pulse through my body. With a sudden rush of energy, I stood up. The nighttime seemed brighter. A cloudburst blew through the desert, washing everything. I was astonished that I could see so well at night. The three-quarters moon was why, but I attributed it to the drug. A jackrabbit racing by stopped and stared. My persistent feelings of anxiety and alienation vanished. I felt an almost overwhelming sense of well-being, a sense that everything would be — *was* — exactly right.

I had to be home by ten, and so I rode back, pedaling without effort. I parked my bike in the garage and entered the house as quietly as possible.

I retreated to my bedroom but was stopped en route. I joined my parents in the kitchen. "Did you bowl a good game?" They didn't have a clue that as I sat with them watching *You Only Live Twice*, the movie of the week, I was tripping my brains out.

*

On the sunny May afternoon, Karen and I are silent as we drive to Nic's school. Students hanging out by the flagpole at the entrance to the campus direct us to the correct office in the lower floor of the science building. We are met by the freshman dean, who wears a T-shirt, khaki shorts, and sneakers. He asks us to sit down, indicating a pair of plastic chairs that face a desk covered with science magazines. Another man, boyish with dark flyaway hair, wearing an open-collared shirt, joins us. He is introduced as the school counselor.

Outside the windows, boys, including some of Nic's friends, are whacking one another with lacrosse sticks on the green athletic field.

The dean and counselor ask how we are holding up.

"We've been better," I say.

They nod. Without making light of Nic's infraction, they take pains to reassure us, explaining that many schools have zero-tolerance policies, but this one has what they hope is a more progressive and helpful approach, taking into account the reality of children's lives these days.

"Nic will have a second chance," says the dean, leaning forward on his desk. "He will be on probation, and if there's another violation he will be out. We also require that he attend an afternoon of drug and alcohol counseling."

"What exactly happened?" I ask.

"Outside the cafeteria after lunch, a teacher caught Nic buying marijuana. The school's policy is that anyone selling drugs is kicked out. The boy who sold Nic the pot has been expelled."

The counselor, his hands folded on his lap, says, "The way we view this is that Nic made a bad choice. We want to help him make better choices in the future. We view this as a mistake and an opportunity."

It sounds reasonable and hopeful. Karen and I feel thankful not only that Nic has another chance, but that we aren't alone in trying to sort this out. The dean, counselor, and other teachers deal with this sort of thing all the time.

During the hour-long conversation, I mention my concern that Nic loves surfing and might be exposed to drugs at the beach. It's a strange paradox that for many kids the high of riding formidable Pacific waves isn't enough. I've seen the surfers on the shore, in wetsuits, passing around joints before heading into the water.

They glance at each other. "We have just the advisor for Nic," says the dean.

He tells us about one of the school's science teachers who is also a surfer.

"We'll call Don."

"He's amazing. Maybe he could be Nic's advisor."

Next they give us details about a center that offers drug and alcohol counseling.

At home, we immediately call and make an appointment for the next day. The three of us meet a counselor, and then Karen and I leave Nic with him for a two-hour session that includes an interview and drug counseling. When we pick him up, Nic says that it was a waste of time.

Don, the teacher, is a compact man with sandy-bronze hair and sea-blue eyes. His face is at once soft and rugged. From what we hear, he is rarely effusive, but guides children with a steady and patient hand and an infectious enthusiasm for the subjects and the students he teaches. He is one of those teachers who quietly change lives. Along with teaching science, he is the school's swimming and water-polo coach. In addition, he has a group of advisees. Nic becomes his newest charge, which we learn a few days after the meeting, when Nic is back in school after his suspension.

"This guy!" Nic says as he runs into the house, throwing down

his backpack and heading for the refrigerator. "This teacher ..."
Nic pours cereal into a bowl and begins cutting up a banana on
top. "He sat with me at lunch. He's amazing." He pours on milk.
"He's a really good surfer. He has surfed his entire life." He grabs
a slice of bread. "I went to his office. It's covered with pictures of
breaks around the world." He slathers peanut butter on the bread,
then grabs the jam from the refrigerator and spreads some on top.
"He asked if I wanted to surf with him sometime."

In a few weeks, the two of them go surfing together. When Nic
returns, he is elated. Don regularly checks in with Nic at school
and he telephones the house. As the school year is about to end,
he begins a campaign to sign Nic up for the swim team, which
will start again in fall. Nic is obdurate. No way. But Don ignores
Nic's rebuffs. Throughout the summer, he frequently phones Nic
in Los Angeles, checking in to see how he is faring. He continues
to ask Nic about the swim team. After a late-summer surf session
back in northern California, he proposes a deal. Come fall, if Nic
will attend one swim-team practice, he will stop harassing him
about joining.

Nic agrees.

Nic is fifteen, a new sophomore, and as promised he shows up at
the initial swim-team practice and then at the next and then the
next after that. With his lanky swimmer's body and arms muscular from plowing through thick waves on a surfboard, Nic is
already a strong swimmer, and he improves rapidly under Don's
coaching. He enjoys the camaraderie of the team. Mostly, he is
inspired by Don. "I just want to please him," Nic tells Karen one
day after a meet.

The swimming season ends around Christmas break. By then
Don has successfully recruited Nic for the water-polo team, too.
Nic is elected cocaptain. Karen, Jasper, Daisy, and I are regulars at

his games — Karen and I sitting with the other parents, Jasper and Daisy climbing up and down the metal grandstands and chiming in at random moments, "Go, Nicky!"

Nic also shows promise as an actor. One night Karen, an assortment of our relatives and friends, and I are astounded by a student-directed performance of *Spring's Awakening*, the 1891 play, often banned or at least censored (but not in this production), by Frank Wedekind. It is a story that faces with frankness the sexual awakening of a group of adolescents unable to turn to the adults in their lives for help. A girl who takes an abortion pill dies; another character commits suicide.

Don encourages Nic's interest in marine biology. As Nic's sophomore year winds down, he tells him about a summer program at the University of California at San Diego devoted to the subject. One day Nic comes home waving a brochure and application printed out from the program's Web site, asking if he can go. Once his mother and I confer, Nic applies.

On a morning in late June, the view out the jet's window is gorgeous. The sky is pink and the Pacific Ocean, where it abruptly meets the coastline, sparkles dreamy blue, as optimistic as Southern California could possibly be. Upon landing in San Diego, we find our suitcases at baggage claim and pick up a rental car. We drive north on Highway 5 through San Diego, until we reach the turnoff for the small beachtown of La Jolla. Exiting the freeway, we drive Nic to the UC campus and check him in. Nic is a bit nervous, but these kids seem welcoming. Like him, a few have brought along surfboards, a comforting sight.

We say our goodbyes. Daisy grabs Nic around the neck with her tiny arms.

"It's okay, bonky," he says. "I'll see you soon."

Nic checks in frequently by phone. He is having a blast. "I may want to be a marine biologist," he says one day. He tells us about the kids in the program and how he and the other surfers get up early before classes to walk down the steep trail to Black's Beach. He says that he has decided to go through the camp's certification program for scuba diving. On a night dive near Catalina Island, he swims with a school of dolphins.

When the program ends, Vicki picks him up and he spends the rest of the summer in LA. It goes by quicker than usual, and soon he is home again, preparing for his junior year.

It is Nic's strongest year in school yet. He has a close-knit group of friends with whom he seems engaged and with whom he shares impassioned concerns about politics and the environment and social issues. Together they protest an execution at San Quentin. A friend of ours who is also there sees Nic sitting on the sidewalk. Tears stream down his cheeks. Nic loves his classes. Writing remains one of his strongest subjects. Along with his creative writing for an English teacher who inspires him to write short stories and poems, he joins the staff of the school newspaper as an editor and columnist. He authors heartfelt personal and political columns about affirmative action, the Littleton, Colorado, shootings, and the war in Kosovo. He attends editorial meetings and stays late into the evenings to help proofread the paper. His columns are increasingly bold. One examines the time he sold out his most highly held ideals. It is about some of our dearest friends, the couple who became Nic's unofficial godparents. One of them is HIV positive. He gave Nic an AIDS bracelet, "one with the same AIDS ribbon that you see all those idiotic celebrities wearing, the one that is handed out at the door as they enter the Oscars," as Nic writes. "To many of those people, that ribbon is probably nothing more than fashionable, but on the bracelet from my friend, it symbolized hope. I was told that the money for it went to finding a cure for the disease."

Nic wrote that he wore the bracelet every day, "but then I got older. Though my feelings about my godparents never changed, I worried what other people would think. I began hearing people at my high school say horrible things about gays ... [and] I began feeling uncomfortable about wearing the bracelet ... Finally, I stopped wearing it." Then, Nic continued, he lost it. "I'm sorry I lost the bracelet," he concluded, "but maybe its absence symbolizes more than its presence would. It symbolizes that I didn't have the strength to stand up for my friend."

Encouraged by the journalism instructor, Nic submits this and other columns to the annual Ernest Hemingway Writing Award for high school journalists. He wins first place. Next he submits a column to the My Turn section of *Newsweek*, which the magazine publishes in February 1999. The piece is a poignant indictment of long-distance joint custody. "Maybe there should be an addition to the marriage vows," Nic writes. " 'Do you promise to love and to hold, for richer and for poorer, in sickness and in health, as long as you both shall live? And if you ever have children and wind up divorced, do you promise to stay within the same geographical area as your kids?' Actually, since people often break those vows, maybe it should be a law: If you have children, you must stay near them. Or how about some common sense: If you move away from your children, you have to do the traveling to see them?" He poignantly describes the effect of his years of our joint-custody arrangement: "I am always missing someone."

Nic's taste in books and music continues to evolve. His onetime favorite authors, J. D. Salinger, Harper Lee, John Steinbeck, and Mark Twain, have been replaced by an assortment of misanthropes, addicts, drunks, depressives, and suicides, Rimbaud, Burroughs, Kerouac, Kafka, Capote, Miller, Nietzsche, Hemingway, and Fitzgerald. One of his favored writers, Charles Bukowski, holds the distinction of the most stolen author in college bookstores. He once summed up his readers as "the defeated, the demented, and the damned." Adolescents may be, or at least feel like, all of those things, but it worries me that these writers, particularly when they glamorize drugs and debauchery, are so compelling to Nic.

At spring break, the two of us set off on a tour of schools in the Midwest and East Coast. We fly to Chicago, arriving on a hazy morning. We have a free afternoon, and so we visit the Art Institute and museums and, in the evening, attend a play. Nic sits in on classes and stays overnight in a University of Chicago dorm. In the morning, we fly on to Boston, where we rent a car. After two days touring schools in the city, we drive to Amherst, where we arrive after dark. We stop in the center of town and eat dinner at an Indian restaurant. Afterward, we ask directions to our hotel. The man we ask bellows urgently in response.

"Go straight!" he shouts. "You will come to two lights." He looks fiercely into our eyes. "Take a right! You *must* take a right, never a left!"

Nic and I follow the instructions exactly, Nic directing me in the same volume and tone used by the man.

"Stop!" he yells. "Right! Right! Right! You *must* take a right, never a left!"

Our final stop is Manhattan, where Nic tours NYU and Columbia.

At home, he fills out his college applications and we plan his summer. He and Karen continue to speak French together. He has an aptitude for language; memorization is easy for him and he has a flawless ear. What he lacks in vocabulary he makes up for in a fluid Parisian accent and, with Karen's help, an arsenal of French slang. Toward the end of the school year, in fact, his French teacher encourages Nic to apply to a summer program in Paris to study the language at the American University there. Vicki and I confer and decide to send him.

Nic spends much of June in LA and then travels to Paris for the three-week session. When he reports in by phone, he says that he's having a great time. His French is improving and he has made good friends. He even landed a part in a student film. "I love it here, but I miss all of you," he says one time before hanging up. "Give my love to the little kiddos."

When the program ends, Nic flies home and I meet him at the airport. Waiting at the gate, I spot him disembarking from the jetway. He looks terrible. He has grown taller, but that's not what I notice first. His hair is shaggy and unkempt. There are black circles under his eyes. Somehow he is grayer. His manner alarms me. I detect a simmering sullenness. Finally I ask what is wrong.

"Nothing. I'm fine," he says.

"Did something happen in Paris?"

"No!" he replies with a flare of anger. I look at him suspiciously.

"Are you sick?"

"I'm OK."

Within days, however, he complains of stomach pain, so I make an appointment with our family doctor. The examination takes an hour. Then Nic comes out and says that I should join him. With his arms folded across his chest, the doctor regards Nic with concern. I sense that there is more he wants to say, but he simply announces that Nic has an ulcer.

What child has an ulcer at seventeen?

7

A fter high school, I enrolled at the University of Arizona in Tucson, even closer to the U.S.-Mexico border. My roommate was from Manhattan. Charles had a trust fund. His parents were dead. I never learned the truth about how they died, but alcohol and drugs were involved. Perhaps suicide. "To have lost one parent, Mr. Worthing, might be considered a misfortune," Charles would say, appropriating the famous line in *The Importance of Being Earnest*. "To lose both looks like carelessness."

Charles was awkwardly handsome with a strong nose, brown curls, and coffee eyes. He had alluring and irrepressible energy. He impressed me and others who met him with his worldliness, stories about Christmases with some Kennedy relations in Hyannis Port and "the Vineyard," and summers in Monaco and on the Côte d'Azur. When he took me and other friends out for dinner at a French restaurant, he ordered — in French — escargot, foie gras, and Dom Perignon. He regaled his audiences with tales of boarding school high jinks that could have (and may have) come out of Fitzgerald; sexual escapades that could have (and probably did) come out of Henry Miller. If you mentioned that you needed a new shirt, he would recommend a tailor in Hong Kong who for years made his father's suits. He claimed to know the best watchmaker on Madison Avenue, bartender at the Carlyle, and masseuse at the Pierre. Mention that you had tasted a good California wine and he would tell you about a Chateau Margaux he drank with a

Rothschild scion. Everything about him was contrived to inspire awe. Including the way he drank alcohol and took drugs. He did both with what at the time I found to be impressive determination.

I discovered that there were two parallel universities in Tucson. One was attended by students who took college with at least some degree of seriousness. The other—the one I attended—was chosen by *Playboy* as one of the top party schools in the nation.

I was an amateur when compared to Charles, who never let school or anything else get in the way of his dissipation, though there would be intermittent hangovers accompanied by guilty resolutions to do better, followed by Champagne or margarita toasts to his new assiduousness.

Charles had friends, also from New York City, who shared a pink adobe house on Speedway Boulevard on the far end of Tucson from the university. They were not on trust funds, but they had money for parties and steak dinners earned by dealing frozen magic mushrooms they smuggled in from the Yucatan.

At the time, Carlos Castaneda's *The Teachings of Don Juan* and its sequels were popular on college campuses. Castaneda, an anthropologist, chronicled his pursuit of the knowledge of a Yaqui Indian shaman who taught him a quasireligious philosophy reminiscent of various Eastern and Western mystical traditions. Integral to Don Juan's spiritual exploration was the consumption of psychotropic drugs, including peyote, datura, and psilocybin mushrooms. My friends and I were intrigued, and the books encouraged us to view our trips on mushrooms or other psychedelics not as debauchery but as intellectual inquiry. Somehow we also justified marijuana, Quaaludes, Jack Daniel's, Jose Cuervo, cocaine, and random uppers and downers.

I recall quite distinctly tripping in the red-rock high desert outside Tucson and watching a Mexican daisy transform into a man's face. Soon it and the daisies around it morphed into the fresh-faced visages of thousands of angels, and then the entire ensemble began whispering the answer to the ultimate question: what is the meaning of life? I moved closer so that I could hear what they were saying, but the murmuring voices gave way to subdued laughter, and the array of somber faces turned into a field of laughing English muffins.

By night, after a full white moon had risen low on the horizon, I decided that if the people in Italo Calvino's book, which we were reading in a lit class, could use ladders to climb onto the moon, why not me, but I gave up the idea when Charles announced that it was time to go clubbing.

Charles bought drugs for studying, and they helped for half an hour or so. Then we would be too high to concentrate on anything other than which bar to visit. Copious amounts of drug and drink never deterred Charles from driving, and he crashed two Peugeots. Thankfully—miraculously—he never harmed anyone, at least as far as I know. I rode shotgun, which now I know was a form of Russian roulette.

He blasted the Rolling Stones. He played his favorite song, "Shine a Light," incessantly and loudly, singing along with Mick Jagger,

> *Well, you're drunk in the alley, baby*
> *With your clothes all torn*
> *And your late night friends*
> *Leave you in the cold grey dawn*
> *Just seemed too many flies on you*
> *I just can't brush them off.*

On a drug-fueled whim, Charles and I decided one night to drive to California to see the sunrise, and so, after packing up an arsenal of drugs, we barreled west to San Diego. It was still dark when we arrived at the beach. Sitting on the sand, blankets over our shoulders, staring out to the horizon, we awaited the sunrise. We smoked joints and talked. After a long while, one of us noticed that it was light. We turned around. It must have been ten or so. The sun had risen hours earlier.

"Oh," Charles said with striking insight. "The sun rises in the east."

Another time, while driving to Tucson after visiting my parents in Scottsdale, we offered a ride to a hitchhiker. When we arrived at her destination, a skydiving school in the middle-of-nowhere desert town of Casa Grande, our rider convinced us to try her favorite sport. The instructional session took place in front of a wall on which someone had painted, "Everything you do on the ground is irrelevant." Our lecturer said, "Your most important job is to enjoy the ride." When he arrived at the finale of his speech, he burst into a cackle and said, "Fuck it. Let's fly."

My parachute didn't open. I was saved at the last possible second when my reserve chute slowed me down. I hit hard but was all right. Charles came running up to me. "Far-fucking out!"

Drug stories are sinister. Like some war stories, they focus on adventure and escape. In the tradition of a long line of famous and infamous carousers and their chroniclers, even hangovers and near-death experiences and visits to the emergency room can be made to seem glamorous. But usually the storytellers omit the slow degeneration, psychic trauma, and, finally, the casualties.

One night, after Charles returned from a two-day bender, I became worried because he was in the bathroom for so long. When he didn't respond to my calls, I broke the lock and pushed open the door. He had passed out, cracking his skull on the tile floor, which was smeared with blood. I called an ambulance. At the hospital, the doctor warned Charles about his drinking and he promised to stop, but of course he didn't.

Later in the year, another of our Hunter Thompson–inspired road trips brought us to San Francisco, where we arrived on a pristine early evening. I had never been there before. We stopped the car atop the city's highest hill. The invigorating wind blew. After a childhood in Arizona, I felt as if I could breathe for the first time in my life.

I applied for a transfer to the University of California at Berkeley. I hadn't yet damaged my transcript and so I was accepted, enrolling for the fall. It was a time when it was not unusual for a student at the university to construct an individual social science field major. My focus was death and human consciousness.

I embraced my studies at Berkeley, but drugs were plentiful there, too. Cocaine and pot were the mainstays of many of our weekends. A friend's father, a doctor, prescribed bottles of Quaaludes because he didn't want his son taking street drugs. I did many drugs, but no more than most of those around me. Somehow we have evolved so that higher education and drunkenness and drugs are, for many students, inextricably tied.

I kept in touch with Charles, whose drinking and drugging escalated in a way that, all these years later, makes me worry about Nic. My drug use was excessive, but I was never like Charles. At one or two in the morning, I would call it a night because I had to get up for class. Charles would look at me as if I were out of my mind. He was just getting started.

After his summer in France, Nic is back in school. The ulcer has healed, but he is different. He still does well in most of his classes, maintaining a high grade-point average, as if that makes his descent more tragic than if he had become a fuckup. However, he quits the swimming and water-polo teams and, eventually, the newspaper. He begins cutting classes, insisting that he knows exactly what he can and cannot get away with. He comes home late, pushing the limits of his curfew. Our concern mounting, Karen and I meet with the school counselor, who says, "Nic's candor, unusual especially in boys, is a good sign. Keep talking it out with him and he'll get through this."

I will try.

It is as if Nic is being pulled by two countervailing forces. Nic's teachers and counselors — and his parents — work to hold him up and keep him from succumbing to another force, one inside him.

After twenty-five years at this school, Don accepts a position elsewhere. No one else has his influence on Nic, not that he — or anyone — could do anything to affect the course Nic is on. Some teachers are still impressed by Nic's acumen and writing and painting talent, including a piece for a student art exhibition, gouache on the inside of a Clue Jr. game, depicting a screaming boy with writing over his face. But though senioritis is common, one day his dean tells me that Nic has broken a school record for most missed classes of any senior — even as we hear from the colleges to which Nic applied. He has been accepted to most of them.

Nic spends as much time as possible away from home. He hangs out with a crowd of boys who are obvious stoners. I confront Nic, but he denies that he is using anything. He is smart enough to justify some outrageous behavior with convincing lies, and he is getting better at covering his tracks. When I discover his dishonesty, I'm confounded because I still think that we are close — closer than most fathers and their sons. Eventually he admits that he is using some drugs "like everyone," "just pot," and only "once in a while." He promises that he never gets into a car with anyone who is high. My advice, pleading, and anger fall on deaf — stoned — ears. He continues to reassure me: "It's no big deal. It's harmless. Don't worry."

"It's not always harmless," I say, repeating a well-worn lecture. "It can become a problem. For some people. I know people who started smoking a little but became potheads and . . ."

Nic rolls his eyes.

"It's true," I continue. "Their ambition was drained because of decades of marijuana smoking." I tell him about another ex-friend, one who was never able to hold down a job and never had a relationship that lasted longer than a month or two. "He once told me, 'I've lived in a cloud of smoke and television since I was thirteen, so maybe it's not surprising that things haven't turned out better for me.'"

"You smoked tons of pot," Nic says. "You're a great one to talk."

"I wish I hadn't," I say.

"You worry too much," he replies dismissively.

On a visit to my parents' for a family party in Arizona, Nic and I go for a walk around the block. Since I lived here, the palm trees have grown thin and absurdly tall, like giraffes with preposterously long necks. A few of the homes have been remodeled with second stories. Otherwise, our street appears the same. I remember when Nic and I took this identical route when he was two or three. I led him with a rope tied to a small plastic car with Nic in the driver's seat. We went to Chaparral Park, where he pulled on the imaginary handbrake, opened the door, and carefully shut it, before running toward the shore of the man-made lake. There he fed pieces of bread to ducks and geese. A ratty old goose bit his finger and Nic wailed.

I know that I am losing Nic, but I still rationalize it: it's typical of adolescents to drift away from their parents — to become surly and distant. "You've got to wonder what Jesus was like at seventeen," Anne Lamott wrote. "They don't even talk about it in the Bible, he was apparently so awful." Still, I try to break through, to get Nic to talk, but he doesn't have much to say.

Finally he turns to me and matter-of-factly asks if I want to smoke some pot. I eye him. Is he testing me, asserting his independence, or trying to reach out — to connect? Maybe all those things.

He pulls out a joint, lights it, and passes it to me. I stare a minute. I still smoke pot, albeit rarely. I may go to a party or a friend's house where pot is smoked as casually as wine is served with dinner. On such occasions, I take a hit. Or two.

But this is different. And yet I accept the joint, thinking — rationalizing — that it's not unlike a father in a previous generation sharing a beer with his seventeen-year-old son, a harmless, bonding moment. I inhale, smoking with him as we walk through my old neighborhood. We talk and laugh and the tension between us melts away.

But it returns. That evening we're right back where we were. Nic is the belligerent, annoyed teenager, miffed at having been dragged to Arizona. I'm the overwrought, worried, and in many ways inept parent. Should I have smoked with him? Of course not. I'm desperate — way too desperate — to connect with him. It's not a very good excuse.

Nic agrees to see a new therapist, one recommended to us as a genius when it comes to working with adolescent boys. Even as we arrive for Nic's appointment, he is filled with unease and a tinge of disgust at the prospect of meeting another shrink. The therapist is tall with a slight bow, heavy-set, and has intense blue eyes. He and Nic shake hands and they disappear together.

An hour later, Nic emerges with a smile and color in his cheeks and a spring in his step for the first time in a while. "That was amazing," he says. "He's different from the others."

Nic begins weekly after-school sessions, though he misses some. Karen and I meet with the therapist, too. In one session, he maintains that college will straighten Nic out. It's a laughable notion — when has the freshman year of college straightened anyone out? And yet I can only hope that he is right.

*

On a sunny late spring afternoon, Vicki comes up and she, Karen, Daisy, Jasper, and I attend Nic's high school graduation. The ceremony is held on the athletic field. Nic has been upset since his class elected to wear caps and gowns. Karen and I will be disappointed, but not surprised, if doesn't show up. But he does. With his hair freshly buzzed, in cap and gown, Nic marches forward and accepts his diploma from the school head, kissing her cheek. He seems jubilant. I leap on each small sign that he might be all right. I think, Maybe. Maybe everything will be fine after all.

Following the ceremony, we invite his friends over for a barbecue. A long table is set underneath a dogwood in full pink flower. In the middle of dinner, during the passing of platters of food, Nic and his friends are up and down and inside and out. Then they say goodbye and leave for the "Safe and Sober" grad-night bash being held at a local recreation center. His friends drop him home late that night — Nic, my high school graduate, who, when I ask about the party, beelines past me into his bedroom, muttering, "I'm exhausted. Good night."

In summer, there is no more pretense of restraint on Nic's part. It is obvious by his erratic behavior and mood swings that he is often high and that marijuana is being supplemented by other drugs. My threats, punishments, and threats of more severe punishments are useless. Nic occasionally reacts with concern and remorse, but more often with disgust. I have become inconsequential. I don't see what more I can do other than warn him, negotiate and enforce curfews, deny him the use of the car, and continue to drag him to the therapist, even as he becomes increasingly furtive, argumentative, and reckless.

We still go to Nancy and Don's for Wednesday night dinners. The adults gather in the kitchen while the grandchildren are usually downstairs in a basement crowded with stored furniture and hanging kayaks and a Folbot, playing Ping-Pong. Or they are swinging in the living room. Nancy and Don's is the only house I have ever seen with a swing inside. It has thick ropes hanging from a rafter beam and a canvas seat. Sometimes the kids use the swing set as a launching pad in a bowling game. First they stack multicolored cardboard bricks into elaborate towers. Then they aim Daisy, sitting on the swing and holding onto the ropes, and let her fly.

A great wooden island with a six-burner range is the main feature in Nancy's kitchen. There's usually something cooking on it, and the room is effused with delicious and exotic and occasionally burned smells of whatever recipe Nancy found in the newspaper, the latest Peggy Knickerbocker cookbook, or *Gourmet*. One night yellow chicken curry is served with white jasmine rice, raita made with yogurt and cucumbers, mango chutney, and flat Indian bread flavored with cardamom. Another menu includes a bubbling Mexican casserole with green chilies and cheese. Or roast pork stewed with lemons and prunes, crispy potatoes, and Brussels sprouts fried with pancetta. When it's time to eat, the kids choose their favorite ceramic plates, each with a different animal. Jasper always chooses the whale. Daisy and their cousin fight over the dog until Daisy relents, settling on the donkey.

Nic still seems to enjoy these festive evenings. Tonight, however, he is acting strangely. He's in the kitchen, uttering a series of non sequitors. "Why *shouldn't* people have sex with whomever they want when they want? Monogamy is an archaic convention," he lectures Nancy, who listens as she stirs a boiling pot on the stove. "Dr. Seuss is a *genius*." He goes on for a while about his latest, frenzied, incoherent philosophies of the type I imagine him spouting late into the night with his friends.

Later, however, it dawns on me that Nic must have been on something. In the morning, I ask him. He denies it. I once again threaten him, but my threats are meaningless. I forbid him to use drugs, but this, too, is useless. When we consult his therapist, he advises me against barring drugs from our house, saying, "If you forbid them, he'll just sneak it. His drug use will go underground, and you will have lost him. It's safer to have him home."

Friends and friends of friends offer contradictory advice: kick him out, don't let him out of your sight. I think: kick him out? What chance will he have then? Don't let him out of my sight? *You* try corralling a seventeen-year-old on drugs.

It is a tranquil midsummer evening, just before his eighteenth birthday. I arrive home and sense that something is amiss. Slowly I realize that Nic is gone, and he has robbed the house of cash, food, and a case of wine. He was selective. He took only very good wine. I am in a panic. I call his therapist, who in spite of this episode reassures me that Nic will be all right, that he is appropriately "exercising his independence." If his rebellion is extreme, it is because I have made it difficult to have anything to rebel against.

Finally someone has said it: so it *is* my fault that Nic has been increasingly saturnine and shadowy and taking drugs and is now lying and stealing. I was too lenient. I am ready to bear this judgment, to accept that I have blown it, though I do wonder about the children in trouble whose parents were overly strict and repressive and those who were far more lenient than me and yet whose children appear to be fine.

Nic is gone two days before he calls. Apparently, he and his friends are in Death Valley on a Kerouacian odyssey fueled by drugs and liquor. I demand that he return home. He does and I ground him. We make an arrangement whereby he will work to pay me back for the thievery. (I do not hold my breath.)

"You're always trying to control me!" Nic shrieks one evening when I tell him he can't go out during the period he is grounded.

He is dressed in baggy green pants held up with a cloth army belt and a white shirt with rolled-up sleeves.

"I have given you ample freedom. You abused it."

"Fuck you." He repeats it with venom. "Fuck you." He storms to his bedroom, slamming the door.

Karen and I have a session with Nic in the therapist's office, a small and comfortable room with a pair of cushioned chairs. Nic sits morosely opposite us, flopped on a couch. The therapist does his best to orchestrate a civil conversation, but Nic is irascible and defensive, minimizing my concerns as stupid and overprotective. He once again lashes out at us for trying to control him.

Afterward, but only afterward, I conclude once again that Nic must have been high. When I call to ask the therapist for his opinion, he says, "Maybe, but adolescent hostility is normal. It's good that he has permission to get it out with you. It's healthy."

We agree to a follow-up session, which is more civil. Nic apologizes and says that he had been angry. He goes so far as to assure us that his partying — he admits to "modest" partying — is a prelude to the hard work of college. "I feel as if I deserve it," he says. "I worked hard in high school."

"You never worked that hard."

"Well, I'll be working hard when I start college. I understand what a great opportunity it is. I won't blow it."

Of course I still want to believe him. I don't think it's simply that I am gullible, but I cannot fathom the implications of his behavior. When change takes place gradually, it's difficult to comprehend its meaning.

It is a fortnight later, on Sunday afternoon, and Karen plans to take all three kids to the beach. I am on deadline, so I'm staying home to write.

The fog has lifted, and I am with them in front of the house in the driveway, helping pack the car. Our friends who are joining them pull up in their car. Next, two county sheriff's patrol cars pull up. When a pair of uniformed officers approach, I think they need directions, but they walk past me and head for Nic. They handcuff his wrists behind his back, push him into the backseat of one of the squad cars, and drive away.

Jasper, who is six, is the only one of us who responds appropriately. He wails, inconsolable for an hour.

8

T he arrest is the result of Nic's failure to appear in court after being cited for marijuana possession, an infraction he forgot to tell me about. Still, I bail him out. "This is the only time," I say. I am confident that the arrest will teach him a lesson.

Nic is moody, but he holds down a job as a barista pulling espressos and steaming milk for caffe lattes in a coffee store in Mill Valley. We go in sometimes — Karen, Jasper, Daisy, and I. Nic stands behind the counter, greeting us with a big smile. He introduces the kids to the rest of the crew and then whips up tall cups of hot chocolate with downy peaks of whipped cream for them.

Nic regales us with workplace stories. He has come to know many regular customers, who fall into one of several categories. "Smarges" order small coffees in large cups. As he explains it, smarges know that the baristas fill up the large cup, so they get extra coffee for free, saving a quarter. "Why bothers" want cappuccinos made with decaffeinated espresso and fat-free milk. "Quads" are maniacs who order quadruple espressos. Unpleasant customers pay dearly for their rudeness. Nic and his coworkers avenge themselves by intentionally mixing up orders, so any particularly nasty customer who specifies decaf gets double shots of leaded espresso, while ones who order regular coffee receive decaf.

Nic dotes on Jasper and Daisy as much as ever. One morning, in an impish mood, Nic does his Agnes Moorehead impersonation—the one from *Pollyanna*—but this time his audience is Daisy.

"Missy, you have a stuffy little nose!"

How often have we been furious with Nic but then have found ourselves disarmed by his kindness and humor? How can both Nics, the loving and considerate and generous one, and the self-obsessed and self-destructive one, be the same person?

Daisy, standing up in an African basket, is furious. "Nic, how did you find me? It's not *fair*."

As usual, her hiding place was the first to be discovered in a game of sardines. Nic found her curled up in the basket near the bookshelf in the living room. "Stop yer caterwauling," Nic says in a new voice, sort of a piratey brogue. "How many baskets go on singin' songs? Next time keep yer singing to yerself."

The two run outside in search of Jasper and their cousins, who are still hidden. It is the end of summer and the maple leaves are maroon, the roses and hydrangea startlingly white and yellow. The air is brisk, and the kids, in the midst of their game, exhale steam.

Nic, this time imitating Karl Malden, a fire-and-brimstone preacher—again from *Pollyanna*—bellows at Jasper, "We'll find you and when we do we'll string you up by your fiddly toes."

"Yeah," Daisy says. "And pour chocolate syrup on your fil-lily head."

Nic plays with the little kids and it seems as if all is well in our house. After his arrest, this paradox baffles me.

Nic has decided on a college, the University of California at Berkeley. On a warm August afternoon, we pile into the car, and Karen and I, with Jasper and Daisy in tow, drive Nic to settle into his dorm. We stop for pizza and then drive him up onto the sprawling campus until we find Bowles Hall, an ancient Tudor dormitory.

"It's a castle!" Jasper says, impressed and envious. "You get to live in a castle!"

We park out front and help him carry his luggage through the stone archway and up two flights of stone stairs, where we find Nic's room and meet his roommates, who are unpacking. They seem serious, studious, and, in one case, nerdy. All seem extremely nice. One boy with scruffy red hair and a light-blue crewneck sweater is assembling an elaborate homebuilt computer system. Another boy, this one in oval tortoiseshell glasses and a striped T-shirt, has George Michael, Celine Dion, Barbra Streisand, and Elton John stacked haphazardly on a small CD player, a selection that does not bode well for harmony in the small room given Nic's uncompromising musical taste.

Nic walks us out to the car. "It will be fine," he says nervously. "It's a cool old building."

He hugs each of us.

I mention the George Michael and Nic laughs. "I'll educate them. It won't take long before they are listening to Marc Ribot." Ribot sings one of Nic's current favorite songs, "Yo! I Killed Your God."

When he calls in a few days, Nic seems engaged by his classes, particularly a painting course. In subsequent calls, however, he admits that he can't build stretcher bars for his canvases. "No matter what I do, they come out all cockeyed," he says. "And I have to lug them across campus. I feel like Jesus carrying his cross."

More phone calls and he is complaining about his other courses, too. "We're taught by TAs rather than real professors," he says. "They're morons."

In some of the conversations that follow, Nic seems distracted, and then he stops regularly returning my calls. I have no idea what is going on, but his silence tells me that things aren't going well.

When finally he checks in— "I've been staying with friends"; "school's cool but I'm really into the underground music scene out here"—I encourage him to take advantage of the opportunity he has at Cal, to weather the initial period. "It will be worthwhile," I say. "It's always difficult at the beginning, but you'll do fine."

I suggest that he meet with school counselors in the health center and, if he wants, check in with his therapist, who has extended an open invitation for Nic to keep in touch as little or as often as he wants. "Lots of freshmen struggle at first," I say. "It's common. Maybe the counselors can help."

He says that it's a good idea. Part of me believes that he will follow through and seek out help, but a bigger part knows that he won't. A week later, one of Nic's roommates calls, telling me that they are worried because Nic hasn't shown up for a few days. I am distraught.

Two days later, on a late fall afternoon, Nic calls, finally admitting that college isn't working. Assuming that drugs are the problem, I say that we need to talk about rehab, but he says that he isn't using anything much. "I wasn't ready for college," he says. "I just need some time. I have lots of work to do on myself first. I've been having a hard time—feeling pretty depressed."

Nic sounds level headed and it makes some sense to me. There's ample evidence that many children use drugs to self-medicate for depression, not to mention a host of mental-health disorders. The drugs they take may become the focal point for both kids and their parents, but they may be masking deeper or conjoined problems. How can a parent know? We consult more experts, but they don't necessarily know, either. Diagnosis isn't an exact science and it's complicated, particularly for adolescents and young adults, for whom some mood changes, including depression, are common. Many symptoms of these disorders appear to be identical to some of the symptoms of drug abuse. Also, by the time experts finally figure out that there's a problem, drug addiction may have exacerbated the initial ailment and fused with it. It becomes impossible to know where one leaves off and the other begins.

"Considering the level of maturity of young adolescents, the availability of drugs, and the age at which drugs are first used, it is not surprising that a substantial number of them develop serious drug problems," writes Robert Schwebel, Ph.D., in *Saying No Is Not Enough*. "Once this happens, the effects are devastating. Drugs shield children from dealing with reality and mastering developmental tasks crucial to their future. The skills they lacked that left them vulnerable to drug abuse in the first place are the very ones that are stunted by drugs. They will have difficulty establishing a clear sense of identity, mastering intellectual skills, and learning self-control. The adolescent period is when individuals are supposed to make the transition from childhood to adulthood. Teenagers with drug problems will not be prepared for adult roles . . . They will chronologically mature while remaining emotional adolescents."

A specialist on child development tells me that children's brains are at their most malleable—that is, the greatest change takes place—before they are two years old and then again when they are teenagers. "The worst time for a person to be tampering with their brains is when they are teenagers," she says. "Drugs radically alter the way teenagers' brains develop." As she explains it, experience and behavior help to set up a cycle that may deepen emotional problems. The biological underpinning may become more acute and more intractable. It enforces and reinforces the psychological problems, which become more firmly established. After that, treating people whose drug use began when they were teenagers is further complicated because deconstructing or rerouting established pathways have biological as well as emotional and behavioral roots.

*

When Nic broaches it, I can believe that he has been suffering from other problems, possibly depression. Could the impressively credentialed shrinks he's seen missed such an obvious diagnosis? If the therapists missed it, perhaps it is because Nic is good at covering it up, just as he was good at covering up his drug use. Depression is a plausible explanation and easier to accept than a drug problem. It's not that depression isn't serious, but unlike drugs, it is not self-inflicted. It is reassuring to imagine that drugs are a symptom and not the cause of Nic's difficulties.

Nic also tells me that Berkeley was a mistake and he would do better at a smaller college. His theory is that he was swallowed up in the impersonal Cal bureaucracy. "I tried to see a counselor," he says, "like you suggested. But I had to wait in line for an hour to make an appointment. I got to the front of the line and they told me that the first appointment was a week later.

"I want to apply to colleges again," he continues. "In the meantime, I think I should take a year off from school, get a job, and get back in physical and mental shape."

Nic moves home again. He promises to follow the rules we establish—he will go to therapy, honor curfews, help around the house, work, and go forward with new college applications. He meets with his therapist, who, afterward, tells me that he supports the plan. Indeed, Nic seems to feel a little better, and so there is reason to believe that things are improving. He applies to a number of small liberal arts schools on the East Coast. His first choice is Hampshire College in western Massachusetts. When we toured the school, he had been inspired by the vibrant atmosphere and bucolic setting. He sat in on English and political science courses and toured the music and drama studios. I, too, felt it was a college made with Nic in mind. Apparently his transcripts are still relatively strong, because, in a couple months, he receives a letter of acceptance from the school. I breathe easier. Nic is on track again on the inevitable (in my view) path that will lead back to college. We've endured a bad period, but Nic will move on. But though he sometimes emerges to play with Daisy and Jasper, or materializes for a meal, when he's not working, Nic spends most of his time at home in his room.

One night when he is at work, I fall asleep early, but wake with a start after midnight. I sense that something is wrong. Maybe it's a parent's sixth sense. Maybe some part of me has detected the early warning signs of imminent trouble. When I get out of bed, it makes the softest rustling sound, enough to wake Karen.

"Is everything all right?"

"Everything is fine," I whisper. "Go back to sleep."

The floor is cold and the room is cold, but I don't stop for slippers or a robe or a sweater because I don't want to make more noise. The hallway is unlit, but moonlight through the living room skylight casts a maroon radiance. I turn on a kitchen light and go to Nic's bedroom. I knock on the door. There is no answer. I open it and peer in. My stomach tightens. The unmade bed is empty.

I am becoming used to an overwhelming, grinding mixture of anger and worry, each emotion darkening and distorting the other. It is a bleak and hopeless feeling. I may know it well, but it is no easier to bear.

Nic has missed his curfew. That is as far as I will allow my worry to go. I anticipate his arrival at any minute and rehearse what I will do. I'll confront him, though facing him is a painful reminder of my inability to alter his behavior.

I tiptoe into the bedroom and try to fall back to sleep, but by then it's futile. I lie awake. Worry is beginning to consume me.

We live at the crest of a small hill, before the road continues up, so that cars driving on the street in front of our house idle as if they might come to a stop before continuing on. One car and then another drives up and pauses. Each time my heart stops. It's Nic. But then the engine pushes on up the hill.

At three, I give up pretending that I will fall back to sleep. I get up. Karen gets up too and asks, "What's the matter?" I tell her that Nic hasn't come home. We go into the kitchen. She tries to reassure me.

"He's probably with friends and it was too late to come home, so he slept over."

"He would have called."

"Maybe he didn't want to wake us."

I look over at her and see the despondence and worry in her eyes. She doesn't believe it, either. The minutes click by. We drink tea and fret.

Early in the morning I call his friends, waking some of them, but no one has seen him. I call his therapist, who even now reassures me—maybe that's how he sees his job, to comfort me—that "Nic is working things out and he will be all right." My panic mounts. Every time the phone rings, my stomach constricts. Where can he be? I cannot imagine, or more accurately, I choose not to. I push away the grisliest thoughts. Finally I call the police and hospital emergency rooms, asking if he is in jail or if there has been an accident. Each time I call, I brace myself for the unthinkable. I rehearse the conversation—the stolid, disembodied voice, and the words: "He is dead." I rehearse it to prepare myself. I go toward the thought, pace around it. He is dead.

Waiting is ghastly, but I can do nothing else.

Later in the morning, Jasper, barefoot and in his pajamas, pads into the kitchen, looking at us with his clear eyes. He climbs onto Karen's lap and chews on a piece of toast. Next Daisy, yawning, marches in, her hair wild.

We say nothing about Nic. We don't want to worry them. We have to tell them soon, though. They know something is wrong. They know that Nic isn't around.

Finally Jasper asks, "Where is Nic?"

I answer with more emotion than I intend to betray: "We don't know."

Jasper begins to cry. "Is Nicky all right?"

"We don't know," I say shakily. "We hope so."

This horror lasts four days.

Then one night he calls.

His voice trembles, but still it brings a wave of relief.

"Dad . . ."

"Nic."

His voice comes as if from down a dim tunnel.

"I." Weakly. "I blew it." A guttural sigh. "I'm in trouble."

"Where are you?"

He tells me and I hang up.

I drive to meet him in an alleyway behind a bookstore in San Rafael. I stop the car and get out near a row of trash and bins strewn with empty bottles, broken glass, torn cardboard, and grimy blankets.

"Dad . . ."

The muffled, scratchy voice comes from behind another series of bins. I walk toward it, pushing aside discarded boxes, turn the corner, and see Nic shakily walking toward me.

My son, the svelte and muscular swimmer, water-polo player, and surfer with an ebullient smile, is bruised, sallow, skin and bone, and his eyes are vacant black holes. When I reach him he goes limp in my arms. I half carry him, his feet shuffling beneath him.

In the car, before he passes out, I tell him that he needs to go to rehab.

"That's it," I say. "There's no choice now."

"I know, Dad."

*

I silently drive home. Nic briefly awakens and mutters in a barren monotone about owing people money, that he has to pay someone back or he will be killed, then he loses consciousness again. Occasionally he awakens and mumbles, but his words are incomprehensible.

Ill, frail, and occasionally still rambling, he spends the next three days shivering as if feverish, curled up in bed, whimpering and crying.

Though I'm terrified, I am also encouraged he said that he will go to rehab. I call the agency that we visited when he was a high school freshman and make an appointment. However, on the morning of the appointment, when I remind him that we are going, he looks at me, revolted.

"No fucking way."

"Nic, you have to go. You told me you would."

"I don't need rehab."

"You promised. You nearly died."

"I messed up. That's all. Don't worry. I learned my lesson."

"Nic, no."

"Listen, I will be fine. I'll never do that shit again. I learned my lesson. I learned how dangerous meth is. It is fucked up. I'm not stupid. I'll never mess with it again."

I stop. Did I hear correctly? No. "Crystal meth?"

He nods.

It sinks in. God no. I am horrified that Nic has used meth. I had an experience with that drug, too, and I will never forget it.

PART II

HIS DRUG OF CHOICE

O God, that men should put an enemy in
their mouths to steal away their brains! That
we should, with joy, pleasance, revel, and
applause, transform ourselves into beasts.

—WILLIAM SHAKESPEARE,
Othello

9

My first summer in Berkeley, Charles moved up from Tucson, enrolling in summer school, and we rented an apartment together. One evening, he arrived home, yanked the thrift-shop mirror from the wall, and set it on a coffee table. He unfolded an origami packet, poured out its contents onto the mirror: a mound of crystalline powder. From his wallet he produced a single-edge razor, with which he chipped at the crystals, the steel tapping rhythmically on the glass. While arranging the powder in four parallel rails, he explained that Michael—Michael the Mechanic, a drug dealer—had run out of cocaine. In its place, Charles had purchased crystal meth.

I snorted the lines through a rolled-up dollar bill. The chemical burned my nasal passages and my eyes watered. Whether the drug is sniffed, smoked, or injected, the body quickly absorbs meth. Once it reaches the bloodstream, it's a near-instant flume ride to the central nervous system. When it reached mine, I heard cacophonous music like a calliope and felt as if Roman candles had been lit inside my skull. Meth triggers ten to twenty times the normal level of the brain's neurotransmitters, primarily dopamine, but also serotonin and norepinephrine, which spray like bullets from a gangster's gun. I felt fantastic—supremely confident, euphoric.

After meth activates the release of neurotransmitters, it blocks their reuptake back into their storage pouches, much as cocaine and other stimulants do. Unlike cocaine, however, which is almost completely metabolized in the body (and has a half-life of forty-five minutes), meth remains relatively unchanged and active for ten to twelve hours. When the dawn began to seep through the cracked window blinds, I felt bleak, depleted, and agitated. I went to bed and slept for a full day, blowing off school.

I never touched meth again, but Charles returned over and over to Michael the Mechanic's. His meth run lasted for two weeks.

Charles could be thoughtful and beguiling and seductively entertaining, but on meth he could, at two or three in the morning, become wretched and mean. Afterward, whether he had turned on a stranger or a friend, he apologized profusely and convincingly, and most people forgave him. For too long, I did, but he moved from Berkeley back to Tucson and we drifted apart. Eventually I lost touch with him. I later learned that after college, his life was defined by his abuse of meth, cocaine, and other drugs. There were voluntary and court-ordered rehabs, car crashes, a house that went up in flames after he fell asleep with a burning cigarette in his mouth, ambulance rides to emergency rooms after overdoses and accidents, and incarcerations, both in hospitals and jails.

Then Charles died on the eve of his fortieth birthday.

Alcohol and heroin are metabolized by the liver, meth by the kidneys. At forty years old, Charles's finally succumbed.

May the good Lord shine a light on you, Charles. Warm, like the evening sun.

When I hear the Stones, I think of him.

And when I hear about meth. So I am sickened that Nic says he has used it.

Integral to my writing process is the research I compulsively undertake. Now that I know that Nic is using meth, I try to learn what I can about the drug. It's more than an attempt to understand it. I sense that there is power in the knowledge of an adversary. The more I learn, however, the more discouraged I am. Meth appears to be the most malefic drug of them all.

The German chemist who first synthesized amphetamine, the forebear of methamphetamine, wrote in 1887, "I have discovered a miraculous drug. It inspires the imagination and gives the user energy." Amphetamine stimulates the part of the nervous system that controls involuntary activity — the action of the heart and glands, breathing, digestive processes, and reflex actions. One effect is the dilation of the bronchial passages, which led, in 1932, to its initial medical use — as a nasal spray for the treatment of asthma. Later studies showed that the drug was also helpful in treating narcolepsy, calming hyperactive children, and suppressing the appetite. In addition, it enabled individuals to stay awake for extended periods of time.

By experimenting with a simple change to the molecular structure of amphetamine, a Japanese pharmacologist first synthesized methamphetamine in 1919. It was more potent than amphetamine and easier to make, plus the crystalline powder was soluble in water, so it was possible to inject it. Methedrine, produced in the 1930s, was the first commercially available methamphetamine. In an inhaler, it was marketed as a bronchodilator; in pill form, as an appetite suppressant and stimulant. An ad read, "Never again feel dreary or suffer the blues."

Meth was widely used in World War II by the Japanese, German, and U.S. military to increase their troops' endurance and performance. Beginning in 1941, relatively mild formulations of methamphetamine were sold over the counter as Philopon and Sedrin. A typical advertising slogan: "Fight sleepiness and enhance vitality." By 1948, these drugs were used in Japan by about 5 percent of the country's sixteen- to twenty-five-year-olds. About fifty-five thousand people had symptoms of what doctors first termed meth-induced psychosis. They ranted and raved. They hallucinated. Some became violent. Mothers ignored or, in some cases, abused their babies.

In 1951, the U.S. Food and Drug Administration classified methamphetamine as a controlled substance. A prescription was required. According to a report published that year in *Pharmacology and Therapeutics*, methamphetamine was effective for "narcolepsy, post-encephalitic parkinsonism, alcoholism, certain depressive states, and obesity."

The illegal speed craze, including the first crank, a meth derivative that is a pale yellow powder that is snorted, and crystal meth, a purer form, the first to be injected (it is snorted, too), hit in the early 1960s. Illicit meth labs emerged in San Francisco in 1962, and speed inundated the Haight Ashbury District, presaging the first national epidemic in the middle to late 1960s. When my research brings me to the San Francisco office of David Smith, the doctor who founded the Haight Ashbury Free Clinic, he recalls the drug's arrival to the Haight: "Before meth, we saw some bad acid trips, but the bad tripper was fairly mellow, whereas meth devastated the neighborhood, sent kids to the emergency room, some to the morgue. Meth ended the summer of love."

Prior to founding the clinic, Smith had been a student up the hill from the Haight at the University of California Medical School. When the hospital emergency room began to see overdoses of this new drug, he started the first clinical research on its effects. He administered small doses to rats, and every one of them died of massive seizures. Rats caged together died on even smaller doses of meth, the effect was quicker, and the cause of death changed. The rats had interpreted normal grooming behavior as an attack, and, as Smith recalls, "they tore each other apart."

In 1967, Smith came down from Parnassus Hill to work in the community. (He went on to become the president of the American

Society of Addiction Medicine and is now the executive medical director of a rehab facility in Santa Monica.) When he arrived in the Haight, he says, "I found a big rat cage—people shooting speed, up all night, paranoid, total insanity, violent, dangerous." Smith issued the original "speed kills" warning in 1968 at a time of meth "shoot-offs" at the Crystal Palace, a bar. A circle of users passed around a needle. "I'd get calls at seven in the morning, when the guy who was the fastest draw was totally psychotic," Smith remembers. The shared needles led to a hepatitis C epidemic. "When I warned the meth addicts about hep, they said, 'Don't worry. That's why we put the yellow guy last.'"

Use of methamphetamine in America waned, waxed, and waned again since the days of the drug's initial heyday. Now many experts say that it's more potent and pervasive than ever. Whereas a few years ago it was concentrated in western cities, meth has now crept across the country, inundating the Midwest, the South, and the East Coast. Meth use is an epidemic in many states, but the enormity of the problem has only recently been acknowledged in Washington, partly because of the lag between the time it took for the newest wave of addicts to fill up the nation's hospitals, rehab facilities, and jails. Former Drug Enforcement Administration chief Asa Hutchinson called methamphetamine "the number-one drug problem in America." It is overwhelming law enforcement, policymakers, and health-care systems.

As recently as early 2006, the Bush administration provoked a political furor when officials with the Office of the National Drug Control Policy downplayed the results of a National Association of Counties survey in which five hundred local law enforcement officials nationwide called meth their number-one problem. (Cocaine was a distant second, and marijuana third.) Later in 2006, the National Drug Intelligence Center published results from a larger, random sample of thirty-four hundred drug enforcement agencies nationwide. For the first time since the organization has conducted the survey, a plurality (40 percent) considered meth their most significant drug problem.

Meth users include men and women of every class, race, and background. Though the current epidemic has its roots in motorcycle gangs and lower-class rural and suburban neighborhoods, meth, as *Newsweek* reported in a 2005 cover story, has "marched across the country and up the socioeconomic ladder." Now, "the most likely people and the most unlikely people take methamphetamine," according to Frank Vocci, director of the Division of Pharmacotherapies and Medical Consequences of Drug Abuse at the National Institute on Drug Abuse.

Internationally, the World Health Organization estimates thirty-five million methamphetamine users compared to fifteen million for cocaine and seven million for heroin. In different places, differing concentrations and forms of the drug are called by many names, including crank, tweak, crystal, lith, Tina, gak, L.A., P., and speed. A particularly devastating form, ice, which is smoked like freebase cocaine, had rarely been seen in U.S. cities other than Honolulu, but it is now turning up on the mainland. Another variety, called ya ba — "crazy medicine" in Thai — is manufactured by the hundreds of millions of tablets in Myanmar, smuggled into Thailand, and, from there, to the West Coast of the United States, where it is sold in clubs and on street corners, sometimes in sweet, colorful pills that are ingested or ground up and smoked.

The most ubiquitous form on the mainland is crystal, which is often manufactured with such ingredients as decongestants and brake cleaner in what the DEA has called "Beavis and Butt-head" labs in homes and garages. Mobile, or "box," labs in campers and vans and labs in motels have been discovered in every state. In 2006, Bill Maher quipped, "If Americans get any dumber about

science, they won't even be able to make their own crystal meth."
For now, however, all it takes is a visit to the Internet where, for
thirty dollars plus shipping, I purchased a thick how-to book
called *Secrets of Methamphetamine Manufacture*. The revised and
expanded sixth edition of "the classic text on clandestine chemistry" has a disclaimer on the title page: "sold for informational
purposes only." This information includes step-by-step instructions to manufacturing a variety of forms and quantities of meth,
plus advice about evading law enforcement.

Home meth brewers get the drug's key ingredient—pseudoephedrine—from nonprescription cold pills, prompting many
states to initiate restrictions, including limits on the number of
packages of Contac, Sudafed, and Drixoral that can be purchased
at a time. As a result, the makers of these drugs are reportedly
working to change the formulas so that they can no longer be
used to make meth. In the meantime, Wal-Mart, Target, and other
stores have moved them behind the counter.

Controlling the supply of cold pills and other sources of ephedrine and pseudoephedrine has had an effect on the domestic supply
of meth, and many STLs—small toxic labs—have shut down.
But the domestic successes have handed a new business over to
Mexican and other international drug cartels, which now smug-
gle in meth along the routes used for cocaine, heroin, marijuana,
and other drugs. While the drug is still often made in garages,
basements, and kitchen laboratories, the majority comes from
superlabs operated by these cartels. *The Oregonian* published an
exposé by reporter Steve Suo that reveals that the government
could have contained (and could still contain) the meth epidemic.
Only nine factories manufacture the bulk of the world's supply
of ephedrine and pseudoephedrine, but pharmaceutical companies—and legislators influenced by them—have stopped every
move that would have effectively controlled the distribution of

the chemicals so they could not be diverted to methamphetamine superlabs. Suo's report suggests that until the government takes on the pharmaceutical companies, the war on this drug is something of a joke. The proof? Users who want meth can find it virtually anywhere and anytime.

The government maintains that overall drug use is down in the United States, but it depends where you look. In many communities, there are more addicts and alcoholics than ever. According to the *Los Angeles Times,* in California, overdoses and other drug-related deaths may soon surpass automobile accidents as the state's leading cause of non-natural death. Numerous barometers indicate a sharp rise in meth abuse. In many cities, meth is behind increasing numbers of addicts entering treatment, showing up at emergency rooms, and drug-related crime. From 1993 to 2005, the number of admissions to rehab for treatment of meth addiction more than quintupled from twenty-eight thousand a year to about one hundred and fifty thousand, according to James Colliver, Ph.D., of the National Institute on Drug Abuse. In its 2006 report, the Substance Abuse and Mental Health Services Administration reported a "surging" of treatment admissions for meth abuse. There also are peaks in crime in communities inundated with meth. Eighty to 100 percent of crime in some cities is meth-related. In some states, law enforcement officials have attributed rising murder rates to the drug. In cities where meth is the predominant drug problem, there are high incidences of spousal and child abuse—indeed, tragic stories of child abuse are common.

As many as half of all meth users, and a larger percentage of ice users, tweak. That is, at some point they experience the type of meth psychosis first identified in Japan in the late 1940s. It is characterized by auditory and visual hallucinations, intense paranoia, delusions, and a variety of other symptoms, some of which are indistinguishable from schizophrenia. The hyperanxious state of tweaking can lead to aggression and violence, hence the following, from a report for police approaching meth addicts: "The most dangerous stage of meth abuse for abusers, medical personnel, and law enforcement officers is called 'tweaking.' A tweaker is an abuser who probably has not slept in 3–15 days and is irritable and paranoid. Tweakers often behave or react violently ... Detaining a tweaker alone is not recommended and law enforcement officers should call for backup."

The report includes Six Safety Tips for Approaching a Tweaker, including: "Keep a 7–10 ft. distance. Coming too close can be perceived as threatening. Do not shine bright lights at him. The tweaker is already paranoid and if blinded by a bright light he is likely to run or become violent. Slow your speech and lower the pitch of your voice. A tweaker already hears sounds at a fast pace and in a high pitch. Slow your movements. This will decrease the odds that the tweaker will misinterpret your physical actions. Keep your hands visible. If you place your hands where the tweaker cannot see them, he might feel threatened and could become violent. Keep the tweaker talking. A tweaker who falls silent can be extremely dangerous. Silence often means that his paranoid thoughts have taken over reality, and anyone present can become part of the tweaker's paranoid delusions."

Tweaking or not, meth addicts are more likely than other drug users (with the possible exception of crack addicts) to engage in antisocial behavior. A successful businessman took the drug to work longer hours, became addicted, and murdered a man who owed him drugs and money. An addict shot his wife, another fatally bludgeoned his victim, and another murdered a couple for a car and seventy dollars. A couple, both meth abusers, beat, starved, and then scalded their four-year-old niece, who died in a bathtub. A Pontoon Beach, Illinois, man was under the influence of meth when he murdered his wife and then killed himself. In

Portland, a woman on meth was arrested for killing her eighteen-
month-old child, strangling her with a scarf. In Texas, a man
high on meth, after arguing with a friend, tracked him down and
murdered him — shooting him six times in the head. In Ventura
County, California, a man under the influence of meth raped and
strangled a woman. Also in California, a meth-addicted mother
was convicted of keeping her two young children locked in a
cold, cockroach-infested converted garage. An Omaha man was
recently sentenced to forty years for murdering his girlfriend's
child after shooting meth. The child had been smothered and
had numerous broken bones. There have been trials in Phoenix,
Denver, Chicago, and Riverside County, California, of mothers
accused of murdering their babies because they nursed them while
they were on meth. The mother in Riverside, during her trial, said,
"I woke up with a corpse."

In addition to crime, methamphetamine causes significant environmental damage in the places where it is made. The manufacture of
one pound of methamphetamine creates six pounds of corrosive
liquids, acid vapors, heavy metals, solvents, and other harmful
materials. When these chemicals make contact with the skin or are
inhaled, they can cause illness, disfigurement, or death. Lab opera-
tors almost always dump the waste. The implications for the central
valley in California, a source of a large percentage of America's
fruits and vegetables and much of its meth, are significant. In the
early 2000s, hospitals in the central valley were treating many
children, often of undocumented immigrants, for conditions related
to the chemical by-products of meth production. As an agent there
told me, "Millions of pounds of toxic chemicals are going into the
fruit basket of the United States. The chemicals are turning up in
alarming levels in ground water samples."

   The health effects of using meth are disastrous. The drug lands more people in ERs than any other club drug, including ecstasy, ketamine, and GHB combined. (And in a laboratory test conducted at the University of California in Los Angeles, eight out of ten tablets sold as ecstasy at clubs in that city contained meth.) Those who don't overdose on the drug may still die from it. Meth causes or contributes to fatal accidents and suicides. After conducting a survey of suicidal tendencies in drug users, psychiatrist Tom Newton, a researcher at UCLA, concluded that "methamphetamine is a uniquely potent drug for inducing depression so severe that people feel like committing suicide."

Many other health risks are related to chronic meth abuse. A doctor who works at a San Francisco emergency room told me about the stream of meth addicts who come in with "blownout" — literally ruptured — aortas. Addicts may cough up chunks of the lining of their lungs. Many meth addicts lose their teeth. Chronic meth use can cause Parkinson's-like cognitive dysfunction, including deteriorating memory and mental acuity and physical impairment, including paralysis — results of meth-induced strokes. One- time use of the drug can be fatal. It can cause the body temperature to sharply rise, leading to lethal convulsions, death from hyperthermia, "arrhythmic sudden death" — the heart no longer has a functional beat — or fatal aneurysms. Serious or fatal conditions may be more likely to occur because of the extended periods of activity that many users engage in. Meth users may not sleep or eat for days. The combination of the drug and fatigue has been shown to contribute to paranoia and aggression. The cycle tends to compound physical, psychological, and social problems; and these all may be further compounded by existing mental health issues, which are common among users.

Nic has used meth. In spite of his protests and promises, I increase my pleas for him to go into rehab, but he will not yield. I check and learn that now that he is over eighteen, I cannot commit him. If he were a threat to himself or someone else, there's a complicated process by which I could commit him to a brief evaluation at a mental hospital, but a parent concerned about a child's drug use doesn't qualify. Had I seen this coming, I would have forced Nic into rehab when I still could have made the decision for him. There is no way to know if it would have helped—he may not have been ready to hear the message of rehab—but at least it may have slowed him down. Now he has to go in on his own.

He sleeps for as much as twenty hours a day for the next three days. After that, he is depressed and withdrawn. Then, without warning, on a cold spring afternoon, he disappears again.

With Nic gone, and our old car with him, I once again call
hospital emergency rooms. I once again call the police to
see if he has been arrested. When I explain that my son is missing,
a police dispatcher, before passing along the phone number for the
jail, tells me that if Nic shows up I should send him to a boot camp
where children, roused and shackled in the middle of the night,
are taken by force. I have been reading about one of these—a
boot camp in Arizona near my parents'. A boy died there over the
summer. At the boot camp, children were beaten, kicked, starved,
chained, and deprived of water in the 114-degree desert.

I talk to other parents who have gone through versions of this
and I am bombarded by their advice, too, much of it familiar and
much of it familiarly contradictory. Once again, one says that
if Nic shows up, I should kick him out. It makes no sense to me
because I know where he would go, to his unsupervised friends'
homes or perhaps to the squalid and treacherous lairs of his drug
dealers. That would be that. All hope for him would be lost. One
mother recommends a lockup school where she sent her daughter
for two years.

Nic has been gone for six days, and my desperation has built to
a frenzy. I have never experienced grief like this. I spend frantic
hours on the Internet reading harrowing stories of children on
drugs. I call parents who know parents who know parents who
have been through this. I try and try to understand what drugs

mean to Nic. He once told me, "Every writer and artist I love was a drunk or an addict." I know that Nic uses drugs because he feels cleverer and less introverted and insecure, and he also carries the dangerous — and fallacious — idea that debauchery leads to the greatest art, whether by Hemingway, Hendrix, or Basquiat.

In his suicide note, Kurt Cobain wrote, "It's better to burn out than to fade away." He was quoting a Neil Young song about Johnny Rotten of the Sex Pistols. When I was twenty-four, I interviewed John Lennon. I asked him about this sentiment, one that pervades rock and roll. He took strong, outraged exception to it. "It's better to fade away like an old soldier than to burn out," he said. "I worship the people who survive. I'll take the living and the healthy."

The living and the healthy.

I do not know if my son can be one of them.

Somehow I never fall apart around Jasper and Daisy. I do not allow myself to; I don't want to worry them any more than they already are. To the kids, we acknowledge that we're concerned about Nic and, in doing so, try for a delicate balance. We don't want to scare them, and yet at the same time, we don't want to pretend that everything is fine when they know — how can they not? — that it isn't. I'm convinced that failing to acknowledge this crisis will be more confusing and more damaging than the truth.

When I am alone, however, I weep in a way that I have not wept since I was a young boy. Nic used to tease me about my inability to cry. On the rare occasions when my eyes welled up, he joked about my "constipated tears." Now tears come at unexpected moments for no obvious reason and they pour forth with ferocity. They scare the hell out of me. It scares the hell out of me to be so lost and helpless and out of control and afraid.

I call Vicki. Our acrimony since the divorce has been pushed aside by our shared worry about Nic. It is with relief that I come to see her not for what separated us but for what unites us. We both love Nic in a way that only parents love their children. It's not that Karen and Nic's stepfather aren't worried about Nic, but in long telephone conversations that no one else can be part of, his mother and I share a particular quality of worry —acute and visceral.

Meanwhile, Karen and I go back and forth switching roles. When I collapse, she reassures me.

"Nic will be all right."

"How do you know?"

"I just know. He's a smart boy. He has a good heart."

Then Karen will lose it, and I console her.

"It's all right," I say. "He's just mixed up. We'll figure this out. He'll come back."

And he does.

On a still, cold, and gray afternoon, a week later, he just shows up at the house. Like the time I went to find him in the alleyway in San Rafael, he is frail, ill, and rambling—a barely recognizable phantom.

I just stare at him standing there in the doorway.

"Oh, Nic," I say. I gaze at him and then lead him by the arm to his room, where, still dressed, he lies on his bed, wrapping up in a comforter. I am glad that no one else is home so that, for the moment, I don't have to explain.

I stare at him.

If all that therapy didn't help, what? Rehab. There is nothing else. "Nic, you have to go into rehab. You have to."

He mumbles and falls asleep.

I know that I must do everything possible to get him into a drug-rehabilitation program, so I call some. I call the place we visited plus counselors and other specialists for recommendations. Nic's therapist now agrees that rehab is essential and calls some of his colleagues who specialize in drug and alcohol addiction. My friends call their friends who have been through this.

Nic sleeps.

I call the recommended facilities in our area, inquiring about their success rates for treating meth users. These conversations provide my initial glimpse of what must be the most chaotic, flailing field of health care in America. I am quoted a range from 25 to 85 percent, but a drug and alcohol counselor familiar with many programs says that the figures are unreliable. "Even the conservative numbers sound overly optimistic," he says. "About seventeen percent of people who go through these programs are sober after a year." An admitting nurse at a northern California hospital may be the most accurate when she tells me the number for meth addicts. "The true number is in the single digits," she says. "Anyone who promises more is lying."

The more I learn about the rehab industry, the more it seems in disarray. Some highly touted, and expensive, rehab programs are ineffective. Many rehabs employ one-size-fits-all-addicts programs. Whether private or public, some are only slightly better than useless when it comes to the treatment of meth addicts, according to Richard Rawson, the associate director of the Integrated Substance Abuse Programs at UCLA, who calls them "the Earl Scheibs of rehab. The paint job doesn't last."

Dr. Rawson doesn't suggest that many programs don't have useful components. They tend to be rooted in the principle of Alcoholics Anonymous, which seem to be essential to staying sober for most, if not all, alcoholics and addicts, no matter the drug. But other than that, they offer a slipshod patchwork of behavioral, psychological, and cognitive therapies. Many programs include lectures, individual counseling sessions, chores with harsh consequences for shirking, and confessional and confrontational group therapy, including badgering patients who resist the gospel of treatment. (According to the drug and alcohol counselors in these programs, resistance means denial, and denial leads to relapse.) Some programs offer life-skills training, such as resumé writing; exercise; group and individual sessions with family; and consultations with a physician and psychiatrists, who may prescribe medication. Some facilities offer massage and nutrition consultations. Some outpatient programs add a relatively new technique called contingency management, a system of positively rewarding abstinence. However, without standards based on proven protocols, patients are often subjected to the philosophies of a program's director, some of whom have no qualifications other than their former addiction. "Having six children doesn't make you a good OB-GYN," says Walter Ling, a neurologist and the director with Rawson of the UCLA program. Even rehabs run by trained doctors and clinicians employ a wide range of treatments, many unproven. Most importantly: many programs fail to take into account the specific conditions of methamphetamine, which is, according to some experts, the toughest addiction to treat. But what else can I try?

I choose a highly recommended place in Oakland called Thunder Road and make an appointment. I steel myself to do the hardest thing I can imagine doing, using what is left of my waning influence—the threat that I will kick him out and withdraw all of my support—to get him to come with me. That I mean it—because I am convinced that this is our only hope—does not make it easier.

The next morning, when Daisy and Jasper are at school, I go into Nic's room, where he still sleeps soundly, his face relaxed and peaceful. A sleeping child. Then, as I watch, he twitches and grimaces and grinds his teeth. I rouse him and tell him where we are headed.

He rages. "No fucking way!"

"Let's go, Nic, let's get it over with," I plead.

He gets up, pushes his hair back with a trembling hand. He holds onto a doorjamb for support.

"I said no fucking way."

He slurs, staggers.

"This is it, Nic," I say firmly. My voice trembles. "We're going. It's not a choice."

"You can't make me. What the fuck?"

"If you want to live here, if you want me to help you, if you want me to pay for your college, if you want to see us . . ." I look at him and say, "Nic: Do you want to die? Is that what this is all about?"

He kicks the wall, smashes his fists onto the table, and weeps.

I sadly say: "Let's go."

He rages some more, but follows me to the car.

PART III

WHATEVER

You're safe, I remembered whispering to
Quintana when I first saw her in the ICU at
UCLA. *I'm here. You're going to be all right.*
Half of her skull had been shaved for surgery.
I could see the long cut and the metal staples
that held it closed. She was again breathing
only through an endotracheal tube. I'm here.
Everything's fine . . . I would take care of her.
It would be all right. It also occurred to me
that this was a promise I could not keep. I
could not always take care of her. I could not
never leave her. She was no longer a child.
She was an adult. Things happened in life that
mothers could not prevent or fix.

— Joan Didion,
The Year of Magical Thinking

11

I drive the old Volvo, faded blue and rusty from the salt air of the coast and dented from Nic's misadventures. It smells of his cigarettes. It is the car he had taken. Nic flops like a rag doll, pressed as close to his door, as far away from me, as possible.

Neither of us speaks.

Nic's electric guitar, buttercup-yellow with a black pick guard, is in the backseat. Another leftover from his escapades lies beside it: an intricately carved bong made of a glass beaker and meerschaum stem. More: a flashlight, a copy of Rimbaud with a ripped cover, dirty jeans, a half-empty bottle of Gatorade, the *Bay Guardian*, his leather bomber jacket, empty beer bottles, cassettes, a stale sandwich.

He tries a few times to talk me out of it.

"This is stupid," he weakly beseeches. "I know I fucked up. I have learned my lesson."

I don't answer.

"I can't do this," he says. "I won't."

He turns livid. Glaring at me, he says, "I'll just run away." He is supercilious and condescending—almost savage. "You fucking think you know me. You don't know anything about me. You have always tried to control me."

He screams until he is hoarse.

In the middle of his ranting, when I notice his slurring, I realize that he is high. Again. Still.

"What are you on today, Nic?" There's incomprehension in my tone.

An angry whisper comes from him. "Fuck you."

I look over at him, look deeply into his impassive face. Nic has many of his mother's handsome features. Like her he is tall and thin and has her fine nose and lips. He had her fair hair before it darkened as he grew up. Even so, sometimes I have looked at his face and it was as if I were peering in a mirror. It was not only the physical similarities that I would see. I saw myself hidden in his eyes, in his expressions. It would startle me. Maybe every child as they grow up takes on their parents' traits and mannerisms and becomes more like them. I see my father in me now in ways that I never did when I was young. In the car, however, I see a stranger. And yet he is a stranger whose every part I know intimately. I recall his soft eyes when they were elated and when they were disappointed, his face when he was pallid from illness and when he was burned red by the sun, his mouth and even each tooth from visits to dentists and the orthodontist, his knees from when he skinned them and I put on Band-Aids, his shoulders from putting on sun block, his feet from taking out splinters—every part of him. I know every part of him just from watching him and living with him and being close to him, and yet driving to Oakland I look at his sullenness and anger and vacancy, his retreat and his turmoil, and I think, Who are you?

I pull up in front of the Oakland rehab and we walk through glass doors into an austere waiting room. As I inform the receptionist that we have an appointment, Nic stands behind me, belligerent on his heels with his arms folded across his chest.

She instructs us to wait.

A counselor, with black eyes and hair tied back in a long ponytail, comes out and introduces herself, first to Nic and then to me.

He acknowledges her with a grunt. As instructed, Nic follows her into another room. He hunches. His feet barely move him forward.

I flip through an old copy of *People*, and then, after nearly an hour, the counselor emerges and says that she wants to speak to me alone. Nic, palpably seething, takes my spot in the waiting room. I follow the woman into a small office with a metal desk and two chairs and a murky fish tank.

"Your son is in serious trouble," she says. "He needs treatment. He easily could die from all the drugs he is using."

"What can . . ."

"At eighteen, he is using and mixing more drugs than many people who are much older. He has a dangerous attitude—he doesn't understand that he's in trouble. He's proud to be so hardcore, wears it like a badge. This program isn't right for him. He is bordering on being too old and is at this point resistant to treatment. We see it all the time. He's in denial. It's typical of addicts, who maintain and believe that everything is all right, they can stop when they want, everyone else has a problem but not them, they are fine, even if they wind up losing everything, even if they are on the streets, even if they wind up in jail or in the hospital."

"Then what—?"

"He has to get into treatment now, whatever it takes. Not here, but somewhere."

She recommends other programs. In her somber tone and expression, I can tell that she holds out no great hope.

Driving home, the tension in the car builds and then explodes. Nic finally yells, "This is bullshit." I think he might leap out of the car as I speed along the freeway.

"It *is* bullshit," I spit back. "If you want to kill yourself, I should just let you do it."

"It's my life," he hoarsely screams. He cries uncontrollably, hysterically. He hits the dashboard with his fists and kicks it with his boots.

We pull up in front of the house, but with Daisy and Jasper home now, I don't bring Nic in. I sit with him in the car for another half-hour until he has exhausted himself. He is remote — somnolent from drugs and anger, his breathing slowed, and then, finally, he falls into a deep sleep. I leave him in the car, checking on him frequently. *Will you check on me every fifteen minutes?* In a while he trudges inside and heads directly for his bedroom. Jasper and Daisy silently watch as their brother's listless body drifts through the living room.

I have to find a program that will take him immediately. Before I lose him.

With Nic asleep in his room, I sit down with the kids. I explain as well as I can that Nic is once again on drugs and ill. I say that I am trying to find a hospital or a drug-rehabilitation program that can help him. I say that kids with a brother or sister or parent with a drug problem sometimes think it's their fault.

"It's not your fault. I promise."

They stare at me, sad and uncomprehending.

"Nic has a serious problem, but we're going to get him the help he needs. With help he can be all right."

Nic seethes and rails in and out of a tormented half-sleep, and I call more rehab programs. One, Ohlhoff Recovery House, in San Francisco, has an open bed. It is a well-respected program, recommended by many experts in the Bay Area. A friend of a friend told me that the program turned around the life of her heroin-addicted son. "He lives in Florida now," she said. "He has a family of his own. He has a job that he loves and, on the side, volunteers to help kids with drug problems."

Parents of addicts live for encouraging stories like this.

When Nic wakes up, I tell him that I have found a program in the city, and he somberly agrees to go in for another evaluation. He grimly follows me to the car.

Ohlhoff Recovery is located in a stately but ancient Victorian mansion with three stories, a central cupola, and a handsome wood-paneled lobby, where I wait while Nic goes in for an interview, this time with the director of the twenty-eight-day primary program — primary as in primary school; it's the initial step into rehab and recovery.

After their session, I am called into the stark room and I sit in the vacant chair. Nic and I face the director, who is behind a wooden desk. From her manner and the look of weariness in her eyes, I can tell that Nic has been as belligerent with her as he had been with the counselor at Thunder Road, but she seems less perturbed.

She begins, "Nic doesn't acknowledge that he is an addict."

"Because I'm not."

Undeterred, she continues, "And says he's only coming to treatment because you're forcing him to."

"I know that," I say.

"But that's all right. Many people don't come here by choice. They have just as much of a chance of getting and staying sober as someone who crawls in here, begging to be treated."

I say, "OK."

Nic glares.

"We will check him in in the morning for our twenty-eight-day program."

Nic hides in his room through dinner. We tell Daisy and Jasper that Nic is going into a treatment program in the morning, but that he is scared.

I sit with them after Karen reads their bedtime story. "I'm so sorry you have to go through this with Nic," I say for the nth time. How else can I help them? "It's such a sad thing to have this problem in our family. I hope you'll talk about it with your teachers and friends at school, at least if you want to. If you have questions or worries, you can always ask me or your mom."

Jasper solemnly nods. Daisy is still. She starts reading a Garfield paperback, which Jasper snatches from her. She scratches him and Jasper pushes her. They both wail.

In the morning, driving to the city, Nic is glowering but drained, hardly saying a word. He is a condemned prisoner, resigned and petrified. He holds back tears.

I park in front of the old mansion and walk with Nic, who carries a duffel bag of clothes. Hidden inside his torn dress shirt and big jeans, his head down, Nic trembles. We walk up the steps, making our way through a pack of cigarette-smoking addicts — at least I presume they are the program's resident addicts — clustered on the front stairs. I shake, too. Noticing Nic's suitcase and his apprehensive, furtive glances, a few of the men address him:

"Hey."

"Yo."

"Welcome to the nuthouse."

Nic meets briefly with the program director in the same wood-paneled office, and he is presented with a piece of paper:

"I, the undersigned, hereby request admission to the Alcohol and Chemical Recovery Program," etc.

He signs.

In the hallway, the director, standing with Nic at her side, says to me, "You may say goodbye now. Phone calls are forbidden for the first week."

I turn to Nic.

We hug clumsily, and I leave.

*

Outside, I feel a barely remembered glimpse of exhilaration from the chill in the air, but driving home, I feel as if I might collapse from more emotion than I can handle. Incongruously, I feel as if I have betrayed Nic, abandoned him, turned him in, though I do take some small consolation in the fact that I know where he is. For the first time in weeks, I sleep through the night.

The next morning, I enter his bedroom and raise high the shades and open wide the window that looks out onto the garden. The gloomy red room is strewn with books, half-painted canvases, grimy clothing, monster speakers, and, on the bed, the yellow guitar. Nic's Sharpie drawings of elongated men and women, their bodies grotesquely contorted, are tacked to the walls. The room has Nic's smell — not the sweet childhood smell he once had, but a cloying odor of incense and marijuana, cigarettes and aftershave, possibly a trace of ammonia or formaldehyde, the residual odor of burning meth. Smells like teen spirit.

Karen watches as I search his dresser and desk drawers and closet and gather up his hidden arsenal — the glass bong, hand-blown meth pipe, cigarette papers, broken shards of a mirror, straight-edge razors, drained Bic lighters, empty bottles — placing them in a black plastic garbage bag, which I carry outside and put in the trash can.

Over the next few days, the barrage of advice from friends and friends of friends continues. A friend of Karen's, when he hears that Nic is in rehab, asks, "For how long?"

Karen explains that it is a four-week program.

Her friend shakes his head. "It's not enough."

"What do you mean?"

He tells the story of his son who had been through two four-week programs before they sent him to one that lasts a year. He is still in the combined rehab and high school. He is seventeen, so they were able to send him by force. Karen's friend says, "Even with a year, we don't know if it's long enough."

Another friend tells us that rehab was the wrong approach, what Nic needed was Outward Bound. Some people believe in therapy, others abhor it. My sense is that the psychologists and psychiatrists who saw Nic over the years gave me useful advice and support, and possibly helped him, too, but in spite of their impeccable credentials and obvious devotion to their work, almost every professional we consulted was inexperienced with drug addiction and failed to diagnose it. Everyone has an opinion; well-meaning advice pours in endlessly. Karen and I listen intently. Though we ignore most of it, we are grateful for people's concern.

A mother of a child at Jasper and Daisy's school calls to recommend a local specialist in drug addiction, claiming that he helped a friend more than any of the other experts she saw. For some reason, we heed this recommendation and make an appointment to see him.

The therapist's office is up a flight of stairs above an art-supply store in San Anselmo. It is modest, shared with a marriage counselor, less formal than the psychologists' offices we have come to know. It seems as if we have seen every drug and alcohol counselor, psychologist, and psychiatrist in the San Francisco Bay Area, where one out of every three people seems to be a therapist of some sort. What does this say about us? Scott Peck said that the sickest and healthiest people are in therapy. Which are we?

The doctor has a calm smile on a lined face. Balding, he wears an open-collared shirt under a wool jacket. He seems solid, gentle, and empathetic; from his appearance and manner and soft voice and eyes, we understand that he knows our despair because he has experienced it.

We tell him all about Nic. We explain he's in rehab at Ohlhoff Recovery. We say that we are unsure if we have done the right thing. We say that we worry about Jasper and Daisy. We say that we have no idea what to do when the program ends.

To our surprise, he doesn't have much advice for us, at least not about helping Nic, though he is supportive of the decision to have him in rehab. Most of his counsel is for us.

"Take care of yourselves," he says. "Pay attention to your marriage. Marriages can be destroyed when a child is a drug addict." He says that we can't and shouldn't try to decide what to do when the program ends — much will happen in the interim. "Take it one day at a time." The cliché works, he says.

Late in the session, he leans forward and speaks with compelling poignancy: "Go out together on a date."

"We are," Karen replies dryly. "This is it."

She and I look at each other, sharing the irony. It is true that we have not been out alone in ages. Traumatized, we have wanted to stay close to home, and we have felt nervous about leaving the children. We finally left the kids with Nancy and Don this evening.

The therapist asks if we have tried Al-Anon.

I say no. "I thought Al-Anon was for . . ." My voice trails off.

He responds, "It might be worth a try."

The telephone may be forbidden, but on his third day at Ohlhoff, Nic manages to call, begging to come home. When I refuse, he slams down the receiver. Worried, I call the counselor assigned to him. She reports that Nic is surly, depressed, and confrontational, threatening to run away. "But they almost always start out this way," she says.

"What if he runs away?"

"We can't stop him. He's an adult."

Karen and I have a series of sessions with the drug and alcohol counselor. He is a good listener, which may be what we need most right now, but it's not only that. He helps us clarify what we can and cannot do for Nic. He says that one of the most difficult things about having a child addicted to drugs is that we cannot control it. We cannot save Nic. "You can support his recovery, but you can't do it for him," he says. "We try to save them. Parents try. It's what parents do."

He tells us Al-Anon's Three Cs: "You didn't cause it, you can't control it, you can't cure it."

Each time we leave his office, he reminds us, "Be allies. Remember, take care of yourselves. You'll be good for no one—for each other, for your children—if you don't."

Now that Nic is safe—for the moment—I am working more. One of my interview subjects is a recovering drug addict as well as a parent of one. I tell him that I have just gotten my son into rehab. He says, "God bless you. I have been there. It is hell. But he's in God's hands." It startles me. I mention that our family never believed in God. "I wish I did," I say. "I wish I could put it in someone else's hands. Someone powerful and benevolent. But I don't believe it."

"You will believe in God before this is over," he says.

I call Nic's counselor at Ohlhoff. I can tell that she is trying to put on the best face, but she seems discouraged. She says: "Methamphetamine is particularly tricky. It's the devil's own drug. It's horrible what it does to them." She pauses, says, "It's early still, though."

This isn't the first time that I have been told that meth is worse than most other drugs. To learn why, I continue my research, traveling to meet with more researchers who study meth. They explain that users of many drugs often binge and increase their dosages in an attempt to recreate the initial high, but for meth addicts, with the depletion of as much as 90 percent of the brain's dopamine, it's no longer possible. As with many drugs, the dopamine deficiency causes depression and anxiety, but it's often far more severe with meth. This compels the user to take more of the drug, causing more nerve damage, which increases the compulsion to use—a cycle that leads both to addiction and relapse. Many researchers hold that this drug's unique neurotoxicity means that meth addicts, unlike users of most other drugs, may never completely recover. For me, this is obviously a chilling conclusion, injecting my research with even more urgency.

The Clinton administration earmarked millions of dollars for research into methamphetamine treatments when the epidemic was beginning to spread, and meth addicts had an unacceptably high rate of relapse and low rate of retention in programs. One of the goals of the research was to determine if addicts' brains were irreparably damaged. If so, as in Parkinson's, the best that could be done would be treating the symptoms or possibly slowing the degeneration. Full recovery would probably be impossible.

In 1987, the Partnership for a Drug-Free America launched the antidrug campaign "This is your brain on drugs." But the human brain on meth does not look like fried eggs. It looks more like the night sky over Baghdad during the first weeks of the war. At least that's how it looks on the computer screen at the desk of Edythe London, a pharmacologist by training, who is a professor of psychiatry and biobehavioral sciences at the David Geffen School of Medicine at UCLA.

When she was an undergraduate, Dr. London took a test that told her that she had an aptitude for medical illustration. In a way, using functional brain-imaging technologies, she does exactly that. In 2000, London created pictures of the brains of sixteen methamphetamine abusers. As with most meth users when they stop taking the drug, her enlisted subjects slept in the hospital for two days after they were admitted. Several days after they awoke, London used positron emission tomography (PET) scans to map their brains. PET scans register brain activity by measuring blood flow and biochemical reactions through the movements and concentrations of radioactive tracers. The results are pictures of human brain function — and the measured activity can be related to emotion. Depending on the compound, or marker, used in a test, a scan can map general activity in the brain or the activity of a specific neurotransmitter. In scanning meth addicts, London's goal was to learn more about the state of users' brains when they are in the initial stages of withdrawal. That is, what shape are they in when they first enter rehab?

Dr. London is a soft-spoken woman with shoulder-length black hair and bangs. While I sit across from her in her small office at the medical center, she rotates her flat-panel monitor so that I can see the image of the functioning (or, more accurately, malfunctioning) addict brain. She explains that the picture is the average of all sixteen addicts' brains, combining PET scans, which chronicle the activity, and MRIs, which provide a highly accurate background structure. These images are stacked upon the average of brains in the control group. London has assigned colors to the images. The result is before me: a map showing the stark difference between addicts' and normal brains. It is a lateral cross-section, with the gray matter — the MRI structure — in gray. Blue patches indicate where the activity in the brain of the meth user is significantly lower than the control group's brains. Yellow to red areas are "hot," meaning that there is significantly more activity in the addicts' than the others' brains.

London stares intently at the image. After a few moments, she sighs. "It's beautiful, but sad."

My mind goes to Nic. Assuming he is an average meth user, the largest sweep of the hottest colors, the size and shape of a small, tailless mouse, is located in the posterior cingulate. Pointing to the patch, yellow in the center radiating out to a circle of Halloween orange, London explains, "What is turned on here is exactly what turns on while people feel pain." The operative word is *while*. She goes on, "A person stops using methamphetamine, and this is awaiting them." Clinicians who work with meth addicts already know that addicts are often depressed, argumentative, anxious, and unwilling to engage in treatment—exactly like Nic—but London's scans reveal that these conditions have a biological basis. In addition, they indicate a level of severity unrecognized before. It led her to conclude that meth addicts may be unable, not unwilling, to participate in many common treatments, at least in the early stages of withdrawal. Rather than a moral failure or a lack of willpower, dropping out and relapsing may be a result of a damaged brain.

She explains that severe cognitive impairments may make patients incapable of participating in therapies that require concentration, logic, and memory. Also, patients with extremely high levels of depression and anxiety, and who are suffering a type of "chronic agony," as London describes it, are at a major disadvantage when taking part in cognitive and behavioral treatments. It's not surprising that Nic, in the first weeks in recovery, wants to flee. In fact, London's research worries me, because it, adding to others' research, shows how long it takes for the brain to return to normal—if it ever does.

After a month of abstinence, the depressive symptoms and pain following meth withdrawal are less severe in many of the abstinent meth users, but in a substantial number, they are far from abated. No wonder the odds are so bad—that is, no wonder the programs available in most rehab facilities in most communities fail most of the time. Some of the places I called are only several-day or week-long detox. Many of the programs, like Ohlhoff, last for twenty-eight days, but few cities have publicly funded long-term programs and few private insurance plans include the coverage for

intensive ongoing treatment. Longer programs, especially inpatient programs, are prohibitively expensive for most people. But
though a meth addict may become well enough in four weeks to
understand the need for ongoing care, he or she may not become
well enough to follow through on it. Dr. London's pictures illus-
trate why programs most likely to be effective would last for many
months. It probably takes at least a couple months for a patient to
recover enough to engage in treatments in meaningful ways.

What should be done for patients when they arrive in these
programs? It would be ludicrous to try to treat heroin addicts
in the few days after their last fix with cognitive and behavioral
therapies, the mainstays of rehab programs. Heroin addicts have a
well-documented physical withdrawal from the drug that includes
shakes, convulsions, and the like. The physical effects of withdrawal from methamphetamine, however, manifest in symptoms
that we usually associate with psychology and emotion, but — and
on Dr. London's computer screen is blue-and-orange proof — they
have physical bases.

There are many spots of "hot" brain activity that correlate
to trait (ongoing) and state (situational) anxiety, far more than
the control subjects. The picture is unique to this drug, London
explains. "Scans of the brains of heroin, cocaine, or alcohol abusers do not show changes like these."

The images also suggest cognitive impairments. A blue patch
in the medial orbitofrontal cortex is worrisome to London because
activity in this area is related to decision-making ability. It is
distinctly blue, with a whitish center. Meanwhile, the posterior
cingulate, related to pain and emotion, isn't activated in the control subjects, but is brightly lit up in the meth users. It is logical
that it would be harder to think when parts of the brain related
to negative emotion are active. "In the meth users, at least in the
first weeks, the cognitive strategies that the brain is using are

abnormal," London says. This means that, in addition to the biologically rooted high anxiety and depression, people getting off meth have severely impaired cognitive functioning.

I check further and come across a study that was conducted three years before London's by Stephen Kish, a doctor at the University of Toronto's Medical Center, who autopsied the brains of meth users. (They were the brains of people who died of a methamphetamine overdose or who had a high level of the drug in their system when they were killed by a gunshot or in an accident.) In slideshows in many generations of high school health classes, the shrunken, dehydrated, eroded gray matter inside the brains of alcoholics has been compared to healthy brains, creamy white and spongy. Unlike alcoholics, there is no damage in the brains of meth addicts that is visible to the naked eye. At the microscopic level, however, the fried-egg "this-is-your-brain-on-drugs" metaphor applies. Researchers have seen that some neuron ends are essentially singed.

Biopsies of brain cells tell more. To analyze them, Kish used biochemical probes and scooped out twenty-milligram chunks of brain. He measured the amount of specific neurotransmitters, and compared them to the amounts in normal brains.

His study showed modestly diminished levels of serotonin and other neurotransmitters but "grossly lower" — by 90 to 95 percent — levels of dopamine. Kish also studied the presence of dopamine transporters, from where the chemical is released. These, too, were depleted. Other scientists found similar depletions when they looked at the brains of meth-addicted monkeys, baboons, mice, and rats, leading to the conclusion that meth is neurotoxic, physically changing the brain, far more than cocaine or most other drugs do. It raised an essential question — my essential question: worrying, pondering my son's future, I want to know, even if Nic stops using, can his brain recover?

It was established that dopamine is dramatically reduced, but not whether there is a physical loss of the dopamine terminals. According to Dr. Kish, if the drug permanently destroys the terminals, there's not much chance of recovery. So in his brain samples, Kish looked at a marker called vesicular monoamine transporter, or V-MAT2. In Parkinson's patients, where there is a permanent loss of dopamine neurons, V-MAT2 levels are extremely low. If it is depleted in meth addicts' brains, it's likely that there is a loss of nerve terminals, and the brain damage is irreversible. However, when Kish tested for V-MAT2, he found normal levels. It was a surprising, and hopeful, finding. This and subsequent research indicate that the "fried" nerve endings probably do grow back, though it may take as long as two years. Two years.

This means that meth addicts can probably recover.

It's good news for a parent of an addict. Of course I want Nic to survive, but I cannot help but to want something more for him. I want him to be all right again. Though inconclusive and still debated, the researchers' findings suggest that he can be, if he stays off the drug. *If* he stays off the drug.

Karen and I eat dinner on Haight Street and then drag ourselves up the hill to what we have come to call the Count Ohlhoff house — Count Olaf is the villain in *A Series of Unfortunate Events*, the Lemony Snicket books we read to Jasper and Daisy. Passing the smokers out front, we go through the wrought-iron gate. After absorbing decades of cigarette smoke and addiction, the courtyard garden we walk through appears unable to sustain life.

We are here to meet with Nic for a family group session. The meetings are held in a dank room. Karen and I, along with other visiting parents or spouses or partners and our addicts, sit on worn couches and folding chairs. A grandmotherly, whiskey-voiced (though sober for twenty years) counselor leads us in conversation.

"Tell your parents what it means that they're here with you, Nic," she says at our first session.

"Whatever. It's fine."

These are stark, haunting, heart-wrenching gatherings. We get to know the other addicts and their families. One of the meth addicts is a nineteen-year-old girl with the face of an ingénue, her tousled hair in a pair of coffee-colored pigtails, and dejected eyes. She has lost custody of her baby — the child was born addicted to meth. She looks like a child herself, other than the track marks. Other patients include heroin addicts, potheads, and an ancient, blotchy *Days of Wine and Roses* alcoholic. We hear their stories. The alcoholic repeatedly left his children and their mother without a goodbye. He would come home and apologize. "After the first four or five times, the apologies meant almost nothing to them," he says. He came to rehab when they left him. One boy, slightly older than Nic, with colorless hair and eyes, is from New York City. He came to San Francisco to study architecture, but, he says, "methamphetamine changed my plans."

It's no surprise that in a San Francisco–based program, nearly half of the patients are gay men whose drug of choice was Tina, their term for methamphetamine. Speed is a disaster in many urban gay communities, "returning them to the 1970s, before AIDS," according to Steven Shoptaw, a psychologist in the department of family medicine at UCLA. Health experts estimate that up to 45 percent of gay men in San Francisco, New York, and LA have tried crystal. Thirty percent of those with new HIV infections are users. Gay men in California who use speed are twice as likely to be HIV-positive as those who don't use the drug. Both straight and gay men and women use meth for sex marathons. "Speed sex" can be long-lasting and intense. Indeed, in the early stages, the drug can make a user feel "energetic, outgoing, self-confident, and sexy," said Gantt

Galloway, a scientist in the Addiction Pharmacology Research Laboratory at the California Pacific Medical Center Research Institute. "But it's soon impossible to become aroused. By then a user is likely to have engaged in the type of sex that he wouldn't engage in without the drug—the type that spreads the virus."

An HIV-positive gay man in the program with Nic, an addict who had been strung out on meth for seven years, speaks in a quavering whisper. "I lost most of my teeth," he says, showing off a lonely pair of north-facing bicuspids. "I have holes in my lungs." With shaking hands, he lifts his T-shirt and juts out his sore-infested, sunken belly. "This shit don't heal. I cough blood. I cough pieces of my stomach. I hurt all the time."

At the third week's family group session, Nic, encouraged by his counselor, tells Karen and me that he won't be going to college. "I was going for you," he says. "I want to work. I want to be on my own for a while. I need to be independent."

When Karen and I leave Count Ohlhoff's, we are greeted by a sharp, biting wind. We pull our coats tighter and take a long walk down Fillmore Street and then over to the Civic Center. Karen is as shocked as I am about Nic's decision to shun college. To be honest, I am still only paying lip service to the idea that Nic is a drug addict. Rehab is necessary, I believe, but he will be fine. I don't look at Nic the way I look at the other addicts in the room. Nic is a smart kid who has gone way out of control. Ignoring the warning from our friend, I have felt that rehab will, in these four weeks, sober him up and scare him enough so that he will understand that he has been on the verge of destroying his life. But that's all. He will return to college, graduate, and have a—a normal life.

Given my quixotic fantasy, I resent the rehab counselors, whose point of view is clear. For them, rehab is all that matters. Everything else must be put aside.

By the end of our walk, I have come up with a new interpretation. Nic is just postponing college. That's all. It makes sense. I adapt to this new scenario. Nic is only eighteen. Many people put off college and do fine.

At the fourth week's family group session, Nic surprises us again. This time he tells us that he has realized that he needs more time in rehab and asks if he can move into the program's halfway house. Dr. Ling had said, "Time off the drug is the best predictor of more time off the drug." As scary as it is—I want this over, I want him cured—it is a sensible plan. Also, I admit, I am afraid of what will happen if he comes home.

And so we agree to let him move into the Ohlhoff halfway house. He does, and three days later, when I call to check on him, I learn that he has vanished.

12

At some point, parents may become inured to a child's self-destruction, but I do not. I do know the drill, though. I call the police and hospital emergency rooms. Nothing. I don't hear a word for a day, another day, and then another. Once more I explain it to Jasper and Daisy as well as I can. All they comprehend is that Nic is in trouble and their parents are wracked with worry. Recalling the incident with the sheriffs in Inverness, Jasper asks, "Is Nic in jail?"

"I called the jails. He's not there."

"Where does he sleep?"

"I don't know."

"Maybe he has a friend and he sleeps there."

"I hope so."

I keep trying to fathom what is happening—not only to Nic, but to our lives, which are preoccupied with him. I am always careful around the little kids, but I snap at Karen. Mostly she tolerates my bursts of anger and frustration, but sometimes she gets fed up with me and my preoccupation with Nic. It's not that she doesn't understand, but sometimes enough feels like enough, and this is interminable. I do not sleep much. She wakes up in the middle of the night and finds me in the living room staring into dim flames in the fireplace. I confide that I can't sleep because I can't block out images of Nic on the San Francisco streets. I imagine him hurt, in trouble. I imagine him dying.

"I know," she says. "I do, too." For the first time, we cry together.

With increasing desperation, I want and need to know that he is OK, and so on a cool, overcast morning, knowing that I am on a fool's errand, I drive across the Golden Gate Bridge with plans to scour San Francisco's Haight and the Mission District, the neighborhoods where I suspect that Nic might show up. After driving aimlessly through the Mission, I cross town, park on Ashbury, and set off walking down Haight Street. I duck into Amoeba, his preferred record store, and peek into cafés and bookstores.

In spite of gentrification, the Haight retains its 1960s-era funkiness, and the air is spicy with burning marijuana. Runaways—dyed hair, tattooed, tie-dyed, track marked, stoned—hang out in doorways. "The street kids still cling to the fantasy of the Haight Ashbury, but it's no longer about peace and love," Nic once observed, "it's about punk music, general laziness, and drugs." (It's also about "all those terrible hippie teenagers from Marin begging for spare change," Dave Eggers adds in *A Heartbreaking Work of Staggering Genius*.) I once heard a recovering addict describe her ex-boyfriend in a way that reminds me of these children: "He had black fingernails and drove a hearse. Everything about him cried out, 'Look at me, look at me,' and when you looked at him, he would snap, 'Who the fuck are you looking at?'" If you subscribe to the idea that addiction is a disease, it is startling to see how many of these children—paranoid, anxious, bruised, tremulous, withered, in some cases psychotic—are seriously ill, slowly dying. We'd never allow such a scene if these kids had any other disease. They would be in a hospital, not on the streets.

Ludicrously, I ask some of them if they know my son. They ignore me or glare. I step over or past them, looking into each one's face and wondering about them, wondering about their parents.

At Stanyan, I cross into Golden Gate Park, into a small forest, dodging rollerbladers and bikers on the pathways. Near the merry-go-round, I stop a police officer and explain that I am looking for my son, a meth addict.

"The tweakers are hard to miss," he tells me. He says that he knows where some may be hanging out and leads me along a path. "Try over there," he says, indicating a grassy knoll under a magnolia tree, where a dozen people are congregated.

I approach a girl who is sitting on a bench apart from the group. She is sylphic and wan, wrapped in a grimy French sailor's sweater. When I get nearer, I see the telltale marks of meth: the tense jaw and pulsing body. I introduce myself and she recoils.

"Are you a cop?"

I say no, but tell her that it was a cop who had pointed her out. I indicate the officer, who is walking away, and she seems to relax.

"He's cool," she says. "He only hassles you if you cause trouble or do drugs near the little kids playing in the playground." She points. Of course I know the playground. Nic used to play secret agent there.

After small talk, I tell her about Nic, and ask if she knows him. She asks me what he looks like. I answer, and she shakes her head. "That sounds like half the guys I know," she says. "I don't know him. You won't find him if he doesn't want to be found."

"Are you hungry? I don't have anything to do for a while. I thought I might get something to eat."

She nods, says, "Sure," and so we walk to McDonald's, where she devours a cheeseburger.

"I've been on the crystal diet," she says.

I want to know how she got here. She speaks in a quiet, halting voice, answering my questions.

"I was not a troublemaker," she says at one point. "I was a sweet kid."

She tells me that she played with dolls, was "the Twister queen," marched in the high school band, liked history, and was good in French. *"Comment allez-vous? Où est la bibliothèque, s'il vous plaît?"* She says that she read voraciously and names her favorite authors, counting them on her thin fingers. It is a list that could have been Nic's, at least when he was younger. Harper Lee, Tolkien, Dickens, E. B. White, Hemingway, Kafka, Lewis Carroll, Dostoyevsky. "Fyodor was my god, *The Brothers K* was my bible, but now I don't read shit." She looks up and says, "Ya know, I was a pompom girl. No shit. I never made that prom, though."

Her giggle is self-conscious, and she covers her mouth with a shaky hand, then pulls at her stringy hair. "No fairy godmother saved the day."

A boy gave her meth when she was fourteen. That was five years ago. She slurps her soda, and then, rocking back and forth in her seat, adds, "Meth . . . Even though I know how fucked up it is, if I had the chance to start all over I would do it again. I can't live without dope, don't want to. You can't imagine how good it gets when it's good, and I need that in my life."

She plucks a few pieces of ice from her cup of Coca-Cola and puts them on the table, flicking them with her fingers and watching them skitter across the plastic. She tells me that her father is a banker; her mother, a real-estate agent. They live in the home in which she grew up in Ohio. "It's white, roses, picket fence — the American experience," she says. Her parents hired a private detective to find her when she ran away from home the first time, catching a ride to San Francisco with a friend. The detective traced her to a homeless shelter and convinced her to return with him. Back home, her parents brought her to a hospital to detox from crystal. "It was hell. I wanted to die."

She stole a jar of Valium, and, the day she was discharged, overdosed on it. After she recovered, her parents checked her into

Hazelden, the well-known Midwestern drug-rehab facility, but she ran away from there, too. Her parents found her again and sent her to a different rehab center. "It's bullshit, a cult," she says of the programs. "All that God shit." She ran away again, scored crank from an old boyfriend, and hitchhiked back to San Francisco, riding most of the way with a meth-smoking truck driver. She settled in the Haight, where she began dealing and "slamming" — that is, shooting — crystal. She says that she lives in a garage with a space heater and no running water, sleeps on an old mattress.

She tells me that she uses crystal almost every day, smokes it and shoots it; stays up for seventy-two or more hours at a time; sleeps, when she does, for days; has "freaky" nightmares. She was in the emergency room three times, once each for pneumonia, some "stomach thing, I was coughing up blood," and for "freaking out." She makes enough money for coffee and cigarettes by panhandling. She stabbed a guy once "just in the leg," and pays for meth by dealing. "When I can't pay, I give a blow job or whatever." She says this and then seems embarrassed, somehow jarred by the memory of an ossified emotion. She turns her head to the side and looks down. In profile, with her unwashed hair hanging down, she looks half her age. "I am a bitch if I can't score," she says. "On meth I'm all right."

"What about your parents?"

"What about them?"

"Do you miss them?"

"Not much. Yeah. I guess."

"You should contact them."

"Why?"

"I'm sure they miss you, and worry. They could help you."

"They would tell me to go back into rehab."

"Maybe it's not a bad idea."

"Been there, done that."

"At least call them. Let them know you're alive."

She doesn't respond.

"Call them. I know they would want to know that you're alive."

I drive home. Without Nic. Wonder about the girl's parents. If they are anything like I imagine them to be— that is, anything like me — whatever they are doing at this moment they are doing it perfunctorily with only a portion of their consciousness. They are never free of worry about their daughter. They wonder what went wrong. They wonder if she is alive. They wonder if it is their fault.

I torment myself with the same unanswerable questions:

Did I spoil him?

Was I too lenient?

Did I give him too little attention?

Too much?

If only we never moved to the country.

If only I never used drugs.

If only his mother and I had stayed together.

If only and if only and if only . . .

Guilt and self-blame are typical responses of addicts' parents. In *Addict in the Family,* a remarkably useful book, Beverly Conyers wrote, "Most parents, when looking back on how they raised their children, have at least some regrets. They may wish that they had been more or less strict, that they had expected more or less of their children, that they had spent more time with them, or that they had not been so overprotective. They may reflect on difficult events, such as a divorce or death in the family, and see these as turning points in their child's mental health. Some may bear heavy burdens of shame over past difficulties, such as an infidelity that damaged the family and caused mistrust. Whatever the parental failings may be, it is almost inevitable that the addicts will recognize these vulnerable spots and take advantage of the parents . . .

"Addicts may have many complaints, including major and minor grievances from years past. Some of their accusations may, in fact, have truth in them. Families may well have caused pain for the addicts. They may well have failed the addicts in some significant way. (After all, what human relationship is perfect?) But addicts bring up these problems not to clear the air or with the hope of healing old wounds. They bring them up solely to induce guilt, a tool with which they manipulate others in pursuit of their continued addiction."

Nonetheless: if only and if only and if only.

Worry and guilt and regret may serve a function—as a turbocharger of conscience—but in excess they are useless and incapacitating. Yet I cannot silence them.

After days without a word from Nic, he calls from the house of a former girlfriend. He is talking fast and obviously lying. He says he has quit on his own and has been sober for five days. I tell him that he has two choices as far as I am concerned: another try at rehab or the streets. My tough talk belies my impulse to rush over and take him in my arms.

He maintains that rehab is unnecessary—he will stop on his own—but I tell him that it isn't negotiable. He indolently agrees to try again, finally concluding, "Whatever."

I drive to the girl's house and wait outside, idling the car on the cul-de-sac. Nic dully climbs in. I notice a black bruise on his cheek and a gash on his forehead. I ask what happened. He looks skyward and then closes his eyes. "It was no big deal," he says. "Some asshole beat me up and robbed me."

I yelp. "And it's *no big deal?*"

He looks weary and empty. He has no suitcase or backpack, nothing.

"What happened to your stuff?"

"Everything was stolen."

Who is he? The boy sitting near me in the car is not Nic nor does he know anything about the child I remember. As if corroborating my observation, he speaks at last. "What the fuck am I doing here? This is bullshit. I don't need rehab. It's bullshit. I'm leaving."

"Leaving?"

"Leaving."

"To where?"

"Fucking Paris."

"Ah, Paris."

"Getting out of this fucking country is what I need."

"What will you do in Paris?"

"Tom and David and I are going to play music in the Metro, set ourselves up with a little monkey, like the old organ grinders."

Over the next twenty-four hours, Nic's mood ranges from agitated to comatose and, in addition to the monkey, his plans include backpacking to Mexico, joining the Peace Corps, and farming in South America, but each time he ultimately comes around to a grim resignation that he will return to rehab. Then he again says that he doesn't need it, he is sober, fuck you, and then he says he needs drugs and cannot survive without them. "Life sucks, which is why I get high."

I am unsure if another four weeks of rehab makes sense, but I know it is worth trying. This time I manage to get him into St. Helena Hospital, improbably located in the Napa Valley wine country.

Many families drain every penny, mortgaging their homes and bankrupting their college funds and retirement accounts, trying successive drug-rehab programs as well as boot camps, wilderness camps, and every variety of therapist. His mother's insurance and mine pay most of the costs of these programs. Without this coverage, I'm not sure what we would do. For twenty-eight days, they cost nearly twenty thousand dollars.

The following morning, Nic, Karen, and I drive past endless yellow fields and green ones—mustard flower, geometric vineyards—on our way to the hospital.

Above the Napa Valley off the Silverado Trail, I turn the car onto Sanatorium Road, which leads to the hospital. Nic looks at the sign, shakes his head, and wryly remarks, "Great. Therapy camp. Here we go again."

I park the car and see Nic looking over his shoulder. He is thinking of making a run for it.

"Don't you dare."

"I'm scared, all right. Jesus!" he says. "This is going to be a nightmare."

"Compared to getting beaten up and almost killed?"

"Yeah."

We enter the main building and follow the signs to the substance-abuse program. We take an elevator to the second floor and from there walk down a corridor. Contrasting with Ohlhoff Recovery, this is a sterile hospital—gray carpeting, fluorescent light, endless hallways, nurses in white, orderlies in blue. We sit on a pair of upholstered chairs near a busy nurses' station, filling out forms. We don't talk.

Then a nurse with a Harpo Marx hairdo and large pink glasses comes for Nic. She explains that he will be interviewed and undergo a physical examination before he is admitted. To me, she says, "It will take about an hour. He'll meet you here."

Karen and I go downstairs to the hospital gift shop and from the meager selection buy him a few toiletries. When we return, Nic says that it is time for him to go to his room. We walk with him a little way down the corridor. He holds onto my arm. He feels almost weightless, as if he could lift from earth.

We all awkwardly hug. "Good luck," I say. "Take care of yourself."

"Thanks, Papa. Thanks, KB."

"I love you," Karen says.

"I love you, too."

He looks at me and says, "Everything." Tears flow.

The program at St. Helena is similar to the one at Count Ohlhoff's, though it includes more exercise, with yoga and swimming in the hospital's kidney-shaped pool, plus consultations with staff physicians and a psychiatrist. It emphasizes education, with lectures and films about the brain chemistry of addiction, and daily AA and NA meetings, plus an expanded two-day-a-week family program. At this point, I am not sanguine about rehab, but I allow myself a sliver of hope. As in the Springsteen song, "At the end of every hard-earned day people find some reason to believe." Mine is a mix of this hope and, once again, tenuous relief because I know where he is.

At home I sleep, though unsoundly. In my nightmares, Nic is on drugs. I rage at him. I plead with him. I weep for him. High, he does not care. High, he stares back blankly and coldly.

Other people visit the wine country for its cabernet and pinot noir, mud baths and good food. Karen and I make pilgrimages for family weekends at the hospital. Before our first St. Helena session, a counselor tells me that an addict's prognosis is far better when his or her family participates. "We worry most about ones without families," she says. "Nic is one of the lucky ones."

"You will find Nicolas greatly changed," she remarks as we walk down a white hallway. "But he's feeling pretty depressed. They all do when they're detoxing, and meth is the worst."

Family sessions at the hospital are structured differently than at Count Ohlhoff's. We first gather in a large room with lines of chairs facing a lectern and TV monitors. The hospital offers four education forums on alternating Sundays. Our first is on the disease model of addiction. This is an alien concept for me. What other diseases include, as a symptom, the willing participation of the victim? Each time Nic does speed, he makes a choice. (Doesn't he?) Smokers may bring on their lung cancer, but otherwise cancer patients are not responsible for their condition. Drug addicts are. (Aren't they?)

The lecturer explains that addiction is genetic, at least the predisposition to addiction. That is, Nic's genes are partly to blame, the potent mix of his ancestry: my dark-complexioned forebears, Russian Jews, mixed with his mother's fair Southern Methodists. Her father died of alcoholism, so we didn't have to look far in the family tree, though no one really knows exactly how the predisposition is passed down. Roughly 10 percent of people have it, the speaker says. If they do, drugs or alcohol "activates" the disease. "A switch is turned on," she says. Once it's activated it cannot be deactivated. Pandora's box cannot be closed.

A man interrupts. "You're letting people off the hook," he says. "No one forced my son to go to his drug dealer, to score, to cook up meth, to inject heroin, to rob us, to rob a liquor store and his grandparents."

"No," she answers. "No one did. He did it himself. But nonetheless he has an illness. It's a tricky illness. Yes, people do have choices about what to do about it. It's the same with an illness like diabetes. A diabetic can choose to monitor his insulin levels and take his medication; an addict can choose to treat his disease through recovery. In both cases, if they don't treat their illnesses, they worsen and the person can die."

"But," the same man interjects, "a diabetic does not steal, cheat, lie. A diabetic doesn't choose to shoot up heroin."

"There's evidence that people who become addicted, once

they begin using, have a type of compulsion that cannot be easily stopped or controlled," she says. "It's almost like breathing. It's not a matter of willpower. They cannot just stop on their own or they would. No one wants to be an addict. The drug takes a person over. The drug, not a person's rational mind, is in control. We teach addicts how to deal with their illness through ongoing recovery work. It's the only way. People who say they can control it don't understand the nature of the disease, because the disease is in control."

No, I think.

Nic is in control.

No, Nic is out of control.

After the presentation, there are questions and answers. Then we meet in another room. We sit in a circle of chairs. Another circle. We are becoming used to these surreal circular gatherings of parents and children and significant others of addicts. We take turns introducing ourselves, sharing abridged versions of our stories. They are all different—different drugs, different lies, different betrayals—but the same, dreadful and heartbreaking, all laced with intense worry and sadness and palpable desperation.

We are dismissed for lunch, to dine with our family member in the program. Nic wanders shakily down a hallway toward us. He is pallid, moving slowly, as if each step causes searing pain. He seems genuinely happy to see us. He gives us warm hugs, holding onto each of us for a long time. His cheek presses against mine.

We choose sandwiches wrapped in plastic and pour coffee into plastic mugs and carry them on trays to an empty bench outside on the balcony. After taking a bite of his sandwich and then pushing it away, Nic explains his lassitude. He has been given sedatives to aid in the come-down process. He says that the medication is distributed twice each day by "Nurse Ratched"—he impersonates Louise Fletcher in *One Flew Over the Cuckoo's Nest*. "If Mr.

McMurphy doesn't want to take his medication orally," he says, with a drawl accompanied by a menacing look, "I'm sure we can arrange that he can have it some other way."

He chortles, but it's a weak performance; he is too sedated to put much verve into it.

After lunch, he shows us his room, with twin single beds and nightstands and a small round table with two chairs. It looks comfortable, like a modest hotel room. Indicating the bed by one wall, he tells us about his roommate. "He's a great guy," Nic says. "He was a chef. A drunk. He's married with a baby. Look . . ."

He picks up a photograph in a bamboo frame on the bedside table. An angelic baby girl, around two years old, and her mother, a beauty with a churned-up sea of yellow curls and a light-filled smile. "She has told him this is his last chance," Nic says. "If he doesn't stay sober, she'll leave him."

On Nic's bedside table is the Alcoholics Anonymous *Big Book* and a stack of recovery literature. There is a small closet and a dresser into which he stashed the small pile of his folded clothes we brought along.

Next he guides us onto the balcony, which looks out over vineyards.

"I'm so sorry about everything," he blurts.

I look at Karen. We do not know what to say.

13

A nother weekend in wine country. The morning lecture is on the "addicted family" — that is, us.

"I probably don't have to tell you that this is a disease that affects families, too," the speaker, a program counselor, begins. "They don't sleep, they don't eat, they become ill. They blame themselves. They feel rage, overwhelming worry, shame. Many people keep their suffering to themselves. If your child had cancer, the support from your friends and family would flood in. Because of the stigma of addiction, people often keep it quiet. Their friends and family may try to be supportive, but they may also communicate a subtle or unsubtle judgment."

Apparently the family dynamics are predictable, illustrated in a mobile that hangs from a ceiling on one side of the lectern. Pointing to the mobile, she explains all of our roles with disturbing accuracy.

Hanging in the center is a paper-doll figure, which represents the addict. Smaller dolls float around the central figure. The figures dangling off to the side represent the kids and Karen, in the periphery, helpless, but inextricably tied to the moods and whims and drug-taking of the central figure. Another figure somewhat precariously hangs between them — me. I am an enabler, propping Nic up; making excuses for him; bending over backward to care for him; trying to protect Karen and Jasper and Daisy from him, and yet also trying to keep them all connected to one another.

"It's not your fault," says the speaker. "That's the first thing to understand. There are addicts who were abused and addicts who from all accounts had ideal childhoods. Yet still many family members blame themselves. Another thing they do is try to solve it. They hide liquor bottles and medication and search for drugs in their loved one's clothes and bedrooms and they drive the addict to AA or NA meetings. They try to control where the addict goes and what they do and who they hang out with. It's understandable, but it's futile. You cannot control an addict."

Later, she says, "An addict can take over the family — take all of a parent's attention, even at the expense of other children and of one's spouse. Family members' moods become dependent on how the addict is doing. People become obsessed. It's understandable, but it's harmful. They become controlling in ways that they never were before, because they are so afraid. People lose their identity because nothing matters except their addicted spouse or child or parent or whoever it is. There is no joy left in their life."

When we meet Nic for lunch, he has some color back in his face and some life back in his eyes. He is freer in his movements, no longer constricted by pain. Nonetheless, he hunches over and seems dejected.

We talk while sitting in chairs on the balcony of his room. "I don't think this is going to work for me any better than last time," he says. "All the talk about God . . ."

He is quiet.

"All the God talk. I can't get past it."

I respond, "They say 'higher power,' not God. There's a difference."

" 'Higher power' is another way of saying God. You have to believe and I don't. You can't get over this unless you believe."

Nic explains his conundrum. "I have no problem with the first step of the twelve steps," he says. "Well, sometimes I do, but I guess it's obvious that I am powerless over drugs and alcohol and my life has become unmanageable. But after that, it's bullshit."

He reads steps two and three from a bookmark.

" 'Two: Came to believe that a Power greater than ourselves could restore us to sanity. Three: Made a decision to turn our will and our lives over to the care of God as we understood Him.' "

I point out, "There's a lot of room in 'as we understood Him.' "

"I don't understand Him to be anything."

For some people, this — his atheism, a gift from his parents, at least me — is enough to explain Nic's problem. I don't believe that any single factor could have changed his fate, but who knows? If a belief in God or a religious upbringing precludes addiction, though, how does one explain all of the people with religious backgrounds and beliefs who have become addicted? The devout are not spared.

Without being solicitous or disingenuous, I try to offer a way that he can conceive of a higher power. Though I raised him without religion, his upbringing was not devoid of a set of moral values. I tried to instill the idea that morality is right for its own sake. The Dalai Lama, writing in the *New York Times,* recently explained this in a way that reflects my thinking: "key ethical principles we all share as human beings, such as compassion, tolerance, a sense of caring, consideration of others, and the responsible use of knowledge and power — principles that transcend the barriers between religious believers and non-believers, and followers of this religion or that religion." To me, those principles are a higher power, one accessible to each of us. My father once explained his concept of God: the "still small voice" inside us — our consciences. I don't call it God, but I too believe in our consciences. When we listen to that voice, we do the right thing. When we don't, we fail to. In my life I haven't paid close enough attention to it — I didn't know how — but I try to now. When I listen to it and act on it, I am more compassionate, less self-obsessed, and more loving. That, I tell Nic, is my higher power.

He is unimpressed. "Rationalizations," he says, "more bullshit. It's a big lie."

Counselors at Ohlhoff, people he has met at meetings, and now the staff at St. Helena have tried to convince him that one's higher power can be anything one imagines it to be — a source of guidance that comes from outside of oneself when it's dangerous to rely on the warped, drug-influenced guidance that comes from one's own brain, the addict brain. "For some, it takes a leap of faith," a counselor told Nic. "You have to trust that there is something bigger than us out there — something that can show us the path that will save our lives. The first step is honesty: my life is out of control. So what are your choices? Continue or submit to a higher power. You have to risk it — to be courageous enough to take a leap of faith and trust that there is something bigger than us that can help."

We once again eat on the deck outside the cafeteria, where Nic introduces us to two friends he has made here. We feel as if we already know them because by now we have been in group sessions with their wives. James is an amiable businessman, handsome with red hair and freckles and the reassuring manner of one of Jimmy Stewart's wholesome characters. He is a Vicodin addict. The drug was prescribed after back surgery. Before checking himself into St. Helena, he was swallowing as many as forty pills a day. Nic's other friend is his roommate, the chef, Stephen, who has apprenticed in some of the Bay Area's most renowned kitchens. According to Nic, the sandy-haired, athletic man with sloping blue eyes abused a variety of drugs, but his primary addiction is alcohol, which has nearly destroyed his marriage and has nearly killed him at least twice. In his early thirties, he has already undergone surgery on his liver and pancreas due to alcohol poisoning. It is shocking to hear his age. He looks fifty.

We sit at long tables with them and their wives, both of whom seem kind-hearted, loving, and exceedingly tired. Nic, James, and Stephen share the same sense of humor and something else: the type of intimacy and affection that normally builds over months or years but is hastened in rehab, where people's souls are exposed. Indeed, afterward, Nic tells us how much it means to have connected with James and Stephen. "Late at night, when everyone else is asleep, we sneak into the hospital kitchen," he says.

"Is that allowed?" asks Karen.

"No one cares," Nic says, speaking quietly. "The other night Stephen made an artichoke soufflé and leek soup. Last night we had chicken cordon bleu. I was sous chef."

We talk to Nic about the morning's and last week's lectures, and I ask if he agrees that addiction is a disease—and he has it. He shrugs. "I go back and forth."

"If a switch was thrown, when did it happen?" I ask. "At Berkeley?"

"God, no," he says. "Earlier. Much."

"How much earlier? When you got drunk in Lake Tahoe? When you first smoked pot?"

After a minute, he says, "Maybe Paris."

I nod and, remembering the ulcer, weakly ask, "What happened in Paris?"

He admits that his language classes at the university couldn't compete with the city's other draws, including an abundance of easily accessible liquor; French waiters thought nothing of serving wine to a sixteen-year-old. As a result, Nic spent much of his time there emulating his drunken heroes—but he forgot the writing and painting part. "One night," he says, "I was so drunk that I crawled into a boat tied to the shore of the Seine and passed out. I slept there, woke up the next day."

"You could have been murdered."

His eyes take me in. "I know," he says darkly. "When I flew home, I snuck some bottles of wine home in my suitcase, but they only lasted a few days. I was fucked. In Paris, I'd been going out to bars and clubs every night, drinking a fucking shitload, but when I got home, I was sixteen, a high school student, living with you guys." He looks down. "It was too bizarre. I couldn't get alcohol, so I started smoking pot every day. It wasn't the same, but it was easier to get."

"What about hard drugs?" I ask, not sure I want to hear the answer. "When did you start?"

"Remember when [he names the boys and his girlfriend] and I left after the barbecue the night I graduated from high school?" He is leaning on the table on his elbows. "There was ecstasy at the party we went to. I took some. I was flying. I felt so close to everyone, going through these long, meaningful goodbyes. After that I took whatever I could find — e, LSD, mushrooms, and then . . ." He looks up. "Then crystal. When I tried it, I felt — I felt better than ever before in my life."

Once again, we gather in the large conference room, patients and family members, for the afternoon group session. More chairs are brought out from a closet to accommodate fifty or so people; the circle stretches into a long, meandering oval, touching the corners of the walls. A counselor leads the session, which starts, as usual, with introductions around the room — a room full of resentment and worry and sadness and rage.

"I cannot think of anything other than my daughter. I cannot let go of it. I dream about it. What can I do? This has taken over my life. People tell me to let it go but how does one let go of their daughter?" The speaker cries and cries. Her daughter sits next to her, stone-faced.

When it is his turn, Nic says, "I'm Nic, and I'm an addict and alcoholic."

I have heard him say it before at other sessions here and in San Francisco and at a couple AA meetings I attended with him, and yet still it jars me. My son the addict and alcoholic. It fills me with a certain pride to hear him admit something that must be extremely difficult to admit. But does he really believe it? I don't. Not really.

Compared to those who gathered at the old Victorian in San Francisco, the crowd at St. Helena is better dressed, though an aged woman appears as if she could have been, hours ago, a derelict on the street. The group therapy begins with patients and their families sharing stories, sometimes commenting on one another's progress. The aged woman shocks me. In a gravelly voice, she explains, "I have a masters degree. I'm a teacher. A good one, I think." She stops and stares vacantly ahead for a moment. "I was a good one. Before speed."

Like me, the addicts' relatives all seem simultaneously hopeless and hopeful.

Sometimes the pain in the room is nearly unbearable. Without respite, we hear, see, and most of all feel with heart-tearing jabs the bleakness of the lives of people whose loved ones have become addicted to meth, though the "drug of choice" hardly matters. Meth, heroin, morphine, Klonopin, cocaine, crack, Valium, Vicodin, alcohol, and, for most, combinations of all of these. The people in the circle are different and yet we are all the same. We all have gaping wounds.

Nic's friend Stephen speaks. He describes his lifelong "dance" with alcohol—he was ten when he got drunk for the first time. His wife cries continuously.

"We love you so much," she says to Stephen when it is her turn, "but I have heard your remorse before. I have heard your promises. I can't live this way."

James's wife speaks about how he has plummeted from "the person I respected most in the entire world, my soul mate" to someone consumed with pills at the expense of everything else. "He went from being the kindest, gentlest—"

The counselor, in a quiet, even voice, interrupts. "Try addressing him directly," she says. "Talk to your husband."

Looking into James's eyes, trembling, she continues: "You went from being the kindest, gentlest man I had ever known in my life to a stranger, yelling at me, listless, depressed, unkind, and unable to share any kind of openness and intimacy. I keep asking myself . . ."

She begins to cry.

And then another and then another. They tell their stories, address their loved ones, apologize, rail at them, and weep. Our similarities are profound. To varying degrees, we have spent years accepting and rationalizing behavior in our loved ones that we would never tolerate in anyone else. We have protected them and hidden their addiction. We resented them and felt guilty for it. We have been furious and have felt guilty for it. We vowed not to take their cruelty or deceitfulness or selfishness or irresponsibility any longer and then we forgave them. We raged at them, often inwardly. We blamed ourselves. We worried—worried incessantly—that they would kill themselves.

Every addict's story has similar themes, too—remorse, out-of-control fury, directed most often at themselves—and a sense of helplessness. "Do you think I want to be this way?" a man screams into the face of his shaking wife. "Do you? Do you? I HATE MYSELF." Both of them cry and cry and cry.

"I'm so proud of him for being here," a woman says of her heroin-addicted husband. "But what happens next? I am terrified." An elderly woman whose sister, a lawyer, is addicted to meth, says, "I no longer give her money, but buy her food and drive her to the doctor and pay for her medications." She sadly adds, "She is incapable of making it across the apartment to the refrigerator." The therapist gently prods her. "She is capable of scoring drugs but she can't make it to the refrigerator?" Then another parent interrupts. "I felt the same way about my son until I realized that he couldn't get to school or work or a therapy appointment but he could get to pawn shops, get to his dealers, get whatever drug he wanted, get alcohol, break into houses, get needles—whatever was required. It's a fairly sophisticated process to cook a batch of methamphetamine, but I felt so sorry for him, thinking, He's depressed. He's fragile. He's incapable. Of course I should pay his bill if he winds up in the hospital. Of course I should pay his rent or he'll be on the streets. So for about a year I paid for a comfortable place for him to get high."

A handsome woman with auburn hair cut short, wearing a silk blouse, cardigan, and wool pants, says that she is a doctor. Deeply sad, she shakily admits that for more than a year she conducted surgeries while high on meth. She initially tried it at a party. "I felt better than I had ever felt before in my life," she says. "I felt as if I could do anything. I never ever wanted to lose that feeling."

She shakes her head. "And you know the rest of the story. I snorted so that I could work all night. I snorted when I wasn't working. I knew that I had a problem," she continues, "but I'm only here because a colleague threatened to report me if I didn't voluntarily deal with my addiction."

Another patient berates her. "You performed surgery while you were high! You *should* be reported. You could have killed someone."

The counselor interrupts and, without raising her voice, says, "Didn't you say that you have had a DUI and you fell asleep at the wheel? You could easily have killed someone, too."

Some stories are beyond my comprehension. A small, jittery woman who almost disappears inside her bulky sweater and sweat pants remembers her son's last birthday. "I was on crack," she recalls. "I left home, left my son, left him with my husband. For crack. He is three."

A woman with pale skin, limp blond hair, and misty golden eyes tells the group that a judge sent her husband to this program as an alternative to jail. Her husband, a GI with buzzed hair and a short-sleeved shirt buttoned up to the collar, sits rigidly on her right. He stares blankly ahead.

She says that high on meth, he attacked her, banged her head against the floor. She managed to dial 911 before she blacked out. Later, when it is his turn to speak, he thanks God that the court allowed him to try rehab instead of jail. "I still cannot believe that I attacked my wife, who I love more than my life," he says. "But now I understand my problem. I am graduating next week and I am looking forward to coming home and beginning a new life."

His wife will not meet his eyes. She looks horrorstruck.

There is a coffee break.

Sitting in the cafeteria, Nic, indicating the woman's husband with a flash of his eyes, tells Karen and me that the wife would be safer if he were locked up. "He is one scary motherfucker," Nic tells us.

The meeting resumes. More heartbreaking stories, more tears.

At the conclusion of each session, the counselor always asks if anyone has anything to say before the group adjourns. Family members often say how proud they are of their loved one and how much better they seem. Fellow patients sometimes cheer on the session's sharers. This day, at the conclusion of our session, in the room of fifty or more people crowded together in chairs around the snaking oval, Nic speaks up. He directs his words to the GI who had attacked his wife.

"I'm sorry, but I have to say something to you, Kevin, because as you said, you're supposed to get out of here next week." Nic stares across the room at him. "I have been in groups with you since I have been here, and whereas everyone else seems sincere and open, genuinely trying to learn about their addiction, there has been no indication that you get what this is about. The program requires humbleness and you are arrogant. It doesn't seem that you really understand and admit that you're powerless over your addiction. You constantly interrupt people. You talk a lot, but you don't listen."

Then Nic looks at the man's wife. Her wide-open eyes pour tears. She trembles like a terrified animal.

Nic speaks to her. "I'm saying this for you, because I'm worried that Kevin needs more time before he comes home. I don't want anything to happen to you."

No one, not even the counselor, says a word. The man looks as if he might lunge across the circle at Nic. Then he and the rest of us stare at his wife, who is gasping for breath between guttural sobs. Through her tears, she finally speaks up, steeling herself, sitting up taller, addressing Nic. "Thank you," she says. "I know. I don't trust him." She cries harder. A woman next to her puts her arm around her shoulder and she weeps more.

She turns toward her husband and speaks sharply, wildly, into his face: "If you ever touch me or the children again—"

She cannot finish her sentence. Her sobs erupt from her roars.

The man looks at his wife. The expression on his face is not one of remorse or love or sorrow. He appears wounded and embarrassed and enraged. He sits erect, his eyes darting around the room.

Finally the counselor speaks, ending the session. She thanks everyone who shared, and she adjourns us. Kevin's wife makes a startling beeline across the circle and, still sobbing, hugs Nic, thanking him.

Her husband, immobile in his chair, glares malevolently across the room.

As we leave, Karen whispers to Nic, "Watch your back."

14

In the program, patients keep journals, and Nic shares an entry with us: "How the hell did I get here? It doesn't seem that long ago that I was on the goddamn water-polo team. I was an editor of the school newspaper, acting in the spring play, obsessing about which girls I liked, talking Marx and Dostoyevsky with my classmates. The kids in my class are in college. This isn't so much sad as baffling. At the time it all seemed so positive and harmless."

It is Nic's third weekend at the hospital, and I am here for another family visit. After the group session in the morning, Nic, on a day pass, will visit the inn where we are staying.

Nic is open and emotional, even expressing his gratitude for the chance to go through this program. He seems sincere. Next he broaches a new subject. He wants to know if college is still an option. He knows that he has made enormous mistakes, but he will do anything if he can still go to Hampshire. He is excited about the school. Because he understands his drug problem, he promises to attend regular AA meetings and to work with a sponsor. He has been told that many colleges have substance-free dormitories and he will request one. He understands that relapse will mean that I will follow through on my threat and withdraw my support and he will be out of college and on his own.

In the car, as we drive to the inn to meet Karen, Jasper, and Daisy, Nic tells me what made him change his mind. Others in his group therapy sessions heard that his parents were willing to send him to college and they ganged up on him. The general consensus was summed up by a man whose drinking and drug addiction had estranged him from his parents and siblings. "Are you out of your fucking mind?" he howled at Nic. "You have *parents?* They love you? They are still willing to send you to college? Go to college. Don't be a fucking idiot. I would do anything for a chance to go to college."

I think over Nic's request. "Karen and I will talk about it," I say. "I'll talk to your mom. We'll have to make our agreement clear. I think it might work if you really want it and think you can pull it off." I still fantasize that everything can be fine. *Nic will stay sober. He understands his problem. Thank God he hasn't done more damage to his life — to his body and brain — to his options for the future. He can still go to college, get a degree, a good job, have a loving relationship . . . Everything will be all right.*

I drive to the inn, a rundown resort with grapevines, a cracked swimming pool, cracked tennis courts, and old horses wandering through the property. Nic is nervous when I drive through the gate. This will be his first visit with Jasper and Daisy since he entered Ohlhoff nearly three months ago.

Nic is elated at seeing Jasper and Daisy and, in spite of their initial reluctance — the last time they saw Nic he was coming down from his high and depressed, angrily leaving for Ohlhoff — they are happy to see him. He plays with them in the icy-cold water and they bat tennis balls back and forth. I sit at a picnic bench under a grape arbor and watch as Karen joins them and the foursome play croquet. As they knock the balls around, Nic asks the kids about school and their friends and he tells stories about a cat that lives on the hospital grounds. When it is time for me to take Nic back to the hospital, Jasper and Daisy seem perplexed. We continually do our best to explain what is going on with Nic, but in their eyes he seems fine. They don't know why he can't come home with us.

On our way back to St. Helena, Nic tells me about two other events of the week. The first is disheartening. Stephen left the program — simply and unceremoniously left one midafternoon, walking down the long road that leads from the hospital to Calistoga. Later the patients learned that he immediately relapsed at a bar. Nic was saddened but not completely surprised. "On the surface, he seemed committed to staying sober," he says. "He knew that he risked losing his wife and that gorgeous baby. But he never took it that seriously. He blamed his wife for their problems. Blamed his parents. Blamed everyone but himself. He never got it."

His other news is harder to believe. Whenever someone completes the twenty-eight-day program, a goodbye ceremony is held among the patients. The graduate asks another patient to "stand up" and speak for him or her, sending them off into the world. These ceremonies are designed to embolden the graduate and inspire newcomers.

The morning Kevin, the GI, was to graduate, he had approached Nic. "You are a brave fucker," he said. "I have to give you that." Then, shocking Nic, he asked him to stand up for him at his departing ceremony. "I respect you," the man said. "I have been watching you and know that of all of us, you're the one who is going to make it. You're young enough not to have fucked up your life too bad. You have a loving family. And you are so damn smart. I want to make it more than anything I have ever done. I'm going to prove that you're wrong. I'm going to make it."

Nic agreed. "So I stood up for him," he says. "I said that I hope and pray that he makes it — that he works his program. I said, 'I hope so for you and for your wife and children.' Later I watched them leave — he and his wife. They both gave me hugs. They were holding hands when they walked away."

*

I am nervous a week later when, following Nic's own graduation, I pick him up. The car windows are down, the air is warm. Nic speaks brightly about the future. His optimism comes through not only in his lucidity, but in the way he holds his body, confident and strong, and in his eyes, which are once again filled with light. He says that he is committed to staying away from drugs. I share his hopefulness, but I know that sobriety is far easier in a safe, structured environment of a rehab program, and so mine is a tentative hope. I need to believe that everything is going to be all right and at the same time I am unable to accept that it will be.

Things are easier at home, though there is occasional tension. I worry when Nic leaves the house for AA meetings. I worry when he seems distracted or down. I worry when, in August, it is time for him to head off to college, this time three thousand miles away.

Hampshire College is on a former apple orchard that retains the feeling of a farm. There are eight hundred acres of sweeping lawns and bucolic vistas. The college offers an impressive, stimulating liberal arts program and hundreds of majors and courses. If those aren't enough, Hampshire is part of a five-college consortium, which includes the University of Massachusetts, Amherst College, Smith, and Mount Holyoke. Nic can pick and choose from the courses offered at the other campuses. A shuttle bus connects them.

Karen and I fly east with Nic to help him settle in and get ready for freshman orientation. We eat at the Indian restaurant Nic and I discovered when we took the college tour more than a year ago.

"Turn right at the light," Nic yells. "Right, right, right!"

In the morning, we drive to campus. It is warm and sunny. Families are busy dropping their children off at their respective dormitories in vans, station wagons, and, in one case, a limousine loaded with suitcases, trunks, a stereo system, a drum set, and several computers.

Nic's room in the sober-living dormitory is small but

comfortable. After dropping off his suitcases, we follow posted signs to the center of campus for the welcoming barbecue. Karen and I survey the incoming freshmen for potential drug dealers.

At the end of the meal, various deans speak to the assembled families. Afterward, I seek out the dean of students and ask her about drugs on campus, explaining that my son has recently been through two rounds of rehab. She admits that marijuana is rampant, but correctly notes the obvious. "Drugs pervade every college campus in America, and every city, so a young adult must learn to live among them."

She directs me to the head of the college's health services, who writes down her name and telephone number and says that she will help Nic in any way that she can. She'll guide him to twelve-step meetings and introduce him to other students in recovery. "He's not the only one," she says. "There is a lot of support for people who want it."

"Hey, Dad," Nic says on the phone after Karen and I are back in California, "it's me, Nic."

He is calling from his dorm. As he speaks, I imagine him wearing a worn-out T-shirt, his pants sagging and dirty, a black belt with metal studs holding them onto his hips, Converse sneakers, and his long curling hair pushed back out of his eyes. He seems excited about his school. Hopeful this time, hopeful as before, I continue my academic fantasy after we hang up, see him on campus, walking to his classes with his backpack on. I can hear his voice speaking out in discussions about dialectical imperialism, Nietzsche, Kant, and Proust.

A month later, he sounds OK, but I detect his nervous breathing. Before he hangs up, I hear him sigh. I know that this is not easy. Nic is giving it the old college try.

Besides classes, he has regular sessions with a drug and alcohol counselor recommended by the school. As we had agreed, he attends AA meetings and finds a sponsor, a grad student at the University of Massachusetts who has a group of students over to his house every Sunday morning for muffins, coffee, and a meeting.

He reports in regularly and the weight on my chest begins to lift. As things get back to seminormal, he tells me more about his teachers. He speaks about new friends. He reports on the AA and NA meetings he attends throughout the week.

A month later, Nic suddenly stops returning my phone calls. I assume that he has relapsed. In spite of his protestations, and maybe (though I'm not sure) his good intentions, and in spite of the room in the substance-free dorm — which was not, Nic claimed with annoyance, substance free (he reported that the sounds of late Friday and Saturday nights included carousing, falling, stumbling, and throwing up) — Nic hadn't stood much of a chance.

It was a gamble sending him to college so soon after rehab, but everyone, including his counselors at St. Helena, cheered the plan, because he was so convincingly devoted to it.

I ask a friend, who is visiting Amherst, to check on him. He finds Nic holed up in his dorm room, obviously high.

I prepare to follow through on my threat and withdraw my support, but first I call to discuss it with the Hampshire health counselor. I imagine her at her desk, the ticking heater, snowdrifts outside the window.

I inform her of Nic's relapse, and when I do, she surprises me. She advises patience, saying that often "relapse is part of recovery."

It is a counterintuitive concept. It's like saying that a plane crash is training for a pilot. At Ohlhoff Recovery and at St. Helena, I heard that it can be more difficult for addicts to recover from subsequent relapses because of the progressive nature of the disease. However, it can and often does take time and mistakes for a person to understand the pernicious power of addiction and, moreover, to understand how easy it is to relapse. I may have heard it, but I have not digested the terrible nature of the illness, including its permanence. But I have also not fully comprehended that failure, even serial failure, may lead to success.

"While it's true that among heavy users, some will go through treatment once and remain clean indefinitely, most will cycle through repeatedly, just as some smokers need multiple tries to kick cigarettes or dieters try over and over to slim down," said Dr. Rawson. "Treatment catches up with you," UCLA's Douglas Anglin, codirector of the UCLA Drug Abuse Research Center, told Peggy Ornstein when she interviewed him for a *New York Times Magazine* article about rehab. "For heroin users with a five-year history of addiction, it may take ten or fifteen years to help them come out of it, but if you start when they're twenty-five, by the time they're forty they're pretty much rehabbed. If you don't, most of them burn out by forty."

This is not comforting. However, if treatment is conceived of as an ongoing process rather than as a cure, a different, more optimistic — and far more realistic — notion of success emerges. According to the National Treatment Improvement Evaluation Study, although addicts may relapse, a year after treatment their drug use decreases by 50 percent and their illegal activity drops as much as 80 percent. They are also less likely than before to engage in high-risk sexual behavior or to require emergency room care. Other studies have shown that they are less likely to be on welfare and their overall mental health improves.

Every relapse is potentially lethal, though. It is an unsatisfying — and terrifying — fact that, yes, an addict may, even after relapse, get and stay sober, if he doesn't die.

*

Prodded by my friend, Nic calls. He admits that he "fucked up," and promises that he will stop using.

"Nic . . ." I hear the tone in my voice, that solemn, castigating, disappointed father tone, and I feel him turn instantly defensive.

"Don't say it, I know," he says. "I had to go through it — to learn."

Waiting is difficult, particularly a coast away, but I know that it will be a significant step if he can pull himself out of a relapse without my dragging him into rehab.

Often relapse is part of recovery. I say it again and again, roll it around in my brain, and wait.

He keeps in close touch and comes home for winter break. It is an easy visit. He seems to be doing much, much better. He slipped, that's all. Often relapse is part of recovery. He bleaches his hair with Clorox, burning his scalp in the process, but he seems all right.

Nic returns to Hampshire for spring semester and, calling home one evening, tells me how excited he is about a writing class taught by a noted author and admired teacher. "It's virtually impossible for freshmen and sophomores to get into the class, but I'm going to try," he says. "I wrote a story — stayed up writing last night — and submitted it." The professor will post a list of accepted students on his office door on Friday.

Late Friday afternoon, Nic calls, elated that his name was on the typed-out list, though his was the only one with an asterisk corresponding to a note at the bottom of the page. The footnote read: "Come see me."

Nic immediately went to the teacher's office. He was nervous — "all butterflies" — when he sat down across from the teacher, who asked, without small talk, if Nic was an addict. He suspected it because of the subject of Nic's submission. He had written fictionalized accounts of some of the memorable characters he met at Ohlhoff Recovery and St. Helena Hospital.

Nic said yes, he was an addict in recovery.

"Here's the thing," the teacher said. "If you stay sober, I'll work with you and help make you a better writer. If you don't, you're out. It's up to you." On Monday Nic shows up, shakes the teacher's hand.

From his telephone accounts, it seems as if Nic is thoroughly engaged in this and other courses. He seems stable, attending regular twelve-step meetings and working with the sponsor. It sounds as if he is still thriving in his classes, and he is newly in love with a girl who drives him to meetings.

I visit Boston in late winter. Nic and Julia, his girlfriend, come in from Amherst to meet me for dinner. It's a snowy night when they arrive at my hotel in Cambridge, bundled up in heavy coats and scarves.

We walk through Harvard Square to find a sushi bar. They have their arms tightly wrapped around each other, the two of them intertwined, walking in step. The three of us have dinner and then we walk more. They talk with excitement about books — Hegel, Marx, Thomas Mann — politics and movies. Nic trounces us in the six degrees of Kevin Bacon game, though Julia nearly stumps him with, of all people, Hulk Hogan. It takes him five of the six degrees.

"OK," says Nic, warming to the challenge. "He was in *Rocky IV* with Sylvester Stallone, who was in *Cop Land* with Ray Liotta, who was in *Narc* with Jason Patric, who was in *Lost Boys* with Kiefer Sutherland." Nic has on a satisfied smile. "And Kiefer Sutherland was in *Flatliners* with Kevin Bacon."

I have traveled to Boston with a close friend of our family's, a subject of a book I am writing, who lives and works in Shanghai. The three of us meet him for coffee. Nic and Julia impress my friend, and before the couple heads back to Amherst, he asks if they're interested in spending the summer in China. He can help set them up with a job teaching English and they can do volunteer work, possibly at a preschool. He even has a place for them to stay. They greet the idea with enthusiasm and gratitude. Flying home, I feel elated. Nic is moving on with his life. He has put his drug problem behind him.

The school year winds down and the China trip is being planned. After working for six weeks in Shanghai, the pair will travel to Yunnan and Tibet. Beforehand, Nic will come home in late May, when he will work to make some money for the trip. Then Julia will arrive and together they will leave for China. Nic seems thrilled with all this and about coming home — most of all about seeing Jasper and Daisy. They are overjoyed, too. His homecoming is marked by some trepidation, but also promise, which is why it is so devastating when Nic confesses the truth: that he has been using the entire time he has been home, using throughout the entire semester.

He leaves, slamming the door behind him. I am stunned. No, I think. No, no, no. When, after school, Jasper and Daisy burst in and can't find their brother, they ask, "Where's Nic?"

"I don't know," I say. I cannot stop my tears.

With Nic gone, I sink into a wretched and sickeningly familiar malaise, alternating with a debilitating panic — every minute feeling his absence.

In the morning, the cross-sticks below the skylight cast striped bars along the countertops. I sit down on a window seat in the living room, reading and rereading a lead paragraph of an article, when Jasper, with scruffy bedhead, comes into the living room holding a satin box, in which he keeps his savings of eight dollars. He looks perplexed. "I think Nic took my money," he says.

I look at Jas, his strong growing body and uncomprehending eyes, and hold out my arms so he can climb onto my lap. How do you explain to an eight-year-old when his beloved big brother steals from him?

PART IV

IF ONLY

Drunkenness — that fierce rage for the slow,
sure poison, that oversteps every other
consideration; that casts aside wife, children,
friends, happiness, and station; and hurries its
victims madly on to degradation and death.

—CHARLES DICKENS,
Sketches by Boz

it's better now, death is closer,
I no longer have to look for it,
no longer have to challenge
it, taunt it, play with it.
it's right here with me
like a pet cat or a wall calendar

—CHARLES BUKOWSKI,
"thoughts on being 71"

15

O n a Wednesday night in late May, Karen and I hire a
babysitter. We are going out. Another date devoted to Nic's
addiction.

We reluctantly drive up to Novato, a rural town on the northern
edge of Marin, to an Al-Anon meeting. These nightly gatherings
are the last place I ever expected to find myself. Like AA meetings,
they fill church basements and libraries and community centers
throughout the country. I am not a joiner. When I can, I avoid
meetings at which attendees are implored to share their feelings.
And yet I am here.

I kept our family's problem a secret for a long time. It wasn't that
I was ashamed. I wanted to protect Nic — to preserve our friends'
and others' good impressions of him. But I have learned that the
AA adage is true: you're as sick as your secrets. I have learned how
much it helps to talk about my son's addiction and reflect on it and
hear and read others' stories. Most counselors in the sessions that
Karen and I attended recommended Al-Anon. Still, it has taken
us a while to go.

The meeting is held in a dingy room, with a dozen people sitting
in plastic chairs set in a circle. Another circle. They serve Folgers
coffee and powdered sugar doughnuts. Overhead, neon tubes flicker
and hiss, and a wobbly fan ticks in the corner. The meeting is called
to order. Clichés, some more annoying than others, spill forth. Al-
Anon, like AA, seems to depend on them. They say: "Let go and let

God." And those three Cs that help even if I cannot always believe them: "You didn't cause it, you can't control it, and you can't cure it." No matter what they say, part of me believes that it is my fault. It was easy for me to stop taking drugs, but Nic could not stop. Maybe I started him off by giving him, along with my hypocritical warnings about drugs, tacit permission to use them. Now I look back in horror on the time I smoked with him. Addicts want to blame someone, and many have plenty of people ready to take the blame. Whatever I did was done naively and stupidly and because of my immaturity, but it doesn't matter. I blame myself. People outside can vilify me. They can criticize me. They can blame me. Nic can. But nothing they can say or do is worse than what I do to myself every day. "You didn't cause it." I do not believe it.

My first impulse in the meeting is condescension. I look around with something bordering on loathing and think, What am I doing with these women in tinted hair and pantsuits and large-bellied men in button-up short-sleeved shirts and chinos? By the time I leave, however, I feel an affinity with everyone here — the parents and children and husbands and wives and lovers and brothers and sisters of the drug-addicted. My heart breaks for them.

I am one of them.

I have no intention of speaking, but then I do. "My son is gone," I say. "I don't know where he is." Tears. I can't get out another word. I am mortified by my public display, but I am also hugely relieved.

As the meeting winds down, they repeat the Serenity Prayer: "God grant me the serenity to accept the things I cannot change, courage to change the things I can, and the wisdom to know the difference."

Please please please grant me the serenity to accept the things I cannot change, courage to change the things I can, and the wisdom to know the difference.

I repeat it silently.

Then they chant, "Keep coming back."

I go back, this time to a swankier neighborhood. There is better coffee. From Peet's. There is, finally, an amusing story. A man in a peach windbreaker says that to keep his medications—the Zoloft, beta-blockers, high-blood-pressure pills, sleeping pills, Viagra—out of his son's hands, he consolidated them into a single hidden bottle. The others in the room nod appreciatively: we know about hiding medications (and liquor) from our relatives.

The man says that one day he had to rush out the door before a presentation and popped a beta-blocker from the bottle. At least, he had planned to take a beta-blocker. Instead, he swallowed a Viagra tablet. It kicked in just as he was about to stand up in front of a group to speak. There was no podium to hide behind.

The mirth evaporates when an extremely shy woman, who mentions her "practice," so maybe she is a doctor or a lawyer, reveals in a fractured voice that she tried to kill herself a few days ago. She has pale, almost green, skin, no makeup, bristly hair, and eyes haunted by sleeplessness and worry. She says that she drove to the Golden Gate Bridge and parked. She then walked from her car out onto the bridge. "The wind cut into me, tears streamed down my face, and I looked down at the water," she said. "I would have had to climb up over a fence and there was a netting on the other side. I would have had to manage to climb over it, too. I decided it would be easier to get a gun. My father has one. He keeps it locked in a drawer near his bed at my parents' home. I have a key. To the house and the drawer. A gun would be quicker. Not so cold."

She walked back along the bridge to where she left her car, but couldn't immediately find it. She thought she must have forgotten where she had parked. She looked around the lot, but her car was gone. She looked up at a posted sign. She had parked in a no-parking zone. The car had been towed.

"It was so sick, I started laughing," she says. "I laughed and cried at the same time. That's when it struck me that I can't take my life as long as I can still laugh."

Tears stream down her cheeks, and the rest of us cry along with her.

I am back in Novato for another meeting in the church. I recognize many of the people here now. We hug one another. Elsewhere, everyone asks how I'm doing. Here, they know.

A mother rocks lightly as she speaks. I stare at the white tiled floor, sitting hunched in the gray metal chair with my hands folded on my lap. The woman, in a plain business suit, sips coffee from a paper cup. Her long hair is plaited, and she wears a touch of peach rouge and black eyeliner. In a shaky voice, she tells us that her daughter is in jail for up to two years after a drug bust. The woman contracts, gets smaller in her chair. She bursts into tears.

Everywhere I go now there are tears.

Tears everywhere.

She says: "I'm happy. I know where she is. I know she's alive. Last year we were so excited that she was enrolled at Harvard. Now I'm relieved that she's in jail."

A white-haired mother jumps in to say that she knows how the other woman feels. "Each day I thank God that my daughter is in jail," she says. "I express my gratitude to God. She was sentenced six months ago for using and dealing drugs and for prostitution." She catches her breath and says to herself as much as to the group, "Where she is safer."

I think: So this is where we get. Not all of us, of course. But some of us come to a place where the good news is that our children are in jail.

*

I can't control it, and I can't cure it, and yet I continue to wrack my brain for something I haven't thought of. "One moment a spark of hope gleams, the next a sea of despair rages; and always the pain, the pain, always the anguish, the same thing on and on," wrote Tolstoy.

I don't hear from Nic and each hour and each day and each week is quiet torture like a physical pain. Much of the time I feel as if I am on fire. It may be true that suffering builds character, but it also damages people. The people in the Al-Anon meetings are damaged, some of them visibly but all of them psychically. At the same time, they also are some of the most open and alive and giving people I have ever met.

As they counsel in Al-Anon, I try to "detach" — to let go and let God. How does any parent let go? I can't. I don't know how.

How could I have failed to know that Nic was using throughout these past months, even when he was in our home? I have been so traumatized by his addiction that surrealism and reality have become one and the same. I can't distinguish the normal from the outrageous anymore. I am so good at rationalizing and denying that I cannot tell where one ends and the other begins. Or maybe it's only that, with practice, addicts become flawlessly gifted liars, and this coincides with parents' increasing susceptibility to their lies. I believed Nic because I wanted to believe him — I was desperate to believe him.

What happened to my son? Where did I go wrong? According to Al-Anon, it is not my fault. But I feel solely responsible. I repeat the litany: if only I had set stricter limits; if only I had been more consistent; if only I had protected him more from my adult life; if only I had not used drugs; if only his mother and I had stayed together; if only she and I had lived in the same city after the divorce.

I know that the divorce and custody arrangement were the most difficult aspects of his childhood. Children of divorce use drugs and alcohol before the age of fourteen more often than the children of intact families. In one study, 85 percent of children of divorce were heavy drug users in high school compared to 24 percent of those from intact families. Girls whose parents have divorced have earlier sexual experiences, and kids of both sexes suffer a higher rate of depression. Since more than half of first marriages and 65 percent of second marriages end in divorce, few of us want to face that divorce is often a disaster for children that may lead to drugs and other serious problems. But maybe it's ludicrous to speculate, since many kids who go through divorces—some far more contentious than mine—don't resort to drugs. And many drug addicts I meet are from intact families. There's no way to know definitively. Were we crazier than most families? Not by a long shot. Maybe.

What else can I blame? Sometimes I think privileged kids are prime candidates for drug addiction for many obvious reasons, but what about the legions of addicts who grew up in dire poverty? It would be easy to blame their poverty, if it were not the case that we encountered children from every socioeconomic class in rehabs and AA meetings. I would blame private schools if public school kids had fewer drug problems. Instead, the research confirms it. Addiction is an equal-opportunity affliction—affecting people without regard to their economic circumstance, their education, their race, their geography, their IQ, or any other factor. Probably a confluence of factors—a potent but unknowable combination of nature and nurture—may or may not lead to addiction.

Sometimes I know that nothing and no one is to blame. Then I slip and feel utterly responsible. Then sometimes I know that the only thing that is knowable is that Nic has a terrible disease.

I still have a difficult time accepting it. I replay the arguments on both sides. People with cancer or emphysema or heart disease don't lie and steal. Someone dying of those diseases would do anything in their power to live. But here's the rub of addiction. By its nature, people afflicted are unable to do what, from the outside, appears to be a simple solution—don't drink. Don't use drugs. In exchange for that one small sacrifice, you will be given a gift that other terminally ill people would give anything for: life.

But, says Dr. Rawson, "A symptom of this disease is using. A symptom is being out of control. A symptom is the need to feed the craving." It is a force so powerful that one addict in a meeting compared it to the "need of a starving baby to suckle his mother—using was no more and no less of a choice than that."

There's a practical reason for people to understand that addiction is a disease—insurance companies cover diseases and pay for treatment. It's good they do, because if you wait until the disease progresses, and it will, you end up paying for replaced livers and hearts and kidneys, never mind the mental illnesses of addicts who descend into psychosis and dementia, and never mind the costs of destroyed families who cannot work, and never mind the costs of addiction-related crime.

Some people remain unconvinced. For them, addiction is a moral failing. Users want to get high, pure and simple. No one forces them to. "I'm not disputing the fact that certain areas of the brain light up when an addict thinks about or uses cocaine," said Sally Satel, staff psychiatrist at the Oasis Drug Treatment Clinic in Washington and a fellow at the American Enterprise Institute. "But it conveys the message that addiction is as biological a condition as multiple sclerosis. True brain diseases have no volitional component."

But I remind myself: Nic is not Nic when he is using. Throughout this ordeal I strive to understand this force that has shanghaied my son's brain, and I sometimes wonder if his recidivism is a moral failing or a character flaw. I sometimes also blame the treatment programs. And then I blame myself. I go back and forth. But I always come back to this:

If Nic were not ill he would not lie.

If Nic were not ill he would not steal.

If Nic were not ill he would not terrorize his family.

He would not forsake his friends, his mother, Karen, Jasper, and Daisy, and he would not forsake me. He would not. He has a disease, but addiction is the most baffling of all diseases, unique in the blame, shame, and humiliation that accompany it.

It is not Nic's fault that he has a disease, but it is his fault that he relapses, since he is the only one who can do the work necessary to prevent relapse. Whether or not it's his fault, he must be held accountable. While this ongoing, whirring noise replays in my mind, I understand when, at St. Helena, Nic admitted that he sometimes wished that he had any other illness, because no one would blame him. And yet cancer patients, for example, would be justifiably disgusted by this. All an addict or alcoholic has to do is stop drinking, stop using! There's no similar option for cancer.

Parents of addicts have the same problem as their children: we must come to terms with the irrationality of this disease. No one who has not confronted it can completely understand the paradoxes. Since most people cannot fathom it, there's no true understanding, just pity that may come with thinly veiled condescension. Outside Al-Anon meetings or apart from the parents who heard what we were going through and called to commiserate, I often felt separate, with a nearly impossible task of stopping my mind from its attempt to understand. Van Morrison sings: "It ain't why, why, why. It ain't why, why, why. It just is."

It just is.

Still, believing that addiction is a disease helps. Dr. Nora Volkow, the director of the National Institute on Drug Abuse, has said: "I've studied alcohol, cocaine, methamphetamine, heroin, marijuana and more recently obesity. There's a pattern in compulsion. I've never come across a single person that was addicted that wanted to be addicted. Something has happened in their brains that has led to that process."

Nic's grandfather once came to visit us — years ago when Vicki and I lived for a year in Los Angeles. On the way to our apartment from the airport, he asked us to stop at a store so he could buy cigarettes. He tried to sneak it, but we saw that he had a bottle of bourbon in the paper sack. By the end of dinner, the bottle was drained. Within two years, he was dead. He had been a kind, loving, and hard-working family man, a farmer, whose life had tragically deteriorated. But because it was alcohol, rather than speed or heroin, his debilitation took decades. He was in his sixties when he died. "Alcohol does the same damage over a much longer term," someone said in a meeting. "Drugs get it over quicker. That's the only difference."

Other than the potency and toxicity of their drugs of choice, ultimately the differences between using addicts and alcoholics become moot; they end up in the same place, similarly debilitated, similarly alone — similarly dead.

I am reading *Brideshead Revisited*, and I'm struck that more than sixty years ago Waugh wrote, "With Sebastian it is different." Julia is speaking about her brother. "He will become a drunkard if someone does not come to stop him . . .It is in the blood . . .I see it in the *way* he drinks."

Brideshead: "You can't stop people if they want to get drunk. My mother couldn't stop my father."

Substitute a few words and they are discussing my son: "With Nic it is different. He will become an addict if someone does not come to stop him . . .It is in the blood . . .I see it in the way he uses."

"You can't stop people if they want to get high."

After you spend some time in recovery programs, you never look the same at a drunk *or* a stoner, whether at a party or in books or movies. Hunter Thompson's accounts of his gluttonous drugging and drinking are no longer funny to me. ("Jesus, that scene straightened me out! I must have some drugs. What have you done with the mescaline?") They are pathetic. There is nothing amusing about Nick Charles quaffing martinis—swallowing them at breakfast; at lunch; at dinner; between, before, and after every meal—in the Thin Man movies. ("Come on, dear, let's get something to eat," Nick says. "I'm thirsty.") In one of these films, Nora jokes that her husband is a dipsomaniac. He is. Many people were charmed by the 2005 movie *Sideways*, about a wine enthusiast, but I was repulsed. To me, it was the story of a wretched alcoholic.

There are functioning alcoholics like there are functioning addicts, at least functioning until they don't. Maybe the only difference between them and winos and drugged-out bums on the street is some money—enough for rent, utilities, a meal, and the next drink.

Some people maintain that designating addiction as a brain disease rather than a behavioral disorder gives addicts, whether they are using alcohol, crack, heroin, meth, or prescription drugs, an excuse to relapse. Alan I. Leshner, former director of NIDA who is now the chief executive officer of the American Association for the Advancement of Science, agrees that addicts should not be let off the hook. "The danger in calling addiction a brain disease is people think that makes you a hapless victim," wrote Dr. Leshner in *Issues in Science and Technology* in 2001. "But it doesn't. For one thing, since it begins with a voluntary behavior, you do, in effect, give it to yourself."

Dr. Volkow disagrees. "If we say a person has heart disease, are we eliminating their responsibility? No. We're having them exercise. We want them to eat less, stop smoking. The fact that they have a disease recognizes that there are changes, in this case, in the brain. Just like any other disease, you have to participate in your own treatment and recovery. What about people with high cholesterol who keep eating French fries? Do we say a disease is not biological because it's influenced by behavior? No one starts out hoping to become an addict; they just like drugs. No one starts out hoping for a heart attack; they just like fried chicken. How much energy and anger do we want to waste on the fact that people gave it to themselves? It can be a brain disease and you can have given it to yourself and you personally have to do something about treating it."

I try not to blame Nic.

I don't.

Sometimes I do.

16

On this sunny June morning, though he promised Jasper and Daisy, Nic is not in the audience at their step-up ceremony.

The head of their school, in a camel-colored sports jacket and bright necktie, has a warm smile, eyes that betray his boundless affection for his charges, and a voice that soothes. He beams along with the children and their parents. Standing behind a microphone, he conducts the ceremony, calling them grade by grade. At his instruction, they stand and then move en masse from the step they're sitting on to the next higher row. Jasper, in a collared white shirt, his brown hair combed down on his forehead, radiates up there among his friends. He is now a third grader.

The headmaster says:

"Will this year's first graders please stand."

They do. And then he says:

"Will next year's second graders please step up."

Now it's Daisy's grade's turn.

"Will this year's kindergarten class please stand."

Daisy, in a soft blue dress with smocking — the dress was Nancy's when she was a little girl — rises along with her classmates.

"Will next year's first-grade class please step up."

There is thunderous applause and foot stomping. This is the school's tradition. Daisy and the other kindergarteners, when they step up to first grade, are greeted by a deafening roar. It's a poignant moment when the bottom tier is empty except for the kindergarten teachers, who are alone, anticipating a fresh group of five-year-olds who will arrive in the fall.

Inside me there is a searing void. The contradiction between the innocence of the children up there and my absent son is almost too much to contain inside one brain at one time.

After the step-up ceremony come speeches and the commencement of the eighth graders, who will begin high school in the fall. I am not the only parent with tears, but I cannot help thinking that mine are unique. I watch Jasper and Daisy dressed up — Jasper in the white oxford with its itchy collar, Daisy in her grandmother's dress, white socks, and Mary Janes — standing with their classmates, immaculate, nervous, and excited, and I remember Nic shining, too, standing tall, his life ahead of him. Where can he be?

Outside, the sky is streaked with smears of blue, but the sign that the storm has passed — and that summer is coming — does not lift my mood. I am in the kitchen boiling water for tea. The phone rings. My anxious reaction is recognizable. Who else would call this early in the morning? It must be Nic. And yet as I reach for the telephone, I tell myself, "No, it's not Nic," so as to ward off the bitter disappointment when it isn't.

It isn't.

"It's Sylvia Robertson," a woman says, her voice chirpy. "I'm Jonathan's mother. I'm the team mom for the Angry Tuna."

Jasper's swim team mom asks if we can work at the snackbar at next weekend's meet.

"Of course. We'd be happy to."

I begin to hang up.

"Go Angry Tuna," she says gaily.

"Go Angry Tuna."

The kitchen is still.

Along with china and teacups and glassware, a photograph dominates the open shelves over the sink. In the snapshot, we are on a boat on a lake somewhere. My father, wearing sunglasses and a fisherman's hat, waves and smiles. Daisy, on Karen's lap, is a baby. Her face is hidden underneath a wide-brimmed sun hat. The boys are in the foreground, smiling at the camera. Jasper, who just got a haircut so that his brown bangs rim his eager face, and Nic, with a short buzz and gleaming braces. My boys. The picture has a stamp on the back, 10 12 '96, which puts Nic at fourteen.

Where is he?

Meanwhile, over the hill, at Karen's parents' canyonside home, Don has just emerged from his lair and he settles into his regular sunny corner of the living room. Wearing old topsiders and a threadbare T-shirt and shorts, he sits in a rattan chair reading about Admiral Lord Nelson. Nancy is busy down the winding pathway in her garden when it dawns on her that the wash is probably done. Her pruning shears tucked into a leather holster on a belt, she trudges up to the house.

Removing her gardening gloves, Nancy enters through the lower door into the downstairs and goes into the packed basement with its distinctive smell of mold and laundry soap. Past the washing machine and the clothes dryer, there is a sewing room and a small bedroom, her son's when he was a teenager. There are bows mounted on the wall that were gifts from friends—members of the Blackfoot Indian tribe—to her parents. The room is now a spare where the grandchildren sleep when they spend the night.

Before she can transfer the load of clean sheets and pillowcases to the dryer, she has to unload the tumble of clean clothes. She piles them, for later folding, on the bed.

And gasps. There's a body under a pile of woolen blankets. Gathering herself, she looks closer, sees that it's Nic, a vibrating skeleton, sleeping, undisturbed by her cry.

"Nic," she exclaims. "What are . . ."

Haunted, with black eyes, fully dressed in jeans and a long-sleeve shirt, Nic looks at her. He sits up.

"What? Nan . . ."

Both of them are stunned.

"What are you doing?"

"Nancy," he begins. "I."

"Are you all right?"

He gets up, grabs his bag, stammers, apologizes.

"Nic, no," Nancy says. "It's all right. It's just that you scared me to death."

"I'm . . . I'm sorry."

"Nic, are you on drugs?"

He says nothing.

"You can stay anytime you want. It's all right. Just tell me. Don't sneak. You almost gave me a heart attack."

He leaves the room and heads up the stairs.

She follows him.

"Have you eaten? Can I make you something?"

"No, thanks. Maybe a banana. If it's all right."

"Nic . . . What can I do to help?"

There are tears in her eyes. She blinks. "Just tell me what I can do."

Nic mumbles something incoherent, an apology, and takes a banana from the basket in the kitchen. He says thank you and mutters I'm sorry and then walks briskly out the front door and up the driveway.

"Nic!"

She hurries after him, calls to him, but he doesn't stop.

By the time Nancy reaches the street, he's gone.

Nancy calls to tell me what happened. By now Don is hovering nearby, listening to the news. Nancy has every right to be furious, but she apologizes to *me*. "I'm sorry," she says. "I didn't know what to do."

I assure her that there was nothing to do.

"I'm sorry he scared you," I say. "I'm sorry you had to see him like that."

Nancy isn't listening. "I tried to get him to stay," she says. "He looked . . ." She stops herself and becomes choked up. "It makes me so damn mad!"

On a crisp afternoon, a few days after the step-up ceremony, I'm at a park, where Daisy's grade is having an end-of-the-school-year party. A friend—a teacher and Daisy's friend's father—is leading the children in a game of his invention inspired by J. K. Rowling. His version of quidditch involves four balls of varying sizes substituting for the bludgers and quaffles and a Frisbee for the golden snitch.

I am present, but I am absent. Parents can only be as happy as their unhappiest child, according to an old saw. I'm afraid it's true.

Out of breath, Daisy runs up to me. "We need you on our team," she says. "Come on." She grabs my hand and pulls me into the game.

There is no news for another week and then Nic calls his godfather, who invites him to come over to his home near Twin Peaks. Aghast at Nic's appearance—"he looks like he could blow away in a strong wind"—he cooks him a pot roast, which Nic devours. He begs Nic to get help.

"I'll be fine, I've stopped using," Nic lies. "I just need to be on my own for a while."

After Nic leaves, my friend calls. He tells me about the visit and then grows quiet. "At least I got him to eat something," he says.

There's no news for a fortnight, nothing but a perpetual state of anxiety.

Again I check jails to see if he has been arrested. Again I call hospital emergency rooms. Then Karen's brother sees him, or thinks he sees him, on Haight Street, huddling on a street corner, shifty, jittery, and suspicious-looking.

I am beside myself—uncomprehending, terrified. Nothing in my life has prepared me for the incapacitating worry when I don't know where he is. I imagine Nic on the streets of San Francisco, like a wild animal, wounded and desperate. Like some off-the-deep-end anesthesiologist presiding over his own brain surgery, Nic trying to manage the flow of drugs in order to achieve a high, which rapidly and necessarily becomes less about euphoria and more about avoiding the hell of withdrawal.

In the drawer of the old desk in his room, I find a scribbled journal entry in a marbled composition notebook that lists a typical day's menu.

1½ grams speed
an eighth ounce of mushrooms
2 klonopin
3 codeine
2 valium
2 hits of e

I try to write, but I'm catatonic. Karen comes into the office and sees me sitting here, staring, and she sighs. She is holding a small slip of paper.

"Look," she says, handing me a canceled check. It is made out to Nic. The shaky signature is an obvious forgery.

I say, "He wouldn't . . ." but even as I say it, I know I'm wrong. Karen dearly loves Nic, and she is stunned and wounded and fuming.

"Poor Nic," I say. "He wouldn't do this if he was in his right mind."

"Poor Nic?"

She angrily turns to leave the room. I call after her, "But this is not Nic."

She looks at me and shakes her head. She doesn't want to hear it. I can't make excuses for him much longer.

I spend several more nights in anguish and dread.

Then, one night, the kids asleep, Karen having read to them from the *Arabian Nights*, she has the newspaper in bed and I am writing in my office when I hear something.

The front door?

With a racing heart, I go to investigate and collide with Nic in the hallway.

He grunts hardly a "hey," then rushes past me, aiming for his bedroom, though he stops briefly when I demand, "Nic? Where have you been?"

He acts put out, snarling, "What's your problem?"

"I asked you a question: Where have you been?"

He responds with all the incredulous indignation he can muster, then peers over his shoulder at me, mumbles, "Nowhere," and continues into his room.

"Nic!" I follow him, entering the smoky red cavern, where Nic is opening and slamming dresser drawers. His eyes scan the bookshelves in the closet. He has on a T-shirt, red, faded, and ripped-up jeans. His red Purcells are untied. No socks. His movements are frantic. He's obviously searching for something—I assume money, drugs.

"What are you doing?"

He glares at me.

"Don't worry," he says. "I've been sober for five days."

I grab his bag, which he has set on the bed, unzip it, and rummage through the pockets of his jeans, unrolling his socks, shaking out blankets, and unscrewing a flashlight. (It is filled with batteries.) While I do this, Nic leans on the doorjamb, blankly watching, his arms folded across his chest. Finally, with a barely perceptible acrid smirk, he says, "You can stop. OK." He gathers up a pile of clothes, stuffs them back into the canvas bag. "I'm leaving."

I ask him to sit down and talk.

"If it's about rehab, there's nothing to say."

"Nic—"

"Nothing to say."

"You have to try again. Nic. Look at me."

He doesn't.

"You're throwing everything away."

"It's mine to throw away."

"Don't throw it away."

"There's nothing to throw away."

"Nic!"

He pushes past me and without looking up says, "I'm sorry." He rushes down the hall.

When he passes Karen, he says, "Hey, Mama," and she stares at him, uncomprehending.

Karen stands with me, still holding the newspaper. We're both looking out the window as he disappears down the deserted street.

Short of tackling him, what can I do?

Though I want to hold onto him and though I dread the haunting vacancy and debilitating worry when he's gone, I don't do a thing.

I am awake at four AM along with other parents of drug-addicted children, children who are—we don't know where.

It is another interminable big-moon night. Suddenly I think, It's Nic's birthday. Today my son turns twenty.

I fight off stabbing urges to second-guess myself. There must have been something I could have tried. I should never have let him leave. I should try to find him.

By now we have been told a hundred times that drug addiction is a progressive disease. I still don't quite get it until the next morning when the phone rings. It's Julia, Nic's girlfriend whom I met last winter in Boston. Now, with Nic gone, their China plans by the wayside, she is calling from her family's home in Virginia, her voice breaking up. She has been crying. "Nic stole hypodermic needles from my mom's house when we visited here last month," she tells me.

"Needles?"

"They were for her cancer medication. He also stole morphine." She sobs.

"I don't know what to say."

"I don't either."

After a pause, she says: "I can tell you one thing. Don't help him. Don't give him any money. He'll try everything to get you to help him. Then his mom. If you help him, it will only kill him faster. It's one of the few lessons we learned from my sister's addiction."

"I had no idea. I'm an idiot. I thought he was doing better. I thought he got through the year at school sober."

"You wanted to believe him just like me."

She is about to hang up the phone.

"From our family's experience with my sister, the best advice I can give you is to take care of yourself."

"You take care of yourself, too."

Even after everything we have been through, I am stunned. Nic is injecting drugs — shooting them into his arms, arms that not that long ago threw baseballs and built Lego castles, arms that wrapped around my neck when I carried his sleepy body in from the car at night.

We have promised to take the little kids to the Monterey Bay Aquarium the next day. The disparity between our two worlds continues to stun and overwhelm. Sometimes it seems as if it is impossible that both worlds coexist.

There is no point in sitting at home waiting for the telephone that does not ring.

We strive to carry on with our lives.

We drive to Monterey, stopping on the way in Santa Cruz, where we hike down a cliff, following a series of jagged footholds, to a cave just above the foaming and churning water. The lower rocks are slippery with seawater. The kids swim nearby at Cowles Beach. My children — all three of them — seem as comfortable in the ocean as on land. They are like dolphins.

At the aquarium, we watch a film of a languid bay and hundreds of feeding cormorants. The birds seem to be playing and splashing in the surf. Then from nowhere the water erupts with evil gray, a mouthful of teeth, a great white shark, and a cormorant is swallowed whole. The shark's tail whips around like a snapping rope and disappears.

I feel like the cormorant. A shark has appeared from the depths. I stare at it and helplessly see the approach — and with it the precariousness of Nic's life — see how close he is to dying. As physically sick as the image makes me, I cannot fend it off.

After the aquarium, we drive south on Highway 1 to Carmel, where the kids play on the beach and then, in a park, climb on an ancient madrone with bark peeling off like an old sunburn. Watching them, I relax for a moment, but anxiety has taken up permanent residence in my body.

We are driving home. We do not talk about Nic. It's not that we're not thinking about him. His addiction and its twin, the specter of his death, permeate the air we breathe. Karen and I try to gird ourselves in case the next telephone call brings with it the worst possible news.

Nic is still gone. Life does not stop.

Karen is working late in her studio, and I take Jasper and Daisy into town to dinner at the Pine Cone Diner. Afterward, we walk over to the grocery store. The Palace Market is nearly deserted. I wheel a cart up and down the aisles. Jasper and Daisy keep tossing Cocoa Puffs and Oreos into the cart and I keep removing them until finally I snap at them to stop. I send them off in different directions for things we actually need, milk, butter, bread. I'm in an aisle vaguely scanning a wall of dried pasta when the Muzak system plays Eric Clapton's song about the death of his son.

"Would you know my name if I saw you in heaven?"

It's more than I can tolerate. I break down crying in the middle of the market. Jasper and Daisy, their arms loaded with the items on their lists, both race around the corner at the same time and catch my tears. They are appalled and afraid.

Here's a note to the parents of addicted children: Choose your music carefully. Avoid Louis Armstrong's "What a Wonderful World" from the Polaroid or Kodak or whichever commercial and the songs "Turn Around" and "Sunrise, Sunset" and — there are millions more. Avoid Cyndi Lauper's "Time After Time," and this one, Eric Clapton's song about his son. Leonard Cohen's "Hallelujah" snuck up on me one time. The music doesn't have to be sentimental. Springsteen can be dangerous. John and Yoko. Björk. Dylan. I become overwhelmed when I hear Nirvana. I want to scream like Kurt Cobain. I want to scream *at* him. Music is not all that does it. There are millions of treacherous moments.

Driving along Highway 1, I will see a peeling wave. Or I reach the fork where two roads meet near Rancho Nicasio, where we veered to the left in carpool. A shooting star on a still night at the crest of Olema Hill. With friends, I hear a good joke—one that Nic would appreciate. The kids do something funny or endearing. A story. A worn sweater. A movie. Feeling wind and looking up, riding my bike. A million moments.

We hear nothing more for another fortnight, when he sends me an email. My initial reaction is relief—he is alive, at least semicoherent, and mobile, if only enough to get to a public library to use a computer. He asks for help, some money so he doesn't have to live on the streets. I write back that I will help him return to treatment, but that is all. I am not parroting any Al-Anon tough-love script, nor have I become calloused. I have been defeated by meth and have given up. Bailing him out, paying his debts, dragging him to shrinks, counselors, and scraping him off the street—it has been futile; meth is impervious. I have always assumed that vigilance and love would guarantee a decent life for my children, but I have learned that they aren't enough.

He declines my offer.

Nic's writing teacher at Hampshire, the one who accepted Nic into his class after they shook hands, hears that he relapsed and writes to me: "Sober Nic sparkles. I've buried too many people over the years not to be sick about this news."

After another anguished week, Nic calls, collect:

"Hey, Pop, it's me."

"Nic."

"How're you doing?"

"That's not the question. What about you?"

"I'm all right."

"Where are you?"

"The city."

"Do you have a place to stay? Where are you staying?"

"I'm fine."

"Listen, Nic, do you want to meet?"

"I don't think it's a good idea."

"Just to meet. I won't lay any trips on you. Just for lunch."

"I guess."

"Please."

"All right."

Why do I want to meet him? No matter how unrealistic, I retain a sliver of hope that I can get through to him. That's not quite accurate. I know I can't, but at least I can put my fingertips on his cheek.

For our meeting, Nic chooses Steps of Rome, a café on Columbus Avenue, in North Beach, the neighborhood where I raised him. Nic played in Washington Square opposite St. Peter and Paul's Cathedral. We would browse City Lights, the bookstore, and walk backward down the nearly vertical streets to the wharf, where we sat on the curb and watched the Human Jukebox play his trumpet and then ate banana splits at the Ghirardelli Chocolate Factory. Across Broadway in Chinatown, we picked up bok choy and melons, and on our way home stopped at Caffe Trieste for coffee and hot chocolate. Sometimes we ate early dinner at a sushi bar, where Nic ordered customized tempura with only orange vegetables (carrots and yams). Or we went to Vanessi's, the Italian restaurant where the waiters, in burgundy coats and creased black pants, lifted Nic and set him, tow-headed and a gap between his front teeth, on a stool at the counter stacked with telephone books. Nic's eyes would grow round while watching the pyrotechnics of the line cooks splashing brandy into saucepans. The liquor ignited, and Nic was thrilled. The cooks had his order memorized: kid-sized Caesar salad, ravioli triangolo, and zabaglione whisked in a banged-up copper bowl. Walking home, we passed the girls who hung out in front of the Broadway strip clubs, whom he knew by their costumes, Wonder Woman, She-Ra, Cat Woman, et al. He was convinced that they were superheroes patrolling North Beach. When he got sleepy, I carried him home, his tiny arms wrapped around my neck.

At Steps of Rome, I sit at a corner table, nervously waiting for him. Since reason and love, the forces I had come to rely on in my life, have betrayed me, I am in unknown terrain. Steps of Rome is deserted, other than a couple waiters folding napkins at the bar. I order coffee, while wracking my brain for the one thing that I haven't thought of that could reach him.

I wait until it is more than a half-hour past our meeting time, recognizing the suffocating worry, and also the bitterness and rage.

After forty-five minutes, I decide that he isn't coming — what had I expected? — and leave. I am unwilling to give up, however, and so I walk around the block, return, peer into the café, and then trudge around the block again. Another half-hour later, I am ready to go home, really, maybe, when I see him. Walking toward me, but looking down, his gangly arms limp at his sides, he looks more than ever like a ghostly Egon Schiele self-portrait, debauched and wasted.

He sees me and stops, then cautiously approaches. We tentatively hug, my arms wrapping around his vaporous spine, and I kiss his cheek. He's chalk-white. We embrace like that, and then sit down at a table by the window. He can't look me in the eyes. No apologies for being late. He folds and unfolds a soda straw, rocks anxiously in his chair, his fingers tremble, his jaw gyrates, and he grinds his teeth. We order. He preempts any questions, saying, "I'm doing — great. I'm doing what I need to be doing, being responsible for myself for the first time in my life."

"I'm so worried about you."

In a moment.

"How are Karen and the kids?"

"They're fine. They're OK, but we are all worried about you."

"Yeah, well."

"Nic, are you ready to stop? To return to the living?"

"Don't start."

"Jasper and Daisy miss you. They don't—"

He cuts me off. "I can't deal with that. Don't guilt-trip me."

Nic scrapes his plate clean with the side of a fork, drinks down his coffee. When he brushes back his bangs, I notice a welt, which he touches with his fingers, but I don't bother asking.

After we say goodbye, I watch him rise and leave.

He's shaking and holding onto his stomach. Through Nic's drug addiction, I have learned that parents can bear almost anything. Every time we reach a point where we feel as if we can't bear any more, we do. Things have descended in a way that I never could have imagined, and I shock myself with my ability to rationalize and tolerate things once unthinkable. The rationalizations escalate. He's just experimenting. Going through a stage. It's only marijuana. He gets high only on weekends. At least he's not using hard drugs. At least it's not heroin. He would never resort to needles. At least he's alive. I have also learned (the hard way because, as it turns out, there's no other way to learn such lessons) that parents are more flexible with our hopes and dreams for our children than we ever imagined. When Nic was growing up, I thought that I would be content with whatever choices he made in his life. The truth, however, was that I fully expected that he would go to college. Of course he would. It was never questioned. I pictured him in a satisfying job, with a loving relationship, and maybe, probably, with children of his own. However, with his escalating drug use I have revised my hopes and expectations. When college seemed unlikely, I learned to live with the idea that he would skip college and go right to work. That would be fine. Many kids take a circuitous route to find themselves. But that began to seem unrealistic, and so I concluded that I would be content if he found a sense of peace. With his ascending drug use, however, I live with the knowledge that, never mind the most modest definition of a normal or healthy life, my son may not make it to twenty-one.

Summer ends.

Every time the telephone rings, my stomach constricts. Long after the euphoria from meth is no longer attainable — Tennessee Williams described the equivalent with alcohol in *Cat on a Hot Tin Roof:* "I never again could get the click" — addicts are agitated and confused and most stop eating and sleeping. Parents of addicts don't sleep, either.

17

I n some towns, noon is marked by ringing church bells or chiming clock towers. In Point Reyes, it is announced by a rooster's crow followed by the harmony of mooing cows from a public address system atop the Western Saloon.

The crowing and moos stop us for a moment.

I'm at the farmers' market at Toby's Feed Barn with Daisy and Jasper and it's like a scene in *Oklahoma*. Our neighbors and friends are buying tomatoes, cucumbers, salad greens, and Cowgirl Creamery cheeses.

Daisy and Jasper sample fresh salsa.

We run into my brother and sister-in-law and their children next to baskets of early girls and basil and other herbs ready for planting lined up along a mural that depicts a scene of locals, including Toby in his knit cap and, when she was a baby, my niece.

By now pretty much everyone we know in town has heard about Nic, so people ask about him with no small amount of nervousness. Laurel, a mother going through this—her daughter, a heroin addict, was in a near-fatal car crash—hugs me and starts crying. I'm glad that Jasper and Daisy are off with their cousins listening to the fiddle-and-bass combo playing bluegrass.

My cell phone rings and I know that Nic is calling. I search for a quiet place away from the crowd and find one near the brooding chicks in a cage inside Toby's barn.

I answer the phone, but no one is there.

I check for messages. There's one—from Nic. His voice is cocky, slurring.

"OK, OK ... sorry. Jesus, this is really hard. Sorry. I'm stopping. But part of crashing out, or whatever, and trying to get focused for work ... I've had to sleep a lot 'cause my body ain't that happy with me. I slept through Friday ... waking up on Saturday, not realizing I'd missed a whole day. So in regards to the rest, I don't know. I'm confused."

Then nothing.

Jasper, in a T-shirt and khaki shorts, runs up:

"Can we buy some ginger cookies?"

He notices something and stops short.

"What?"

He looks at the phone in my hand with worried eyes and asks, "Is it Nic?"

A week or so later, Nic contacts his mother, asking for help. "Honestly you would be quite appalled at my lifestyle and I've got enough negative shit coming my way as it is," he writes in an email. "I'm in trouble. It has been a crazy couple months, ultimately resulting in my getting kicked out of the house. I had no money, nothing ... I'm banned unless I go back to rehab. This is not an option. I have that education already ... aa and a higher power don't work for me. They leave me just as horribly empty as ever—"

It cuts off, ends there.

Another email to Vicki. "I'm pretty screwed up physically and mentally, so forgive me if I'm less than perfectly eloquent," he writes. "I'm going to call you once it's late enough, but I wanted to get a few things down on paper just to lay it all out." He explains that he has stolen some checks from the mother of a friend. "I may have a warrant out for me and I need to pay them back or I'm just going to have to remain in hiding."

Vicki and I disagree about the best way to proceed. I understand her fright, but I'm disconcerted when she helps pay his debt. It's a natural and even laudable instinct, but I fear that her support while he's using will simply postpone the inevitable, allowing him to continue on his hazardous course. At least she has said that paying his debt is one thing but she won't give him cash. Giving cash to a using addict is like handing a loaded gun to someone on the verge of suicide.

When I tell Karen about the emails and how incomprehensible it is for me that Nic would do something so abhorrent—so self-destructive—she reacts with fury.

"I'm so sick of all this."

"What am I supposed to do?"

"I'm just sick of it." She walks out of the room.

Nic disappears again, reappears again, keeping sporadic touch with his mother, not with me.

When old family friends from New York happen to be visiting San Francisco, Vicki arranges for Nic to meet them. She pleads with him to go to their hotel.

He does. Disheveled and obviously high, he's not allowed into the lobby until he convinces a security guard to call our friends.

When he, an ashen skeleton, twitchy and rambling, wobbles unsteadily into their room, they are horrified both by his debilitated condition and the track marks on his arms. They beg him to come to New York, where he can stay with them and detox.

Maybe his romance with the San Francisco streets has passed, maybe he is tired and frightened, or maybe it's just that relocating to New York City intrigues him. He agrees to go, but not before he flees one more time, scoring. His dealer gives him a going-away present, an obscene pile of meth, and Nic snorts it before boarding a cross-country flight.

In New York, our friends convince Nic to see a psychiatrist who specializes in addiction. The doctor prescribes sleeping pills and Nic sleeps for most of a week. He endures the physical withdrawal accompanied by the mental anguish— "remorse, shame, disbelief, wanting to use, wanting to die," as he says when he calls me.

Other than telling him that I love him and that I am sorry it is so difficult, I am unsure what else to say.

It's a week later. I answer the telephone. A representative of a bank I used to have an account with is calling. Someone wrote a check for five hundred dollars on the closed account.

Each new betrayal brings with it a new eruption of emotions, many of them clashing inside my skull. Being robbed is a visceral, traumatizing experience anyway. To have it be my son . . . First Karen, now me.

After a month or so, when Nic calls he sounds somewhat less desolate. Vicki helps him move into an apartment in Brooklyn, and he gets a job. After having concluded at one point that college was stupid, Nic has decided that working minimum-wage jobs is even stupider, and so he says that he plans to return to school. "This time I'll do it on my own," he says. "I've blown my chances before, but I won't blow this one."

Nic tells me that he can never again use crystal, he knows that, but, according to him, his doctor says that it's fine that he smokes pot or has a glass of wine; they help him "keep even." So once again I brace myself. I have reason to worry. A UCLA study has shown that an addict is twelve times more likely to relapse on meth if he smokes pot or drinks alcohol.

Nonetheless, I'm unprepared for the phone call at five on a Sunday morning. I leap up and my heart pounds. Karen lifts her head and looks at me. "What is it?"

I grab the phone and weakly say hello.

It's Nic's stepfather. Nic's stepfather? I have talked to him only a few times in twenty years. At this hour? He says that a doctor just called from Brooklyn. Nic is in a hospital emergency room after an overdose. "He is in critical condition and on life support."

I have been waiting for this telephone call, and yet it is no easier for having previewed it so often.

I hang up and tell Karen.

"Will he be all right?"

"I don't know."

I begin praying, pleading with a god I have never believed in. "God, don't let him die. Please don't let him die."

I call the doctor, who explains that someone—one of the kids with Nic when it happened last night—called 911 because Nic went unconscious. An ambulance had been dispatched to Nic's apartment. When he saw the ambulance, Nic's landlord called Vicki, who is on Nic's lease.

The doctor tells me that if the EMT team hadn't responded right away, Nic would have been dead already. Now there is a chance.

I have learned to live with tormenting contradictions, such as the knowledge that an addict may not be responsible for his condition and yet he is the only one responsible. I also have accepted that I have a problem for which there is no cure and there may be no resolution. I know that I must draw a line in the sand—what I will take, what I will do, what I can't take, what I can no longer do—and yet I must also be flexible enough to erase it and draw a new line. And now, with Nic in the hospital, I learn that I love him more, and more compassionately, than ever.

I make arrangements to fly to New York and throw some things in a suitcase.

The telephone rings again. It's the same doctor. He has a serious but empathetic voice. He tells me that Nic should pull through. His vital signs are returning to normal.

"He's a very, very lucky boy," the doctor says. "He'll have another chance."

My son will have another chance. For the first time since the early morning phone call, I breathe.

Jasper and Daisy are awake. They come in and see the state I'm in. We tell them. We tell them that we all just have to hope that Nic makes it.

I call the hospital and ask if I can speak to Nic. The doctor says no, Nic is asleep, I should try in a couple hours. I pace. I walk in the garden. Vicki and I talk a few times, commiserate. Our child has nearly died. Jasper and Daisy again ask if Nic is going to be all right.

I call the hospital in an hour's time, and I'm put through to a telephone next to Nic's bed. He is hardly coherent enough to talk, but he sounds desperate. He asks to go into another program, says it is his only chance. I tell him that I'm on my way to New York.

In another hour, I leave for the airport. While driving, I call the hospital to see how he's doing.

The on-duty nurse tells me that he has checked out.

"What do you mean he checked out?"

"He checked out against doctor's orders."

He pulled out the IVs and catheter, and he left.

I hang up and pull off the freeway. I know that if this overdose isn't enough to stop him, nothing will.

Shaking, I return home.

At night I lie in bed, smell the star jasmine through the open window, stare into the dark.

"Are you awake, Karen?"

"Are you?" she asks.

There is no sleeping for either of us.

I cannot comprehend what could have happened, but the most likely scenario is that withdrawal was too much for Nic or the prospect of recovery was too much for him or the pain was too much and he went out to score. Another known terror plays out in my brain. Nic, overwhelmed by the newest events and feeling physically as well as psychically defeated, has gone to kill himself.

No answer on his telephone, nothing.

He calls in the morning. He sounds groggy and deeply depressed.

"Nic . . ."

"Yeah, I know."

"Where are you?"

He tells me he's at his apartment.

"But what happened? Why did you leave the hospital?"

"I was freaked out. I don't know. I had to get out of there."

I imagine him in the basement apartment of the Brooklyn brownstone where I last visited him — devoid of decoration or furniture other than a mattress on the floor and a dresser that Nic found on the street — with shades drawn fast to keep daylight out. Except for throwing off the boots he had snatched from the closet in his hospital room, he has not troubled to undress. He still has the remnants of tape on his arms that had held the IVs in place. He had reached his apartment and made his way inside and fallen face-down on the mattress, as though diving headlong into a burial plot.

He asks if I'm coming. Will I come?

"What are you going to do?"

Without coercion this time, Nic chooses to return to rehab. He begs.

Is this what hitting bottom means? The experts all say that an addict hits bottom and then engages in recovery in a new way.

I fly to New York to help him check into Hazelden's Manhattan center. I take a taxi in the rain under a dusky lavender sky, and on my way into town I try to anticipate what I will feel when I see him. Overjoyed to see him alive. Furious because of how close he came to throwing away his life.

I wait for him in the lobby of my hotel, where we plan to meet. Suddenly he's standing before me.

"Hey, Pop!"

It is always a dramatic moment when Nic arrives.

In spite of his attempt at putting on a brave façade, he looks like someone who survived a famine. His face is like crepe paper, ghost-white. He wears a torn sport coat over a T-shirt, torn jeans, and busted-up sneakers. We hug stiffly. My affection for him is tempered by my fear of him.

He stays in my hotel for the night. To kill time, we go see a movie, *Punch-Drunk Love,* and eat pasta in a café. He tries to explain what happened, but we're biding our time because this trip is about the morning, when he will check into rehab. Again.

After dinner, Nic and I watch TV. It's the stupidest show ever on television. Young men film one another doing ludicrous, humiliating things. Professional baseball pitchers have been enlisted to hurl one-hundred-mile-per-hour fastballs at the crotches of greasy-haired boys. When the balls hit, the boys double over in pain. Why would they do this? Why would someone put this on TV? Why are we watching?

We have two double beds with thick white comforters, and our heads rest on fat pillows. *Letterman* is on. In the middle of the show, Nic says that he has some business to attend to before he can go to Hazelden. I look at him as if he's out of his mind, which he is.

"Business? What kind of business?"

He says, "It's fine. I'll head out and be back soon."

"No," I say. "Any business you have to attend to now is trouble."

"I have to," he says. "I have to take care of a few things."

He pulls on his sneakers.

I'm unable to dissuade him, so I say, "I'll come."

I throw on my shoes, too, and we go into the cold night. We take the subway to the East Village, stopping at seedy apartment buildings, buzzing buzzers that are (thankfully) not answered. We follow an Indian woman carrying groceries into a building and ascend five flights. I stand with Nic as he pounds on a door. He says that he has some money to retrieve.

Finally he gives up. I am relieved when, near two in the morning, a taxi finally drops us back at the hotel. Riding in the elevator, we stare up at the tiny television screen showing a Tweety and Sylvester cartoon.

In the morning, we walk around until his admission appointment at Hazelden, which is located in a stately brownstone overlooking Stuyvesant Park. While he is interviewed, I wait in the park, sitting on a bench. I watch a group of boys huddled in a corner of the park near a metal gate. A drug deal goes down.

Hazelden is probably the nation's most well-known drug and alcohol rehabilitation center. Its main location is in Minneapolis, but there are programs in New York, Oregon, and Chicago. This is not a primary program. Nic has tried two of those. This one is an ongoing program of six months, perhaps longer, depending on how Nic does. Rather than a crash course of rehab 101 fit into four weeks, patients are required to work or attend school. The idea is that they will learn to integrate recovery into their lives. There are regular meetings with a staff therapist, group therapy, and required AA meetings. There are chores. There is a long list of rules, but unlike the other programs, patients can come and go as they please as long as they are present at dinner and required meetings and appointments and in before curfew.

Nic signals me from the building's open door. It's time. I come upstairs, and we sit in the large foyer lined in cherry bookshelves.

There's not much to say, but we sit there for a while in leather sofas. When an attendant calls Nic—says it's time for him to check in and say goodbye—we stand and look at each other.

We hug. His body feels brittle, like it could break into pieces.

18

I watch the weeks and then months of his recovery from afar. Biding my time, I continue my research into meth, this time canvassing the nation's preeminent researchers and asking them what is to me the bottom-line question. What would you do if a family member were addicted to this drug?

They agree that the first step should be assessment. If an addict is in methamphetamine psychosis, sedatives and other medication should be administered. ("They sometimes are as crazy as a loon, and that needs to be dealt with," said UCLA's Dr. Ling.) Though meth addicts are three to four times more likely than others to have attendant psychiatric conditions in addition to addiction, the symptoms are difficult to distinguish from meth withdrawal. Some doctors would routinely treat addicts for depression. That is an expensive proposition, and some researchers suggest that patients should be off meth for at least a month before they are diagnosed and treated for secondary illnesses.

The experts are divided about whether inpatient or outpatient programs are more likely to work. The former are expensive, but they provide a safe and controlled environment where a patient can be closely monitored. However, it may be difficult to transfer rehab to the real world, and discharged patients often relapse. Outpatient programs integrate recovery work into an addict's life, but there are many opportunities to slip. The majority of experts said that they would ideally choose as long of an inpatient program as possible, to be followed by a gradual transition to a comprehensive outpatient program that would continue for a year or more. This would begin with four or five daily or evening sessions for an initial period, followed by fewer sessions, tapering off to once a week.

These experts agree that, whether in an inpatient or an outpatient setting, it makes little sense to initiate behavioral and cognitive therapies for the initial withdrawal period. Palliatives such as massage, acupuncture, and exercise programs, along with carefully monitored sedatives, may do as much as anything to help patients make it through the worst stages of withdrawal. Addicts in outpatient programs seem to benefit when they get help making a schedule they can follow until their next session. Drug testing, with severe penalties for relapse, is, the experts claim, essential. Behavioral and cognitive therapies should be added slowly. When they are, they should be monitored so that they reflect an addict's ability to participate in them. Some doctors advocate psychotherapy, but many do not. "It probably has little effect," says Dr. Rawson at UCLA. "Talk just can't penetrate the wiring problems." Dr. Ling adds, "Understanding things will not change an addict's life. Doing things differently will." The doctors however prescribe psychotherapy and psychopharmacology when dual diagnoses are apparent, whether depression, bipolar disease, acute anxiety, or other conditions.

The initial goal is to retain addicts in treatment long enough for them to participate in cognitive and behavioral therapies that train, or retrain, them. A range of these therapies has been implemented and tested at Matrix, the drug-rehabilitation centers founded by Rawson and his UCLA colleagues. The Matrix program, developed for cocaine addicts, has been adapted for methamphetamine. It includes therapies that teach addicts to avoid, if possible, or "reframe," if not, situations that previously would have led to relapse. In theory, new behaviors eventually become habitual.

At Matrix-based programs, addicts are trained to interrupt their normal reactions to anger, disappointment, or other emotions. They are taught about components of addiction such as priming and cueing, which often lead to relapse. Priming (as in priming a pump) is a mechanism that launches a single or incidental drug use into a full-blown relapse. Since addicts may slip at certain stages of their recovery, the program trains them to reframe the incident. Rather than responding to priming, an addict can stop the process at a "choice point." The moment can be viewed as an opportunity to try an alternate activity. Cueing leads to drug use when an addict encounters a trigger that starts a cycle of intense craving that often results in using. I came to understand the way a cue works when I thought about Nic's and my different reactions to the movie *Requiem for a Dream*. Nic loved Darren Aronofsky's relentlessly dismal story of a boy and his mother, a heroin addict and speed freak. I found it unbearable. Even the people I know who liked the movie were depressed by its bleakness and depravity, but Nic was thrilled by it. Nic later told me that the drug scenes, accompanied by throbbing music from the Kronos Quartet, which are cautionary, nearly unstomachable for most people, made him want to get high.

Studies have shown that cues dramatically change an addict's vital signs. They don't have to be as obvious as a needle. A cue can be anything from the smell of a chemical reminiscent of meth burning in a pipe to "the people, places, and things" associated with the drug to, for some addicts, payday, a street corner, a song, or a sound—subtle and hidden from everyone but the addict. Many meth addicts associate the drug with sex. As the high school Casanova in the pilot of *Six Feet Under* put it, meth "just makes everything burn a little bit brighter, and it makes sex totally primal." Though most heavy users eventually are unable to have sex, arousal—anything from pornography to a sexual situation—can remain a powerful trigger. "Trying to interrupt drug use at that stage is like trying to get in front of a train," Dr. Rawson said. However, Dr. Shoptaw at UCLA has worked on specific therapies designed to help gay addicts who associate meth with sex to reframe their responses to arousal. The idea is that any behavior, including behaviors that seem automatic or compulsive, can become conscious and can then be interrupted. A user can be taught to stop the moving train and call an AA sponsor or drug counselor, attend a recovery meeting, work out in a gym, or other constructive choices. Once again, time in treatment—time measured in many months if not years—is usually required for dramatic change. In the process, the user's brain is probably regenerating, and dopamine levels may be normalizing. A cycle of abstinence replaces a cycle of addiction.

Recent clinical trials have shown that meth addicts respond to the Skinnerian approach of rewarding clean (that is, drug-free) urine specimens with small cash payments or vouchers for anything from immunizations for an addict's child to a pass to an ice-skating rink to a certificate good for the repair of a broken lawnmower. In a UCLA study, these contingency management strategies, when added to a cognitive and behavioral therapy program, produced two to three times as much abstinence as the cognitive behavioral therapy programs alone.

Medications may help, too. There is currently no methadone for meth users. Nor are there medications to neutralize meth in case of overdose, counteract most symptoms, treat its neurotoxicity, or interrupt the high—all of which would be useful at different stages of treatment. Part of the reason may be that there hasn't been as much research into methamphetamine as into heroin and cocaine, which have long been pervasive on the East Coast, particularly in New York and the beltway. Meth hasn't been directly in the faces of policymakers who allot research money, though this has been changing as meth creeps eastward. Another factor may be the molecular structure of heroin compared to methamphetamine. "Methamphetamine is dirtier," a researcher explained. Whatever the reason, because of the unique level of harm this drug causes, even compared to heroin and cocaine, plus the dismal record of current treatments, clinicians are desperate for medications that would help up the odds for addicts, whether they would replace dopamine, help heal the nerve damage, or treat or manage symptoms. However, the top researchers in the field admit that their efforts warrant little optimism. At the beginning of a trial of a medication that could help with withdrawal, the doctor in charge admitted, "Success for me? Modest effect in a minority of patients. My expectations are nil to minimum, so I'll be really happy with minimum." And he was working on one of the more promising drugs.

Since depression is prominent in the early stages of withdrawal, some researchers maintain that antidepressants would help. However, preliminary tests of Prozac, Zoloft, and other SSRIs suggest that those drugs have little effect. Researchers are currently investigating other antidepressants, including bupropion (Wellbutrin), which interacts with specific subsystems of serotonin and dopamine transmitters and receptors, and a drug called ondansetron. Numerous other trials are planned. Researchers throughout North America told me about dozens of drugs that might help. One is levodopa (L-dopa), which is used to counteract the degeneration of Parkinson's. It essentially replaces missing dopamine, though the effect seems to diminish over time. When tested with cocaine addicts, the drug made no difference. However, researchers conducting a trial posit that the drug may have a stronger effect on meth addicts, because their dopamine levels are nearly bankrupt, compared to slight reductions in cocaine users.

Even if medications turn out to aid in meth withdrawal or at other stages of recovery, researcher Gantt Galloway is convinced that they will never play more than a peripheral role. "There's never going to be a drug that will make you check the peephole before you answer the door, so if it's your dealer you won't answer it," he says. "And even if you do perfect detox and great pharmacotherapy and you get somebody's brain precisely where it was before they started using meth, then the clock starts rolling forward again. It's Groundhog Day. You have to intercede at that point, using behavioral and cognitive therapies to teach people an alternative way to live their lives."

Nic checks in from time to time. He attends AA meetings each evening with a band of Hazelden patients. He describes their outings with his typical dry humor. "We're a sight walking through the city," he says, "a gang of grateful misfits."

I return to my own meetings: Al-Anon. These gatherings are no cure-all, but once again it's comforting, though always so sad, hearing others' stories. After one lunchtime meeting, at which I briefly speak — I shakily begin, "My son is in rehab again" — a woman approaches and timidly hands me a pamphlet called "3 Views of Al-Anon." "It helps me," she says.

At home, I read it. From "Letter from an Addict" in the pamphlet: "Don't accept my promises. I'll promise anything to get off the hook. But the nature of my illness prevents me from keeping my promises, even though I mean them at the time ... Don't believe everything I tell you; it may be a lie. Denial of reality is a symptom of my illness. Moreover, I'm likely to lose respect for those I can fool too easily. Don't let me take advantage of you or exploit you in any way. Love cannot exist for long without the dimension of justice."

With Nic in recovery again, Karen and I get books for children about addiction from the library and read them to Daisy and Jasper. We do our best to encourage the kids to talk about their feelings — to get them out. We meet with their teachers to discuss how they're doing. So far, we're told that they seem all right.

In December, Hazelden's New York inpatient program closes its doors. The organization, which continues to run an outpatient program in Manhattan, blames the economy — it can't fill the brownstone's three dozen beds with paying customers. Nic is wary of the Bay Area, which he associates with meth, and chooses, helped in his decision by his counselor, to move to Los Angeles to live near Vicki.

Herbert House, a sober-living house in Culver City, is actually a series of bougainvillea- and rose-draped bungalows, white-washed and cheerful, with small porches with loveseats and rocking chairs, all facing a central brick courtyard with palms, picnic tables, and garden furniture — sort of a Melrose Place for addicts.

Nic settles in and likes it there. He makes good friends with other patients, and he becomes especially close with the director of the program, a compassionate man named Jace who has dedicated his life to helping addicts and alcoholics. Herbert House has strict rules and requires chores, plus residents must attend nightly meetings. Nic also participates in a nearby outpatient program, meets with a new psychiatrist, and works with another AA sponsor, a man with whom Nic goes on long bike rides along the Pacific Coast Highway. Randy has intense blue eyes; he has been sober for more than fifteen years. Nic says that Randy inspires him, "shows me how good life can be."

On the phone, he sounds like the old Nic, Nic in his right mind. It is almost impossible to reconcile this Nic with the person he was on drugs. I think, by trial and error and persistence, helped by the months at Hazelden, the support of those at Herbert House, the outpatient sessions, AA, Randy, and his friends in recovery, Nic has constructed a comprehensive program that, according to what I have learned from the researchers, reflects the one that should be available for all meth addicts.

Nic's AA friends help him find a technician job at Promises, another renowned drug and alcohol rehabilitation program, this one based in Malibu. He drives patients to meetings and doctors' appointments, dispenses medication, and assists counselors in a wide range of other duties. It is fulfilling work. He has something to offer — he can help others even as the work helps him.

In July, Nic turns twenty-one. To celebrate, I visit him in Los Angeles. It is a warm summer afternoon when I pick him up in front of Herbert House. Nic leaps into the car. We hug. He appears whole again. Twenty-one is a milestone in everyone's life, and it is a milestone for parents when their child turns twenty-one. For me, it feels like another miracle.

It takes a while before Karen says she is ready to see him. In addition, we haven't allowed him to see Daisy and Jasper yet. We don't want them to get hurt again. We all are still torn apart by the warring between our fear and our love. We want to protect Daisy and Jasper, and yet they love him and he loves them. Once again we wonder: how do we know when we can trust him?

Finally, near the end of summer, Karen and the kids come along with me when I drive down the coast on an assignment in LA. The family is reunited on the beach, where Nic, Jasper, and Daisy make sand castles and play in the surf. After that, we come to see him on a series of weekends. We visit him at work and he introduces us to his colleagues, who clearly adore him and whom he seems to adore back. He takes us to another beach, a secluded spot near Malibu that is reached after a hike down a steep trail. Another time we hike through a canyon with his mother and stepfather's dogs, Payson and Andrew. (Nic is dog-sitting them.) We walk up a trail until we reach a lookout from where we can see all the way from Hollywood to the ocean. We rent cruisers and he meets up with us on his racing bike and together we ride down the Venice boardwalk, stopping to watch graffiti artists and weightlifters. As always, we go to museums and galleries—a Royal Art Lodge show at MOCA and at Angles Gallery in Santa Monica an exhibition of thousands of photographs by Nick Taggart of his wife and collaborator, Laura Cooper, taken of her just before she woke up every morning for thirteen years. We usually eat dinner at the same restaurants, a Korean barbecue or tiny sushi bar where loud reggae music plays. We spend most of our time on the beach, but, as always, we see movies. Nic has seen *The Triplets of Belleville*, but he goes again because he wants Jasper and Daisy to see it, too. After the film, together Jasper and Nic sing, with an Indian accent, exactly as in the pre-movie commercial.

Nic begins, "Is the movie sold out, my husband?"

Jasper: "Chitra, my queen, I've used Fandango."

Nic: "My happiness is a golden poem."

Jasper: "I'll get the popcorn."

Nic calls frequently. We have a close telephone relationship. Sometimes we just yak about nothing, sometimes about his recovery. We always talk about movies and books. Especially movies. We cannot wait to talk after one of us sees a new release by one of our favorite directors, whether Spike Jonze, David O. Russell, Todd Solondz, the Coen Brothers, P. T. Anderson, Wes Anderson, Pedro Almodóvar, or Robert Altman, as well as anything written by Charlie Kaufman. I recommend films for him to rent—*Rivers and Tides*—or he recommends them for Karen and me—François Ozon's *8 Women* and his current favorite, Fassbinder's *Die Bitteren Tränen der Petra von Kant*. "Have you read Anthony Lane on the new *Star Wars*?" Nic asks one day. He reads aloud: "'Also, while we're here [on Yoda], what's with the screwy syntax? Deepest mind in the galaxy, apparently, and you still express yourself like a day-tripper with a dog-eared phrase book. "I hope right you are." A fucking break give me.'"

Sometimes he reports successes that for other people are no big deal but to him are Herculean. Little things: he has a bank account and secured a credit card. He is saving some money. He buys a fifth-hand four-hundred-dollar Mazda and, later, a new bike. He moves into an apartment, renting a room from Randy's sponsor, an extremely kind, silver-haired and bearded man who walks with a cane. Ted has been in recovery for thirty years and has helped many young addicts.

Yet some days are excruciating for Nic. I hear it in his voice. He is lonely. He has Randy and good friends, but he would like someone special in his life. He becomes overwhelmed with worry about the future. His moods swing, and he craves drugs. He describes these ups and downs to me sometimes with stoic determination, other times holding back tears. "Sometimes all I can think of is using," he says. "Sometimes it's too difficult. I feel as if I just can't do it. But I call Randy. It really does help if you do what they tell you."

In September, Nic celebrates his year of sobriety. As much as a child's birthday is important to a parent, as much as twenty-one meant to me, a year in recovery means more.

In fits and starts, Nic tells us about a new romance with a girl, Z., but then one day he calls and is near tears. She has broken off the relationship. Earlier, Nic would have called a dealer or one of his druggie friends or scrounged a joint or beer. Now he calls Randy.

"Get over here, Nic," Randy says. "We're going on a bike ride."

They ride for three hours—up Temescal Canyon. Twice. Afterward, Nic calls and sounds elated. "I'm going to be all right."

*

It is a month later. Nic stops returning my calls. Something is wrong.

In our last conversation, he admitted that he was still reeling from the heartbreaking split. He said, "I cannot stop thinking about her."

It is the morning of the third day since then. After French toast, Daisy and Jasper play in their room for a while and then, though it's drizzling, head outside. By the time I corral them, we're running late. They shower and dress, and I remind them to brush their teeth. Daisy asks if she can use an acoustic toothbrush.

"Acoustic toothbrush?"

"A regular one. Not the electric."

Daisy takes her brushing seriously now that her braces are off. There's a retainer to contend with, though. "I can't stop fiddling with it with my tongue," she says.

"Try not to," I say.

"It's too tempting."

The kids race through the house, collecting homework and cleats, stuffing them into their backpacks. Karen takes on Daisy's tangled braids, and then heads out to drive them to school. When they're gone, I am left to fall apart. Again.

How do I know that something is wrong? It's not only that he hasn't called me back. Is it a parent's intuition? Were there warning signs that slowly seeped up into my consciousness? Were there clues in what he said that I detected on a subliminal level? Or was it the laconic pauses between his words?

Where is he? I will not accept the most likely answer: that he has relapsed.

He has been doing well. It's not perfect, but he has a coterie of supportive friends and a good job. He is biking and writing. He attends AA meetings, including some at Herbert House, where he sees Jace and his friends. With Randy, possibly his closest friend ever, he is devotedly working the twelve steps of self-evaluation, atonement, and what he has described as "new character building." Overall, he seems enthusiastic about his life. I know that sometimes he is lonely, but who isn't. Sometimes he is down, but who isn't. Sometimes he feels overwhelmed, but who doesn't.

And yet he must have relapsed. What else could explain his disappearance? Am I being paranoid? I have reason to be hyper-vigilant, alert for any sign that something could be wrong, but I must allow him to move on and have a life. Maybe he has a new girlfriend. Maybe he's just down and needs some time without being in touch; there have been times when I have needed to withdraw from my parents.

I call Vicki, who reassures me that she saw him a day or two ago and he was fine.

Still, I ask her to go to Nic's apartment to check.

When she calls back in an hour, she says that his roommate hasn't seen him, his bed hasn't been slept in. We call Promises and a coworker says that he has not shown up in two days. We call his friends, who have not heard from him. Yesterday one had a date to meet Nic for lunch and a bike ride, but he never arrived. I call the police to see if there has been an accident. Once again. I call hospital emergency rooms. His mother drives to the Santa Monica police station and files a missing person's report.

He is:

Male.

Caucasian.

Twenty-one.

His baby blond hair settled into a coppery brown. He has tear-drop-shaped green-brown eyes and sun-bronzed olive skin. He has an easy smile. He is just over six feet tall, thin with the muscular upper arms and chest of a swimmer and the strong thighs and calves of a cyclist. When not in bike shorts and shirt, these days he normally wears an outfit of T-shirt, jeans, Converse. He has a strawberry birthmark on his right shoulder.

I try to keep it together—to appear all right—in front of Jasper and Daisy.

Karen and I don't want to tell them about Nic until we know more. We don't want to worry them more. They are only seven and nine years old. What will we say? "Your brother has vanished. Again. He may have relapsed. Again. We don't know."

But we will have to say something soon. We can't for much longer conceal the anguish and hysteria that is, again, taking over our home. It takes a prodigious effort to go through the motions of ordinary days with my constricting stomach, racing heart, and the inescapable, high-definition *CSI* video clips playing inside my skull: the grimmest, most sordid scenes of the worst things that happen to children on the streets at night.

I continually try Nic's cell phone but each time reach his deadpan voicemail: "Hey, it's Nic. Leave a message." I repeatedly check with his mother for news, but there is none. On a whim, I call the 800 customer-assistance number for our shared cell phone company to ask if there have been any recent calls to or from Nic's phone, but an operator says that she can't access the information. However, she explains that she can tell me if his cell phone is currently connected to the network. "It's against regulations," she says. "But I'm a mother of a teenager." After some clicking on a keyboard, she reports, "Yes, the phone is on. It's accessing a tower in Sacramento."

Sacramento?

I call his mother and his friends. No one knows why he would be in Sacramento. No one knows of any friends there.

Two hours later, the operator calls back. "I checked again," she says. "The phone is on still. It's now in Reno."

Reno?

A police detective tells me that Reno is a meth capital, which could explain it, though it seems farfetched because he wouldn't have to go to Reno to score the drug.

No, he cannot have relapsed. He just celebrated his seventeenth month off of meth. Not only that. He works at a rehab center, helping addicts.

I try to work but can't. There is no news throughout the day. After school, Karen and I ferry Jasper and Daisy to lacrosse at two different fields. Daisy has started lacrosse after watching Jasper's games. She finds the required skirt sexist, but she reluctantly wears one. After practice, a thrown-together dinner, homework, baths, and bedtime stories, the children are asleep.

I call the wireless operator again — she has given me her private cell phone number. She says that she will call in the morning from work, so I wait the interminable hours of another night. She calls and tells me that Nic's phone is still on, but now it's in Billings, Montana.

I wrack my brain for a plausible explanation. Has he been kidnapped? Is he dead in the trunk of the car of some psycho who is fleeing east across the country? I call the Billings police and the FBI.

19

It is raining outside. The children are still at school. Karen and I sit on the concrete kitchen floor with Moondog. The vet is here, too, also sitting on the floor. The dog's head rests on Karen's lap. She strokes his velvety ears.

Moondog's cancer has taken over—he can barely stand. He trembles and cries out from pain. It's time to put him out of his misery, but we are devastated. Karen shakes and weeps. The doctor has come here to do it at home. As the vet injects Moondog with something that puts him into a deep sleep, tears come from me, too. His breathing is labored. A second injection, and there are no more breaths. The vet sits with us awhile and then she leaves. Karen and I struggle to carry a blanket with Moondog's heavy body on it to a hole we dug under a redwood tree in the garden, where we bury him.

When Daisy and Jasper come home from school, they work with Karen in the rain making a shrine for Moondog. We cry for Moondog and for all of the sadness in our home. At their bedtime, we read to them from a picture book called *Dog Heaven*: "So sometimes an angel will walk a dog back to earth for a little visit and quietly, invisibly, the dog will sniff about his old backyard, will investigate the cat next door, will follow the child to school . . ."

Where is Nic? It is late morning on the fourth day since he disappeared. I continue to try his cell phone. Finally someone answers. A male voice. Not Nic.

"Ha-llo?"

"Nic? Is this Nic?"

"Nic's not here."

"Who is this?"

"Who is *this?*"

"Nic's father. Where is Nic?"

"He gave me his phone."

"He gave it to you? Where's Nic?"

"How the fuck should I know?"

"Where was he when he gave you the phone?"

"I don't even know him. He was at the bus station in LA. Downtown. He gave me his phone and I haven't seen him since then."

"He gave you his phone? Why would he give you his phone?"

Silence. He hangs up.

I call the cell phone operator and ask her to disconnect the telephone, telling her that it has apparently been stolen, thanking her for her help and her compassion.

Vicki and I are frantic. Once again. We make phone calls, hoping for some — any — news. Finally Vicki tries Z. and yes, she just heard from him. Nic called her — from San Francisco. Here we go again. She says that when he called her, he was high. Of course.

I want this to stop. I cannot bear it. I wish that I could expunge Nic from my brain. I yearn for a procedure like the one Charlie Kaufman invents in a movie he wrote, *Eternal Sunshine of the Spotless Mind*. A doctor provides a service for people who suffer from the pain caused by a traumatic relationship. He literally erases every trace of the person. I fantasize that I could have the procedure, have Nic wiped from my brain. Sometimes it feels as if nothing short of a lobotomy could help. Where is Nic? I cannot take this any longer. And yet every time I think I can't take anymore, I do.

Utter despondency is followed by a frantic impulse to do something, anything. I know better, but I am desperate to find him. When she hears the plan, Karen shakes her head. "It won't help to find him if he doesn't want to be found," she says. She looks at me with concern and — what is it? Exasperation. Sorrow. "You'll just be disappointed."

I say, "I know," and I don't say anything more, even as my brain calculates: it won't help to find him if he doesn't want to be found, but he could die and then it will be too late. Waiting is ghastly. Karen, sensing my anguish, finally succumbs. "Go ahead," she says. "Look for him. It can't hurt." I can tell that she's trying hard not to judge me or Nic, but she is increasingly angry and frustrated by the relentlessness, and she resents the impact on Jasper and Daisy. On us. On me. She resents that she has lost me to worrying. "Go on," she says. "Maybe you'll feel better for trying."

And so I am in the city again, driving along Mission Street, peering into the open doorways of shops and taquerias and bars. I examine every face, continually seeing Nic. Every other person looks like him. Next I park on Ashbury and slowly walk along Haight Street, zigzagging back and forth across the street, checking head shops and bookstores and a pizza place and café and Amoeba. I return to Golden Gate Park, making my way to the clearing where I met the meth-addicted girl from Ohio. Except for two women, whose toddlers play on a blanket, it is deserted.

Back home, I dial Randy. He listens patiently to the anguish in my voice and then assures me: "Nic won't stay out long. He's not having any fun." I hope he's right, but I am no less worried that he could overdose or otherwise cause irreparable damage.

Nic is gone a week. Then another. Interminable days and nights. I try to keep busy. I try to work. We make plans with friends — the same ones who were going to the beach with Karen and the kids when Nic was arrested. With bikes strapped onto racks that hang from the backs of our cars, on a pristine Saturday morning we meet them at the parking lot at Bear Valley. Between our two families, there are eight bikes, ranging from fancy fourteen-speeds to the littlest girl's tiny, rattling Schwinn.

Bear Valley is gold and verdant and the sky, filtered through the trees, is a blue-white canopy. We pedal along a dirt trail to a meadow and from there down a rocky path toward Arch Rock. To reach it, we have to leave our bikes and hike the last mile.

The forest trail, which follows a stream, is edged with fir and Bishop pine and chinquapin and gnarled and twisting oaks. At the end, we climb up to a sheer cliff with a startling lookout on the sea, where seals poke their heads up near a jagged rock that emerges like a glacier from the ocean.

Now we follow another path, this one lined with sticky monkey flower, myrtle, and iris. Rust-colored moss grows on granite boulders. Jasper says it's like being in *Lord of the Rings* on Frodo's quest. At the bottom, under Arch Rock, timing it so that we can run past a crashing wave after it has been sucked back into the ocean, we traverse a rocky point and climb down onto a fingernail of beach. The floor is polished quartz and spongy seaweed.

The path leads back to the trailhead. Jasper and I are the first to arrive. We mount our bikes and continue ahead. The plan is to meet up again at the meadow.

When we reach it, we lean our bikes against a tree and rest on a fallen log under an oak. Jasper points out into the meadow— "Look!" There's an astonishing swath of shocking pink flowers, exotics left over from a long-abandoned garden: pink ladies, pink like cotton candy.

We sit there quietly, listening to birdsong and wind in the leaves. Suddenly I am flooded with déjà vu. I have been here before. Sitting on this same log. But with Nic. More than a decade ago. My heart pumps and my eyes water. Nic climbed this tree. Climbing, he called to me: "Dad, look at me! I'm way up here!"

He absentmindedly sang: "All mimsy were the borogoves, and the mome raths outgrabe."

He climbed higher up and then began to shimmy out onto a thick branch that reached over the meadow. "Look at me, Dad! Look at me!"

"I see you."

"I'm up in the sky."

"Fantastic."

"I'm higher than the clouds."

He slid farther out along the gnarled limb. "Pulling weeds," he sang. "Picking stones. We are made of dreams and bones." A puff of wind shook the tree; its leaves trembled and branches swayed. "I want to come down," Nic said suddenly.

"It's OK, Nic. You're fine. Just take it slowly."

"I can't," he called. "I'm stuck."

"You can," I said. "You can do it."

"I can't get down." He began crying.

"Take your time," I said. "Find one foothold at a time. Go slowly."

"I can't."

"You can."

He wrapped his gangly legs and arms tighter around the branch. "I'll fall."

"You won't."

"I will."

I stood directly underneath and yelled up to him, "You're fine. Take your time." I said it, but I was thinking, I'll catch you if you fall.

Sitting here with Jasper, remembering, a few tears slide from my eyes. Jasper immediately notices. "You're thinking about Nic," he says.

I nod. "I'm sorry," I answer. "I was just reminded of him. I remember when he was your age we were here."

Jasper nods. "I think about him a lot, too." We sit together under the ancient tree saying nothing until Karen, Daisy, and our friends call out to us.

On a morning the following week, Karen notices that something is amiss in our house. Just a few things out of place. A hairbrush on the floor. Some books and magazines strewn on a couch. A sweater is missing.

I am working in my office, but I join her in the living room. "What are you talking about?" I ask. Immediately I am protective. My knee-jerk reaction is that Karen is overreacting, paranoid — always ready to blame Nic.

"No. Someone —" She stops. "Come look."

I follow her, and my mind clicks from defensiveness to acceptance. Nic has been here. He broke in. Together we check throughout the house and find, in our bedroom, a broken dead-bolt on a French door. The door's redwood astragal is splintered beyond repair. Only then do I notice that my desk drawers have been ransacked.

Each time Karen or I discover another violation, we are hit anew by a combination of sadness and fury. How could he do this? We closed our bank accounts when he forged our names on our checks, closed credit card accounts when he stole them. We'll have to do it again. Now I call a locksmith and burglar-alarm company.

I also call the sheriff, reporting the break-in. If anyone had told me that I would be calling the sheriff on my son before I encountered addiction I would have thought that that person was the one on drugs. I don't want Nic arrested. Imagining him in jail sickens me. It sickens me. Could anything good come of it? Suddenly I share the feelings of the parents I met in some of the Al-Anon meetings whose children were in jail and who said, "At least I know where she is." And: "It's safer." The sad irony is that as violent as jail can be, as bleak and hopeless, it is probably safer for Nic than the streets.

The locksmith who comes to our house is a burly man in jeans and a work shirt. I show him the locks on the doors and windows that we want him to change. It's an expensive and humiliating experience, because I'm honest when he asks, "Just a precaution or have you had any problems?"

My voice catches when I reply, "My son."

The next day, we hear from friends who live in Inverness below Manka's, the former hunting lodge that is now a renowned restaurant. A workman arrived this morning, meeting his crew, and saw two boys duck out a window of their house. The boys cut along the side and retreated in a rattling old sun-faded red Mazda. The boys were quick in their flight, but the man, whom we know, recognized Nic. I go over to their house. The remnants of Nic's night are untouched: he and his friend slept on the living room floor. Nothing much is disturbed, but there are cotton balls, silver foil packets, and other accoutrements of smoking and shooting meth.

Where else might Nic break in? It's never easy to fathom exactly what motivates a drug addict, but I am struck that Nic is drawn back to places where he is loved — our house, our friends', his grandparents'. It's probably merely convenience, when he doesn't know where else to go, but could it be an unconscious desire to return home to safety? Whatever the reason, when he inflicts his craziness upon us, it becomes even more difficult to feel compassion. We become afraid of him.

*

It is the next morning and Karen is outside, when, surreally, she sees Nic drive by in his old Mazda, smoke billowing from the tailpipe. They make eye contact. He steps on the gas, gunning the car, which creeps up the hill past the house.

Karen, puzzled, does a double take. Yes, it is Nic. She calls to me.

I jump in the car and chase him. What will I do? I suppose I will just tell him how heartbroken we are. And warn him that the police have been called. He had better stop, get help, call Randy.

I drive the winding hillside streets above our home. There was a wildfire here ten years ago. Forty-five homes and more than twelve thousand acres burned. The returning oaks, pine, and Douglas fir are now the size of small Christmas trees. I drive streets that snake through canyons and on the ridge side, but I can't find him.

I head back down the hill to our house and pull into the drive-way, noticing that our other car is gone. I run inside. Jasper and Daisy tell me that Karen saw Nic driving down the hill—somehow I had missed him—and she leaped in the car. She is following his ancient car in our own ancient car, the beat-up, rusted-out Volvo station wagon that can hardly reach forty miles per hour.

I try Karen's cell phone, but it rattles and rings in the bedroom, a few feet away from me. The kids look worried, so I reassure them. By now they know that Nic has relapsed, but how can they understand what it means that their mother has jumped into the car, left them home alone, and driven off in pursuit of their brother?

She doesn't come home for almost an hour, by which time I am crazy with worry, but for the kids' sake pretending that this is normal, again reassuring them. We wait in the living room. When Karen pulls into the driveway, we rush outside. She says that she followed Nic down Highway 1 and up over the mountainous Stinson Beach Road. Finally she realized that it was ludicrous—what would she have done if she had caught him?—and so she stopped.

"What *would* you have done if you caught him?" Jasper asks.

"I'm not sure," she says. She looks beleaguered; she has been crying.

Later, when we're alone, she confides to me, "I wanted to tell him to get help, but mostly I was chasing him—chasing him away from our house—from Jasper and Daisy."

It's not that we need a reminder, but the absurd morning tells us how out of control our lives have become. It was foolish to try to chase him, but we have succumbed to the irrationality that festers along with addiction.

Three days later, on Sunday morning, the phone rings but no one is on the other end. Then it happens again. There's a number on the caller ID that I don't recognize.

Using the reverse lookup feature on anywho.com, I learn that the phone is under a familiar name. It takes a while for me to place it. It's the parents of a girl Nic knew in high school. I call but reach an answering machine, on which I leave a message. "I'm trying to reach my son. His name is Nic Sheff. He called from this number."

The girl's stepmother returns my call. I am astounded by what I hear. "You're Nic's father? It's so nice to talk to you," she says. "What a great son you have. He's a pleasure to have around. We've been so worried about April, and he's such a good influence on her."

"A good influence on her?"

I sigh and tell her about Nic's relapse and disappearance. She is stunned. She explains that her stepdaughter has been in and out of rehab for drug addiction and Nic has seemed so supportive of her recovery.

In the afternoon, Nic calls. He tells me everything—he has relapsed, is using meth and heroin. I have rehearsed my response. I shakily tell him that there's nothing I can do. It's up to him. I say that the police are searching for him, that his mother reported him missing to the Santa Monica police, and that the Marin sheriffs are patrolling our home and the home of our friends where he broke in. I say, "Do you want to wind up in jail? That's where you're headed."

"God," Nic says. "Please help me. What do I do?"

"All I know to tell you to do is what you already know. What do they tell you in the program? Call your sponsor. Call Randy. I don't know what else to say."

He is crying. I say nothing. This isn't how I want to respond. I want to drive to the city to get him. But I repeat, "Call Randy." I tell him that I love him and hope that he gets his life together. I may sound resolved or resigned, but I'm neither of those things.

I hang up. My stomach is tight and my temples pound. I want to call back. I want to tell him I'm coming. But I don't.

Randy calls in a half-hour or so. He says that he heard from Nic and encouraged him to return to LA. "I told him that I miss him," Randy says. "I do. I told him to get his ass back here — I'm waiting. He sounds ready to come in."

I breathe. When I thank Randy, he says, "No need to thank me. This is how I stay alive." He adds, "And I really do miss that knucklehead."

Vicki and I talk. We are both relieved to hear that Nic has agreed to go back to LA, to Randy — to the program. However, we're both shell-shocked, unable or unwilling to accept that everything may be all right again. It's all too precarious.

In the evening, Vicki calls. Nic, who had enough money left for a taxi to the airport and a plane ticket, made it back to LA. She picked him up at the airport and dropped him off at his apartment, where his roommate welcomed Nic home with a pat on the back.

Nic immediately retreated to his bedroom, where he fell asleep. When I call, Ted tells me that Nic is sleeping it off. "Detoxing isn't any fun, but he has to go through it," he says. "There's nothing you can do. Just pray."

Nic calls in the morning. His voice is hoarse. When I ask how he feels, he gruffly responds, "How do you think?" He recounts his departure from San Francisco. "I did what Randy told me to do," he says. "I prayed. I just kept saying, 'Please help me.' I kept repeating it. When I was getting ready to go, April saw me and freaked out. She grabbed onto my leg and was crying and screaming that I couldn't leave. But if I stayed, we'd both die. I told her, but it didn't help." He cries. "I fucked up bad."

Over the following days I try to be optimistic, but I'm in a confused frenzy. I still act as if I'm OK around Daisy and Jasper, but I break down with Karen.

I go to an Al-Anon meeting in a room at a church in Corte Madera. I am shaking, unable to restrain myself, and when it's my turn, I blurt out a reconstruction of the past couple weeks. As I'm speaking in a rush of tears and panic, I think, Someone else is talking. This is not my life. Finally, drained, I say, "I don't know how all you people in this room survive this." And I cry. So do many of the others.

After the meeting, as I help fold and stack the metal chairs, a woman whom I have never met comes up to me and hugs me and I horrify myself by weeping in her arms. "Keep coming back," she says.

Sometimes it startles me that life goes on, but it does, inexorably. Jasper comes into my office. He wears short flannel pajamas and furry slippers. Daisy, her slept-on hair messy, has on a T-shirt and rainbow-striped pants and she carries Uni, her stuffed unicorn. Then Karen, the kids, and I make waffles. After eating, Jasper and Daisy launch a game of hide-and-seek. Jasper is it, and Daisy zooms down the hallway. He calls, "Ready or not," and hunts her down. He discovers her, coiled like a cat inside the same basket she always hides in. Jasper tips the basket and spills her out onto the concrete floor and then trips over her sprawled body and falls on top of her. They laugh like hyenas. Daisy uncoils and leaps up, making a run for it, with Jasper in hot pursuit. They careen by us and dive into Nic's vacant bedroom, designated base in spite of the bad memories that seem permanently soaked into the walls.

Next they dress and go outside and throw a lacrosse ball back and forth. Within minutes, however, like always they lose the ball. The garden has a mystifying power of attraction for balls: lacrosse balls, whiffle balls, tennis balls, soccer balls, footballs, baseballs —and not only balls, but shuttlecocks, paper gliders, model rockets, Frisbees. They look under bushes and hedges for a while but the ball is gone into the garden's black hole. The kids give up and sit on the gravel, from where we overhear their handclapping game: "Lemonade, crunchy ice. Beat it once, beat it twice." Next we hear Jasper say, "Do you think that Nic looks like Bob Dylan?" The other night, we watched a video that had in it a performance by Dylan in Greenwich Village at twenty or so years old.

Daisy doesn't respond directly, but asks, "Do you know why that guy does drugs?"

Jasper says, "He thinks it makes him feel better."

"They don't. They make him feel all sad and bad."

Jasper responds, "I don't think he wants to do them, but he can't help it. It's like in cartoons when some character has a devil on one shoulder and an angel on the other. The devil whispers into Nicky's ear and sometimes it gets too loud so he has to listen to him. The angel is there, too," Jasper continues, "but he talks softer and Nic can't hear him."

In the evening Nic reports that Randy almost literally dragged him out of bed and onto a bicycle. "I felt like I wanted to die," he says, "but Randy didn't take no for an answer. He said he would pick me up, so I got ready. Randy was there and I got on my bike and felt like shit, didn't think I could pedal down the block, never mind up the coast, but then I felt the wind and the memory in my body took over and we rode for a while." There is some life back in Nic's voice, and I am left with a hopeful image: Nic on his bike in the Southern California sunshine riding along the beach.

On the weekend, when Nic calls again, he is eager to talk. He expresses astonishment that he relapsed. "I was sober for eighteen months," he says. "I got cocky. It's this trick of addiction. You think, My life isn't unmanageable. I'm doing fine. You lose your humbleness. You think you're smart enough to handle it." He admits that he is ashamed—mortified—about this relapse and claims that he is redoubling his efforts. "I've been going to two meetings a day," he says. "I have to start the steps all over." Of course I am relieved (once again) and hopeful (once again). I'm always evaluating, What's different this time? Is it different? Indeed, he is making progress, the kind you learn to measure day by day. Randy helps him get a new job. Together they begin to work the twelve steps again. Each day before or after work, they go on long bike rides.

At home in Inverness, Karen and I work on an analogous recovery. Through Al-Anon and the therapist Karen and I continue to see on occasion, we understand the ways that our lives have become unmanageable, too. Mine has. My well-being has become dependent on Nic's. When he is using, I'm in turmoil; when he's not, I'm OK, but the relief is tenuous. The therapist says that parents of kids on drugs often get a form of posttraumatic stress syndrome made worse by the recurring nature of addiction. For soldiers back from battle, the sniper fire and bombs are in their heads. For parents of an addict, a new barrage can come at any moment. We try to guard against it. We pretend that everything is all right. But we live with a time bomb. It is debilitating to be dependent on another's moods and decisions and actions. I bristle when I hear the word *codependent,* because it's such a cliché of self-help books, but I have become codependent with Nic — codependent on his well-being for mine. How can a parent not be codependent on a child's health or lack of it? But there must be an alternative, because this is no way to live. I have come to learn that my worry about Nic doesn't help him, and it harms Jasper, Daisy, Karen — and me.

A month passes. Two. In June, I am going to LA to conduct an interview. I ask Nic if he wants to meet me for dinner.

I pick him up in front of his apartment. We hug when we see each other. Stepping back, I look at him and try to take in what is there. By now I have learned enough to know that at some point, addicts, especially meth addicts, don't recover — at least for a long, long time. Some never recover. The physical, never mind the mental, debilitation can be permanent. But Nic's eyes are light-filled brown, and his body seems strong again. He's young enough to bounce back, or at least it seems that he has. His laugh seems easy and honest. But I have observed this transformation before.

We take a walk and make small talk — the upcoming election, stuff like that. Movies are always safe. "I want to apologize," he says, but his voice catches and he is silent. For the moment it seems to be impossible for him. Maybe there is too much to apologize for.

We meet again the next evening and I accompany him to an AA meeting. While drinking tepid coffee from paper cups, we introduce ourselves. "I'm Nic, a drug addict and alcoholic," he says. When it's my turn, I say, "I'm David, father of an addict and alcoholic, here to support my son."

The meeting's speaker says that he has been in recovery for a year. There is applause. He tells stories about the impact on his life. Last week, he says, he found himself alone with a friend's girlfriend, to whom he had been attracted for years. She began to come on to him. Any other time in his life he would have been elated and wouldn't have thought twice about sleeping with her, but he started to kiss her and then stopped himself. He said, "I can't do this," and he left. Outside her apartment building, walking home, he began crying uncontrollably. He says, "It dawned on me. I have gotten my morals back." Nic and I look at each other with . . . what? Tentativeness. And for the first time in a long time, tenderness.

I am continuously reminded that nothing is easy for Nic. My heart goes out to him. I want to do something to help, but there's nothing to be done. I want him to acknowledge the traumatic past and promise that it will never happen again. He can't. When we talk, in fact, I realize that Nic has discovered the bitterest irony of early sobriety. Your reward for your hard work in recovery is that you come headlong into the pain that you were trying to get away from with drugs. He says that he sometimes feels optimistic and fine, but other times he is depressed and desolate. "Sometimes I don't think I can make it," he says. He feels overwhelmed by this relapse. "How could I have fucked up so badly?" he asks. "I can't believe I did it. I almost lost everything. I don't think I can face starting over again."

Nic admits that sometimes he fantasizes about relapsing. He dreams about it. Again. Always. His dreams are vivid and ghastly. He feels at once abhorrence and the seduction of drugs. He can taste them. He tastes crystal, smells it, feels the needle pierce his skin, feels the drug coming on, and the dream turns into a nightmare because he cannot stop.

He wakes up panting, in a sweat.

I know that being sober is more difficult for Nic than I can comprehend. I feel sympathy and pride for his hard work. When I get angry about the past—the lies, the break-ins, the betrayals—I restrain myself from saying anything or even reacting. It does no good. I think it was in New York that Nic and I saw *The Royal Tenenbaums* together. Nico—her voice pained—sings Jackson Browne's "These Days." I hear her sing the haunting lyric: "Don't confront me with my failures. I have not forgotten them." I have to remind myself that if Nic's relapses horrify me, it's worse for him. I suffer, Vicki suffers, Karen suffers, Jasper and Daisy suffer, my parents suffer, Karen's suffer, others who love Nic suffer, but he suffers more. "Don't confront me with my failures. I have not forgotten them."

Today was particularly tough, Nic says when he calls. Indeed, he sounds depleted. His car broke down on his way to an interview for a job he's excited about. As a result, he missed the interview. I always worry if these normal, everyday frustrations will be too much for him, but he and Randy went riding. They rode for hours and talked about the program, AA, the twelve steps, and how difficult it is to open up to the world, but how much there is to gain when you do. Sobriety is only the beginning and is the only beginning.

Though they have spoken on the telephone with Nic, Karen, Jasper, and Daisy have not seen him since the relapse. We continue to try to explain it to Jasper and Daisy. "He has a disease" doesn't begin to comfort them. It's a wholly unsatisfying, confusing explanation. From their perspective, the symptoms of a disease are things like coughing, fevers, or a sore throat. The closest they get to understanding is Jasper's image of the devil and the angel, competing for Nic's soul. Regardless, Daisy and Jasper miss him. Karen and I are unwilling to let Nic visit us in Inverness. We need more time. Nic seems to understand. We are not ready to have him come home again—not after this last time. Not after the stolen checks, the car chase, the traumatic break-ins at our and our friends' homes, the thefts, the trauma of not knowing—imagining him in the trunk of a car driving west across the country, Sacramento, Reno, Billings, Montana. But in late summer, we are taking a vacation to Molokai, Hawaii, staying in tent cabins above a beach, and Karen suggests that we use some frequent-flier miles and invite Nic to join us. Finally she's ready to see him. For us both, it feels safer to meet on neutral territory, and a vacation is a less complicated time to try to begin to reunite.

On the day of Nic's arrival, the four of us drive to the single-runway airport on Molokai to meet him. As always, the reunion combines excitement with intense nervousness.

"Daisy, you have a stuffy little nose, missypants," Nic gushes when he sees her, picking Daisy up in a bear hug and spinning in a circle. "It's so good to see you, little boinky.

"And you, mister," he says, squatting down to meet Jasper's full eyes. "I have missed you more than the sun misses the moon at night." He squeezes him too.

During the long drive to the camp, there is some diffidence and awkwardness, but then Jasper asks for a PJ story, and we are back in safe territory.

Nic begins: "PJ Fumblebumble, London's greatest detective, awoke." He uses a British accent that borrows pitch and tenor from the narrator of *Rocky and Bullwinkle* cartoons. "As everybody knows, PJ Fumblebumble is the greatest detective in all of London. However, for those of you who have spent your whole life living in a cave or in a hut buried beneath snow, I'll just say that if anything were to ever go amiss for you—a missing parakeet, a burglar in the bedroom, no syrup for your pancakes—there's only one man that you need bother to call. That man, as you probably guessed, is the one, the only, Inspector PJ Fumblebumble. Children want to be him, men are fiercely jealous of him, and women swoon at the very mention of his name."

Nic has been telling installments of these stories about PJ and the Lady Penelope for years. The kids love them. "The man is tall and thin," Nic continues, "lanky and lean like a lollipop stick with legs and a carefully groomed handlebar mustache. His nose is enormous and hooked. It can follow a scent as well as a common bloodhound. His ears are equally keen and oversized. His hair is beginning to gray and fall out on top, while his eyes require the aid of round, wire-rimmed spectacles. Dashing and bold, he is aging with distinction. The man's hands are large, with fingers of knotted rope. His Adam's apple is round and protrudes marvelously."

PJ takes most of the ride to the coastside campsite. After the conclusion — PJ arrests the vile Professor Julian "Poopy Shoes" Pipsqueak — the kids update Nic about school and their friends.

"Tasha has gotten meaner and she always copies me," Daisy is saying. "She ignores Richard, who follows her around. It makes him cry."

"The snobby little prig," answers Nic, still British from PJ.

We drive along and gaze out on red-earth vistas. In a moment, Jasper quietly asks: "Nic, are you going to use drugs anymore?"

"No way," Nic says. "I know you worry, but I'll be all right."

They are quiet. We stare at the red clay and spy the first glimpse of the breaking surf.

At the beachside camp, the five of us ride rental bikes, play in the sand, and swim together in the waves. Karen reads aloud *Treasure Island* in the shade of palm trees.

One afternoon we go to town for ice cream to a shop with chairs with twisted wire backs and legs. The assortment of flavors is uniquely Hawaiian, sweet potato, green tea, and macadamia nut swirl.

It is striking to me how our dual realities once again blur. It's probably a vestigial survival mechanism. Now, instead of recalling the overwhelming calamity and evil, I am swept up in the loveliness of the children here together and the natural beauty. I feel as if we are all being washed clean by the ocean and warm tropical breeze. Feeling hopeful about Nic's future, I can tuck the darkness of his addiction away — not to forget it, but I set it aside — and meanwhile appreciate the sublimity. A sunset, the clear green water, poetry in the music that plays on CDs in the car — Lennon singing "Julia," Van Morrison's "Astral Weeks." For the moment, evil is at bay.

The night is filled with the sounds of crickets and mice skittering across the wood floor. From their tent with three single beds, we also can hear Nic reading to Jasper and Daisy. He has picked up *The Witches* where he left off more than two years ago.

After goodbyes at the airport, we board separate jets, Nic for LA, us for San Francisco.

A week later, I am with Jasper in Point Reyes Station, where we pick up the mail. There's a stack of bills, letters from their school with a schedule for the new year, and a letter for Jasper — from Nic. Jasper opens the envelope carefully. He unfolds the letter and holds it in his hands, reading aloud. In his neat script on paper torn out of a notebook, Nic writes, "I'm looking for a way to say I'm sorry more than with just the meaninglessness of those two words. I also know that this money can never replace all that I stole from you in terms of the fear and worry and craziness that I brought to your young life. The truth is, I don't know how to say I'm sorry. I love you, but that has never changed. I care about you, but I always have. I'm proud of you, but none of that makes it any better. I guess what I can offer you is this: As you're growing up, whenever you need me — to talk or just whatever — I'll be able to be there for you now. That is something that I could never promise you before. I will be here for you. I will live, and build a life, and be someone that you can depend on. I hope that means more than this stupid note and these eight dollar bills."

PART V

NEVER ANY KNOWING

JOEL
How exactly is this going to work tonight?

(*As Mierzwiak talks, the room colors start to fade, Mierzwiak's tone of voice is also affected; it becomes dry and monotonous.*)

MIERZWIAK
We'll start with your most recent memories and go backwards — There is an emotional core to each of our memories — As we eradicate this core, it starts its degradation process — By the time you wake up in the morning, all memories we have targeted will have withered and disappeared. Like a dream upon waking.

JOEL
Is there any sort of risk of brain damage?

MIERZWIAK
Well, technically, the procedure itself is brain damage, but on par with a heavy night of drinking. Nothing you'll ever miss.

— CHARLIE KAUFMAN,
Eternal Sunshine of the Spotless Mind

M y article "My Addicted Son" appears in the *New York Times Magazine* in February. Nic and I both hear from friends and strangers, sharing the feedback. Both of us are encouraged, because it seems as if our family's story has touched many people — and, according to some, helped them, especially those who have been through some version of this, or who are going through it now.

When Nic is asked to write his memoir, he enthusiastically goes forward. And the reaction inspires me to want to write more about it — to go deeper. Soon I have a book deadline, though I would continue writing without one. Writing is enormously painful, and writing this story is sometimes excruciating. Writing every day I go through the emotions I felt at the time of the story I'm remembering. I relive the hell. But I also relive the moments of hope and miracle and love.

Later in February, we plan to spend the weekend skiing at Lake Tahoe. Nic gets a few days off work so he can join us. The kids ski together. In the evening, Nic tells them PJ stories by the fire.

When we talk about it, Nic seems emphatically committed to his sobriety. I have learned to check my optimism, but still, it's good to hear Nic discuss the life he is rebuilding and building anew in LA. In addition to his book, he is writing short stories and movie reviews for an online magazine. It seems so fitting that he's reviewing movies since they are such a big part of his life. Every day in LA, Nic bikes, swims, or runs. Sometimes he does all three. Nic and Randy ride up and down the coast from Santa Monica. They ride through the canyons, up hillsides, through the city, and along beaches.

When I drive him to the airport after his visit in the mountains, he tells me that he loves his life. He uses those words. "I love my life."

He says that his rides with Randy enliven and sustain him. "The high is so so so so much better than drugs ever were," he says. "It is the high of a full life. Riding I feel it all." Yes, I am optimistic. Do I stop worrying? No.

It is June 2. A few days before this year's step-up ceremony at Daisy and Jasper's school — she is stepping up to fourth grade, Jasper to sixth. Karen and I are home in Inverness. Suddenly I feel as if my head is exploding.

People use this as an expression. Not this time. I really feel as if my head is exploding.

"Karen, call 911."

She stares at me a minute, doesn't comprehend what I'm saying. "Are you . . ."

She places the call.

It takes ten or fifteen minutes for three men, carrying boxes and machines and a stretcher, to arrive. They set up near me in the living room. They ask questions and perform a preliminary examination while strapping on a blood-pressure and heart monitor. They ask which hospital I prefer.

I am in the back of an ambulance.

I lie in the ambulance with two men hovering over me. They talk to me. I cannot understand. I am sick, repeatedly throwing up into a plastic receptacle, apologizing.

When the ambulance arrives at the hospital, Karen is waiting in the emergency room with her father. An admitting doctor or nurse discusses options when I hear Don quietly say something.

"Have you considered a subarachnoid hemorrhage? Maybe you should do a CT scan."

The doctor or nurse eyes him with some uncertainty but says, "Yes. We'll do a CT right away."

I am wheeled down a corridor and into an elevator. I am not panicked or fearful that I will die because I am too confused for such a straightforward thought. I feel a strange peacefulness.

I am moved from my gurney onto a long plastic board and from there onto another gurney that moves like a conveyor belt until my head is inside a small tunnel. I am told not to move. White light, a clonking noise, blue light.

I am wheeled back to the emergency room. By then, I don't know. I don't know.

My condition worsens. I hear the phrase *cerebral hemorrhage*. I know only that I have heard of it and can roughly decipher the words *cerebral*, the brain; *hemorrhage*, bleeding.

Late at night Karen goes to her parents', where Jasper and Daisy are asleep. In the morning, early, the telephone rings. Karen, who has not slept much, answers it. A nurse—my nurse—is calling. "I should warn you. He can't speak."

At the hospital, a neurosurgeon takes Karen aside and tells her that he wants to drill a hole into my skull and insert a shunt. "It will alleviate the pressure." She gives her permission.

Karen's sister is a nurse at the University of California Medical Center and her close friend is a neuro-oncologist there. The doctor visits me at the hospital and, after consulting with my surgeon, arranges for me to be moved to the neuro ICU at UC in San Francisco. I take another ambulance ride, this one over the Golden Gate Bridge into the city.

The neuro ICU.

I am crawling out of my skin—too hot, unable to lie still, with drugs to combat drugs—antinausea, antiswelling, anti-coagulant, antipain, blood pressure made higher by the anxiety, requiring more medication that causes more anxiety. I am taped and strapped and stuck with needles and tubes protrude from my body—from my arms and my penis and the top of my head—like Neo in the *Matrix*. At some point my pubic hair is shaved for angiograms. I itch from the morphine. I am blasted by harsh lights and hear/feel ceaseless pounding from shrill monitors.

Nic.

Where is Nic? Where is Nic? Where is Nic? Where is Nic? I must call Nic.

I cannot remember his telephone number.

Three one zero.

What comes next? I wrack my brain.

On a time cube on the bedside table, shimmering numbers, radioactive blue-green, re-form so that the two morphs into a three and the five and nine dissolve into a pair of boxy zeros. Three in the morning.

Three one zero. That is his area code.

If only I could quell the incessant sonarlike pinging. If I could extinguish the humming ice-white lights. If I could recall Nic's telephone number.

The nurse berates me for fiddling with the shunt that sticks out of the top of my head.

I forgot. I'm sorry.

When she's gone, I reach up with my unencumbered hand and trace the plastic tube from where it juts out like a pear stem from the shaved patch at the top of my skull.

The thin hose loops upward like a curling flume to an S hook that dangles from a metal stand. From there, it makes a swan dive, plunging into a sealed plastic bag.

I move my head to the right. A fraction. When I do, I see the tube like an errant artery carrying a trail of clear fluid tinged with red. The liquid, slowly dripping into the bag, is draining spinal and brain fluid. The red is the hemorrhaging blood. A nurse explains again: I am bleeding deep inside my brain in the subarachnoid space. When this happens, it is almost always caused by an aneurism, a weakened spot on an artery that leaks blood. I surmise that often the bleeding is lethal; it can also cause temporary or permanent brain damage.

A new nurse. She pushes buttons on the monitors. "Please, will you help me call my son? I cannot remember his telephone number. I have to call him."

"Your wife will be here in the morning," she says. "She will have the number."

I need the number now.

"Get some sleep. It's too late to call him now anyway."

Voices drone from the nurses' station.

Three one zero.

The telephone number begins three one zero, the area code nearest the beach in Los Angeles.

The beach.

White sand.

Nic is running. He turns onto a fire trail that leads through brush above the canyon near a deserted cove overlooking Malibu. His lanky long body and strong legs running.

In a headband.

Big sneakers and running shorts and a T-shirt tight around his muscular chest.

His eyes the color of tea and clear.

I rely on his voice on the telephone to calm my agonizing

worry even though I know that his voice is adept at deception. I no longer know the truth and yet I will choose to be reassured if I can hear him.

Hey, Dad, it's me. What's happening? Are you all right?

I'm sure he is all right. I am never sure that he is all right.

Three one zero and.

Some of the times when Nic wasn't all right it got so bad that I wanted to wipe out and delete and expunge every trace of him from my brain so that I would not have to worry about him anymore and I would not have to be disappointed by him and hurt by him and I would not have to blame myself and blame him and I would no longer have the relentless and haunting slideshow of images of my lovely son, drugged, in the most sordid, horrible scenes imaginable. Once again: I wished in secret for a kind of lobotomy.

I was in wretched anguish and yearned for relief.

I longed for someone to scrape out every remnant of Nic from my brain and scrape out the knowledge of what was lost and scrape out the worry and not only my anguish but his and the burning inside like I might scrape out the seeds and juicy pulp of an over-ripe melon, leaving no trace of the rotted flesh.

It felt as if nothing short of a lobotomy could alleviate the unremitting pain.

It sinks in: I am in the neuro ICU after a cerebral hemorrhage, not a lobotomy but near enough.

I am in a white room in the Medical Center at the University of California, San Francisco, haunted by sonar monitors and kind nurses asking me if I can remember my name (I cannot) and the year (two thousand fifteen?).

I have had a kind of brain scraping, a potentially lethal one, and I cannot recall my name and the year and yet I am not spared the worrying that only parents of a child on drugs—I suppose any parent of a child in mortal peril—can comprehend.

Is he in mortal peril? His beautiful brain, poisoned, possessed, on methamphetamine. I wanted to remove him erase him elide him from my brain, but he is there, even after this hemorrhage. We are connected to our children no matter what. They are interwoven into each cell and inseparable from every neuron. They supersede our consciousness, dwell in our every hollow and cavity and recess with our most primitive instincts, deeper even than our identities, deeper even than our selves.

My son. Nothing short of my death can erase him. Maybe not even my death.

What is his telephone number?

Nic.

A monitor like a mallet hitting my skull.

"Get some."

"What?"

"Some sleep."

A nurse. Rousing me.

"Nic?"

"Calm down, dear. It's all right. Your blood pressure is up."

More pills and a paper cup of water with which to wash them down.

"Nic—"

"Get some sleep. It will help more than anything."

"My son?"

"Get some sleep."

"Will you please help me dial—"

"Get some sleep."

I am agitated and—apparently—tearing at the shunt. The nurse, looking fatigued and discouraged, is here, having rushed in. She says she will give me another injection of pain medication.

The drugs do not allay my terror. I want to call him to be sure that he is all right. I need to call him. I cannot remember. What is his number? It begins with three one oh.

"Please, dear, go to sleep."

In the morning, Karen is here. A doctor enters. "Can you tell me your name?"

Once again I sadly shake my head.

"Do you know where you are?"

I ponder this for a long time and then ask, "Is that a metaphysical question?"

The doctor doesn't immediately respond. When he finally does, he has decided that, no, a straightforward answer would suffice.

Karen is in tears.

"Who is the president of the United States?"

I stare blankly.

I say: "Will you tell my editor about the suitcase? It is broken. Tell him that the locks don't work."

"The suitcase?"

"Yes, the locks don't work. The suitcase is broken."

"All right. I'll tell him."

The broken suitcase, my brain. Filled with everything I am. I cannot remember my name and I do not know where I am and I cannot remember his telephone number, the digits have spilled from the suitcase with the noise and mess of an overturned bucket of Legos or Nic's collection of tiny seashells from China Beach when he was—was he four? They have spilled out because the lock has broken.

My son is in danger. I cannot forget it even now with my brain awash with toxic blood.

Nic.

"What is your name?"

The nurse again.

"Can you dial my son?"

"What's his telephone number?"

"Three one."

"Yes?"

"I can't."

The nurse injects me with a sedative and painkiller and a thick warm wash fills up my toes and legs and pours into my limbs and it bubbles up like oozing tar. It fills up my belly and chest up through my shoulders and down my arms and into the base of my neck and up the back of my neck and up into my damaged head, soothing. Deathlike sleep beckons like the descent of a dead man with a concrete block on his feet who has been thrown into a bottomless lake and I fall down and down and down and yet even now I wrack my injured brain, What comes after three one zero?

I have my own room, but there is no privacy. The door is open. It is always light. Once or twice I ask Karen or a nurse to open a window for air, but then I get ice cold. Karen's sister visits when she has a few minutes between her rounds in other wards. I feel better when she is here.

And mostly I feel better when Karen is here. She rests on my bed under the neon tubes enclosed in plastic underneath the square white ceiling panels with a constellation of pin-sized holes. She rests with me and she reads to me and I fall asleep. She is juggling the kids, everyone else, everything, our lives, but I want her with me, need her with me. When she is here, everything else falls away—worry, fear. Lying with me, Karen holds my hand and we watch the only television channel that I can tolerate—the only plot that I can follow—a broadcast of an unchanging picture of a mountain.

I miss step-up day. I miss Daisy's birthday.

A succession of doctors ask: What is your name? What is the date? Where are you? Who is president? They instruct me to hold out my arms, palms up. How many fingers am I holding? Wiggle your toes. Put pressure against my arm. Now with your feet.

Test after test. They reveal that there is no aneurism. Ten percent of people who come in with a subarachnoid hemorrhage have no aneurism.

More tests.

Today I can answer the doctors' questions.

David Sheff.

June 11, 2005.

San Francisco at the Medical Center.

I twist completely inside out from feeling extremely unlucky — how did I get here? — to feeling like the luckiest person in the world. If I need confirmation, it comes when they tell me that I am ready to begin to move a bit. I try walking. I am shaky. With a nurse's help, I drag myself out of my room and move down the drab yellow neon-lit corridor past a YOUR SAFETY IS OUR GOAL sign. I see into other patients' open doors. One man is unconscious in his hospital bed. He has scars like the stitching on a football on his shaved skull. Another man sits up in bed rambling. A woman, knocked out, and then a man and then another man have blackened eye sockets, almost as if their eyes have been gouged out.

On my walks, I see the ill and maimed, the frightened and feeble, fighting to stay alive. There is a window near the ICU that looks out at San Francisco — you can see the new, twisting, copper-skinned De Young Museum in Golden Gate Park, rows of Victorian houses and blocky apartments. I look at them and then back at the faces that pass by me in the corridor — a tremulous, shrunken yellow-haired ghost with palsy, grasping a metal walker in his white claws, and a shriveled woman with petrified eyes on a gurney pushed by an aide.

Jasper and Daisy come to see me. Their light fills the room. I reassure them. I'm going to be fine. They scramble into my bed. I can't respond too much and I worry that it scares them, but I can't do anything other than tell them I love them. I thought it would be good for them to see me, that I'm all right, but maybe my judgment isn't the best it has ever been.

Nic calls.

Nic calls.

Nic.

Is fine.

Nic has been speaking to Karen every day since I arrived in the hospital. He jokes about the hole in my head. He says that he is coming up to visit me.

Nic is fine.

After two weeks, Karen drives me home. From bed, I see the garden through the room's glass doors. I am stunned by color, the greens of every leaf, plant stalk, and cypress needle. And soft white. Hydrangeas. Sun yellow. Roses. Lavender. Violets growing from the cracks on the terraced stepping stones. I watch a small bird with purple feathers preen and flutter its wings in the birdbath.

I eat ripe peaches. They are all I want to eat.

I sleep most of the time, but play Crazy 8s and Nickels with Jasper, and Daisy reads to me. Every day. Nic and I talk on the phone. Karen and I lie in bed together side by side, she reading the *Times* and me trying to read a sentence in a magazine. Finally I make it through a capsule review in *The New Yorker*. When I make it through a Talk of the Town piece I feel as if I have earned a Ph.D.

Karen and I hold hands. I am swept over by the elusive, pure, and precious feeling that settles here with us in bed.

Karen and I walk together through the garden.

"Nic called. He'll be here in a couple hours. How do you feel about seeing him?"

"I can't wait."

Nic pops through the front door and is met by barking Brutus, followed by charging Daisy and Jasper. I can hear them from my room.

"Hi, Nicky."

"Nic."

"Bop!"

"Nickypoo!"

"Dais!"

"Hey."

"Ouch."

"Nicky."

Barking.

"Boinkers."

"Poopyboy."

Then Karen.

"Hey, Mamacita!"

"Sputnik."

"KB."

"So good."

"And you."

"To see you."

"How was?"

"Quick. Fine."

"Good."

"The drive."

"You, too."

"I got a football."

"Foosball?"

"Do you want to draw?"

"But."

"Football."

"To play?"

"Yes, but."

"I have chalk."

"Chalk? In a."

"Will you tell us a PJ?"

"Yes, yes, yes. But."

"Are . . ."

"Where's the old man?"

Trailed by the kids and Karen, Nic comes into my bedroom. I want to greet him properly. I shakily stand and we hug.

"So."

"So."

"Hey, Pop."

"Hey, Nic."

"So good to see you."

"You, too."

I sleep for long chunks of every day, but Nic sits with me and holds my hand. When I sleep, he goes off for a bike ride. He brought his bike, threw it in the back of the car he recently bought from an AA friend. Standing there in bike shorts with their padded bottom and a shirt with a Motorola logo and calf-high socks and bike shoes that clip onto the pedals. He leaves the house for a ride down our road and then west along the Tomales Bay. I imagine him riding along the bay where he played and grew up and kayaked and swam and did drugs with his friends on the beaches riding out along the peninsula, along the long bay out past ranches and the Estero where we surfed.

Back from the ride, he checks on me, peeking in, sits with me. He says: "I thought we were going to lose you."

I eye him closely. "That's a switch."

I am ready to sleep, and Nic goes into the kids' room to play with Jasper and Daisy. Then the next day, too quickly for us all, he has to get back to work. He leaves in the evening, drives south again, back to LA.

Each day I seem to feel a little better for a little longer. "Many patients with a subarachnoid hemorrhage do not survive long enough to reach a hospital," according to a medical Web site I find online. "Of those who do, about 50 percent die within the first month of treatment."

In the mornings and again before dark, Karen encourages me to walk with her in the garden. I complain, but make it as far as her studio before I return to bed exhausted.

I am trying to make sense of what happened and what will happen. I don't even know what I want to happen. Somehow I want to get back to normal and yet I don't. I don't want things to go exactly back to normal. That is, I do not want to get back to the normal of worry about Nic.

Sometimes I panic about the future. Sometimes I feel weak and pained about the past. But for today, Jasper and Daisy are fine. He is at camp for the week. She swims in the morning and then comes home. She reads me a book, *Love, Ruby Lavender.* Nic has moved again, this time into an apartment in Hollywood. He's excited to have a place with friends. He called this morning on his way to meet Randy for a bike ride down the coast.

I turn my time in the hospital around and around in my recovering mind. I cannot forget when I couldn't remember his number, and I am struck anew that a brain hemorrhage—even that—could not remove the worry about him. I recall the many occasions when he was gone, on the streets, God knows where, when I fantasized that I could scrape him out of my brain, if only

I could get a lobotomy, the eternal sunshine of a spotless mind, and I would no longer agonize about him, and agonize for him. I am grateful now to have it all — even the worry and the pain. I no longer want a lobotomy, no longer want him erased. I will take the worry in order to take what has come through as the most important emotion after my hemorrhage.

Some people may opt out. Their child turns out to be whatever it is that they find impossible to face — for some, the wrong religion; for some, the wrong sexuality; for some, a drug addict. They close the door. Click. Like in mafia movies: "I have no son. He is dead to me." I have a son and he will never be dead to me.

I do not relish but I am used to the perpetual angst and humming anxiety and intermittent depression that comes with Nic's addiction. I don't remember me before this. I am accustomed to the way that joy can be fleeting and I can sometimes fall into a dark pit. However, living with this over time, I am now being allowed — allowing myself? — to crawl up out of the pit and lift the veil that covers it and to witness, with visual and aural and tactile acuity, a slightly altered world, slightly brighter, richer, and vivider. I well up with tears for it. For all of it. On the one hand: the uncertain future. The possibility of another hemorrhage. The chance that my children will be killed in a car accident. The chance that Nic will relapse. A million other catastrophes. On the other: compassion and love. For my parents and family. For my friends. For Karen. For my children. I may feel more fragile and vulnerable, but I experience more consciousness.

People who go through life-threatening experiences like mine talk about how everything becomes clear for them. They describe a revised understanding of what's important and what isn't. They usually say that they appreciate more than ever their loved ones and their friends. These survivors say that they have learned to cut out the extraneous in their lives and live for the moment. I don't feel as if everything is clear. In some ways, everything is less clear. Rather than less to consider, I have more—because of a heightened sense of mortality. Yes, I'm no less certain that my loved ones and friends mean more than anything. That was never a problem for me; I appreciated them from the start. I am no less certain that I should enjoy the moment—appreciate what I have. I am no less convinced that I am lucky for so many things and most of all lucky to be alive. I have glimpses of the grandeur and the miracle, even as I feel the inexorable slide of time. The children growing up, with both the sadness and excitement of it. Mostly the inevitability of it. I feel it all.

I am getting out more now. I take long walks in the solitary, mysterious woods tranquil and silent and see more intensely the color—still more greens, an infinite number, and the shoots and buds on woody branches before they open. I see a darting rabbit and, overhead, red-tailed hawks, great blue herons, and an osprey. God or no god, this barely ponderable and impossible-to-understand system of complexity and beauty is profound enough to feel like a miracle. Consciousness feels like a miracle. The constellation of these impulses that we call love feels like a miracle. The miracles do not cancel out evil, but I accept evil in order to participate in the miraculous. Nic, do you have a sense of your higher power now?

He has been sober for more than a year. Again. A year and a half.

He called this morning on his way to meet Randy for a bike ride down the coast. Jasper and Daisy and their cousins are outside playing on a homemade Slip n' Slide. Their laughter filters in through the light-filled leaves. I am left with a hole in my head, though my doctor has told me that it will grow together. I am left with a thought about Nic's head, too, a hopeful one. I recall Dr. London and her computer scans. Now that Nic has reached the year and a half anniversary of his last experience with meth or any other drug, I have in my mind Dr. London's PET scan on her computer screen — the brain of her control group with a balanced chemistry and the normal fluctuations of the neurotransmitters in proportion to life events. I wonder if it is once again a picture of my son's brain.

D aisy sits near me on a boulder alongside the Big Sur River. It's late summer on a cool evening inside a cathedral of towering redwoods. They have furrowed bark like a topographical map and thick, sweet-smelling canopies that shoot skyward like medieval church spires. The day is gray with fog. We are sitting outside of our tent, which Jasper and I managed to set up. This is no small accomplishment for us.

After the hospital stint and recovery time at home, having missed much of June and July, I am trying to squeeze every last drop out of summer, clawing into the waning season, desperate to slow its departure. I am as ready as I ever will be to fully return to the living. It's time. The kids are going back to school in a week. My head is, they tell me, mended. The lock on the suitcase is repaired. And so I step out beyond the garden, beyond Inverness. Karen, Jasper, Daisy, and I fit in a few days' hiking and playing on the beaches of the Big Sur coast. Sitting at our camping spot aside the river, under these glorious trees, Daisy pronounces it a "beauteous day."

We plan a hike, stopping first at a store to buy sandwiches. "It's a convenience store, but it's not very convenient," observes Jasper. "It's closed." We drive on and play a modified version of twenty questions. In the kids' game, seventy or more questions are allowed.

Jasper is a "thing" that begins with h. It's taking us forever to guess what he is.

We try another store. It's open.

Back in the car, Jasper reminds us, "I start with an *h*."

"Are you edible?"

"Are you bigger than Brutus?"

"Are you man-made?"

"Are you a hole?" Daisy says.

"What?"

"A hole."

"How did you guess?"

"I peeked."

"You peeked into my brain?"

With a pack filled with a picnic lunch, we hit the trail, walking through a forest of Monterey cypress. We turn a corner and see, on a boulder near the trail, a California condor. In 1982, there were fewer than twenty-five of these magnificent creatures left in the wild, but now, because of the efforts of environmental groups devoted to preserving them, there may be more than two hundred. Here is one: a survivor, hope for its species, cocking its head, staring at us, and then, dramatically unfolding its expansive wings, gliding out onto a wind current over the Pacific.

Just as we arrive back to the car, my cell phone rings.

"Yo, what's happenin'?" It's Nic.

We talk awhile and then he asks to say hi to the others. I pass the phone around. Nic tells stories about the people with whom he works. The kids and Karen tell Nic about our adventures in Big Sur. He wishes them a happy new school year.

It's late in the day, with the sun setting. Time to return home. Our vacation is over. We drive on.

"Pause," says Daisy. In spite of our admonitions, she clicks her retainer in and out.

"I have been thinking," she says, apropos of nothing. "On the last day of my life, I would eat tons of sweets, because it wouldn't matter if you got cavities or if the food was bad for you, would it?"

She continues: "Actually it would be sad to be old, because you guys would be dead." She is indicating Karen and me. "Even Jasper, because I'm the youngest. But you know, I don't think I will be so scared to die. I think it's like today: the end of a vacation when you are ready to go home."

On Tuesday morning, Jasper and Daisy have first-day jitters. On Tuesday afternoon, though, they are enthusiastic, telling us about their teachers and their friends. Jasper is in sixth grade now. It's the first year that he changes classes for math, English and history, science, and other subjects. Daisy adores her new teacher, who has asked the students to write a letter to her about their lives so she can get to know them better.

"Dear Laura," Daisy writes. "I'm really looking forward to fourth grade. I want to get better at math. Spanish is not my cup of tea, but Señor Leon is funny. I do like science. I really like to read . . .

"I just got a retainer and it's hard to say G. I'm getting better at it, though. It's still hard not to flip it around in my mouth."

There's lots more—about her favorite foods and the dogs. "Jasper used to call Moondog Moongoggy," she writes. "Moondog died of cancer." The letter concludes: "My brother was a smoky guy, but he stopped. Don't worry it's not Jasper. It's Nic. He lives in LA. My dad David got a brain hemrij but he's better. Jasper flipped over on his bike. I don't want to tell you too much bad news, but I zippered my eye in my jacket. Now it's fine. Everything is A okay now. Love, Daisy"

After summer hours, mornings are a challenge, but we get the kids to school on time today.

I'm writing again. I am writing again after being unable to write a word.

This afternoon, Jasper has soccer (biding his time until lacrosse season, he joined the school's team), and Daisy and I go for a walk. After collecting Jas, we head to Nancy and Don's for the weekly dinner.

The kids are playing on the indoor swing. "Put on some shoes," Nancy scolds. "You'll get a splinter."

After a roast with Yorkshire pudding, peas, and scalloped potatoes, we decide to spend the night so we don't have to drive back to Inverness. The kids do their homework — Daisy is practicing her multiplication tables and spelling words like *cormorant*, and Jasper is writing a book report on *The Giver* — and then they read. Afterward, the four of us gather in the downstairs bedroom where Karen reads aloud. We are on to the new Harry Potter.

Dumbledore says to Harry, "Numbing the pain for a while will make it worse when you finally feel it."

And then we come to this.

All in all, the temptation to take another gulp of Felix Felicis was becoming stronger by the day, for surely this was a case for, as Hermione put it, "tweaking the circumstances"?

Finally Harry takes the drug.

"What does it feel like?" whispered Hermione.

Harry did not answer for a moment. Then, slowly but surely, an exhilarating sense of infinite opportunity stole through him; he felt as though he could have done anything, anything at all . . .

He got to his feet, smiling, brimming with confidence.

"Excellent," he said. "Really excellent. Right . . ."

The kids are asleep.

Karen and I walk up the narrow staircase to the drafty third-floor corner bedroom that looks out over trees that creak like rocking chairs. I check my answering machine in Inverness. I hear Nic's voice. It's brittle, breaking up.

He is crying.

No. Why.

"Please call me," he says.

I check the time. He called about three hours ago.

Nic answers on the second ring.

His voice is slurry, sticking to itself, his tongue in the way.

"I want to tell you what's been going on," he says. "I want to tell you the truth. Three days ago we were at a party. Z. did a line. She asked me to do some with her. And I did. If she was going to go out, I was not going to let her go alone."

Z. is the girl who broke his heart after their short time together. Before he relapsed last time. He's with her again, moved from his new apartment into hers.

"Nic. No."

"We've been high since then. Speed balls and meth." Speed balls are a combination of heroin and cocaine.

"Now I took a sleeping pill to come down. I know I fucked up. I'm going to stop."

I tell Nic the only thing I know to say and what I know he isn't ready to hear.

"You know who to call. Get help. Before it's too late. You and Z. both need help. You can't be together until you are well and sober."

He hangs up.

No. No. No. No. No. No. No. No. No. No. No. No.

What was it this time? Approaching two years. The researchers said that it can take two years for a user's brain to fully recover. Nic has never made it two years since all this started.

An eruption of the same old worry—all that could happen to him—but then I become overwhelmed by fatigue and fall asleep, my worry settling into a newly carved-out nook in my remodeled brain. Maybe this reflects something else that shifted in the hospital—the character if not the volume of the worry. Lying in the neuro ICU, I came to another startling realization when it dawned on me that Nic—and not only him, but Jasper and Daisy, too—would survive my death. It's not that they would be unaffected, but they would survive it. Possibly because there's a time in their lives when children are dependent on their parents, we tend to forget that they can and will survive without us. I did. By now, though, through Nic's addiction, I have learned that I am all but irrelevant to Nic's survival. It took my near death, however, to comprehend that his fate—Jasper's and Daisy's, too—is separate from mine. I can try to protect my children, to help and guide them, and I can love them, but I cannot save them. Nic, Jasper, and Daisy will live, and someday they will die, with or without me.

In the morning, I contemplate whether to tell the kids about Nic. In Daisy's letter to her teacher, she wrote, "My brother was a smoky guy." I suppose that is her way of summing up the drugs. And she said: "Everything is A okay now." I want everything to stay A-okay for her for at least a little while.

I had so much wanted to end my book with Nic's letter to Jasper. It served too perfectly as a neat bow on the package, a happy ending. I wanted it to be the happy ending of our family's story about meth. I wanted to move on from it. I wanted this now to be the post-Nic's-addiction phase of our lives. But no. It is still so easy to forget that addiction is not curable. It is a lifelong disease that can go into remission, that is manageable if the one who is stricken does the hard, hard work, but it is incurable.

Nic's latest relapse is an undeniable measure of the relentlessness of this disease. It's not a new revelation, but a different iteration. Everything was going well for him. He had a girlfriend, so we cannot blame his loneliness. We cannot blame work that bores him, because he seems to enjoy his job and adore his coworkers. He considers them his good friends. He has a book deal and a shot at a job as an assistant editor at a magazine. His movie reviews have led to a few interviews and a review for *Wired* magazine. Perhaps most significant, he has a close group of friends who seem dear to one another.

All of this is irrelevant now.

Despite my knowledge that addiction does not respond to logic, I have held onto a vestige of an idea that the trappings of a life — girlfriend, job, money, solid friendships, a desire to do right by those you love — can make it OK, but they don't.

Please God heal Nic.

When I was in the hospital, many people told me they prayed for me, and I am enormously grateful to them. I never prayed. Perhaps I cannot pray because I never have, I do not know how, and I cannot conceive of a god to pray to. But as John Lennon said: "God is a concept by which we measure our pain." Here I am with Nic using again and I know that there is nothing I can do and I cannot believe that we are here again and that the next telephone call could be the one I have feared for the past half-dozen years, and I am praying.

Please God heal Nic. Please God heal Nic. Please God heal Nic.

It's my plea to whatever higher power there is, the one they — they in the endless rehabs, the endless meetings — the one they promise is out there listening. I repeat it inside my head sometimes even without knowing I am saying it: Please God heal Nic.

I pray even as the news in the papers makes my prayer seem insignificant in scale and wholly selfish. There is a devastating hurricane and flooding and suicide bombers and crashes and tsunamis and terrorism and cancer and war—endless and brutal war—disease and famine and earthquakes and everywhere there is addiction, and today the heavens must be overwhelmed with the noise of all the prayers.

Here is one more.

Please God heal Nic. Please God heal Nic.

The descent is quick. Nic shows up high at work and loses his job. His phone is disconnected because he does not pay his bill. He deserts every real friend. Saddest, he has deserted his best friend and his sponsor, Randy.

In one message he says that he and his girlfriend have sold their clothes to pay for food. I don't know how they have paid their rent. I don't know how they will pay next month's rent, but soon, unless they have a benefactor or are dealing drugs, they will be homeless.

Today Vicki cannot stop herself, and she drives from the west side of town to his apartment in Hollywood. She wants to see for herself. She wants to see if he is alive.

I pretend that I am not waiting by the phone to hear from her.

She parks her car and apprehensively walks into the apartment building. She pulls open the screen and knocks on the door. There is no answer. The window shades are down. She knocks again. No answer. She knocks again. The door opens a crack. Then wider. The place is filthy—squalor. There is a pool of brown water on the floor. Trash everywhere. Nic, blocking the flood of daylight with his hands, shakily steps into view. Behind him, his girlfriend does, too. It is a scene familiar to me, but new to his mother. Vicki has never seen Nic like this: gaunt, white, nearly yellow, trembling limbs, sunken black circles around vacant eyes.

Z.'s legs are bleeding. When she notices that her legs are uncovered and that Vicki is staring, Z. stammers, "A light bulb broke on the floor. We were cleaning it up."

Nic tells his familiar lies: "We had to go through this. We're done now. We're getting sober."

He asks his mother to leave and to not come back.

Vicki calls and tells me. She sounds like I have felt on many occasions before. She sounds furious and wretched and horrified, emotion so overwhelming that she cannot yet cry.

A week goes by.

It is Sunday and I am driving Daisy to the city to meet a friend and her mother at Washington Square. We meet up with them and walk through the park, from where we watch the Columbus Day Parade. A float is filled with a dozen girls dressed as Queen Isabella. Nic is here. He is six years old. Queen Isabellas float by. This is our neighborhood. Nic is one of the children running toward the climbing structure, climbing up to the tip top, watching the parade from that crow's nest, waving at the queens.

I drive Daisy and her giggly friend across town to a birthday party being held at a ceramics studio. The girls, strapped into the backseat, play a game inspired by the picture book *Fortunately* by Remy Charlip.

The book reads:

Fortunately Ned was invited to a surprise party.

Unfortunately it was a thousand miles away.

Fortunately a friend loaned Ned an airplane.

Unfortunately the motor exploded.

Fortunately there was a parachute on the plane.

Unfortunately there was a hole in the parachute.

"Fortunately she had a very delicious sandwich," says Daisy's friend in the girls' game.

And Daisy's turn:

"Unfortunately she dropped it on the dirty street and along came a slobbery dog, who ate it up."

"Fortunately he threw up the sandwich and it was as good as new."

More giggling.

"Unfortunately a little fuzzy hamster scurried in and grabbed it and took it with him and then he disappeared into a crack in the wall and was never seen from again."

My own version plays in my head.

Fortunately I have a son, my beautiful boy.

Unfortunately he is a drug addict.

Fortunately he is in recovery.

Unfortunately he relapses.

Fortunately he is in recovery again.

Unfortunately he relapses.

Fortunately he is in recovery again.

Unfortunately he relapses.

Fortunately he is not dead.

22

Another week.

Vicki, with whom I speak daily, says that she is numb. I am, too. It's not that I don't worry about Nic — I think about him all the time — but for the moment I am not incapacitated.

Is this where parents wind up?

I walk past more people on the streets, this time in San Rafael. I walk past them and step over them, people alone and abandoned, and, when I do, like always, I think, Where are their parents?, but this time I wonder, Is this the answer? Am I becoming one of them — a parent who has accepted defeat? My agonizing has not helped Nic in the slightest.

I am not pretending that this isn't happening. I am doing all that I can do.

I wait.

A downward spiral.

It's a degenerative disease. I imagine the downward spiral.

No, I am not numb. I wish I were. Sometimes I feel overwhelmed.

I brace myself.

Randy continues to call Nic and leave messages on his dead cell phone. Randy was Nic's lifeline.

Using Z.'s phone, which is still working, Nic calls and leaves more messages. "I just want you to know we're safe. I'm doing fine. We're going to meetings. I'm getting sober."

He claims that the relapse was a one-shot, three-day mistake and he's fine. But the longer he talks, the more it becomes obvious that his voice is the voice of Nic on something.

I wait.

It's like watching from afar, perhaps through binoculars with imperfect lenses, the moments before a train wreck. All of us who love him commiserate. Karen and I. Vicki and I. Randy. We all know. And yet there's nothing we can do. I call Nic back. "Nic, don't forget how dangerous it is when you aren't attending meetings," I say. "Don't forget when you listen to the logic of your brain when it's under the influence."

In recovery, working with Randy, Nic was the one who explained the insidiousness to me: "A using addict cannot trust his own brain—it lies, says, 'You can have one drink, a joint, a single line, just one.'" It tells him, "I have moved beyond my sponsor." It says, "I don't require the obsessive and vigilant recovery program I needed when I was emerging from the relapse." It says, "I am happier and more complete than I have ever been." It says, "I am independent, alive." And so Nic said he couldn't trust his own brain and needed to rely on Randy, meetings, the program, and prayer—yes, prayer—to go forward.

Nic, you have come so far.

Let me quote *you:* "Everything I have will be gone if I don't stay with the program."

Two days later, on Wednesday, Nic calls up slurring and asks for rent money. No. He says that he knew I would say no. He saved it for the end of the conversation, after, "I love you so much. I'm safe. We really fucked up but we're going to be fine now. I just took a little something to help me come down from the meth and coke and smack and . . ."

Vicki says no, too.

Now it is Friday. Nothing on Saturday. Nothing on Sunday. Nothing until Monday when an email arrives.

"hey pop, we're in the desert. Z is doing a commercial, out by joshua tree . . . my phone doesn't get any reception here and I just borrowed this computer for a second from some guy on the set . . . sorry . . . this came up really suddenly . . . anyway, i'll call you when i find a phone that works . . . it's hot, hot here and boring . . . z just doing wardrobe and i'm writing in the shade here . . . don't fret . . . i may have some exciting news too . . . love ya . . . nic"

Joshua Tree.

A respite. An oasis. Maybe Nic will stop on his own. Maybe he'll be OK.

Nothing for two more days, but Nic is in the desert, writing in the shade. There are drugs in the desert, too.

At night, Karen and I switch off reading to the kids. We are nearing the end of Harry Potter. Professor Dumbledore died. He is dead. More than one of the children we know cried for hours when they read this — Albus Dumbledore, Harry's protector with whom these children grew up, is dead. Evil is winning, and I feel weakened by the ceaseless battle.

On Thursday, Jasper has a soccer game after school. Daisy has swimming. Karen and I divide the driving.

I have found a quiet place in a corner of the clubroom near the pool to write. Looking up, out the window through the slats of shutters, I see a dark form curve up and break the water, followed by a pair of kicking feet: Daisy doing her laps. The coach, poised and tanned and lithe, a former All-American swimmer who has taught all three of our children, crouches at the end of the lane, encouraging Daisy and the other swimmers. I lose sight of her among the lines of bodies in their blue suits until she returns back down the lane in the opposite direction, her powerful arms pulling in arching freestyle strokes. I remember when it was her big brother Nic in the water, his lean dolphin body cutting through the pool.

"Hey, you, mister, let's skedaddle."

It is Daisy, dripping after a shower, wrapped in a beach towel.

There is no news.

Some of the panic in which I lived during these crises seems to have lifted. I worry, but I am not sick with worry. I'm getting better. I'm letting go. I'm in abject denial.

It must be like a soldier in a trench in a bombing raid. I have shut down every unessential emotion — worry, fear — concentrating every neuron in my new brain on the moment in order to stay alive.

I am in a silent war against an enemy as pernicious and omnipresent as evil. Evil? I don't believe in evil any more than I believe in God. But at the same time I know this: only Satan himself could have designed a disease that has self-deception as a symptom so that its victims deny they are afflicted, and will not seek treatment, and will vilify those on the outside who see what's happening.

After dinner, Jasper asks me to quiz him on math and his words of the week. Then he and I read a *Mad* magazine together.

In bed, I grab one of the novels on the tottering stack on the nighttable. I will never get through all the books. I'm so tired at night that I read a page, maybe two, and fall asleep. Karen joins me.

A page. Two pages. I am asleep.

The telephone rings. I ignore it. In my half-consciousness I have decided that it's a serviceman we called for an estimate on some repairs. I think, It will wait until morning.

The phone rings again. I'll get the messages tomorrow.

No, Karen says, you had better check.

The first call is Nic's godfather. Nic just called him and left a message. "He's in Oakland." My friend's voice is in a state of alarm. "He says he's in trouble and needs help. I don't know what to do."

My heart pounds.

The next message is from Vicki. Nic called her, too, leaving a similar message. "I lied about Joshua Tree because I didn't want you to worry that I was in Oakland. I'm sober. Please, we're in trouble. We need plane tickets back to LA." He tells a convoluted story about how they got there, but the bottom line is that he and Z. are at the home of a crack addict in Oakland who is out of his mind and they have to get out.

Nic is in Oakland.

Brutus stiffly follows me upstairs, shuffling his weary paws along the concrete. I fill the teakettle and place it on a flame on the stove.

I return Vicki's call. She is unsure what to do — whether or not to pay for a plane ticket. I understand, but, no, I say. If it were me, I would not help unless he wants to go into rehab. Then maybe.

I hang up.

I call my friend. He is calmer than when he left the message. He says, "Listen," and plays the message on his answering machine over the telephone. We hear the slur in Nic's voice. "I need help. I can't call my dad. I don't know what to do, please give me a call." He leaves Z.'s cell phone number.

"It's so sad," my friend says. "Part of me wants to drive to Oakland to get him and part of me wants to wring his neck."

Once again, Nic is here and he is high. For some reason, I'm aberrantly calm as I think, If he is here, what might he do? Might he come to our house? What do I do if he does? Would he go back to Karen's parents' like that time Nancy found him in the downstairs bedroom? Would he break in again?

Karen emerges from our bedroom. She asks, "Do you think he might go back to Nancy and Don's?"

She is worried about the same thing. He probably wouldn't go there, but, would he? We debate whether we should call them. It would worry them. But it would be worse not to warn them and then to have Nic show up. We call them.

Where else might he go?

The next day, Nic leaves another message for his godfather and one for his mother, this time saying that the girlfriend of the crack addict with whom they were staying showed up and gave Nic and Z. money to fly home.

I'm working at the Corte Madera library, a stack of books at my side.

I have brought my laptop and I'm writing and writing, an attempt to contain something that is fast (once again) spiraling out of control.

The phone is on vibrate because of the library and it starts its mad shaking and rattling as if possessed. I pick it up from the table so that the noise doesn't disturb anyone. On the screen, in sickly green letters, I see that it's Nic's girlfriend's phone.

I have no desire to hear more lies. I turn it off.

Later, as I am driving to pick up the kids from school, I listen to the message. Nic says that he and Z. are driving back from Joshua Tree and are finally in cell phone range. He says, word for word: "Hey, Pop, we're driving back from Joshua Tree and we're finally in cell phone range again . . ."

I am struck not just by the lie, but by its intricacy. He could have said, "I'm back in LA." He could have checked in without saying any more than hello. But he thought through the original lie and built on it, bejeweling it with detail so that I would never question it. And I would not have if I didn't already know it was a lie. By now I have heard about the web of lies by addicts. "Substance abusers lie about everything, and usually do an awesome job of it," Stephen King once wrote. "It's the Liar's Disease." Nic once told me, quoting an AA platitude, "An alcoholic will steal your wallet and lie about it. A drug addict will steal your wallet and then help you look for it." Part of me is convinced that he actually believes that he will find it for you.

I listen to the message a few times. I want to remember it.

Did he forget that he called his mother and his godfather and told them that he was in desperate peril in Oakland? After everything, does he assume that my dear friend would not call me if he was worried about Nic, if Nic was desperately in danger in an Oakland crack house? Does he not know by now that his mother, with whom I have ridden this hellish rollercoaster, will of course call to check in with me to talk about what, if anything, we should do? And not only about what to do. Just to talk to the other person who loves Nic like she does.

The message continues. He's not slurring. He sounds fine. He says he misses and loves me.

23

"Hey, papa, it's me, Nic. I just found out that you know the truth of what happened."

I check my messages. Nic called. Again. There's a slurriness. He has talked to Vicki, and he knows that I know that he was in Oakland, not Joshua Tree, and he tries to cover his tracks. "I just didn't want to worry you," he says. "And also I didn't want to be pressured to come see you while I was in the Bay Area and I had no idea this guy was going to turn out to be such a psycho. And neither did Z. We got out of there the best as we could . . . I'm safe now . . . Anyway, I'm sorry I lied to you."

I am in the living room sitting on the couch. Something catches my eye: a pile of newspapers on the floor. On top is an *SF Weekly*. I look closer. A *Bay Guardian* and a flyer from Amoeba Records, his favorite store. I stare at them and it sinks in. No.

I ask Karen if they are hers. No, aren't they yours?

Nic broke in again. I'm certain.

Karen is certain.

We are certain.

No.

Our hearts pound. We start looking around the house.

Karen stops and asks if they could have been left by a friend who was visiting from New York, staying with us last weekend. Could they be his? I call him. The newspapers are his.

We are paranoid and crazy. It's not only the addict who becomes paranoid and crazy.

I haven't returned Nic's calls because I just can't face talking to him now, not until he is sober. Off every drug. Not "I'm just using Klonopin to get off the meth," or "just a Valium to help me come down."

I love him and always will. But I cannot deal with someone who lies to me. I know that sober and clear-headed and in his right mind and in recovery Nic would not lie to me. In a way, I am grateful for the blatancy. It has taken away one thin layer of my uncertainty. Normally I am in some hellish purgatory, not knowing what is true and what isn't, whether he is using or not, but now I know.

I have, above my desk, photographs leaning against books on a shelf. There's a recent picture of Karen and another of her when she was a child, a ruminative, dark-complexioned girl with short hair and a striped sailor shirt on a beach somewhere. She looks like Daisy, or, rather, Daisy, with her sparkling gaze and dark eyes and hair, looks like her. There are also pictures of Daisy. In one she wears moccasins and blue underwear and is closely inspecting Moondog's tolerant face. There's a picture of Jasper when he was an infant in Karen's arms and Jasper dressed up in a red flannel loden coat, silk purple raja pants, a knitted green flannel hat with gold tassels and fluffy pompoms, and, on his feet, genie shoes embroidered with gold thread with curled-up, pointy tips. There are team pictures of Daisy and Jasper posed in their swim goggles and Jasper posed with a lacrosse stick. There are pictures of Nic. In one he is about ten, wearing jeans, a blue zippered sweatshirt and blue sneakers. His hands are in his pockets and he looks at the camera with a gentle smile. There is a more recent picture of Nic, too. A broad smile, in baggy trunks and bare-chested, from when he met us in Hawaii. It's my son and my friend Nic in recovery, and he is all right.

I cannot bear to have it stare down at me. I put it in a desk drawer.

Jasper has become adept with Garage Band, a music recording and mixing computer program. He has constructed a haunting and beautiful song.

"It's a sad song," I say as I enter the room where it's playing.

"Yes," he replies quietly.

"Are you sad?"

"Yes."

"About?"

"We ran the mile at school today. I couldn't think about anything but Nic."

I tell Jasper that there are places we can go where other kids with brothers or sisters or parents with alcohol or drug problems go.

"What do you do there?"

"You don't have to do anything. You can just listen to what other kids say. It can help. If you want you can say something."

"Oh."

"Do you want to try it?"

"I think so."

He hugs me tighter and longer than he ever has before.

In the morning, the sun shines through a hole in a gray-black sky. It's like a klieg light is shining on the garden. There is a yellow circle surrounded everywhere by a diffused patchwork of gold, rust, and dying white hydrangea — the dying colors of autumn. The poplar trees are nearly bare; all but a few leaves are gone and the trees' naked white branches reach skyward into the gray shimmering light. Only the magnolia has blooms — three white flames.

A load of firewood was delivered for the winter season. This morning my goal is to stack it with the kids. As we work, I am thinking about, what else, Nic. I am neither optimistic nor pessimistic. I don't know what will happen. I believe deeply in his good soul and brain and at the same time I have no illusions about the severity of this illness. No, to be honest, right now I do not feel optimistic at all.

It comes down to where Nic is. I'm optimistic — not overly optimistic but optimistic — when he's in recovery, disconsolate and pessimistic when he isn't.

Strangely, the thought of being cut off from Nic used to send me into a panic, but now — today, at least, today at this moment, at least — I am all right with the concept. But then I think, Nic could die. Stacking wood, I think, Nic could die. I stop for a moment.

I would miss having Nic in my life. I would miss his funny phone messages and his humor, the stories, our talks, our walks, watching movies with him, dinners together, and the transcendental feeling between us that is love.

I would miss all of it.

I miss it now.

And here it sinks in: I don't have it now. I have not had it whenever Nic has been on drugs.

Nic is absent, only his shell remains. I have been afraid — terrified — to lose Nic, but I have lost him.

In the past, I tried to imagine the unimaginable and I tried to imagine bearing the unbearable. I imagined losing Nic by overdose or accident, but now I comprehend that I have already lost him. Today, at least, he is lost.

I have been terrorized by the fear that he would die. If he did, it would leave a permanent crack in my soul. I would never fully recover. But I also know that if he were to die, or for that matter, if he stays high, I would live on — with that crack. I would grieve. I would grieve forever. But I have been grieving for him since the drugs took over — grieving for the part of him that is missing. It must be grief. At least it feels exactly like Joan Didion describes it in *The Year of Magical Thinking:* "Grief comes in waves, paroxysms, sudden apprehensions that weaken the knees and blind the eyes and obliterate the dailiness of life." (Ah, so that is what they are. It's a relief to know.)

I grieve, but I also continue to celebrate the part of him that is untouchable by meth or any other drug. I will never let a drug take that from me.

"Insanity is the insistence on meaning," wrote Frank Bodart in a poem. Yes, but this human brain of mine requires meaning—at least an approximation of meaning. The meaning I have come to is that Nic on drugs is not Nic but an apparition. Nic high is a ghost, a specter, and when he is high my lovely son is dormant, pushed aside, hidden away and buried in some inaccessible corner of his consciousness. My faith, such as it is, comes with a belief that Nic is in there and he—Nic, his essence, his self—is whole, safe, and protected. Nic strong and clear and filled with love—Nic may never again emerge. The drug may win the battle for his body. But I can live knowing that Nic is in there somewhere and that the drug cannot touch him where he is in there somewhere he is there.

Whatever happens I will love Nic. Somewhere in that place he knows this. And I know.

I look over at the pile of unstacked wood. We have barely made a dent in it. The kids are whining and don't want to work. They look dejected and sullen. Jasper's head falls back, his eyes are closed, and he exhales loudly. He grumpily tosses a log onto the sagging pile. My head rings. I hear a truck grinding up the hill.

There is currently no ongoing Al-Anon group for kids as young as Jasper and Daisy. (Alateen is for older children.) So I call around for recommendations of other places to go for help. I want them to know that they aren't alone, it's not their fault, and that though the drugs have stolen Nic from them, they can still love their adored and adoring brother. I want Jasper to try to understand that Nic meant everything he wrote in his note to him. But Nic's illness is bigger than his best intentions — his desire to do right by himself and others. The Nic who wrote the note is gone, at least for now. We need to figure out a way to help the little children grieve for their brother.

The devoted librarians at their school send out a request to a network of their fellow librarians at schools around the country. The response is overwhelming. I am forwarded a list of books about kids dealing with a situation like ours — about the guilt and responsibility one feels and the questions that adults can hardly comprehend, never mind children. The counselor at their school tracks down a therapist who works with families and specializes in addiction. Karen and I will meet with him and then, if it feels as if it might be useful, bring Jasper and Daisy with us to meet him.

One day I am driving Daisy and Jasper home from school. As we reach the crest of the hill above Olema, gold and dry in autumn, marking the entrance to West Marin, Daisy looks up from the scarf she's making and says, "It's like Nic is like my brother who I know and this other guy who I don't."

She puts her knitting aside. Then she says that yesterday they discussed drugs in Girls on the Run, a group of fourth-, fifth-, and sixth-grade girls who run and talk about personal and social issues — everything from body image to nutrition. The girls split into groups to discuss why kids start drinking alcohol, smoking, or using drugs.

"What were the reasons?" I ask.

"They are mad at themselves," she says. "Monica says peer pressure. Janet said, somebody gets stressed, and I thought, because you want to get out of yourself.

"We talked about ways to deal with stress or sadness or things like that and said it would be smarter to think of ways to feel good about yourself and to do things that make you feel happy, like running, rather than to do drugs."

Jasper has been quiet, thoughtful. He says, "I was talking about drugs on my field trip, too." His grade just returned from spending the night on icy-cold and fogbound Angel Island. He says that he and a friend, shivering through the dark night, talked. "He asked me how Nic is doing," Jasper says. "I said that he is using drugs again."

His friend, who had read the *Times* article, said, "But your brother seems so smart and like such a nice kid."

Jasper says, "I told him, 'I know. He is.'" He repeated the story about the cartoon angel and devil on Nic's shoulder and also said that he is going to talk to someone about it—a person who helps people who have addicts in their families learn how to deal with it.

In the past, Jasper and Nic have sent each other messages from my cell phone to Nic's—one-line greetings. Now Jasper, thinking about his brother, asks if he can send one.

He writes: "Nic, B smart. Love, Jasper."

He sends it even though Nic's cell phone has been shut down. "Maybe he'll turn it back on," Jasper says.

So much about this disease is grieving. Grief is interrupted by hope, hope by grief. Then our grieving is interrupted by a new crisis. From the Shakespeare by the bed, I read:

> Grief fills the room up of my absent child,
> Lies in his bed, walks up and down with me,
> Puts on his pretty looks, repeats his words,
> Remembers me of all his gracious parts,
> Stuffs out his vacant garments with his form;
> Then have I reason to be fond of grief.

I rage against his struggle and pain and how his addiction has caused so much pain in our lives—ours, his—and I am also filled with boundless love for him, the miracle of Nic and all he has and all he has brought to our lives. I rage against this God I don't believe in and yet pray to and thank him for Nic and for the hope that I have—yes, even now. Maybe it's that my brain is bigger now: it can hold more than it could hold before. It can more easily tolerate contradictions, such as the idea that relapses can be part of recovery. As Dr. Rawson said, it sometimes takes many of them before an addict stays sober. If they don't die or do too much damage, there's a chance, always a chance.

I look back at the dismal statistics I was given years ago by a nurse about the success rates for rehab of meth addicts—single-digit success. I understand that it's unrealistic to think that many addicts will stay sober forever after one or two or three or however many tries at sobriety, but maybe the more meaningful statistic is this, related by one of the lecturers at a rehab: "More than half of the people who enter rehab are sober ten years out, which doesn't mean that they haven't been in and out of sobriety."

It's a sad, sad time, but I am grateful for the miracle that Nic is alive and has a chance. Maybe it will take a bigger miracle to save him. When we named him, we consulted my father. His full name is Nicolas Eliot Sheff. His initials spell the Hebrew word for "miracle." I pray for a bigger miracle, but in the meantime I am grateful for the one we have. Nic is alive. Writing about his son, Thomas Lynch described the unexpected conclusions parents reach when we confront something as overwhelming as a child's addiction: "I could be thankful even for this awful illness—cunning, baffling, and powerful—that has taught me to weep and laugh out loud and better and for real. And thankful that, of all the fatal diseases my son might have gotten, he got one for which there is this little sliver of hope that if he surrenders, he'll survive."

*

In the morning, Jasper, wearing a berry-colored sweater, sits at my desk, where he plays a new computer game. Along with the sound of computer-generated music, crashing cymbals, a French horn, and booming bass, Jasper talks to the screen. "What? Eh eh eh. Gotcha."

Daisy closes her book and moves to the round table where Karen is working on a collage. Soon she is cutting, painting, and pasting paper, too.

Nic called and left another message last night. He said that he and his girlfriend "brought things way too far" and now plan to get sober. He explained that he talked to a doctor about it and was given some medication to help.

Of course I don't believe it. His meaningless words these days are another sad fact of his addiction, belying their genuineness when he is sober.

I wait. For Nic to hit some sort of bottom. It sinks in after everything we have been through and everything I have read and heard. Addicts ultimately recover when they hit bottom. They become desperate and hopeless and terrified; they must be so desperate and so hopeless and so terrified that they will be willing to do anything to save their lives. But how could Nic's overdose in New York, when he was rushed to the emergency room—unconscious, near death—not have been hitting bottom? How could his subsequent nightmarish relapse not have been hitting bottom? I don't know. All I do know is that Nic is back in a state of drugged fantasy, holding onto the illusions that allow him to deny the seriousness of his situation. It's what addicts do. I am fearful knowing that Nic will remain in this deluded state until the next dramatic event. What event? We must wait for it, meanwhile knowing that it might never arrive. Before many addicts hit bottom, they die. Or some wind up half-dead, paralyzed or brain-damaged, after a stroke or something similar.

This is true of most drugs and certainly with meth, which can turn a brain into misfiring mush.

Parents want only good things for their children. Yet here, in mortal combat with addiction, a parent wishes for a catastrophe to befall his son. I wish for a catastrophe, but one that is contained. It must be harsh enough to bring him to his knees, to humble him, but mild enough so that he can, with heroic effort and the good that I know is inside him, recover, because anything short of that will not be enough for him to save himself.

A friend whose mother was an alcoholic told me that he spent a decade hoping for a "near miss" — something dramatic enough to bring his mother into treatment for her illness, but not too dramatic — nothing permanently debilitating. The near miss never came. His mother died two months ago. When my friend and his sisters cleaned his parents' home, they uncovered empty vodka bottles hidden in the backs of cupboards behind china and empty bottles buried under neatly folded sweaters in closets. When she died, his mother had thirty times the legal driving limit of alcohol in her body.

I wish for a near miss for Nic.

I pray for a near miss.

24

There's nothing to be done, we have to do everything we can do. We have done everything we can do, we have more to do. Vicki and I agonize over it.

After Nic calls again, high, asking for money, Vicki says, "We have to try."

I wonder about an intervention, but think that after everything we have done, it's ridiculous and hopeless.

"You can't control it."

But I cannot let Nic go. Not yet. Soon? Not yet.

I cannot let Nic go.

I will not let Nic go unless I am forced to. I may be.

You didn't cause it, you can't control it, you can't cure it.

I know.

There's a lot I don't know, but I have learned some lessons about addiction. Though there are some wrong courses of action to take, there is no predetermined right course. No one knows. Since relapse is often part of recovery, Nic still may get it. Nic can still be OK.

I go over the endless stories of people I have met in the rehab groups or at AA and Al-Anon meetings and the stories of friends of friends for whom it took multiple tries. Some of them hit bottom — unthinkably horrible bottoms — and literally dragged themselves from crack houses, from gutters, from dealers' dens, from pools of their own blood into rehab or detox or to an AA meeting or to their parents' doorstep. Others got to rehab because their wives gave them an ultimatum; the court ordered them; their parents forced them; or their friends and family orchestrated interventions. A woman who hears about our plight calls and says, "I just want to say don't give up. My son would be dead if I had given up. I decided to do it one last time. This is after seven rehabs and hospitals and arrests and two suicide attempts. Now my son, who is twenty-five, has been sober for three years and he is better than he has ever been in his entire life. People told me to give up on him, but I didn't. How does a mother give up on her son? If I had, he wouldn't be here now. That's a guarantee. He would have died. I called just to tell you this story. Do not give up hope and do not give up on him."

If it were legal, I would hire someone to kidnap Nic and forcibly take him to a hospital for detox with the hope that sober again—at least with a window out of the deranged and deluded drugged state of mind—he would try. I have heard stories about parents who hired people to kidnap their adult children. I would consider breaking the law and suffering the consequences if I thought it would work, but I don't think it would. Nic would flee. If he was unready to be treated, he would flee. Yet it feels too risky to wait for him to bottom out.

Karen and I decide that we will help pay the cost of rehab if we can get him to go. Again. His mother says that she will, too. We have decided to pay one more time. Yes, we know that it could be wasted money. We agree that this is the last time, because rehab can become a lifestyle for some addicts. After this, if Nic relapses and wants help, he will have to do it on his own, relying on the sorely limited public resources available to addicts. Maybe it would be more useful if he crawled on his hands and knees into a publicly funded program begging for help. Would he do so? There are programs in many cities, but they are overcrowded. There are waiting lists. It's likely that it would take Nic two to four months to get into one.

We may not have that long.

Sometimes I am all right. Is this what they call letting go? I have let go if letting go means that I am all right sometimes. I leave the crisis behind for periods of each day. I enjoy the time I spend with Karen and Daisy and Jasper and our friends. Yesterday Daisy and I had our book group. Last evening Jasper and I went on a thrilling bike ride past egrets and curlews on the trails through Corte Madera Marsh. Sometimes I am fine, sometimes I am not.

I consult more experts. After our experience, I am not naive enough to believe that any expert has the answer to our family's problem. But I am not arrogant enough to think that I know the answer, either. I will not blindly follow anyone's advice, but I gather information and will weigh it and decide what, if anything, to do. I know more than I did at the start of this thing. I know that no one knows the answer to what is right for Nic or any other addict. No one knows what will work. No one knows how many times. This neither compels a loved one to act nor impels him not to.

Over the past few years, I have come to know and respect and trust a few of the experts more than others. Dr. Rawson at UCLA knows as much about methamphetamine as anyone. As a researcher, he has no agenda other than fact and truth. He is devoted to his work for one reason, to help addicts.

I email him and ask if he thinks that, after everything we have been through, trying an intervention is crazy, an exercise in futility. I fully expect to hear back the conventional wisdom—Nic has to hit bottom. I expect him to tell me that I should do my best to let go.

Instead, he warns me that intervention is no cure-all. He warns me that it is risky. In addition, he says that he doesn't know of data that would support (or shoot down) intervention. "But," he writes, "my impression is that some [interventionists] are quite good at organizing a family's response and creating a process and intervention event that results in a resistant addict getting into treatment more quickly than if they had waited until the addict 'hits bottom.' This is not an insignificant contribution, since 'hitting bottom' is a tautology. When a person finally gets sober and remains sober for an extended period, the bad stuff that happened immediately prior to that is referred to as 'hitting bottom.' Similar periods of awfulness that are equally awful but don't lead to sobriety are, by definition, not hitting bottom. Some people die before they 'hit bottom.' I don't think 'hitting bottom' is a useful construct. So I do think interventions can be helpful in getting resistant people into treatment. However, they don't give guarantees of outcomes at 1, 5 or 10 years post intervention. And they can be expensive."

Then he says what decides it for me. Forget theory, forget statistics, forget efficacy studies. What would he do if Nic were his son?

"If I had a child who was addicted to meth and I had done everything I could think of to get them help and they still were engaged in the dangerous, life threatening behavior of meth (or heroin, cocaine or alcohol) use, I would seriously consider using an interventionist. My thinking about this is the same as if I had a kid who had a relapsing chronic illness of other types, I would keep pushing them toward treatment to the extent I had resources to do it. All of my support would be linked to their entry into treatment."

It seems mad to try again—how can you help someone who doesn't want to be helped? But it doesn't matter. We will try again. His mother and stepfather and Karen and I will try again.

An AA saying is that trying the same thing and expecting different results is the height of insanity. But a repeated message of rehab is that it may take multiple tries for someone to get and stay sober. I think of the children of the people who wrote to me — "my beautiful, lovely daughter, twenty years old, the gentlest soul on Earth, overdosed last year and died," a father wrote — and I wonder how and when we should try one more time to get Nic into treatment. "If I had a child who was addicted to meth," Dr. Rawson wrote. I do.

One morning, Nic calls and informs me that he has a new plan. Addicts always do. Again and again, they reframe the world to fit into their delusion that they are still in control. Nic tells me that he and his girlfriend finished off their stash of meth and that's it, it's over. He isn't going to succumb to my manipulation to go back into rehab. He promises that this time is different — "she won't let me use, I won't let her, we made a vow, we'll call the police on each other if we slip, she'll leave me if I slip" — more of what he has said the many times he promised that this time would be different.

He hangs up.

I call some interventionists recommended by Dr. Rawson and a counselor at Hazelden's 800 number. Then I receive another phone call, this time from a friend who offers the counterargument. He has been in recovery from drugs and alcohol for nearly twenty-five years. He says that it's a mistake to intervene and a mistake to try rehab. "The rehab industry is like the auto repair industry," he says. "They want you to come back. And people always do. It's a thriving industry because no one gets well. They tell you, 'Keep coming back.'" He laughs grimly. "That's what they want. I had to hit bottom when there was no one and nothing and I had lost everything and everyone. That's what it takes. You have to be alone, broke, desolate, and desperate."

Yes, that might be what it takes. Yes, the odds are that neither intervention nor another try at rehab will work. But they may.

We will not keep coming back. We have neither the emotional nor the financial resources to keep coming back. My brain already burst once, and sometimes it seems as if it could do so again.

But here I am, making calls to interventionists as Nic leaves hardly coherent messages on our machines. And after everything we have been through I am still confused, in a familiar place between the opposing messages from outside me and inside me — leave him alone, let him suffer the consequences of his actions, try anything to save his life.

The first interventionist I reach claims that he has a 90 percent success rate, and I politely thank him for his time. He could be telling the truth, but I am doubtful. Another one is more modest. "There are no guarantees, but it is worth trying," he says. He proposes a scenario in which Nic's mother and I, along with Karen, his friends, and his girlfriend, if she is willing, confront Nic and offer him a chance to go to rehab. A bed would be waiting. Nic would be encouraged to get into a car and immediately go.

"I can't imagine that he would go," I say.

"It often works," he explains. "The psychology of intervention is that an addict feels overwhelmed and vulnerable in the presence of his family and friends. He may agree to go because of guilt or shame or because his loved ones break in enough so that he can glimpse the truth of his circumstance — the people who love him would not lie. They are motivated by one thing. To save him."

After a pause, he asks the usual question:

"What's his drug of choice?"

"He uses just about every drug on the streets, but he always gravitates back to methamphetamine."

The voice on the telephone lets out a deep sigh.

"I work with all drugs, but I hate to hear about meth. It's so destructive and unpredictable."

I tell him that I will consult with Nic's mother and call him back.

From *Addict in the Family:* "None of this is easy. Addicts' families walk an unhappy path that is strewn with many pitfalls and false starts. Mistakes are inevitable. Pain is inevitable. But so are growth and wisdom and serenity if families approach addiction with an open mind, a willingness to learn, and the acceptance that recovery, like addiction itself, is a long and complex process. Families should never give up hope for recovery — for recovery can and does happen every day. Nor should they stop living their own lives while they wait for that miracle of recovery to occur."

When will it occur? Will it occur?

In the meantime, seemingly miraculously, the sun rises each day and sets each evening. The globe does not stop spinning, and there are spelling tests to prepare for, swim team and lacrosse carpools to drive, math homework; there are dinners to be made and, afterward, dishes to wash. There is work — articles to be written for inflexible deadlines.

In a week Nic leaves another message.

"It has been eleven days now. I'm sober. Eleven days."

Is it real? Will it last to twelve days?

How many times have I promised myself never to do this again, never again live in a state of panic, waiting for Nic to show up or not show up, to check himself in or not check himself in. Doing the same thing repeatedly and expecting different results is the definition of insanity. I will not do it again.

I am doing it again.

Up and down. Twisted and depressed. Distraught and then all right.

I keep the interventionist's number handy.

One Saturday, after lacrosse, Jasper leaves for a boy's birthday party, a sleepover. Karen is in the city hanging her paintings for tomorrow's opening and so it is the two of us, Daisy and me, at home in Inverness. Brutus is breathing hard on the couch near the fireplace after his daily game of chase with a bevy of quail that have taken up permanent residence in the garden. He may be decrepit, but his shaky legs don't stop him from this exhausting sport. Now he is too tired to flee from Daisy, and so he is at her mercy. Using Klutz Press nail polish — nontoxic purples and pinks — she paints his claws. She has been making folded-paper cootie-catchers, a game of fortune-telling. Now she makes one for Brutus. Normally these contain colors and numbers and fortunes for humans, but Brutus makes his choices with a "yawn," "twitch," or "pant." "Come here, big brown fluff ball," she says. His fortunes: "You will have a nice day of sleeping and eating." "You will bump into a great dane and become friends." "You will steal a steak and get in trouble." Fog like steam and thick cotton has blocked out the sun, but a fire still palely burns.

In the evening, Daisy and I read together — the book is by one of our favorite children's authors, Eva Ibbotson. Daisy leans on my shoulder. She pushes her retainer out between her lips, sucks it back in, and clicks it into place. She dislodges it again, pushes it out, clicks it back.

"Stop playing with your retainer."

"It's entertaining." She clicks it again.

"The orthodontist said it's a bad idea. Stop."

"Fine." She clicks it again.

We close *The Star of Kazan* and I kiss Daisy on the forehead. She goes off to bed.

I am in my bed reading when the phone rings.

Nic.

He says that he is good and things are going well, but I can tell that he is high.

I say so.

He insists that it's the medication for getting off meth and coke and heroin.

"I'm only using Klonopin, Seboxin, Strattera, Xanax."

"Only?"

He insists that a doctor prescribed them. If this is true, I cannot comprehend the difference between him and Nic's other drug dealers.

Nic says, "I know that on these drugs I'm not 'AA sober,' but that's bullshit anyway. I'm sober."

"Call me when you're AA sober," I say. "We'll talk then."

In the morning I check my email before leaving to pick up Jasper from the sleepover.

Nic's girlfriend has sent an urgent message.

"He left me at the market this morning to go to his moms said he'd be back in 15 minutes. Took my car, my purse is in it with my inhaler. He never came back to the market I waited for 4 hours until my friend sent a cab for me.

"Please call me at [her phone number]. Emergency."

25

I t is November, but the morning is warm. A thin moon still hangs on the daylight. Staring at it earlier, Daisy called it a sideways smile. Karen has taken Daisy with her to the city, and I am driving to pick up Jasper from the overnight, having arranged to collect him at the soccer field near the windmill at Golden Gate Park.

As my car crests Olema Hill, I call Z.'s number. She is out of breath, frenetic—angry and worried. In this state, she reveals more than she had in her email, explaining that Nic dropped her off at a market in the Palisades at 5:45 AM. He took her car to his mother's. He was going to break in and steal Vicki's computer. She says it as if he were going over to borrow sugar. Nic had promised to be back in fifteen minutes, but he had not returned for four hours. Presuming that he'd been arrested, she called the police, but they had no record of him.

She is sobbing.

"What could have happened to him in five blocks from the market to his mother's house?"

I tell her what I know from my experience with Nic. Every time that he disappeared I imagined every possible scenario—that he had been in a fatal accident or, absurdly, been kidnapped—but he had relapsed.

I ask, "Could he be driving to San Francisco?"

"He has no money."

"Then he probably went to a dealer in LA."

"And just left me on the street?"

"For drugs. What else can it be?"

I tell her that I'll check with Nic's mother and call back.

The phone awakens Vicki. When I explain, she says that Nic hasn't shown up. "There's no sign of him," she says.

In a half-hour, she calls back.

"He's here. He is in the garage. He broke in and was robbing us, piling things in shopping bags. He got confused and somehow managed to lock himself inside. He's panicked and crazed. He's ranting."

"Tweaking," I clarify.

By the time I call Z., she has heard from Nic, who called from a telephone in the garage. Enraged, she is packing up his clothes. "I've had it," she says. "If you talk to him, tell him his clothes will be outside on the front porch."

Vicki, after discussing it with her husband, tells Nic that he has a choice. The police will be called and he will be arrested or he can go back to rehab.

Driving to get Jasper in the city on the sunny morning, I reel.

He has broken into his mother's house. He is out of his mind. Meth again. Tweaking. Since he relapsed, I have known that something like this was coming, but now the dam bursts and I am flooded with emotion.

Please God heal Nic.

Is it too late?

Relapse is part of recovery.

Please heal Nic.

There's Jasper with his friends on the soccer field. When he sees me, he waves and then runs to the car. He throws his bag of clothes and sports gear in the backseat and climbs in.

"We stayed up until midnight having a pillow fight."

"Are you exhausted?"

"I'm not even tired."

He is asleep in minutes.

With Jas sleeping beside me, I make more phone calls — calls to decide where to send Nic. If he agrees to go. I call Jace, the director of Herbert House, who knows Nic and cares about him. Jace has helped many addicts. He knows the rehabs. He says that whatever we do, we should get Nic out of LA and in an inpatient program that lasts for a minimum of three or four months, preferably longer. He says, "Hazelden is expensive, but it's as good as they come." Hazelden has a four-month program, and so I call the 800 number for the organization. An intake counselor tells me that there is no bed in the Minnesota location, but there is one in Oregon, and so I am transferred to a counselor there.

He must speak to Nic, but it seems likely that Nic, if he is willing, can go there.

Karen's opening is in the city. Jack Hanley, the gallery in the Mission, is crowded. Daisy, wearing a wool knitted cap, and Jasper, in shorts in spite of a cold wind, play outside with other kids until they leave early with my brother and his family.

I take a break to get air. I walk around the block. When Karen first moved in with us, Nic and I lived a few blocks from here. We walked this and the neighboring streets for tortillas and mangoes at the Mexican markets. On weekends, we would go to Inverness.

I recall a school holiday in October of that year — 1989 — when we stopped at the corner market to stock up and then drove out for a night in the country. In the afternoon, we met up with a friend for a walk on miles-long Limantour Beach. We were hiking under a sapphire sky. Suddenly Nic pointed to the nose of a seal that had popped up through the choppy surf. Then there was another, then another. Soon ten or a dozen seals were peering at us with black eyes, their long necks jutting out of the water. Next it was as if someone grabbed the beach and shook it out like an old rug. The sand rolled, as wavy as the ocean, up and then down and up again before collapsing.

We steadied ourselves and tried to take in what had happened. An earthquake.

We headed back to the cabin, where we used a cell phone (the land lines were out) to call our friends and family, making sure that everyone was all right and assuring them that we were. The cabin had a Honda generator that powered a few light bulbs and an old black-and-white television, on which we watched footage of the devastation in San Francisco, including flattened apartment buildings in the Marina District and cars squashed by a fallen ramp connecting to the Bay Bridge.

School was canceled and so we stayed in Inverness for a few days. Finally when it resumed, we headed back home. The teachers talked to the children about the earthquake and other things that scare people. The children wrote about their experiences. "I was at the beach," Nic wrote. "I was looking down into a sand pit. I heard that a person was thrown out of a swimming pool. The earthquake made me feel dizzy." At recess, a boy stood on the playground, rocking and swaying. When the principal asked if he was OK, the boy nodded and said: "I am moving like the earth so that if there's another earthquake I won't feel it."

As I walk around the block crowded with people out on a Saturday night, I remember the little boy and feel like he felt. I navigate through each day like him, on guard, wary of the next upheaval. I protect myself as best as I can. I move like the earth in case there's another earthquake. Like now, bracing myself when I flip open the cell phone and call Z., prepared for whatever comes.

She hands the phone to Nic.

"So it looks like there's a bed at Hazelden in Oregon. You will have to call and speak to a counselor in the morning."

"I've been thinking about it. I don't have to go. I can do it myself."

"You tried that and it didn't work."

"But now I know."

I sigh. "Nic . . ."

I can hear Z. in the background. "Nic, you have to go."

"I know, I know. All right. Yeah, I have to go. I know."

After the initial burst of bravado, Nic seems resigned. He also seems mystified. "I thought that I could stay sober because I wanted to," he says. "I thought that being in love like this could keep me sober, but it couldn't. It freaks me out." After a pause, he says, "I guess this is what it means to be an addict."

Moving like the earth so I don't feel this new earthquake — this latest relapse. I walk under streetlamps, an austere sky overhead. Cars streak by. I walk back to the gallery.

On Monday, Nic speaks to a counselor at Hazelden and afterward he tells me that he is going to Oregon.

I book a flight knowing that he may not show up.

Next I hear from him that he is packed and ready to go.

His girlfriend is driving him to the airport. I call Hazelden to be sure that someone will pick him up when he arrives, but the man who answers the phone says that there is no record that Nic is arriving. When I protest, I am transferred to a supervising counselor, who explains that Nic was not approved for admission.

"What do you mean he's not approved for admission? He's on his way."

"Why is he on his way? He was not approved."

"No one told us."

"I'm not certain why, but this is the decision."

"But you can't . . . He is on his way to the airport. We have to get him into a program while he's willing to go."

"I'm sorry, but—"

"Can he come tonight and begin detoxing while we figure out where he'll go next?"

"I'm sorry."

"What am I supposed to do?"

"If he flies up here, no one will be meeting him."

"What am I supposed to do?"

"We have some recommendations of other programs." She gives me the names.

I hang up and call Jace. He says he'll make some calls. Jace calls back with the name of a hospital in the San Fernando Valley where Nic can detox.

I call the doctor who runs it and arrange for Nic to be admitted. Then I call Z.'s cell phone again and explain what happened. Instead of going to the airport, I say that Nic should go to the hospital. I provide the address. At least he will be safe in a hospital. If he shows up.

John Lennon sang, "Nobody told me there'd be days like these." Nobody told me there would be days like these. How do people survive them?

After midnight, Z. drops him off at the hospital. Nic is given medication to begin detoxing. As the nurse explains, he will spend most of the initial few days sleeping. The alternative to medication is the well-documented hell of cold turkey, which many addicts cannot endure. Crawling out of their skin, depressed and distraught, feeling hopeless and in acute pain, they will do anything to feel better—they will find drugs.

I regularly check in with the nurses on the ward, who assure me that he's doing all right. One says: "Given the quantity and variety of drugs in his system, it's a miracle that he made it in. I don't think his body could have survived another month."

His mother and I explore options for where he can go next. Once again I ask Dr. Rawson for advice, and he queries some friends and colleagues. I check on the programs recommended by the supervisor at Hazelden. We ask the doctor who is detoxing Nic for his suggestions. Over the course of these days, Vicki and I each make dozens of telephone calls. We talk to admissions reps and check Web sites. We continue to get contradictory advice. Some programs charge forty thousand dollars a month, but the experts agree that Nic will need many months in treatment this time. We can't afford forty-thousand-dollar months. Some people we speak to are as pushy as used-car salesmen. One place recommended by Hazelden sounds appropriate and is more affordable than many others. Then someone tells me that it is a hardcore program in which punishments for breaking rules include cutting the grass with scissors. This may be useful therapy for some people, but Nic would go crazy. Maybe I'm wrong. I have been wrong about so much.

At least he's safe for the weekend.

I talk to another nurse attending to Nic. His blood pressure has been extremely low, though it is better today. He hasn't eaten much since he arrived.

She asks Nic if he is up for coming to the telephone. He walks to the nurses' station and picks up the phone.

"Hey, Dad."

His voice is hardly audible. He sounds extremely, extremely depressed.

"How's it going?"

"It's hell."

"I know."

"But I'm glad to be here. Thanks. I guess this is what they mean by unconditional love."

"Just go through this. This is the worst, but it will get better."

"What should I do next?"

"We'll talk about it when you're feeling a little better. Your mom and I are working on it."

In fact, Vicki and I are overwhelmed trying to find a place that will give Nic the best chance. Dr. Rawson continues making calls and sending emails to his colleagues around the country on our behalf. He tells me that "this experience in advising you has made me more convinced that making a selection of programs in the mental health/substance abuse service system is like reading tea leaves."

Nic calls on the third morning of his detox and asks me to call him back on the pay phone down the hall.

"It's worse," he says, sounding weak and miserable. I imagine him standing in a hospital hallway — well lit, white — tethered to a pay phone by its metal cord. Slumped over. Supported by the wall.

"I'm tired. All the fears come in. Confused. What is happening? Why? Why does this keep happening to me?"

He cries.

"What is wrong with me? I feel as if my life has been stolen."

He cries.

"I can't do this."

He cries.

"You can do it," I say. "You can."

More calls today. Vicki and I have conference calls with the intake people at rehabs around the country, in Florida, Mississippi, Arizona, New Mexico, Oregon, and Massachusetts.

We finally choose one in Santa Fe. I am uncertain. After sifting through what Dr. Rawson calls "a non-system comprised of rumor, marketing bullshit, best guesses and fiscal opportunism," we made the best choice we could, but I'm unsure. Is it the right one? How can anyone know?

Nic calls again. He says that he should stay in LA and, at most, work in an outpatient program.

I counter: "I know, and I think that a part of you knows, that you need to go somewhere and stay there until you have done the hard work of figuring out what is wrong and what you can do."

"Why do you still care?"

"I still care."

"Why can't I do it myself? Why do I need to go into another program?"

"So you can have a future. Last week when I knew that you could die at any moment, I couldn't bear it. I live with the knowledge that you could black out or overdose or go psychotic or do some irrevocable damage or die—it could happen at any moment."

He answers, "I live with it, too."

Together we weep. It's a startling moment for me. In the trenches these past months, I have held back tears, but now they pour forth. Nic is in the hallway of a hospital somewhere, leaning against a wall, and I am on the kitchen floor, crying.

Before hanging up, he weakly says, "I cannot believe that this is my life." Then he breathes in and says, "I'll do whatever it takes."

Early on Tuesday morning, his mother picks him up at the hospital in the valley and drives him directly to the airport, where she convinces a security agent to allow her through the checkpoint so that she can escort him to the gate and onto the flight to New Mexico.

She calls me from the lounge. Nic has boarded the plane. It is backing up from the jetway. I see her standing there with her cell phone to her ear looking out the window. I see Nic on the plane. I see him as he is—frail, opaque, ill—my beloved son, my beautiful boy.

"Everything," I say to him.

"Everything."

Fortunately there is a beautiful boy.

Unfortunately he has a terrible disease.

Fortunately there is love and joy.

Unfortunately there is pain and misery.

Fortunately the story is not over.

The jet pulls away from the gate.

I hang up the phone.

I see a small lilac box with tulips painted on the top and sides. A music box. Daisy's. I open it and a ballerina springs upright. She dances. I inspect the inside of the box. It has small compartments, all empty.

Like a jumbo assortment of Sees Candy, the box has hidden layers. I carefully remove the topmost felt tray. Under it, set on black felt like an artifact in a museum, is a plastic syringe. I hold the syringe up and turn it over in my hand, examining it, and then put it aside. I pull up the next felt layer and see, in one of the small compartments, tiny packages the size of small stones, each one wrapped in Kleenex. I pick one up and examine it, unwrap it slowly. It is Nic's tooth. There is blood on the root. I pick up the next small package and unwrap it. Another tooth.

I wake up.

I go into the kitchen, where Brutus is flat on the floor, his hind legs splayed out. He cannot move. Karen places a towel under his belly and, using it as a sling, slowly lifts him, helping Brutus stand. His frail hind legs tremble, but he is able to move forward.

The vet prescribes a new medicine. We cannot contemplate putting him to sleep. Not Brutus. I don't think Daisy, who every evening before bed wraps herself around him, could take it. I don't think Karen could. Or Jasper, who for hours a day would sit in a chair in the garden and throw a tennis ball for Brutus, who would retrieve it, return to Jas, and spit it out onto his lap. None of us could. If we have to, we will. This, too.

After school, Karen, Jasper, Daisy, and I enter the office of the family therapist. We feel enormous trepidation. The kids sit hunched on a leather couch. They squirm in their seats, almost literally crawling into their sweatshirts like turtles retracting into their shells.

The doctor is a young man with a trimmed beard and dark eyes. He speaks in a soft, reassuring voice. "Your mom and dad and I met," he says to the kids. "They told me a little about what's going on in your family. They told me about your brother, Nic, and about his addiction. It sounds as if you have had a hard time."

Jasper and Daisy stare at him, intently listening.

"It's very scary to have a brother who uses drugs," the therapist continues. "For a lot of reasons. One of them is that you don't know what will happen. I know you're very worried about him. Do you understand where he is now?"

"He's in rehab," Jasper says.

"Do you know what that means?"

The therapist explains and then tells the kids about other children like them who are in this situation — about how hard it is. "It's normal to feel confused if you have a brother who you love and who you may be afraid of, too."

The kids eye him sharply.

The doctor leans forward and rests his elbows on his knees. He looks closely at Jasper and Daisy. "I'm going to tell you a word you may not have ever heard before," he says. "The word is *ambivalence*. It means that it's possible to feel two things at once. It means ... It means that you can love someone and hate them at the same time — or maybe hate what they're doing to your family — and to themselves. It means that you can want to see them very badly and at the same time be very afraid of them."

The kids look uncomfortable, but less so. Then Jasper speaks. "Everybody is worried about Nic." He looks over at me.

"You're looking at your dad," the therapist says. "Does he worry about Nic?"

Jasper nods.

"Do you worry about your dad? Especially after the hospital? They told me about that, too."

Jasper looks down and offers a barely observable nod.

In his office on this wintry evening, the children's initial hesitation is replaced by what feels to Karen and me like a cautious sense of relief. The more we talk, the taller they sit up in the couch. We talk about things that are undeniable and yet have never been adequately acknowledged.

The therapist says that even though Nic is safe for the moment in rehab, it's probably scary to think about the future. Plus just because he is safe doesn't mean that everything is fine.

"After Nic's thefts, whenever something is missing, I go into a state of panic thinking Nic has been in our house again," Karen says.

"Panic is the exact right word," responds the therapist. "You return to the state when you felt under attack."

We describe the stack of our friend's newspapers by the fireplace. Karen and I both felt that they were papers that Nic would have brought into the house. Before we discussed it, we went into a state of high alert. I did not want to worry her. She did not want to upset me. But both of us thought: Nic was here. Will he break in again? It turned out fine, but it took a toll.

The doctor explains how triggers like the newspapers can return us to a state of panic. He then asks about other triggers, and it dawns on me. Of course.

"I think it happens when the phone rings," I say.

"The phone?"

The kids are staring.

"The phone, when it rings, brings on the same state of panic. I am always worried that there is news of another crisis. Or it's Nic, and I don't know if he will be sane or high. Or it won't be him, and I'll be disappointed. My body tenses up. Oftentimes during meals or when we're hanging around in the evening, I let the phone ring until the answering service picks it up, because I don't want to deal with whatever might be coming. I think that everyone feels tension. Jasper always asks why I don't answer the phone. I think it makes him nervous."

Jasper is nodding.

The doctor says, "And so it is not only something rare and random that comes into your house like the stack of newspapers. The phone must ring all the time. You must all be in a fairly constant state of worry and tension. That mustn't feel very good." He turns to the kids. "Does that sound accurate?"

They both nod vigorously.

It seems to be a profound acknowledgment. To me, the doctor says, "Maybe you can shut off the ringer for periods of time. You can always call people back." He then says: "And now that Nic is in rehab, maybe it would be useful to you and to Nic to establish a time — whenever, once a week or more — when you will speak on the phone. Then you will know. Establishing borders like that can help you both. You both will be freed from a continual state of anxiety that he should or has or hasn't called you. It may help all of you. Your family will know when it is time for you and Nic to talk, and then they can be assured he's all right, but it won't feel like a constant threat."

I respond, "That's a good idea," but then I admit, "My heart is pounding. The idea of shutting down communication is terrifying."

"You're not shutting it down, you're making it safer for everyone."

We leave the session, descend the flight of concrete stairs from the nondescript building, and the children seem to have been unbound. Their cheeks are flushed and their eyes sparkle.

"What did you think?" Karen asks them.

Daisy says, "It was—".

Jasper finishes. "Amazing."

"It was," Daisy says.

I begin to monitor my telephone use, shutting off the ringer in the evenings and on weekends. I make a plan to speak to Nic once a week. Small things. They seem enormous.

It has been three weeks since Nic has been back in rehab. He sounds unwell. As he explains, the initial weeks of his treatment have been devoted to stabilizing him. The week-long detox in the valley wasn't enough to clear his body of all the drugs. Even now, after three weeks, he remains in acute mental and physical pain. He has had intermittent convulsions. Once he was rushed to a local hospital. His body writhes, he is desolate, and he can't sleep. The pain goes on and on, proof, as if I need more, of the deathly grip of the drugs on his body.

Nic calls on Sunday. He sounds cold and angry, blaming me for where he is. He asks for a plane ticket home. "This was a mistake," he says. "It's a disaster. It's a waste."

"You have to give it time."

"Will you or won't you send a plane ticket?"

"I won't."

He hangs up on me.

He calls back the next day to say that he is feeling a little better. He slept soundly last night for the first time since he arrived from LA. He is sorry for yesterday. "I still cannot believe that I relapsed," he says. "I cannot believe that I did what I did." He tells me that he feels guiltier about it than he can say.

"I'm afraid to say anything at all because I don't know what will happen. I don't want to open you and Karen and the kids up and then disappoint you again."

He tells me a little about the treatment program's different approach from the other rehabs. "In my first group, a counselor asked me why I am here. He asked, 'What's your problem?'"

"I said, 'I'm a drug addict and alcoholic.'"

"He shook his head. 'No,' he said, 'that's how you have been treating your problem. What is your *problem?* Why are you here?'"

Fine, I think, but I am past being hopeful. I don't know if he is too far gone, if there is too much damage from the drugs. Even if not, I am unable to allow myself hope.

Another week. Another. Christmas. New Year's.

Another week. A month. Nic is safe in rehab, but I remain skeptical.

It is Thursday. I pick Jasper up from after-school World Beat Band practice, where I sit in and listen from the upper corner of the theater while they play. Jasper plays congas for "Oye Como Va." An eighth-grade boy wails on guitar like Carlos Santana.

I drive him home and say goodbye to him, Daisy, and Karen. They are going to their cousin's eleventh birthday party. I throw my suitcase in the car and drive in heavy rush-hour traffic to the Oakland airport, where I check in and eat a quick dinner.

I board a packed Southwest flight. When I arrive in Albuquerque, I walk past the gates through the airport. I have a vivid image, Nic's arrival here eight or so weeks ago, after his mother watched the plane take off in LA. I see the terminal through his eyes: southwest art, Indian rugs, the ENTERING O'KEEFFE COUNTRY sign. In my mind he glances up at Thunderbird Curio and Hacienda New Mexican cuisine. I think, Nic would have been disdainful of being here in this themed terminal if he were in shape to be disdainful of anything.

Outside, I imagine the driver from the Life Healing Center waiting for Nic with a sign that says NIC SHEFF, but there would have been little doubt who Nic was, the young man off the LA flight, wearing in his colorless face and dull eyes and listless body his months-long binge and the week of torturous detox from a dozen drugs.

I rent a car. It is supposed to be a nonsmoking car but it smells like cigarettes. Driving on a wide highway, I turn on the radio, and the first thing I hear is the opening riff of "Gimme Shelter."

I drive for an hour and find my motel and check in. I try to sleep. I would be more at ease if I were here for a convention of dental students practicing their first root canals on me.

Swimming might calm me down. I leave the room and drive around until I find a mall where I buy a bathing suit. Then I return to the motel and find the pool closed, yellow tape surrounding it as if it were a crime scene.

In my room I pick up the *The New Yorker* and read the fiction and Hertzberg and Anthony Lane. I wonder if there are copies of *The New Yorker* at Nic's rehab? Finally I fall asleep for a while, wake up at eight, and get ready.

I have not seen Nic since June, right after the ICU. I hardly remember his visit, only the ensuing barrage. The slurred voice, telephone calls, lies, terror, his mother's visit to his apartment, the email from—ostensibly from Joshua Tree, but, as I learned, from Oakland.

Why am I here? A weekend cannot undo these years of hell, and a weekend cannot turn Nic's life around. Nothing I've done made a difference. Why am I here?

The therapists in his program counseled him to ask his mother and me to come. If we're trying this one last time, trying one last time to give him another chance, I will do what they tell me. I know that nothing will help, probably nothing will help, but I will do my part. Frankly and to be completely honest — don't tell anyone, don't tell him — I am also here to see him. I have been afraid, but a cautious and well-guarded place inside of me misses him like crazy, misses my son.

The morning blue sky is marred only by a smoke line from a jet.

I drive through the town, following the directions that arrived in the mail from the treatment center. I turn down a dirt road lined with sagebrush and scrawny pines. It's like a scene in an old western. The place looks as if it once was a ranch. There are bunkhouses and a chow hall and a ramshackle main house and out-buildings sided with split logs. A line of log cabins on a ridge that looks onto the high desert. The place is rustic and modest, unlike Count Ohlhoff's old Victorian mansion or the austere modern hospital in the wine country or the stately brownstone on Stuyvesant Park in Manhattan or Jace's LA Melrose Place.

I fill out forms in a small office and then wait outside for Nic. It is cold, but I have a thick coat.

There. Nic.

Deep breath.

Standing under a sagging awning on a low porch of a rundown cabin, Nic.

Nic in an army jacket and purple scarf with paisleys.

Nic in a faded T-shirt and cords with tiny leather patches and black leather sneakers.

His gold and brown hair is curly and long. He pushes it out of his eyes.

Nic walks down the rickety steps toward me. His face: thin and angular. His eyes flash at me with —?

"Hey, Dad."

If I admit how good it is to see him, I may be accused of forgetting the fury and terror, but it is good to see him. I am scared to death.

He walks over. Reaches out his arms. I smell his smokiness and embrace him.

While we wait for Vicki, we make small talk. Then Nic looks shyly up at me and says, "Thanks for coming. I didn't know if you would."

I walk with him up to an outside smoking area under a wood roof with a few weathered chairs and a fire pit.

I'm afraid and I don't want to want to see him and I don't want to be happy to see him.

We meet some of his friends. There's a girl with pierced ears and inch-short bleached hair and a boy with no hair and a boy with curly black hair. A man who looks as if he spent his life in the sun comes over and shakes my hand. His skin is rough, brown wrinkled leather. He shakes my hand and tells me what a great son I have.

Nic smokes. We sit near the fire pit and he says that things are changing.

"I know you've heard it before, but this is different."

"The problem is that I have heard *that* before, too."

"I know."

We go inside to meet with his chief therapist and wait there for his mother, who comes in, too. Vicki wearing a beige jacket, her hair long and straight. I glance over at her. It is difficult to look her in the eyes even after all these years. I feel guilty. I was a child—exactly twenty-two, a year younger than Nic is now—when we met. I can try to forgive myself, whether or not she forgives me, because I was a child, but some things you just live with because you cannot go backward. I have been nervous to see Nic, but I was also nervous about seeing Vicki. We may have become closer over these past few years, we have, but though we talk on the phone and console each other and support each other and debate interventions and worry about the lack of good insurance (she is working now to get him back on her policy), we have not been in the same room for more than a few minutes since our divorce twenty years ago. Come to think of it, last week was our wedding anniversary, or would have been. The last time we were together for more than five minutes was Nic's high school graduation, when Vicki and I sat next to each other and Jasper sat on my other side. Afterward, Jas whispered, "Vicki seems nice."

The therapist says that in her view Nic is doing well, is where he should be considering everything, asks us to notice how things compare and contrast from his previous times in rehab. She asks us all to think about what we would like to get out of this weekend. She wishes us luck.

Nic, Vicki, and I have lunch. There's a spread of food. Tamales, salad, fruit. Nic eats a bowl of cereal.

Nic leads us to another building, into a room with two wood-paneled walls and two white walls covered in patients' artwork. The floor tiles are off-white, some of them buckling. It smells of coffee that has been sitting all morning on a burner.

A circle of chairs waits for us.

I look over at Vicki. She has been a journalist for more than twenty years, but when we met she was working in a dental office in San Francisco. The office was below the northern California headquarters of the newly founded *New West*, where I was an assistant editor, my first job after college. It was an office devoted to New Age dentistry designed for pleasure, not pain, airy, with a vaulted ceiling supported by exposed rough-hewn wood beams; Italian lights dangled from crisscrossing wires; and a jungle of hanging potted ferns. Music—Vivaldi, Windham Hill—was piped in through patients' headphones, nitrous oxide through their masks. Vicki wore a white smock over a Laura Ashley print dress. She had dawn-blue eyes and Breck-girl hair. She was a recent arrival from Memphis, where she had an uncle who was a dentist, which somehow qualified her for her job as a dental assistant. It took her four tries before she got my x-rays right, but I thought, Blast away, because, on nitrous with her levitating before my eyes, I was content. We married the following year. I was twenty-three—exactly Nic's age now. The check to the pastor of the pretty white church bounced. No one but two friends were there in Half Moon Bay. We have not seen those two friends since. I was twenty-three, and three weeks ago I turned fifty. My hair is no longer gray, it is white. It's getting like my father's cotton-white hair.

The chairs are filled. I look around the circle. The patients and their parents and one's brother. Here we go again.

Two therapists lead us. One has dark hair, one is light blond, both wear scarves, and both have eyes that are kind and intense. They take turns speaking. They set forth ground rules and expectations.

I think, This is bullshit. I have been here and done this and it did no good whatsoever.

First there is a questionnaire to fill out. Each of us. I set to work. After a half-hour or so, we take turns reading our answers. One mother, responding to the question, "What are your family's problems?" reads, "I didn't think we had any problems, but I guess if we didn't we wouldn't be here. I thought we had a good family." She begins crying. Her daughter puts a hand on her mom's knee. "We do have a good family." Once again I'm back in a room with people like me, people hurt by addiction and uncomprehending—baffled and guilty and angry and overwhelmed and terrified.

Next is art therapy.

Art therapy!

I have been through too much to be sitting on the floor finger-painting with Nic and my ex-wife. I am raging inside. Why did I come? Why am I here?

We are given a piece of paper divided, for our family, into three wedges. Nic, Vicki, and I sit on the floor around the paper in a triangle. A triangle.

As instructed, I start drawing. I choose chalk. I just start pushing the chalk around on the paper.

The heater is turned up too high. There is not enough air.

Vicki, using watercolors, paints a pretty scene like a beach or whatever it is. I am still raging. She is drawing a sunset. Bright and light blue and swirls. She is drawing a pretty picture, as if we were here together at family art day at Nic's preschool with a blue sky and a green grassy field. But then I look over at Nic's third of the paper. Using ink, he draws a heart. Not a valentine heart, not Cupid's heart, but a heart with muscle and tissue and ventricles connecting to an aorta, a pumping heart inside a body. His body. Attached to the aorta, a face, and then more faces at different angles with expressions of fury and desolation and horror and faces in pain. I draw with my chalk. I have made some kind of thick line coming up from the bottom of the paper, some river coming up, but then it splits open and flows into the two top corners of the page. I push so hard that the chalk disintegrates into powder.

What's the point, it's a waste of time. Now Vicki has — here it comes, dark watery black is on her brush now and the pretty light blue sky is gone, covered with the watery swashes of black and sweeping, pouring brushstrokes. Nic begins writing hard, a word, *I*, two words, *am*, three words, *sorry*, writes them again, writes them again, writes them again, writes them again. He cannot, it feels like, stop writing them. It is bullshit, a cheap attempt at — it is not bullshit — he is trying with excruciating desperation, which I can feel coming from him, to say something, to get out something, that he cannot get out.

It's easy to forget that no matter how hard it is for us, it is harder for him.

My drawing—now there are drops, tears, from the two branches of the tributary and six circles above it. Then I know—I have drawn the opening up of my brain and all that is in there—tears pain blood rage terror. The broken suitcase with the circles, its contents—me, former me—spilling out.

His mother has drawn a small red smear in the center and there is a drip from it—blood there, too.

Nic is writing *I am sorry,* and I want to cry. No, I think, don't let him in again. No don't let him in again. No don't let him in again.

We take turns family by family describing what's on the pages and what it felt like working next to one another. Vicki's red isn't blood, it's a red balloon that she wants to hold onto to take her away from the black storm. Nic looks at her and says how remarkable it is that she is here. I look up at her and here she is. I look at Nic. Here is Nic with his parents. I feel sadness, overwhelming sadness, that she has gone through so much and mostly sadness that Nic has gone through so much and then me, us, and I am mortified to feel sadness, mortified to feel . . . Oh, Nic, I am sorry, too, so so sorry.

Nic says that the work he's doing here isn't about finding excuses for his debauchery or his craziness and it isn't about blaming anyone. It is about healing. His therapists have told him that he has to work through whatever it is that causes him to harm himself, to put himself in danger, to turn from those friends who love him, to lash out at his parents and others who love him, to lash out at himself, mostly at himself, to try to destroy himself. He is an addict, but why besides the luck of the gene-pool draw, what is it? They want him to face it all so that he can heal and move forward.

People in the other family groups talk about their pictures, what they evoke, what working on them was like. Then we comment on one another's. One girl, Nic's friend, says how different the images are in our family's pictures and how intense each one is, but she

says that Nic's heart leads into ventricles and my stream of chalk
looks like a broken artery.

Somehow I am crying. Nic's hand is on my shoulder.

When we emerge before sunset, an imperious moon hovers over
the mountain. I look at it and understand that I have not held out
hope for this new program not because I do not hope that it works
and not because it cannot work but because I am terrified to my
core to hope again.

I go to a bookstore and buy Zadie Smith's novel *White Teeth*.
I want to escape for tonight, and I want to hide in someone else's
story. The first thing I open to back in my motel room is the
epigraph from *Where Angels Fear to Tread* by E. M. Forster. I read
it and read it again. "Every little trifle, for some reason, does seem
incalculably important and when you say of a thing that 'nothing
hangs on it' it sounds like blasphemy. There's never any knowing — how am I to put it — which of our actions, which of our
idlenesses won't have things hanging on it for ever." I am almost
shaking. I think, How innocent we are of our mistakes and how
responsible we are for them.

This is about healing, not blaming. Is it possible to get beyond
blaming? At one point Vicki says that she used to carry around so
much anger toward me that it was as if she had on a backpack filled
with bricks. "What a relief no longer to be carrying them around,"
she says. After some of her comments in our next group session, I
tell her, "Maybe there are still a few bricks in there." She acknowledges, "Yes, maybe there are." But we are now united in one of the
most primal of human behaviors, trying to save our child. The therapist says that the weekend is not about blaming, but about moving
beyond lingering resentment. A father here says, "Resentment is
like taking poison and waiting for the other person to die."

*

In the morning, I again drive up to the treatment center. There's Nic in a New York Art Academy T-shirt, bell-bottom jeans with frayed cuffs, and a multicolored coat. He wears a knit cap low over his eyes. We drink coffee.

The families have a collective group therapy session. It's an appallingly vulnerable position — group therapy with an audience. But I admit that it's a relief to say what's on my mind. When Nic speaks, I feel a range of emotions — anxiety, fear, exasperation, anger, sorrow, remorse — and there are bursts of pride and dangerous flashes of memory of what we have had and of love. I want to open up and hear Nic and believe him but I am unwilling to tear down the fragile dam that I have constructed to protect myself. I am afraid that I will be drowned.

I'm a sucker. Parents are suckers. I am a sucker to contemplate opening to the idea of healing. And yet . . . Suddenly I recall when I prayed for Nic. I never planned to pray. I just looked back and realized I had been praying. What did I pray for? I never said stop taking drugs. I never said stay away from meth. I said, Please God heal Nic. I prayed, Please God heal Nic. Please God heal every ravaged person in this room, the dear ravaged people on this planet, these dear, wounded people. I look around at them. They are brave. They are here. However they got here, they are here. They are here and so there is a chance.

On the final session of the last day, we are instructed to think about the future. The future. The future is fraught with danger. We map it out. Literally. Our leaders give each family large sheets of paper with a shape drawn in the bottom left-hand corner representing one piece of land — where we are — and a shape on the top right corner representing our destination. Between them are small circles, stepping stones.

The instructions. Indicate where you are today. And where you want to go. Indicate the steps — concrete steps — you can take to get there. Think about the next few months, not the rest of your lives. Where do you want to go, and what steps will you take to get there. "And oh," she says, "the rest of the area of the paper is a swamp. To get across it from where you are now to where you want to go, using the stepping stones, you must avoid the perils in the swamp. Indicate the pitfalls lurking there, waiting for you."

Nic, in thick red marker, has no trouble identifying the perils. There are so many — all the old mistakes, habits, the temptations of drugs. He draws a hypodermic needle. There is so much red that it is almost impossible to find room to write on the small circles, the stepping stones. The stones look so small, so unsteady, in comparison. But on them, Nic writes our family's plan and his plan. How we will go slow, taking small steps forward. How we will support but not impede one another. Nic's stepping stones include AA and other conscientious work that will, he hopes, repair his relationships. He mentions Karen and looks up at me. "I really love Karen," he says. "We are friends — I miss her." With Jasper and Daisy. "I know that it will take a long time," he says. There's a lot to write. When the map is complete, it is clear that his mother's and my tasks are not inconsiderable — to step back, be supportive, but let Nic's recovery be his recovery as we work on disentangling and have healthy, as Nic describes them, loving and supportive, but independent relationships. But most of the hardest work falls on Nic's shoulders, because the perils are looming, waiting for him, enticing him to fail. The perils in slashing red marks are pernicious and ubiquitous and sinister. It is a swamp, and it will take a miracle for Nic to navigate it. Just as I think that, I look over at Nic's mother and I look at Nic. We three are here together, and I think, This is a miracle. Is it too much to hope for others?

*

I fly home. I feel as if someone has sawed through my chest and made a series of cuts from my clavicle to each shoulder blade, then back at the center, cut southward through the middle of my chest and stomach to just above my groin and then more horizontal cuts from the tip of one pelvic bone to the other. Then with plastic-gloved hands, they reached into the flaps of flesh and pulled them back on one side and then the other, tearing the sinews and muscle and skin so that I am here with my guts exposed.

The feeling does not abate. I am home again and Karen is off with Daisy at the orthodontist, which leaves me alone with Jasper, who is playing guitar — what he terms the "pluckage" for a song he is recording on Garage Band. He adds drums, other percussion, and synthesizer. Next he records his voice, improvising funny lyrics. For the chorus, he repeats the word *doughnuts* as if it is the dénouement in the libretto of an opera. When the raucous composition is complete, he burns it onto a CD.

It's time to ferry him to lacrosse. Driving, we listen to his music and then to the White Stripes. When we get to the field, he leaps out of the car, throws on his uniform, and runs to his friends.

I stand on the sidelines. The boys in their gladiator gear breathe vapor like dragons because of the chill. They race after the small white ball, scooping it up into the mesh pockets at the end of their sticks, hurling it forward to one another on the field.

My cell phone is in my pocket, but it is off, a state formerly unthinkable. As the doctor noted, the phone connected me to Nic, and each shrill ring provided a jolt to my heart like a defibrillator. Apparently it jolted each of our hearts. Every call fed my growing obsession with the promise of reassurance that Nic was all right or confirmation that he was not. My addiction to his addiction has not served Nic or me or anyone around me. Nic's addiction became far more compelling than the rest of my life. How could a child's life-or-death struggle not? Now I am in my own program to recover from my addiction to his. The deep work occurs in therapy, but I take practical steps, too. Like turning off my cell phone.

After practice, Jasper and I go to a sporting goods store. He has grown out of his cleats and needs new ones. To help pay for them, he uses a gift card left over from Christmas. Standing by the cashier, when he retrieves the card from his wallet, a piece of paper falls to the floor.

"What's that?" I ask Jasper, as he bends over to pick it up.

"The letter Nic wrote me."

He quickly folds it back up and puts it into his wallet.

We drive home.

Now the children are asleep. Karen and I are in bed reading. Brutus is running in his sleep. I put down my book and lie here, trying to comprehend exactly what it is that I am feeling. Parents of addicts learn to temper our hope even as we never completely lose hope. However, we are terrified of optimism, fearful that it will be punished. It is safer to shut down. But I am open again, and as a consequence I feel the pain and joy of the past and worry about and hope for the future. I know what it is I feel. Everything.

Epilogue

Oh, what'll you do now, my blue-eyed son?
Oh, what'll you do now, my darling young one?

—BOB DYLAN,
"A Hard Rain's A-Gonna Fall"

Ha Jin writes: "Some great men and women are fortified and redeemed through their suffering, and they even seek sadness instead of happiness, just as van Gogh asserted, 'Sorrow is better than joy,' and Balzac declared, 'Suffering is one's teacher.' But these dicta are suitable only for extraordinary souls, for the select few. For ordinary people like us, too much suffering can only make us meaner, crazier, pettier, and more wretched."

I am no great man, but I do not feel meaner, crazier, pettier, or more wretched. There were periods when I did, but now I feel fine, at least much of the time.

Nic completed three months at Santa Fe and his counselors recommended that he next go to a program in northern Arizona where he would continue his work in recovery, plus get a job and volunteer. He said no. He told me: "I know this will worry you, but I have to get on with my life." He tried to reassure me. "It will be all right."

At first I said, "No, you can't," but then I remembered: It's your life.

Nic caught a bus east. He went to see a friend he met at the program. We didn't speak for a while, but then we began talking again. Now we check in with each other fairly regularly. He met someone new. She's an art student. They got a place together. Nic is working at a café, serving decaf (he says) when a customer asks for it. And he's writing again. He's back writing his book. Now he has more to say about how hard it is to stay sober.

We talk about our writing. We talk about our lives and the news and books we read, music and movies (*Little Miss Sunshine*!).

I calculate that it has been — what, a year since he left LA. As far as I know, he's a year sober again. After everything, do I trust that he has remained sober? Do I deny what we have been through? Do I ignore how difficult it is and will continue to be? Never. But I hope. I continue to believe in him.

In the immediate aftermath of my brain hemorrhage, I complained that I had missed out on what I imagined might be a benefit of surviving a near-death experience — that is, beyond the ultimate perk: still being alive. As I said, I have often heard and read survivors describe the epiphanies that came from tragedy. Their lives transformed, became simpler, with clearer priorities. They had a new appreciation for life. But as I also said, I always appreciated life. Instead, for me, the brain hemorrhage made life seem scarier. I learned that tragedy could hit any of us — or our children — at any moment and without warning.

I was judging too early. Things have shifted since then. Just as there are stages of grieving or dying, there must be stages after a trauma, because the lessons of the neuro ICU sank in over time.

I turned fifty in December. At the time, I was speaking to a therapist about the past few years. When I told him that the neurologists had all dismissed the idea that my brain hemorrhage was related to the stress in my life, he looked at me indulgently and said, "Well, it sure didn't help." He pointed out that before my head literally exploded, it often felt as if it could explode. For years, I had lived with intense and relentless worry about Nic. I had rationalized it: no conscientious parent of a drug addict could expect to be happy for long. I was grateful for the moments of relief — when Nic seemed better, at least when he was OK. In the meantime, I did my best to enjoy my life — Karen, Jasper, Daisy, and the rest of my family and friends, the respites, however exiguous and short-lived.

The doctor pointed out that I could make a different choice. Without invoking AA or Al-Anon, he basically restated the Serenity Prayer. I could decide once and for all to accept the things I cannot change, have the courage to change the things I can, and the wisdom to know the difference. The key was the second of those. Did I have the courage to change the things I could?

"I've tried," I said. "I have tried for years."

"Apparently you haven't tried hard enough."

The doctor asked why I was in therapy only once a week. I said that I didn't have the time or money for more.

Of the financial excuse, he responded, "If during these past few years, someone told you that Nic needed more therapy in order to get well, would you have found a way to pay for it?"

I answered honestly: "Yes."

"Is his mental health more important than yours?"

I got the point.

As to the question of time for therapy, he asked, "How much time is it worth to end a person's suffering? How much time do you waste suffering now?" Then he summed: "You almost died. You are fifty years old. How do you want to spend the rest of your life? It's up to you."

My brain hemorrhage ultimately has made me appreciate, rather than fear, the profound truth of this cliché: our time here is finite. This realization impelled me to listen to the doctor and do whatever I could to get past my obsessive worry about Nic. I could not change Nic, only me. And so instead of focusing on Nic's recovery, since then I have focused on mine.

I attended Al-Anon meetings. I also had twice-weekly therapy sessions and, for the first time ever, I lay down on the doctor's couch. The difference has been profound — like disassembling a multilevel Lego building with hidden rooms and attics, dismantling it brick by brick, examining each one — a meticulous, often frightening process. I learned that at some point, focusing on Nic's perpetual crises became safer territory than focusing on myself. It was even safer to have a near-fatal brain hemorrhage.

As anyone in intensive therapy knows, though it's not easy, there can be a deep transformative benefit to the work. I have been uncovering layers of guilt and shame that help explain why I was so willing to take on the responsibility for Nic's addiction — for his life, in fact. As a result, those other clichés of Al-Anon and recovery no longer feel like clichés. I still don't fully accept the initial C. Instead, I recognize that I will never know how much I caused or contributed to it. Recently in the *New York Times Magazine*, William C. Moyers, the son of the journalist Bill Moyers and a recovering addict, said, "Recovery is . . . about dealing with that hole in the soul." What made the hole? No one knows. How innocent we are of our mistakes, but how responsible we are for them. I accept that I made terrible mistakes raising Nic. I don't absolve myself — even now. As you know, Nic, I am so sorry.

I have accepted the other Cs. I cannot control it and I cannot cure it. "For all their tears and heartache and desperately good intentions, most families of addicts are defeated in the end," writes Beverly Conyers. "Addicts persist in their self-destructive, addictive behavior until something *within themselves* — something quite apart from anyone else's efforts — changes so radically that the desire for the high is dulled and ultimately deadened by the desire for a better life." It's one thing to read this. It's another to evolve toward a true acceptance of it. I am confident that I have done everything I could do to help Nic. Now it's up to him. I accept that I have to let him go and he will or will not figure things out. I imagine that Nic, too, may be relieved that I have stopped trying to take on his recovery. It sets the stage for a different kind of relationship for us — like the one he envisioned in Santa Fe. Rather than codependent and enabling, with me trying to control him — even if to save him — our relationship can evolve into one of independence, acceptance, and compassion, with healthy boundaries. The love is a given.

The brain hemorrhage helped me understand the distinction. It was something that I knew intellectually, but it has sunk in and I now know it emotionally. My children will live with or without me. It is a staggering realization for a parent, but one that ultimately frees us to let our children grow up.

I wish I had gotten here quicker, but I couldn't. If only parenting were easier. It never will be. If only life were easier. It isn't — nor is that my goal any longer. Once I desperately wanted things to be simpler, but my worldview was broken over the course of Nic's addiction and my stay in the ICU. From them, I learned another lesson: that I can accept — in fact am relieved to accept — a world of contradictions, wherein everything is gray and almost nothing is black and white. There is much good, but to enjoy the beauty, the love, one must bear the painful.

There have been practical lessons, too. Since it has gotten around that our family has gone through this, friends, friends of friends, friends of friends of friends, as well as strangers, come to us.

Apparently people still read my article, because I get more letters. Every other person seems to be in the middle of some version of the hell of addiction, their own or their child's, spouse's, sibling's, parent's, or friend's. Often they ask for advice. Even now, my advice is tentative.

I agree wholeheartedly with the foremost recommendation of every rational antidrug campaign: talk to your kids early and often about drugs. Otherwise, you're leaving it to someone else to instruct them. Should you be open and honest about your experience with drugs? It's an individual decision, because every parent and child is unique. I would be careful never to glorify drug or alcohol use and would consider children's ages, never giving more information than they can comprehend at the time. But in the end, I don't know if it matters if or how much you tell them about your experience. Other things matter much more. Where do I come down on this for my family? I believe that kids don't need to (and shouldn't) know every personal detail of our lives, but I will never lie to my children, and I will answer their questions honestly. Sooner or later, Jasper and Daisy will read this account. It won't surprise them — they have lived through it. We have an ongoing conversation not only about Nic, but about drugs, peer pressure, and the other issues in their lives. They will know about their father's drug history, the toll it took. They already know about their brother's.

More than anything else, parents want to know at what point a child is no longer experimenting, no longer a typical teenager, no longer going through a phase or a rite of passage. Since it's unanswerable, I have concluded that I would err on the side of caution and intervene earlier rather than later — not waiting until a child is wantonly endangering himself or others. Looking back, I wish I had forced Nic — while he was young enough so that legally I could have forced him — into a long-term program of rehabilitation. Sending a child — or adult, for that matter — to rehab before they are ready and able to understand the principles of recovery may not prevent relapse, but from what I've seen it cannot hurt and may help. In addition, a period of forced abstinence during the formative teenage years is better than that same time spent on drugs. Forced treatment in a good program accomplishes at least one immediate goal. It keeps a child off drugs for the time they are in treatment. Since the less they do, the easier it is to stop, the longer they are in treatment the better.

Where should one send a child? What type of program? Though they may help some children, I would be wary of programs that employ harsh discipline. It's not that I don't understand the impulse to send a child to a boot camp. Parents give up and say, "You fix my kid." However, there is no convincing evidence that boot camps or similar programs help children, and they may hurt them. The National Institute of Justice once funded an evaluation of boot camps in eight states that concluded, "Common components of boot camps, such as military-style discipline, physical training, and hard labor, do not reduce recidivism." A report by the Koch Crime Institute in Kansas found that "fear of being incarcerated at a boot camp has not deterred crime," and three out of four children are back in some form of detention within a year after camp. On its Web site, the National Mental Health Association reports that "employing tactics of intimidation and humiliation is counterproductive for most youths," "boot camp graduates are more likely to be re-arrested or are re-arrested more quickly than other offenders," and, detailing the more serious problem with boot camps, there are many "disturbing incidents" of abuse. In 1998 in Georgia, a U.S. Justice Department investigation concluded, "The paramilitary boot camp model is not only ineffective, but harmful." Beyond some cases of deaths and abuse, "a dangerous situation is created, one that is often psychologically damaging," said Mike Riera, an author and psychologist renowned for his work with teenagers whom Karen and I met with about Nic. "If the anger and confusion underlying the child's problems are forced underground, there is a strong chance that they will become pathological, showing up in an inability to maintain relationships or in violence, depression, or suicide. Also, abuse breeds more abuse."

Then what? I have heard success stories from people who sent their children away to various types of programs — inpatient, outpatient, month-long programs like Ohlhoff Recovery, St. Helena, Sierra Tucson, Hazelden, and hundreds of others; three-month wilderness programs; six-month programs like the ones offered by Ohlhoff, Hazelden, and other treatment centers around the country; and year-long high school or post–high school programs. For many addicts, long-term stays in sober-living communities such as Herbert House changed — that is, saved — their lives. There is no single or easy answer, because no one knows what will help a particular individual. It is difficult to get reliable professional advice, but I would seek it out. I would insist on second and third opinions. I would confer with doctors, therapists, counselors in and out of schools — making sure they have experience with drug and alcohol addiction. I would weigh their advice while remembering that this is not an exact science, and every child and every family is unique.

In almost every case, sending a child into rehab against his or her will was the hardest decision parents ever made. The mother of one of Nic's grade-school friends told me that she hired a man to abduct her seventeen-year-old son who was using and dealing meth. Trained specialists grabbed him and escorted him, handcuffed, to a three-month-long wilderness program. She wept for three days. Since he graduated from the program, he relapsed once, but he now says that her intervention saved his life.

I heard similar stories at AA meetings I attended with Nic.

Addicts in recovery remembered the time their parents orchestrated interventions or forced them into treatment. "I hated them at the time. They saved my life." I heard about failures, too. "I tried, but my son died." With addiction, no outcome is guaranteed. Statistics are almost meaningless. You never know whether your child will be one of those in the 9 or 17 or 40 or 50 or whatever percent that is the true number who make it. At the same time, the statistics are useful in a sobering way. They inform us that our adversary is formidable and they guard us against irrational optimism.

Sometimes, when Nic relapsed, I faulted his counselors, therapists, the rehabs, and, of course, myself. In retrospect, I have come to understand that recovery is an ongoing process. He may have relapsed, but rehabs interrupted the cycles of using. Without them, Nic could easily have died. He has a chance now.

This informs another question. Yes, I would help a child of mine return to rehab after a relapse. I'm not sure how many times. Once? Twice? Ten times? I don't know. Some experts will disagree with me. They will advise you to not help them at all. They feel that an addict must come to recover on his own. They may be right when it comes to some children. Unfortunately, no one knows for certain.

I have learned a few other things. Rehab isn't perfect, but it's the best we have. Medications may help some addicts, but they cannot be expected to replace rehab and ongoing recovery work. I would not in any way help someone using drugs to do anything other than return to rehab. I would not pay their rent, would not bail them out of jail unless they went directly into rehab, even then would not repeatedly bail them out, would not pay their debts, and would never give them money.

In 1986, Nancy Reagan, who started the "Just say no" antidrug campaign, famously said, "There is no moral middle ground.

Indifference is not an option ... For the sake of our children, I implore each of you to be unyielding and inflexible in your opposition to drugs."

I don't know any mature person in favor of drugs like meth. We must instead understand the complex world in which our children are growing up and help them as best we can.

People said to Nic, "Well, just stop."

I have learned that it's not that easy.

People told me to let go of my worry because there was nothing I could do. "Put it out of your mind." I never could. I finally learned to do the hard work it took to put it in perspective, because it does not help anyone — the addict, the rest of the family, you — when it becomes the only thing in one's life. And so my advice: do whatever it takes — therapy, Al-Anon, lots of Al-Anon — for you to contain it. And be patient with yourself. Allow yourself to make mistakes. Be easy on yourself and extra loving toward your spouse or partner. Do not keep secrets. As they often repeat in AA, you're as sick as your secrets. Though it is not a solution, openness is a relief. Our shared stories help us remember what we're dealing with. Addicts need ongoing reminders and support, and so do their families. It helps to read others' stories. And it helps to write, at least it did for me. As I said, I wrote frantically. I wrote in the middle of the night and made it to morning. If I were a painter like Karen, I would have painted what I was going through. She often did. I wrote.

I am no longer preoccupied with Nic. This could change, but at the moment I accept and even appreciate that he is living his life his way. Of course I will always hope that he stays sober. I hope that our relationship continues to heal, knowing that this can happen only if and while he's sober.

Where has my worry gone? I have a mental image of it. The artist Chuck Close once said, "I get overwhelmed by the whole."

He learned to break down images into a grid of small, manageable squares. Painting one square at a time, he creates mesmerizing wall-sized portraits. I was often overwhelmed by the whole, too, but I learned to contain my worry about Nic in a square or two of the grid that would be there if Close were to paint my life. I check into them once in a while. When I do, I feel an entire range of emotions, but they don't overwhelm me.

Sometimes I still freak myself out about the future, but far less than I used to. I'm better about taking it one day at a time. It may sound simplistic, but it's as profound as any concept I know. I can still worry what will happen to Nic in five years, in ten—to Jasper and Daisy, for that matter—but then I return to today.

Today.

It is June. Daisy's birthday. She is ten today. Ten! It's also step-up day—Daisy stepping up to fifth grade, Jasper to seventh.

Their graduation song this year is "I Believe in Love," with verses written by the children with the help of their teachers. The World Beat Band plays. "Fourth grade was the door," sings Daisy and her friends, "and knowledge was the key. The fiesta was fantastica. We sang in harmony. Gold country and Ohlone Days kept us in the groove. Fourth grade time is over; we're fifth graders on the move. I believe in music. I believe in love . . ."

Jasper's grade stands and the children sing their verse: "Sixth grade was heck-a-gnarly, the Angel Island trip kind of scarred me. Ancient Egypt, China, and Greek philosophies. And nothing really rhymes with Mesopotamia. I believe in music. I believe in love . . ."

In the evening, our weekly dinner at Nancy and Don's is devoted to celebrating the kids' graduation, Nancy's and Daisy's birthdays, and my anniversary. It has been exactly a year since my brain hemorrhage.

The kids are at the kitchen table playing Chinese checkers with Nancy, who is losing and not taking it well. "That's not fair," she huffs when Jasper wins.

Jasper, Daisy, and their cousin drag out an old piano dolly tied to a long rope. They take turns pulling one another on it, almost as if they're water-skiing. The rider goes careening around the living room. In the kitchen, Nancy tosses a handful of chopped shallots into a skillet of melted butter. When they're crispy and brown, she adds red wine vinegar. After stirring it, she leaves the sauce to simmer on the range and goes onto the deck. Looking up into the trees, she makes a funny bird call. Crows and jays come down for crackers.

Don climbs up the path from the garden, where he has been watering. He wears a pocket radio with earphones. The kids charge into the kitchen, trailed by the pack of barking dogs, including Brutus, who makes his slow way behind the others. Nancy made a leg of lamb with the vinegar-and-shallot sauce and white beans with kale, fresh thyme, and garlic. Karen's brother carves. For dessert, her sister made a lemony cake with pale pink and blue icing and tiny monkeys, elephants, and bears with candles in them. We sing happy birthday to Daisy and Nancy, who blow out the candles. Afterward, Jasper, sitting next to me at the table, says, "I can't believe it's summer."

Summer. Surfing in Santa Cruz. We are here with our dear friends on a quiet day at the hook at Pleasure Point. The waves are small, so most of the hardcore locals have stayed home. But the silky, gently peeling sets are perfect for the children. The water is clear and warm. Sitting on my board, awaiting the next set, I take a moment to survey the grid inside my head until I reach the squares in which Nic resides. He and I spent so much time here together.

On the drive home up the coast, Jasper chooses a CD. Like his older brother when he was younger, Jasper's favorite musician of the moment is Beck, and he hands me *Midnite Vultures* to slide into the player. The car is sandy and we are all sandy and salty and the sea air rushes in the open windows and Beck is singing — Jasper and I along with him. Daisy complains, telling us to turn it down. I look out at the blue ocean, feel Nic so strongly.

At home, Jasper is sitting on the deck with Daisy, consoling her. She is upset because she watched a video about global warming. "I feel like I am standing against a wall and a giant monster is coming slowly toward me and I want to stop it but I can't," she says. She's actually teary. "I want to fly up there and sew a patch on the ozone layer." If that wasn't enough, she also overheard that Pluto is no longer considered a planet. "The poor little nugget," she says, wiping a teardrop. But soon she pushes aside her sadness about Earth and Pluto, and Jasper is directing her and himself in a play they wrote called *Queen Mean*.

I am in my office writing when an email arrives from Nic's girlfriend. She has attached some photos from their recent road trip. Nic, his hair longer, wears big sunglasses, a newsboy cap, a black T-shirt, and bell-bottoms. He stands by a river. He's in front of a geyser at Yellowstone National Park. He smiles — a joyful smile.

In the morning, the garden is swathed in lacy fog. Karen got up early to drive Daisy to swim-team practice. Jasper is upstairs noodling on the guitar. I call Nic to say hi. We talk awhile. He sounds — he sounds like Nic, my son, back. What's next? We'll see. Before hanging up, he says, "Give Karen, Jas, and Daisy my love." Then he says he has to go.

Postscript for the UK edition

In its most recent report, the International Narcotics Control Board (INCB) indicates that methamphetamine remains the world's number-one drug problem. "Demand for methamphetamine ... continues to steadily increase in both the industrialized and developing world," it summed. The meth epidemic is worsening in many Asian nations. In Thailand, where the government's war on the drug has resulted in the death of thousands of people, it has been estimated that an astronomical and almost inconceivable 9 to 11 percent of all adults are "dependent" on meth. Both cities and rural areas in Japan, Thailand, North Korea, South Korea, China, Myanmar, and the Philippines, are being devastated by the drug. Meth is also turning up in many African nations and the INCB report notes that "over the past year, methamphetamine production increased, and drug-related violence and homicides escalated" throughout the western hemisphere.

Indeed, meth is a growing concern throughout Europe. Evidence of its prevalence has been found through an unlikely source: euros. Banknotes are often rolled up and used to snort the drug. As a result, they can retain a trace of the sulphates that are used to produce meth. These chemicals can cause banknotes to corrode. German banking officials told *Der Speigel* Magazine that an increasing number of euros are "crumbling" after being withdrawn from cash machines. Much of Germany's supply of crystal, most smuggled in from the Czech Republic, Lithuania,

Moldova, and Slovakia, has high concentrations of sulphates, which spread between contaminated and clean notes in wallets and purses. According to the spokesman for the banking industry, "A 2003 report by the Institute for Biomedical and Pharmaceutical Research in Nuremberg found that 90% of German euros were contaminated with cocaine. Now we are finding meth."

Australia and New Zealand have steadily growing rates of meth abuse. A recent report by the New Zealand Police Force noted that the drug is readily available; is being used by a greater cross section of society than in the past, and is increasingly linked to domestic violence and horrific crimes. Similarly, more young Australians are using methamphetamines than ever before. According to one report, an estimated one hundred thousand Australians used meth in the week the survey was conducted and five hundred thousand used it in the previous month—up twenty-eight percent from six months earlier.

Until recently it looked as if Britain was being spared from the devastation wrought by methamphetamine, but this is changing. The drug is turning up in the London nightclub scene with regularity and there is a well documented epidemic in the nation's gay community. In addition, there have been a number of busts of meth labs in England. Similar circumstances presaged the current epidemic in the US—and indeed, the drug has now been reported in many towns throughout England including Torquay, Luton, Sunderland and Huddersfield. As a result of an increase in meth-related hospital admissions and crime, in early 2007 the British government reclassified the drug as class A, joining heroin on the list of the most dangerous illegal substances. In addition, there is a movement in Britain to ban or control some common cold medicines that can be used to cook meth—at a time when the drug is reportedly becoming easier to get in bars and clubs and from many of the same dealers who supply crack, cocaine, and heroin. The cost: £35–£75 for a gram—more than enough to start an addiction.

In the US, meanwhile, the number of meth users has been on a slow decline in some communities, but it has surged in others. Recently there have been troubling reports of a new variety of meth that is flooding many cities. Called "strawberry quick," the methamphetamine is flavored with sugary powder so that it tastes like candy. It is being marketed to younger children.

Meth may be particularly neurotoxic, but, as I have said, it would have been no easier to see my son strung out on heroin or cocaine or any other drug. All of these drugs lead to broken families and destroyed lives as well as crime and death. There are an estimated twenty-three million addicts and alcoholics in all in the US. The UK number is currently believed to be around five and a half million. According to the Partnership for a Drug Free America, abuse of prescription and over-the-counter medicines "has become entrenched in teen culture." In a recent survey, one in five teens (or four and a half million) reported abusing prescription medications to get high, while one in ten teens reported abusing cough medicine. There are also reports of rises in the use of heroin, ecstasy, and PCP.

These alarming trends may be discouraging, but as our family learned, everyday people get sober. Everyday lives are saved. On occasion I still attend Al-Anon or AA or NA meetings. The stories I hear are still heartbreaking—many of them unbearably so—but many are hopeful.

"That was ten years ago," a girl in her mid-twenties says at a meeting, describing the time she woke up in an alleyway. On heroin, she had been repeatedly raped. She had multiple fractures, including a concussion. "I have stayed sober since then. My life now is a blessing." She describes the appreciation she has for her family and friends. She describes a better life than she ever dreamed possible.

A boy who was captain of his high school football team — whose life descended when he became addicted to meth — says, "My last relapse landed me in jail. Thank God, because I wound up in rehab. Now I'm back in school. I've got friends, a good relationship with my parents. I love my life." His fellow addicts in the room applaud. They understand what it feels like to say, "I love my life," after periods of hating it.

Jeanne, a thirty-two-year-old teacher, shakily confessed to a friend that she was in trouble. Her drug use had, she says, "gone way out of control." It began casually. She snorted cocaine occasionally, "on weekends just to loosen up and party." Not now. "I've been using it every day," she confided, "first thing. I need it to get through the day." She choked on her words and continued, "I never understood what it meant to be addicted to something. I thought drug addicts were homeless and derelicts and criminals. Like . . ."

She looked at her friend and immediately felt self-conscious. Jeanne had chosen this friend to confide in because her former boyfriend was an addict. And, yes, a criminal. He wound up in jail, but not before her friend tried to help him get sober. Three or four times.

Her friend said, "Rehab's a waste of time and money." Instead, she said that she had read about a new treatment for cocaine addiction — what she called "anti-addiction drugs" — offered at a clinic. "It takes a month and works miracles," she said. But when Jeanne asked another friend — an alcoholic in recovery — he told her to go into rehab. "There's no shortcut," he said. Jeanne's sister said she just needed some time away and recommended a meditation retreat. She asked her family physician, who prescribed sedatives. She filled the prescription, but ignored the other advice. One evening, high on the pills and cocaine, she ran a red light and was stopped by a police officer who administered a sobriety test.

She failed. The officer searched her and her car and discovered two grams of cocaine. Arrested, Jeanne spent the night in jail and later, in court, pleaded no contest to possession and charges of driving while under the influence. She no longer had a choice about treatment: a judge mandated a rehab program. That was seven years ago. "I never expected to be able to say this," she said recently. "But what at the time seemed like the worst thing that could ever happen to me was the best—a gift. To anyone out there who is struggling with alcoholism and addiction, I would tell them, 'At first, yeah, it's really hard, but it gets easier. I promise. Not only that, but at the start of the process of recovery, the rewards of a better life may seem impossible to imagine. Once you choose to face your problem and treat it, however, everything in your life can improve. You can have the life you always dreamed of. I do."

Afterword

In the decade since *Beautiful Boy* was published, I've heard from thousands of people. Many were addicted or loved someone who was. As I had been when this all began, they were isolated and scared. Many said that hearing my story gave them comfort and encouraged them to share their own stories.

Beautiful Boy was preceded by an article I wrote for the *New York Times Magazine*. Before it appeared, a friend read it and warned me not to publish it. She said that people at Jasper and Daisy's grade school would look at our family differently and even treat our kids differently. They'd judge us. So I braced myself. The article was published, and guess what?

If there was any negative judgment at the kids' school or elsewhere, I have never seen or felt it. What I did see was an immense outpouring of concern, help, commiseration, and kindness. I connected deeply with people I'd never known. As I walked through their campus one day soon after the article appeared, a mom I didn't know grabbed my arm and pulled me aside. Before she could say a word, she was crying. She had grown up with an alcoholic father. She was worried about her child, an eighth grader, because she'd caught him smoking pot. She hadn't told anyone until then.

A father told me that his daughter was in treatment for an eating disorder and addiction. His voice cracked and his hands shook. He whispered it as if there was shame in having a child suffering a serious illness. Since this book was published, I've heard thousands of stories like these. The details of those stories break my heart, but I am honored to have heard every one of them.

Anne Lamott advises, "Try not to compare your insides with other people's outsides." That is, it may look as if everyone else is doing great, their kids are sailing through. But no one sails through.

When we tell others about our struggles, we find tremendous relief. We find comfort. We get help. We are reminded that life is hard for everyone. All of us are united by our suffering and by the support we give each other.

People also wrote to me because they'd felt as I had throughout the years of Nic's drug use: desperate for help. Some were overwhelmed by the prospect of raising children in a culture in which drugs are ubiquitous. People asked me how to prevent their children from using in the first place, how to interrupt drug use if it had begun, and how to prevent early stages of drug use from becoming addiction. Like me, they had no idea where to turn, and most were subjected to America's disastrous addiction-treatment system.

For a book I wrote after *Beautiful Boy*, *Clean: Overcoming Addiction and Ending America's Greatest Tragedy*, I continued to research addiction and learned that 90 percent of people who need help never receive it. Indeed, people with addiction are more likely to wind up in prison than in rehab. Those who do get treatment enter a broken system that's almost impossible to navigate. Whether they're trying to help a loved one or seeking help themselves, most people are in crisis when they first encounter this system. They're immobilized by fear and anxiety, and yet in this compromised state, they must make one of the most complex and important decisions of their lives.

Because they don't know where to turn, people in need of help go online. A Google search for drug treatment programs turns up seventy-three million results. Programs promise miracle cures and inflate their success rates. Many Web sites that purport to provide objective information are disguised advertisements for treatment programs, and some of those cost more than fifty thousand dollars a month.

People may seek the advice of professionals, but few know what to recommend. They often do what I did at first, which was rely on the testimonial of a friend of a friend—hardly the way to find treatment for a serious, potentially fatal disease.

As I wrote in *Clean*, "Of course, many people recommend rehab, but what is rehab, exactly? There's no standard definition; it's a generic word for a wide variety of treatments, including many that are harmful. Some rehabs employ threats and harsh and humiliating punishments. Some are run by self-anointed 'experts' with no training or credentials, unless you count their own recoveries from addiction. In many states, anyone can open a rehab. There are online guides such as 'How to Open a Drug-Rehabilitation Center.' Some programs are operated by cults and many actively reject science- based treatments, including medications like Suboxone and methadone, even though they are by far the most successful treatments for opioid addiction.

"Often, the more information people get, the more bewildered they become ... and they become increasingly disillusioned, skeptical, and distrustful, because most treatments are a haphazard collection of cobbled-together, often useless, and sometimes harmful recovery programs based not on medical science but on tradition, wild guesses, wishful thinking, and pseudoscience, some of which borders on voodoo. (I've heard of a program that claims to treat addiction by exorcism and past-life reintegration.)"

Finally, I heard from people who reached the last page of *Beautiful Boy* and were worried about Nic, because the book ends without a clear resolution.

Whether in person or through letters or private Facebook and Twitter messages, people asked as gently and tactfully as they could. Some apologized in advance, fearing that they might open a wound. They asked if Nic survived.

I thanked them for writing and assured them he had.

The journey was still challenging. Nic relapsed in 2010 after two years of sobriety. Of course, as with every other relapse, I was devastated and scared. But something important had changed. Other relapses quickly led to catastrophe, and I had to intervene, but Nic stopped this one on his own. He recognized he'd relapsed, realized he needed help, and checked himself into a residential treatment program. From there he enrolled in outpatient treatment.

Following that relapse, Karen and I went with Nic to see a new psychiatrist. The doctor spent an hour with Nic and then called in Karen and me. He said aloud what we had feared: that the last relapse was proof that Nic's addiction still posed a serious threat.

Contrary to the common message that relapse is part of recovery, this doctor insisted that we shouldn't accept it as inevitable. Rather, we should assume there were reasons beyond addiction itself for Nic's continuing relapses. The doctor asked to see the results of Nic's psychological tests.

I asked, "What psychological tests?"

The doctor was incredulous. "Do you mean to tell me that Nic has been in a dozen treatment programs, and he's seen all those therapists"—about a dozen of those, too—"and no one had him tested?"

No one had.

He identified a major problem in the addiction-treatment field: the majority of those who become addicted have co-occurring psychological disorders and have experienced some form of trauma. If those issues aren't addressed, continued relapse is likely.

The doctor ordered tests, and the results were definitive: Nic has severe bipolar disorder and depression. In the years after his mother and I divorced, I'd taken him to see therapists, and some recognized depression and anxiety, but none identified the intensity of those afflictions, had him tested, or offered treatments that worked.

After he was diagnosed, Nic moved back to Los Angeles, where he began working with a doctor to treat his psychiatric disorders as well as his addiction. He still sees her for therapy and takes medications she prescribes and monitors. He religiously takes the antidepressants and bipolar medications, plus Suboxone, the drug I mentioned earlier that blocks craving of and prevents overdose on opioids.

He hasn't relapsed since then.

Nic and I have speculated on how his life might have been different if he'd undergone psychological testing when he was younger. What if his illnesses had been diagnosed and treated then? Would he have become addicted? Even if he had, would his drug use have been as extreme? Would he have been as treatment-resistant? Would he have continued to relapse?

There's no way to know, but we both believe that diagnosis as a child or as an early teen would have spared him some or most of the torments he's since endured.

When I researched addiction, I found evidence that many people use drugs to self-medicate for psychological problems. It makes sense that someone with untreated depression and bipolar disorder would use drugs. When Nic felt depressed, getting high was not just the easiest remedy; it was the only one. When his anxiety felt unbearable, he used drugs to ease the angst and pain. When he suffered the terrible highs and lows of bipolar disorder, he used drugs to feel sane. Since he's been in consistent treatment for his psychological disorders, he's stayed sober.

As of this writing, Nic has been sober for eight years.

*

Six years ago, Nic got married. His wife, Jette, had been his best friend when he was in sixth and seventh grade. She was the girl I mentioned in *Beautiful Boy* when I wrote about taking Nic and some friends to the beach and then back to our house for a sleepover. I called her "Skye": "Their preteen awkwardness dissolves as they play like much younger children, laughing without self-consciousness, tumbling and wrestling in the sand. Before dark, we drive back home, where they play Twister and Truth or Dare, with risqué questions like, 'Do you think Skye is cute?' (Nic does: She's the big-eyed, brown-haired girl whose name, when he mentions it, makes him blush. He talks to her on the phone at night, sometimes for an hour or more at a time.)"

Skye—*Jette*—is my daughter-in-law.

Nic hadn't seen Jette for a decade since his drug use and addiction began. As many people do when they become addicted, Nic had shed his old friends, including Jette, replacing them with ones who used.

Nic and Jette both happened to be visiting their parents in the Bay Area and ran into each other at Karen's opening at an art gallery in the city. A friend of mine who witnessed their reunion came up to me at the opening and whispered in my ear, "They're going to get married."

A year later, they did.

Jasper was Nic's best man. Daisy did what she'd do for no one but her big brother: wear a flowery pink dress.

Nic and Jette live in LA. Nic works as a writer. Besides his two memoirs, *Tweak* and *We All Fall Down*, he's written a novel and has worked as a writer on several TV shows. He sometimes speaks about addiction and recovery to students and other groups. (We often speak together.)

And, of course, Nic isn't the only one who's grown up. Jasper is twenty-four, and Daisy twenty-two. The three of them live within fifteen or twenty miles of one another. They often hang out at each other's houses and have dinner together, or go to movies, or to the beach.

It sounds like a happy ending to a nightmarish story of addiction, and it is. What I'm saying is, as bad as it gets, there's usually hope. People usually recover. To those in the throes, I say: Addiction is a complicated disease that's often further complicated by co-occurring psychological disorders. Living with it is always a challenge, and sometimes a torment. But those diseases are treatable. I'll say it again: Don't give up hope.

I started shaking when I typed the words "don't give up hope." As I wrote them, my head filled with a cacophony of voices and a flood of tears. They're the voices and tears of the people I've met and corresponded with who have no hope.

I hear from these parents and other loved ones every day. And I meet them—devastated people. I can see it in their eyes before they say a word. They show me photographs and say, "He was the light of my life" and "She was my angel." Child after child killed by this disease because they never got the treatment they needed.

There's no hope for them.

Even as I'm grateful that my son is alive, my heart breaks for these other parents, children, siblings, partners, husbands, wives, and others who've lost someone they love.

After completing *Beautiful Boy*, I planned to go back to writing a business book I'd been working on. But because of the people who'd lost their loved ones, I couldn't. There was too much suffering. Here was a problem that was devastating families, and almost no one was talking about it. And when addiction strikes, no one knows what to do. So I set out to learn whatever I could about drug use and addiction, and to learn why we fail so miserably in our efforts to stop these scourges.

My research resulted in *Clean*, in which I reported on the devastation, but also on the progress that was being made, which gave me hope for the future. I described the changing paradigm of addiction prevention and treatment, rooted in the knowledge that addiction is a disease rather than a character flaw. Although the changes were slow, I saw movement, the evolution from archaic attempts to prevent and treat addiction to modern methods based on science.

I believed things were improving, and they were. But they've since gotten worse.

The year *Beautiful Boy* was published, thirty-six thousand people in America died of drug overdoses. In 2013, when I wrote *Clean*, the number was about forty thousand. In 2017 there were sixty-four thousand. One hundred and seventy-five people died every day—that's eight an hour. The number is predicted to be higher in 2018. The main culprits have been opioids, including prescription pain medications like OxyContin and Vicodin, and street drugs like heroin and fentanyl. They're the number-one killers of people under fifty. More people die of opioid overdoses than car accidents, suicide, or any other nonnatural cause. In the meantime, even as the nation focuses on the opioid crisis, the use of methamphetamine and cocaine is rising.

The opioid overdose epidemic has many causes. Pharmaceutical companies claimed their opioids were nonaddictive, and partly as a result, doctors overprescribed them. Even when properly prescribed, they were often accessible to kids; the most common place they got these drugs was their parents' medicine cabinets. (Dispose of yours or lock them away!) In many cases people who used pain medications couldn't get more because they were unavailable or expensive, and they discovered heroin and fentanyl, which are related and cheap, which explains the spike in the use of—and overdose on—those drugs. Fentanyl is fifty times stronger than heroin. Another concern is an opioid called carfentanil, which is as much as one hundred times more potent than fentanyl. According to the *New York Times*, an amount smaller than a snowflake could kill a person.

The current crisis is rooted in America's half-century-old war on drugs.

Most people know that President Nixon inherited the war in Vietnam, but few remember that in 1971 he initiated the war on drugs. Without question, the war has been a failure, costing far more than a trillion dollars, while drug use, and the resulting morbidity and death, has risen steadily.

The government's handling of the problem would be laughable if the implications weren't so horrific. In addition to the deaths, consider the related tragedies that can result from drug use—crime, accidents, suicide, sexual assault, abuse, drug- and alcohol-caused illnesses, lost productivity—and you'll begin to fathom the enormity of the problem, much of which is hidden.

It's hidden because many addiction-related deaths are officially ascribed to other causes: suicide, homicide, accidents, heart attacks, hypertension, pulmonary disorders, strokes and other brain hemorrhages, hepatitis and other infections, HIV/AIDS, liver disease, respiratory disease, kidney disease, septicemia, and on and on. Because payment of life insurance may be denied if drug or alcohol abuse led to death, doctors and medical examiners do grieving families the "favor" of citing a death's immediate cause—an accident or ailment—rather than the underlying, primary one. And apart from these more practical reasons, addiction remains a secret because of the shame associated with it. When the scion of a prominent Midwestern business family died suddenly, newspaper accounts cited the cause of death stated on the coroner's death certificate: injuries sustained in a motorcycle accident. The lethal dose of heroin in the young man's bloodstream was never mentioned.

While we go on denying the ubiquity of addiction, we marginalize and stigmatize its victims. According to a national survey called "The Face of Recovery," one quarter of the people in recovery have been denied a job or a promotion or have had trouble getting insurance; seven in ten reported that they had experienced shame or social embarrassment. In our society, addicts are viewed as having a character deficiency rather than a serious illness. We often ignore their condition except to criminalize it and the dangerous behavior it can lead to. In addition, the threat of arrest and prosecution makes it less likely that addicts will admit their problem and seek early treatment. So the disease progresses, making it more likely that addicts will become criminals.

The opioid epidemic has made politicians finally discuss the nation's drug problem, and some have acknowledged that the war-on-drugs approach was counterproductive. President Obama called the war on drugs an "utter failure." As I reported in an op-ed in *USA Today*, "His administration emphasized treatment-and-prevention programs based on scientific advances that have shown addiction to be a brain disease with biological, psychological, and environmental determinants. The president championed landmark legislation that funded mental health and addiction treatment programs and research ... A godsend to sufferers of substance-use disorders, the Affordable Care Act [ACA] mandated that insurance plans cover mental health, including addiction care, in parity with other diseases."

I reported that Obama's first attorney general, Eric Holder, ended the draconian mandatory minimum sentencing that filled prisons with people convicted of nonviolent drug crimes, and his drug czar, Michael Botticelli, called for replacing "the failed policies and failed practices" with evidence-based prevention, treatment, and harm reduction. Obama's surgeon general, Vivek Murthy, released a groundbreaking report on alcohol, drugs, and health that made science-based prevention and treatment a national priority.

When he was a presidential candidate, Donald Trump called America's drug crisis "a crippling problem." He said, "This is an epidemic that knows no boundaries and shows no mercy, and we will show great compassion and resolve as we work together on this important issue."

In the op-ed I wrote, "However, as president he's largely abandoning the addicted and their families."

After he was elected, Trump signed an executive order establishing the President's Commission on Combating Drug Addiction and the Opioid Crisis. The commission released a list of fifty-six recommendations, including expanding access to treatment, but as of the publication of this new edition of *Beautiful Boy*, the administration has provided almost no money. In fact, Trump proposed slashing six billion dollars from some of the agencies that address drug use and addiction.

"Of immediate concern to Americans who meet the diagnostic criteria for the disease of addiction," I wrote, "and the 40 million regularly misusing alcohol and other drugs who are at risk and may require some form of treatment, the president is determined to dismantle the ACA. In addition . . . at least thirty-seven states are trying to end mandates that require insurance plans to cover the treatment of mental illness, including addiction."

In the meantime, Trump has returned to failed drug-war policies. Attorney General Jeff Sessions has reinstated mandatory minimum sentencing. He said, "You have to able to arrest people and then you're intervening in their destructive habit. Many people never ever recover from addiction—except by the grave."

In fact, most of them would recover if they received proper treatment. I wrote, "Any policy that throws sick people in prison is inhumane and harmful."

Meanwhile, addiction continues to devastate families and communities. Yet when it strikes, people are caught off guard. Given the enormity of the suffering, it's astounding that we—the collective we—are doing so many things wrong in our fight against this disease. We fail miserably when it comes to education about drug abuse and addiction. The day- or weeklong education sessions provided at school pale—in quality and quantity—in comparison to messages that promote use and abuse. We fail at prevention, too, because we're inept at diagnosing and treating the psychological and social problems that create fertile ground for addiction.

Stigma and prejudice have also limited financial support for research into addiction and limited access to evidence-based treatments. Thus addiction carries a relatively poor prognosis, which reinforces its stigma. (Many people think those afflicted with addiction can't get well, but again, with proper treatment, most can.)

The afflicted who manage to find a good program may find it impossible to pay for it. In spite of ACA provisions that require insurance companies to cover mental illness, including substance-use disorders, in parity with other diseases, it's rare that plans pay for needed treatments. Good publicly funded programs are scarce.

As a result, few of the addicted get the long-term, comprehensive care they need. And by the time they seek treatment, if they do, they're usually in crisis, which makes it more difficult and expensive to treat them. At that stage, many are belligerent, angry, depressed, or even violent, so doctors, nurses, counselors, and social workers don't always want to treat them. Some caregivers admit they'd rather spend their energy, as a nurse put it, "on appreciative patients rather than antagonistic ones who'll likely be back in the ER in a week or month or two."

The war on drugs wasn't the only one Nixon declared in 1971. In his State of the Union address that year, he also declared war on cancer. "I will ask for an appropriation . . . to launch an intensive campaign to find a cure for cancer," he announced. "The time has come in America when the same kind of concentrated effort that split the atom and took man to the moon should be turned toward conquering this dread disease. Let us make a total national commitment to achieve this goal." By the end of that year, he had signed into law the National Cancer Act, declaring, "I hope in the years ahead we will look back on this action today as the most significant action taken during my Administration."

Cancer hasn't been eradicated, of course, but the illness, once a death sentence, is now often treatable. The incidence of cancer began dropping in 1990 and has continued to fall every year since then. Since 2004, the death rate from cancer has decreased at double the rate of the previous two decades.

I believe we need an all-out war on addiction modeled on the war on cancer. We could save millions of lives and billions of dollars now squandered on, and by, addiction. But we won't make a dent in this problem unless we decide to fight the right war.

What would such a campaign look like? Like the war on cancer, it would have to be well coordinated and lavishly funded, comprehensive, multifaceted, and long term. "The war on cancer supported basic research handsomely," noted Dr. Vincent DeVita, a professor of medicine at the Yale Cancer Center. "It set up application programs and U.S. clinical trials programs. The measure gave the National Cancer Institute unique autonomy within the National Institutes of Health to fund and coordinate research."

The war on addiction should include significant money for

research as well as similar application and clinical trials programs. Researchers have hundreds of promising ideas for medications, cognitive and behavioral therapies, and combination treatments, and a flood of money into the field would allow a far wider range of study and draw in new researchers who will learn more about the mechanics of addiction and develop and test promising treatments.

In addition, there must be an overhaul of the treatment system. Much as physicians and hospitals are, addiction-treatment practitioners and programs must be required to be licensed, and they should be monitored. Programs that offer substandard treatment should be put out of business. And evidence-based care—in doctors' offices as well as outpatient and residential treatments—must be available to anyone who needs it. Insurance, include Medicaid, must pay for quality, long-term care.

Meanwhile, there's resistance to some of the most effective treatments we have now. For example, I mentioned that Nic takes Suboxone, which lessens craving, blocks an opioid high, and prevents overdose. This and other addiction medications are by far the most successful treatment for opioid addiction, but many treatment providers ignore the evidence and refuse to use it.

The final component of a war on addiction should be prevention, the current buzzword for dealing with obesity, heart disease, and many other illnesses. We could save billions of dollars and untold lives if we intervened early and prevented the progress of addiction and its effects. Addiction prevention would identify and face head-on the risk factors, including social and psychological conditions and mental illness, that often lead to addiction.

In addition to lowering morbidity and mortality, the war on cancer changed the way we look at the disease and treat its sufferers. Cancer is no longer the "Big C," a secret shame. Addiction, destigmatized, would come to be thought of as a serious illness, best recognized and treated early. This might be the biggest breakthrough of all.

Can we cure addiction? Again, despite forty-five years of aggressive research, many cases of cancer resist treatment. But we have made dramatic progress. And in the process we've relieved incalculable suffering, saved hundreds of millions of dollars, and saved millions of lives. A war on addiction would do the same— and more. By dramatically decreasing emergency room visits and prison populations, we would eventually free up funds to treat other illnesses, improving health care across the board. We'd eliminate much homelessness and dramatically reduce violence, including child abuse, spousal abuse, sexual assault, and violent crime. We'd help families stay together and repair broken neighborhoods. We'd alleviate immeasurable suffering.

In spite of the current crisis, I'm still hopeful, in part because science continues to progress and evidence-based treatments are slowly being adopted by treatment professionals. I'm hopeful because more people are learning that addiction is a disease, not a choice. I also find hope in the launch of national organizations founded to address addiction and in a grassroots movement started by parents who've lost their kids. In cities across the country, these parents have banded together and organized programs to educate the public about drugs and addiction and successfully lobbied legislators to fund prevention campaigns, treatment programs, and enact "911 Good Samaritan" laws in many states. In the past, people have died because they overdosed in the company of friends who didn't call 911 because they feared getting arrested, which they could have been. These laws protect people who call authorities in order to save a life. They've also successfully lobbied to make a drug called naloxone, or Narcan, widely available. This drug can temporarily revive a person who's overdosed on opioids, giving time for EMTs to arrive.

As I've traveled around the country, I've met many of those parents who've devoted their lives to ending addiction. They're using their anguish so that other parents won't have to suffer what they're suffering. They are saying "Enough!" They will no longer tolerate ignoring this disease. They are fighting back against the stigma and refusing to hide in the shadows. They are supporting one another and working tirelessly to end this crisis.

And me? Not a day goes by when I don't realize how lucky we are—Nic and I and our family. I know that luck is the only reason my son is alive while other people have had to bury their children. Even as we go on, I think of these people every day.

I'm so proud of the work Nic has done and continues to do on himself, but of course there are no guarantees. I'm optimistic because of research that shows that time off drugs predicts more time off drugs. But there's always a risk: I've heard about people relapsing after twenty years or more of sobriety.

As I write this, Nic is thirty-six years old.

After what we went through, thirty-six feels miraculous.

Acknowledgments

With great respect, I would like to thank Steve Shoptaw, Edythe London, Walter Ling, and especially Richard Rawson, all at the Integrated Substance Abuse Programs at the University of California, Los Angeles, for helping me to understand addiction. I also would like to thank the people who vetted sections of the book and offered their corrections and suggestions. Along with Drs. Rawson, Shoptaw, and London, they include Dr. Judith Wallerstein and Gayathri J. Dowling, Ph.D., Deputy Chief, Science Policy Branch Office of Science Policy and Communications, National Institute on Drug Abuse.

This book grew out of an article that appeared in the *New York Times Magazine*. I cannot adequately express my thanks and deep respect to my editors there. They guided me with immaculate skill and flawless consciences. They are Katherine Bouton, Gerry Marzorati, and, in particular, Vera Titunik.

It is even more difficult to fully express my gratitude when I get to my friend Eamon Dolan, the editor of this book. It is impossible to overstate his contribution. At every stage, I was inspired by, and learned from, his wisdom, intelligence, and elegant editing. I am also grateful to Suzanne Baboneau and Janet Silver for their devotion to *Beautiful Boy*. Reem Abu-Libdeh contributed her skillful and artful copyediting. Jeremy Butcher created the jacket and design. I would also like to thank Ian Chapman, Rory Scarfe, and Emma Harrow in the UK and Bridget Marmion, Lori Glazer,

Megan Wilson, Carla Gray, David Falk, Lois Wasoff, Sasheem Silkiss-Hero, Chester Chomka, Sanj Kharbanda, Michaela Sullivan, Melissa Lofty and Elizabeth Lee in the US. Binky Urban, my agent, lived through much of this story and provided unwavering support and guidance through minefields. Also at ICM, thanks to Ron Bernstein, Jacqueline Shock, Karolina Sutton, Molly Atlas, and Alison Schwartz. Thank you, too, to Jasper Sheff for his insights and corrections, and Daisy for your suggestions.

At UCSF Medical Center, I am indebted to Michael Lawton, Susan Change, and Lisa Hannigan as well as the many other doctors and nurses there and at Marin General Hospital. Throughout the past few years I have been awed by the brave and dedicated people who work to help addicts and their families. We were counseled, guided, and supported by David Frankel; Paul Ehrlich; Rick Rawson; Jace Horwitz at Herbert House Sober Living Environment, and humble saints who prefer to be mentioned only by their first names, Randy and Ted. I reserve special, and boundless, gratitude for Mary Margaret McClure and Don Alexander.

Finally, I would like to thank the remarkable teachers and families at our children's schools; the wondrous people of Point Reyes Station and Inverness, and of course my dear family and friends. If they got sick of our endless crises, and how could they not have — I did — they never once showed it. Thank you Peggy, Armistead, Christopher, Steve R., Sarah, Mike, Ginny, Annie, Sue, Nan, Lee, Heidi, Bo, Jenny, Jim, Mike M., Marshall, Jennifer, Suning, MK, Laura, Ginee, Fred, Jessica, Peter, Ilie, Jeremiah, Vicki, Susan, Buddy, Mark, Jenny, Becca, Bear, Susan, Lucy, Steve, Mark, Nancy, Don, Debra, Sumner, Joan, and Jamie, Kyle, Dylan, and Lena. On one of the worst days, I checked my voicemail and Jamie had called from New York. "I want to fly home and build a retaining wall around you," he said. You and Kyle did. And with my boundless love, thank you Daisy, Jasper, Nic, and Karen.

Resources

For further reading and help. This is by no means an exhaustive list, but the following books, articles, and websites may be useful.

Addiction. HBO Series. Produced by John Hoffman and Susan Froemke. DVD available. www.hbo.com. Home Box Office, 2007.

Al-Anon and Al-Anon Family Group Headquarters. *The Al-Anon Family Groups — Classic Edition*. Virginia Beach, VA: Al-Anon Family Group Headquarters, Inc., 2000.

Al-Anon and Al-Anon Family Group Headquarters. *Alateen — Hope for Children of Alcoholics*. Virginia Beach, VA: Al-Anon Family Group Headquarters, Inc., 1973.

Al-Anon and Al-Anon Family Group Headquarters. *Courage to Change: One Day at a Time in Al-Anon II*. Virginia Beach, VA: Al-Anon Family Group Headquarters, Inc., 1968, 1972, 1973.

Al-Anon and Al-Anon Family Group Headquarters. *One Day at a Time in Al-Anon*. Virginia Beach, VA: Al-Anon Family Group Headquarters, Inc., 1968, 1972, 1973.

Al-Anon and Al-Anon Family Group Headquarters. *Paths to Recovery — Al-Anon's Steps, Traditions, and Concepts*. Virginia Beach, VA: Al-Anon Family Group Headquarters, Inc., 1997.

Black, Claudia, Ph.D. *Straight Talk from Claudia Black: What*

Recovering Parents Should Tell Their Kids About Drugs and Alcohol. City Center, MN: Hazelden Publishing, 2003.

Brown, Stephanie, Ph.D., Virginia M. Lewis, Ph.D, with Andrew Liotta. *The Family Recovery Guide: A Map for Healthy Growth*. Oakland, CA: New Harbinger Publications, 2000.

Burgess, Melvin. *Junk*. Puffin Teenage Fiction, 1997.

Burton-Phillips, Elizabeth. *Mum Can You Lend Me Twenty Quid: What Drugs Did to My Family*. Piatkus Books, 2007.

Cheever, Susan. *My Name Is Bill: Bill Wilson — His Life and the Creation of Alcoholics Anonymous*. New York: Washington Square Press, 2005.

——. *Note Found in a Bottle*. New York: Washington Square Press, 2006.

Conyers, Beverly. *Addict in the Family: Stories of Loss, Hope, and Recovery*. Center City, MN: Hazelden Publishing and Educational Services, 2003.

Didion, Joan. *The Year of Magical Thinking*. New York: Knopf, 2005.

DrugScope. *Drug Abuse Briefing: A Guide to the Non-medical Use of Drugs in Britain*. DrugScope, 2002.

DrugScope. *Drugs: Your Questions Answered: A Student Reader*. Drug Scope, 2002.

Emmett, David, and Graham Nice. *Understanding Street Drugs: A Handbook of Substance Misuse*. Jessica Kingsley Publishers, 2005.

Fitzgerald, Hiram E., Barry M. Lester and Barry Zuckerman ed. *Children of Addiction*. Garland Science, 2000.

Ganeri, Anita. *Drugs*. Scholastic Point, 1996.

Gilvarry, Eilish. *Young People and Substance Misuse*. RCGP, 2005.

Hoffman, John, and Susan Froemke, eds. HBO's
 Addiction: Why Can't They Just Stop?
 New York: Rodale Press, 2007.

Johnson, Vernon. *Intervention: How to Help Someone Who
 Doesn't Want to Be Helped*. Center City, MN: Hazelden
 Publishing, 1986.

Kellermann, Joseph L. *A Guide for the Family of the Alcoholic*.
 Center City, MN: Hazelden Publishing and Educational
 Services, 1996.

Ketcham, Katherine, and William F. Asbury, with Mel
 Schulstad and Arthur P. Ciaramicoli. *Beyond the Influence:
 Understanding and Defeating Alcoholism*. New York:
 Bantam Books, 2000.

Lamott, Anne. *Bird by Bird: Some Thoughts on Writing and Life*.
 New York: Anchor, 1995.

—. *Plan B: Further Thoughts on Faith*. New York: Riverhead
 Trade, 2006.

—. *Traveling Mercies: Some Thoughts on Faith*. New York:
 Anchor, 2000.

Lawson, Sarah. *Everything Parents Should Know About Drugs
 (Overcoming Common Problems)*. Sheldon Press, 1995

Lynch, Thomas. "The Way We Are," from *Bodies in Motion
 and at Rest: On Metaphor and Mortality*. New York: W. W.
 Norton and Co., 2001.

Mackie, Judy. *Drugs: A Parent's Guide to the Facts (Need2Know)*.
 Need2Know, 1997.

"The Meth Epidemic." *Frontline*. DVD. PBS, 2005.

Milan, James Robert, and Katherine Ketcham. *Under the
 Influence: A Guide to the Myths and Realities of Alcoholism*.
 New York: Bantam Books, 1983.

Mnookin, Seth. "Harvard and Heroin." Salon.com,
 Aug. 27, 1999.

——. "The End of My World As I Knew It." Slate.com, Dec. 31, 2004.

Mnookin, Wendy. "My Son the Heroin Addict." Salon.com, Aug. 27, 1999.

Moyers on Addiction: Close to Home. Directed by Bill Moyers. VHS. Curriculum Media Group, 1998.

Moyers, William C., and Katherine Ketcham. *Broken: My Story of Addiction and Redemption*. New York: Viking, 2006.

Naik, Anita. *Drugs (Wise Guides)*. Hodder Children's Books, 1997.

Oliver, Dr Ian. *Drug Affliction: What You Need to Know*. The Robert Gordon University, 2006.

Orenstein, Peggy. "Staying Clean." *New York Times Magazine*, February 10, 2002.

Recovery of Chemical Dependent Families (booklet). Center City, MN: Hazelden / Johnson Institute, 1987.

Schwebel, Robert. *Saying No Is Not Enough: Helping Your Kids Make Wise Decisions About Alcohol, Tobacco, and Other Drugs*. New York: Newmarket Press, 1989.

Shannonhouse, Rebecca. *Under the Influence: The Literature of Addiction*. New York: Modern Library, 2003.

Sheff, Nic. *Tweak*. New York: Ginee Seo Books/Atheneum, 2007.

Singer, Mark. "The Misfit: How David Milch Got from *NYPD Blue* to *Deadwood* by Way of an Epistle of St. Paul." *The New Yorker*, February 14 and 25, 2005.

Stark, Margaret M., and Jason Payne-James. *Symptoms and Signs of Substance Misuse*. Greenwich Medical Media Ltd, 2002.

Sweet, Corinne. *Overcoming Addiction: Positive Steps for Breaking Free of Addiction and Building Self-esteem*. Piatkus Books, 1999.

Tyler, Andrew. *Street Drugs*. Coronet Books, 1995.

Wallerstein, Judith S., and Sandra Blakeslee. *What About the Kids: Raising Your Children Before, During, and After Divorce*. New York: Hyperion, 2003.

Wallerstein, Judith S., Julia M. Lewis, and Sandra Blakeslee. *The Unexpected Legacy of Divorce: The 25-Year Landmark Study*. New York: Hyperion, 2000.

Websites for more information and referrals, including twelve-step meetings in your area

Addaction; gives details on individual projects, research and development, training courses and access to networks
www.addaction.org.uk

Addiction Recovery Foundation; registered charity
www.addictiontoday.co.uk

Adfam; national charity working with families affected by drugs and alcohol
www.adfam.org.uk

Drugs Information UK; dedicated to, and for the help of, people who are struggling with the substance misuse of a friend or family member
www.drugs-info.co.uk

DrugScope; charity providing an online encyclopaedia of drugs and directory of help sources
www.drugscope.org.uk

Families Anonymous; for relatives and friends concerned about the use of drugs or related behavioural problems
www.famanon.org.uk

Life or Meth; methamphetamine awareness, prevention and empowerment resource for gay men and their friends
www.lifeormeth.com

Narcotics Anonymous; information on the fellowship, details
of meetings nationwide, and access to the helpline and
discussion forum
www.ukna.org/

The National Treatment Agency (NTA); a special health
authority, created by the Government in 2001 to improve
the availability, capacity and effectiveness of treatment for
drug misuse in England
www.nta.nhs.uk

Parents Against Drug Abuse (PADA); information and support
group for parents
www.pada.org.uk

Release; national legal and drugs advice service
www.release.org.uk

Tackling Drugs; the Home-Office website
www.drugs.gov.uk

Talk to Frank; builds on the work of the National Drugs
Helpline and provides free, confidential drugs information
and advice 24 hours a day
www.talktofrank.com

Credits

The author wishes to express his thanks to the artists and license holders of the following song lyrics, movie scripts, books, and poems for their permission to use their copyrighted work in this book. All rights are reserved by the copyright owners to the following:

Excerpts from "God," "Beautiful Boy (Darling Boy)," and "Nobody Told Me," written by John Lennon, copyright © 1970, 1980, and 1980, Lenono Music. Used by permission. All rights reserved.

Special thanks to Yoko Ono.

Excerpt from "It's All Right Ma (I'm Only Bleeding")), written by Bob Dylan, copyright © 1965 by Warner Bros., Inc. Copyright renewed 1993 by Special Rider Music. All rights reserved. International copyright secured. Reprinted by permission.

Excerpt from "A Hard Rain's A-Gonna Fall," written by Bob Dylan, copyright © 1963 by Warner Bros., Inc. Copyright renewed 1991 by Special Rider Music. All rights reserved. International copyright secured. Reprinted by permission.

Excerpt from "Reason To Believe" by Bruce Springsteen, copyright © 1982 Bruce Springsteen (ASCAP). Reprinted by permission. International copyright secured. All rights reserved.

For help with these rights, thank you to Marilyn Laverty at Shoreline and Glen Brunman at Sony BGM.

Excerpt from "Shine a Light," written by Mick Jagger & Keith Richards, published by ABKCO Music, Inc., © 1972 ABKCO Music, Inc., www.abkco.com.

Excerpt from "Tears in Heaven," words and music by Eric Clapton and Will Jennings. Copyright © 1992 by E. C. Music Ltd. and Blue Sky Rider Songs. All rights for E. C. Music Ltd. administered by Unichappel Music Inc. All rights for Blue Sky Rider Songs administered by Irving Music, Inc. International copyright secured. All rights reserved.

Excerpt from "These Days," words and music by Jackson Browne. Copyright © 1967 (renewed) Open Window Music. All rights administered by Wixen Music Publishing, Inc. All rights reserved. Used by permission of the publisher and Alfred Publishing Co., Inc.

Excerpt from "In the Neighborhood," written by Tom Waits and Kathleen Brennan, copyright © 1983 Jalma Music (ASCAP). All rights reserved. Used by permission.

Excerpt from "Smells Like Teen Spirit," words and music by Kurt Cobain, Krist Novoselic, and Dave Grohl. Copyright © 1991 EMI Virgin Songs, Inc., The End of Music, MJ Twelve Music, and Murky Slough Music. All rights for The End of Music and Murky Slough Music controlled and administered by EMI Virgin Songs, Inc. All rights for MJ Twelve Music controlled and administered by Songs of Universal, Inc. All rights reserved. International copyright secured. Used by permission.

Excerpt from "Territorial Pissings," words and music by Kurt Cobain and Chet Powers. Copyright © 1991 EMI Virgin Songs, Inc. and The End of Music. All rights controlled

and administered by EMI Virgin Songs, Inc. All rights
reserved. International copyright secured. Used by
permission.

Excerpt from "Dumb," words and music by Kurt Cobain.
Copyright © 1993 EMI Virgin Songs, Inc. and The End
of Music. All rights controlled and administered by EMI
Virgin Songs, Inc. All rights reserved. International
copyright secured. Used by permission.

Special thanks to Peter Asher for the permission to use Nirvana's
lyrics. Thanks also to Shari Wied at Hal Leonard
Publishing.

Excerpt from "Countryside in England" by Van Morrison used
by kind permission of Exile Productions © Van Morrison.
All rights reserved.

Excerpts from *Addict in the Family,* by Beverly Conyers,
copyright © 2003 by Hazelden Foundation. Reprinted by
permission of Hazelden Foundation, Center City, MN.

Excerpts from the script for *Eternal Sunshine of the Spotless Mind*
by Charlie Kaufman are courtesy of Universal Studios
Licensing LLLP. All rights not specifically granted by
Universal herein are reserved.

Excerpts from the script of *One Flew Over the Cuckoo's Nest,* ©
1975 the Saul Zaentz Company. All rights reserved. Used
with permission.

Excerpt from *Welcome to the Dollhouse,* copyright © 1996
Suburban Pictures, Inc.

Excerpt from Fandango Bag Puppet commercial reprinted
with the permission of Fandango Inc., © 2004. All
rights reserved.

Excerpt from the script of *Do the Right Thing,* by Spike Lee,
used by permission of Spike Lee and Seven Acres and a
Mule Productions. All rights reserved.

Excerpt from "thoughts on being 71" from *Open All Night: New Poems* by Charles Bukowski, copyright © 2000 by Linda Lee Bukowski, reprinted by permission of HarperCollins Publishers.

Excerpt from "Bella Notte (This Is the Night)" from Walt Disney's *Lady and the Tramp*. Words and music by Peggy Lee and Sonny Burke, © 1952 Walt Disney Music Company. Copyright renewed. All rights reserved. Used by permission.

You've read the story of the father who loves him;
now, in an exclusive extract from his own book
Tweak, hear from the *Beautiful Boy* himself . . .

Simon & Schuster is proud to publish
David's son Nic's companion memoir,
Tweak, also available now.

Day 1

I'd heard rumors about what happened to Lauren. I mean, I never even knew her that well but we'd sort of hung out a few times in high school. Actually, I was sleeping with her for about two weeks. She had moved to San Francisco when I was a senior and we met somehow – at a party or something. Back in high school it was just pot, maybe I'd do some acid and mushrooms on the weekend.

But I smoked pot every day. I was seventeen and had been accepted at prestigious universities across the country and I figured a little partying was due me. I'd worked hard those last three and a half years. Sure I'd had some problems smoking weed and drinking too much when I was younger, but that was all behind me. I was smart. I was on the swim team. My writing had been published in *Newsweek*. I was a great big brother. I got along with my dad and stepmom. I loved them. They were some of my best friends. So I just started smoking some pot and what harm could that do me anyway? Hell, my dad used to smoke pot. Most everyone in my family did. Our friends did – it was totally accepted.

But with me things were different. In high school I was rolling blunts and smoking them in the car as I drove to school. Every break in classes had me driving off to get high. We'd go into the hills of Marin County, dropping acid or eating mushrooms – walking through the dry grass and overgrown cypress trees, giggling and babbling incoherently. Plus I was drinking more and more, sometimes during the day. I almost always blacked out, so I could remember little to nothing of what'd happened. It just affected me in a way that didn't seem normal.

When I was eleven my family went snowboarding up in Tahoe, and a friend and I snuck into the liquor cabinet after dinner. We poured a little bit from each bottle into a glass, filling it almost three-quarters of the way with the different-colored, sweet-smelling liquid. I was curious to know what it felt like to get good and proper drunk. The taste was awful. My friend drank a little bit and stopped, unable to take anymore. The thing was, I couldn't stop.

I drank some and then I just had to drink more until the whole glass was drained empty. I'm not sure why. Something was driving me that I couldn't identify and still don't comprehend. Some say it's in the genes. My grandfather drank himself to death before I was born. I'm told I resemble him more than anyone else – a long face, with eyes like drops of water running down. Anyway, that night I threw up for probably an hour straight and then passed out on the bathroom floor.

I woke up with almost no memory of what I'd done. My excuse for the vomit everywhere was food poisoning. It scared me, honestly, and I didn't drink again like that for a long time.

Instead I started smoking pot. When I was twelve I was smoking pot every day – sneaking off into the bushes during recess. And that pretty much continued through high school.

Lauren and I really never got very close back then. When I heard later that she'd been put in rehab for cocaine abuse and severe bulimia, I guess it wasn't that surprising. We'd both been really screwed up all the time and I had a history of dating, well, not the most balanced girls. I remember being ashamed to bring her to my house. I remember not wanting my parents to meet her. We'd come in late, late and leave early in the morning – whispering so as not to wake up my little brother and sister. Maybe it was them I wanted to shield from Lauren the most. Or, not from Lauren so much as, well, the person I was becoming. I was ashamed of my behavior, but still I kept going forward. It was like being in a car with the gas pedal slammed down to the floor and nothing to do but hold on and pretend to have some semblance of control. But control was something I'd lost a long time ago.

Anyway, Lauren was not someone I thought about a whole lot. When she approaches me, I don't even recognize her at first. It's been five years. She yells my name:

'Nic Sheff.'

I jump, turning around to look at her.

She is wearing big Jackie O sunglasses and her dyed black hair is pulled back tight. Her skin is pale, pale white and her features are petite and delicately carved. The San Francisco air is cold, even though the sun has broken through the fog, and she has a long black coat pulled around her.

So I think ... think, think. Then I remember.

'L-Lauren, right?'

'Yeah, don't pretend like you don't remember me.'

'No, I ...'

'Whatever. What're you doing here?'

It's a good question.

I'd been sober exactly eighteen months on April 1st, just two days ago. I'd made so much progress. My life was suddenly working, you know? I had a steady job at a rehab in Malibu. I'd gotten back all these things I'd lost – car, apartment, my relationship with my family. It'd seemed like, after countless rehabs and sober livings, I had finally beaten my drug problem. And yet there I was, standing on Haight Street, drunk on Stoli and stoned out on Ambien, which I'd stolen from the med room at that rehab.

Honestly, I was as surprised by my own actions as anyone else. The morning of my relapse, I had no idea I was actually going to do it. Not that there weren't ominous signs. In the twelve-step program they tell you to get a sponsor. Mine was a man named Spencer. He was around forty, strong, with a square face and hair that stood on end. He had a wife and a three-year-old daughter. He spent hours talking with me about recovery. He helped me get into cycling and walked me through the twelve steps. We'd ride our bikes together along the Pacific Coast Highway, up Latigo Canyon, or wherever. He'd relate his own experience getting sober from chronic cocaine addiction. But I stopped calling him as often. Maybe I felt like I didn't need his help anymore. I seldom went to meetings, and when I did, my mind would talk to me the whole time about how much better I was than everyone else — or how much worse I was, depending on the day. I'd stopped exercising as frequently. I'd stopped taking the psych meds they had me on — a mixture of mood stabilizers and antidepressants. I'd started smoking again. Plus there was Zelda.

Zelda was a woman I thought I was madly in love with. She was fourteen years older than I was and, well, she was also engaged to marry another guy, a wealthy real-estate broker named Mike. When I started sleeping with her, I tried to justify it to myself. I figured it was her decision and I wasn't really doing anything wrong and it was just for fun and blah, blah, blah. Basically, I thought I could get away with it. I mean, I thought I could stay detached emotionally.

I couldn't.

She came to represent for me everything I thought would make my life perfect. After all, she'd been married to this famous actor and was an actress and grew up in Los Angeles, raised by her famous uncle who was also in the movie business. Everyone seems to know her in L.A. She's sort of a celebrity, you know? Being with her became my obsession.

Ultimately, however, she wouldn't leave her boyfriend for me and got pregnant with his child. I was crushed. I mean, I just couldn't handle it. So yesterday I relapsed, driving up the 5, drinking from a bottle of Jäger.

So now I'm standing on Haight Street and Lauren, this girl I haven't seen or thought about in five years, is here, in her long black coat, asking me what I'm doing.

I'd driven up from L.A. the night before and slept in my old, falling-apart Mazda, parked in a lot on the edge of the Presidio – a great expanse of forest and abandoned army housing that stretches out to the cliffs overlooking the Pacific and the San Francisco Bay. A friend of mine, Akira, had once lived there. He occupied a basement apartment on the edge of the Presidio. I'd hoped to find him still living there, but after I wandered around the house some – looking into the dust-smeared windows – it was clear that the place was deserted. It was Akira who'd actually introduced me to crystal meth when I was eighteen. He was a friend of a friend. He did a lot of drugs and we immediately gravitated toward each other. Somehow that always seemed to happen – we addicts can always find one another. There must be some strange addict radar or something.

Akira was like me, but more strung out at the time. He had dyed red, curling hair and dark, dark eyes. He was thin, emaciated, with hollowed-out features and narrow, dirty fingers. When he offered me that first line of meth, I didn't hesitate. Growing up I'd heard, you know, never to do heroin. Like, the warnings were everywhere and I was scared – do heroin, get hooked. No one ever mentioned crystal to me. I'd done a little coke, Ecstasy, whatever – I could take it or leave it. But early that morning, when I took those off-white crushed shards up that blue, cut plastic straw – well, my whole world pretty much changed after that. There was a feeling like – my God, this is what I've been missing my entire life. It completed me. I felt whole for the first time.

I guess I've pretty much spent the last four years chasing that first high. I wanted desperately to feel that wholeness again. It was like, I don't know, like everything else faded out. All my dreams, my hopes, ambitions, relationships – they all fell away as I took more and more crystal up my nose. I dropped out of college twice, my parents kicked me out, and, basically, my life unraveled. I broke into their house – I would steal checks from my father and write them out to myself to pay for my habit. When I had a job at a coffee shop, I stole hundreds of dollars from the register. Eventually I got arrested for a possession charge. My little brother and sister watched me get carted away in handcuffs. When my then seven-year-old brother tried to protect me, running to grab me from the armed policemen, they screamed for him to 'get back.' His small body crumpled on the asphalt and he burst into body-shaking tears, sobbing and gasping for breath.

Then there were the treatment centers, two in northern California, one in Manhattan, and one in Los Angeles. I've spent the last three years in and out of twelve-step programs. Throughout all of it, the underlying craving never really left me. And that was accompanied by the illusion that, the next time, things would be different – I'd be able to handle it better. I didn't want to keep hurting people. I didn't want to keep hurting myself. A girlfriend of mine once said to me, 'I don't understand, why don't you just stop?'

I couldn't think of an answer. The fact was, I couldn't just stop. That sounds like a cop-out, but it's the truth. It's like I'm being held captive by some insatiable monster that will not let me stop. All my values, all my beliefs, everything I care about, they all go away the moment I get high. There is a sort of insanity that takes over. I convince myself and believe very strongly that this time, *this time*, it will be different. I tell myself that, after such a long time clean, these last eighteen months, I can go back to casual use. So I walk down to the Haight and start talking to the first street kid who asks me for a cigarette.

This turns out to be Destiny. He is a boy around my age, twenty or twenty-one, with snarled dreads and striking blue eyes. He has the narrow face of a fox or coyote and he's hiding a can of beer indiscreetly in the sleeve of his oversize jacket. He is distracted and out of it as I'm talking to him. I keep trying to get him to focus on what I'm saying. Eventually, he agrees to introduce me to a friend of his who deals speed, so long as I buy him another beer.

'Dude,' he says, his voice thick and strained, 'I'm gonna tell you straight, man, I'm fo'realze. My boy's gonna hook you up fat, that's no joke. You ask anybody, homes, they'll tell you, Destiny is all right. Everyone's cool with me 'cause I be cool with everyone.'

He rambles on like that, pausing only to high-five pretty girls as they pass. As for me, the vodka and sleeping pills have calmed me down enough to keep me breathing through all this – though the blind hungering for the high that only meth can bring has me pretty anxious. There'd been times, in the past, where I got burned copping drugs on the street. On Mission Street I tried to buy some heroin once and came away with a balloon filled with a chunk of black soap.

I smoke cigarettes, one after the other, trying to keep Destiny on point – getting the phone number of his connection. It was right before Lauren stopped me that Destiny told me to wait while he went and got his 'boy's' number from a friend. He walked off down the street and then Lauren is standing there, asking me what I'm doing.

My first instinct, of course, is to lie. The wind is blowing the street clear and Lauren takes off her sunglasses, revealing those transparent green eyes of hers. What I say is, 'Actually, I just moved back here from L.A. where I'd been sober over a year, but now I'm doing the whole relapse thing and I'm just waiting to hook up some meth. I heard you had some trouble like that too. Is that true?'

If she's surprised, she doesn't show it.

'Yeah,' she says, her voice light and soft. 'How much are you getting?'

'A gram, I hope. What are you doing here?'

'I was going to get my tattoo filled in. But, well, now I guess I'm going with you, aren't I? You need any money?'

'Uh, no.'

She puts her glasses back on. 'What about a car?'

'Uh, yeah, we could use your car. Mine's over on Lake Street.'

'All right, then.'

What I said about the money is sort of true. I have three thousand dollars saved up and, for me, that is a lot of money. I'm sure that it'll be enough to get me started on a life working and using in San Francisco. The rehab I'd worked at in Malibu catered to wealthy, often celebrity, clients. They paid well and, sober, I had few expenses. I can afford a sixty-dollar gram. In the next couple days, I'll start looking for work. I mean, I've got it all figured out. Really.

We stand watching the people on the street, walking from shop to shop.

'What've you been doing?' I ask. 'It's been a long time.'

'Five years. But, like you said, I had some trouble. I'm working now, though – for my mom. I have about four months clean.'

'But you're over it.'

'Hell, I've just been waiting for the right person to go out with.'

'Really?'

'I don't know.'

'You look good.'

'Thank you. It's nice to see you, too.'

'Yeah.' I put a hand on her shoulder, feeling her body tense up. 'Here he comes.'

Destiny is sort of strutting or limping or something down the street. I introduce him to Lauren.

'Rockin',' he says. 'We can go meet him in, like, half an hour. Here's his number.' He hands me a crumpled piece of paper. 'You gonna get me that beer, right?'

'Of course.'

'I'll go get my car,' says Lauren.

I walk into the liquor store on the corner and buy two 40s of Olde E and another pack of Export As. Lauren pulls her green Nissan around and we pile in – me in front, Destiny in back. I pass him one of the 40s and drink a bunch of mine down. Lauren refuses to take it when I offer her some, but she pops a few Klonopins 'cause she says she's gonna freak out if she doesn't. She gives me one and I figure it won't do anything since I used to take so much of it, but I chew it up anyway, hoping it might take the edge off or something.

Destiny directs us out of the Haight, and lower Haight, down Market and up into the Tenderloin. The rows of Victorian houses give way to corporate high-rises and then the gritty, twisting streets of the San Francisco ghetto – cheap monthly hotel rooms, panhandlers, small-time hustlers, dealers, and junkies. Neon signs, off during the day, advertise strip clubs and peep shows. The sky has blown completely blue, but the sun is blocked by the falling-down buildings, leaving everything cold and windswept and peeling.

We stop the car on the corner of Jones and Ellis, watching the scourge of walking dead as they drift down the street. One man – a skinny white guy with no hair on his head, but a lot on his face – stands in front of an ATM machine. He turns his head toward the sky every minute or so, screaming, 'Please! Please!' Then he looks back at the ATM. Nothing comes out.

'Here they come,' says Destiny, getting out of the car with the 40. 'Thanks a lot, kids.'

'Cool, man, thanks.'

'Have fun,' he says, nodding toward Lauren knowingly. She maybe blushes a little.

A young kid greets Destiny and then jumps into Lauren's back-seat. He is accompanied by a tall, skinny white man with gray hair and a face that looks like a pile of pastry dough. The boy is thin, but strong, with a round nose and darting eyes. He wears a black bandanna tied around his head and ratty, baggy clothes.

'Yo, what's up? I'm Gack,' he says.

The fat older man says nothing.

'Hey, I'm Nic. This is Lauren.'

'Cool, cool. You wanna G, right?'

His voice comes out in quick, hoarse bursts. I just nod.

'Word,' he says. 'Yo, this is my dad, Mike.'

Mike waves stupidly.

'Anyway,' continues Gack, 'you're gonna give me the money, and I'm gonna go get yo' shit. My dad'll wait here.'

'Dude, there's no way. I'm not letting you walk outta here with my money.'

'Come on, yo, there's no other way. My dad'll stay here and, look, here's my cell phone, and my wallet, and I'll leave my skate-board. Just wait two minutes, okay?'

I look at Lauren. She shakes her head, but I say, 'Fuck, all right.'

I hand him sixty bucks and he leaves. Part of me expects never to see him again, but he returns ten minutes later with our sack. He comes all out of breath.

'Yo, I'm hookin' you up so fat,' he says, handing over a very not fat Baggie of white crystals.

'Dude,' I say, 'this is fucking pin as hell.'

'No way, man.'

I take out one of the pieces and put it in my mouth. The bitter, chemical sour makes me shudder, but it tastes familiar. 'All right, fine,' I say.

'Word.'

'You have any points?' asks Lauren.

I'm proud of her. I hadn't even thought about getting rigs and there she is, coming right out and saying it.

'Uh, yeah. You all don't mess around, huh?'

'No,' we both say at the same time.

Out of his pocket, Gack pulls a pack of maybe five syringes held together by a rubber band.

'Those are cleans?' I ask.

'Fo'sure.'

'All right,' I say. 'We'll take those and we're cool on the short sack.'

'Dude, that sack is fat.'

'Whatever.'

'All right, well, call if you need more.'

'We will,' I say.

And with that, Gack and his dad leave the car and Lauren and I drive off with fresh needles and about a gram of crystal methamphetamine.

I remember Lauren's dad's house from the time we'd been together back in high school – but I also remembered it from when I was much younger. The place is a European-style mansion in Sea Cliff. It is four or five stories high, sort of boxy, with giant bay windows bordered by faded green shutters. Vines climb the gray-washed walls and white roses grow along the sloping stairway. It looks out on the ocean – rough and pounding, relentless. The top story, a bright, sun-drenched loft, used to be the playroom of my best friend and sort-of brother, Mischa.

See, the divorce went down like this: My dad had an affair with a woman, Flicka, then left my mom for her. Mischa was her son. We all moved in together when I was five. Mischa was my age, with long, white-blond hair, blue eyes, and a famous actor father. He threw tantrums and would bite me, but we were also very close. His father was the one who had lived where Lauren's father lives now. I would go over there and play video games with Mischa, or build Lego spaceships, or draw, or whatever.

Walking in the door with Lauren – backpack full of drugs, drunk and stumbling – I can't help but feel a tightness in my stomach, thinking back to the child that I had been. I remember going on walks with my dad out to Fort Point, a jetty that stretches out underneath the Golden Gate Bridge. I remember eating sushi and tempura in Japantown, playing on the ships docked off Hyde Street, riding my bike through Golden Gate Park, being taken to the old Castro movie theater, where a man played the organ before every show. I remember my championship Little League team in Sausalito, birthday parties at the San Francisco Zoo, going to art galleries and museums. I'd been so small that my dad would shelter me from the cold by hiding me in his sweater. Our heads would stick out of the stretched-out wool neckline together. I remember the smell of him – that indescribable smell of dad. He was so there for me always – especially when my mom moved down south. Sober and living in L.A., I'd talked on the phone with him almost every day. We talked about everything – from movies, to art, to girls, to nothing at all. I wonder how long it will be before the calls start coming in – how long before he knows I've gone out, relapsed, thrown it all away.

Lauren's room is in the basement – basically just a large canopy bed and TV and not much else. There are books and clothes and things all over the place. The shades are drawn over the windows, and Lauren plugs in a string of Christmas lights above the built-in shelves along the wall. She puts a CD in the player, something I've never heard before.

'Come on, let's hurry up,' she says. 'My parents will be home soon and I wanna get out of here before they come.'

'Cool. You know, my parents' weekend house in Point Reyes will be empty tonight. We can go stay out there.'

'I gotta work tomorrow morning,' says Lauren.

'That's fine. We'll get you back.'

'My parents are gonna freak out if I don't come home tonight.'

'Make something up.'

'Yeah, fuck, all right.'

'Can I use this?' I ask, holding up a blown-glass jar, maybe an inch high, swirled with streaks of white and green.

'Sure, whatever.'

'You gotta Q-tip?'

'Fuck, yeah, but let's go.'

'All right, chill.'

She rummages around and gets me the Q-tip. I rip off the cotton from one end. I go to the sink in her bathroom and fill the jar with a thin layer of water. I pour in a bunch of the crystal and crush it up with the back of a Bic lighter I have in my pocket. I hold the flame to the base of the jar until the liquid starts to smoke and bubble. I drop in the cotton and then pull it all up into two of the syringes. I pass the one with less over to Lauren and set about making a fist with my right hand, watching the veins swell easily. My body is so clean, so powerful – over a year needle-free and my veins reveal themselves instantly. I think back to how difficult it'd once been to hit – when the veins all began collapsing, hiding under the skin. But now the veins jump up right away. I pull back the plunger, watch the blood rush up into the mixture, and then slam it all home.

I cough.

The chemical lets off this gas as it reaches your heart, or brain, or whatever and it rushes up your throat, choking you.

I cough, choking like that.

My eyes water – my head pounding like maybe I'll pass out, my breathing going so fast.

'Goddamn, goddamn,' I say, the lights dimming out and really, I mean, there's no feeling like it. The high is perfection.

I turn and see Lauren push off and as it hits her I kiss her without saying anything and she kisses back and it is all so effortless, not like being sober and consumed by worry and fear and inhibitions. I kiss her harder, but she pushes me back, saying, 'Come on, let's go to the beach.'

We get outta there fast and then we are walking in the sunlight, back toward Lauren's car. It is a different world, man, heightened, exciting. I light a cigarette and my fingers move spasmodically and I start talking, talking, talking. The waves of the drug keep sweeping through me and my palms turn sweaty and I grit my teeth. I tell Lauren about the book I've written and the job I want to get at this magazine in L.A. and suddenly it doesn't seem like these are impossible dreams anymore. I feel like it is all happening – that my book is getting published and I can get any job I want and I'm gonna take Lauren along with me in my new life. Nothing, I mean nothing, can stop me.

'You know,' says Lauren, 'my parents are going out of town next week, so you should stay with me in my house, unless you have somewhere else to go.'

'No, no,' I say, everything fitting together perfectly in my world, in my mind, in destiny, and fate and blah, blah, blah. 'That'll be great.'

'They're gone for two weeks.'

I laugh.

Baker Beach is mostly empty. We pull into the parking lot and look out at the pounding shore break, sucking up the brown, coarse sand and dashing it to pieces against the slick, jagged rocks. The Golden Gate Bridge looms up to the right, and across the channel are the Marin Headlands – lush, green, rolling hills dotted with eucalyptus and oak, the red earth cliffs dropping down to the swirling water below. We get out of the car and I take Lauren's cold little soft hand in mine. We walk down along the dunes and the wind is blowing sand in my face, and suddenly I stop and strip off all my clothes down to my boxer briefs and run, headlong, into the surf. I hear Lauren giggling behind me, then nothing but the roar of the ocean and the cold, cold, cold.

The current is strong and I'm immediately struggling against it, ducking the swells and feeling the pull out the mouth of the bay. But I'm a good swimmer. I navigate past the rocks and begin paddling into the waves as they break along the beach. Growing up I'd surfed all along this coastline. My friends and I would stay out sometimes five or six hours. In the end I'd gotten very comfortable in the water, able to ride the big waves off Ocean Beach or down in Santa Cruz. I'd watch the pelicans riding the updrafts of the swells, or sea otters eating crabs, floating on their backs. I'd wake up early, heading out before the sun rose to get the morning glass. But as I got deeper and deeper into my using, my surfboards went untouched on their racks in the garage. I lost interest. There's something devastating about that, though I try not to think about it.

I mean, here I am, bodysurfing the breakers at Baker Beach, feeling my breath catch in my lungs from the frigid water. The muscle memory is all there, in my arms and chest. I look back at Lauren, stripped and lying in the warm sand. I take another wave in, then run up to her, kissing the white of her stomach and listening to her laugh and shiver. Then I run on, up and down the beach. Fast, freezing, but not feeling it, really. I look at everything, the trees, and shells, and tall sea grass. It all seems so new and exciting. My little sister, Daisy, never failed to point out the delicate flowers or intricately shaped stones as we went on walks together. She was so present and filled with wonder. Meth gives me that childlike exuberance. It allows me to see, to really see. The world appears miraculous and I laugh and run down the beach until I'm gasping for air – then back to Lauren.

She smiles at me and I kiss her some more.

That night I drive her car through the winding back roads out to our house in Point Reyes. The drive is so familiar. I know every turn. It's the same route I'd used to get back from school every afternoon. We pass the little towns of San Anselmo and Fairfax, curving beneath the redwood forest of Samuel P. Taylor State Park. Then we come out on the green pastureland, obscured by the darkness and fog. We turn up our street, steep, steep, bordered by dense woods on either side. The car sputters some, but makes it – taking me home.

My parents' house isn't huge or anything, but it is designed by some famous architect. It's sort of very Japanese and minimalist, with mirrors and windows all over the place. It looks out on maybe half an acre of garden – wild, tangled vines, hedges, oaks, poplars. Gravel paths twist through the brush and in the spring and summer there are flowers everywhere.

Seeing that the driveway is empty and the lights are out, I creep along to the different doors and windows and things. It's all locked. I climb the faded wooden gate, wander over to the back doors until I find one that isn't dead-bolted solid. I yank it open, breaking the base of the door where it has been secured to the floor. Turning on as few lights as possible, I go through the house to the front and let Lauren in.

'Jesus,' she says. 'I remember these paintings.'

My stepmother is an artist. The walls of our house are covered with giant, swirling canvases. The oil images are dark yet organic – eyes, organs, branches, shapes repeated over and over.

'They're beautiful,' I say. 'So haunting, right?'

'Yeah.'

We go up to the living room and I put music on the stereo – some electronic stuff I left the last time I'd been home. I open a bottle of sake I find in the closet and pour a glass. Lauren looks at all the art books and things on the shelves. I look at the photographs of my little brother and sister on the windowsill. There is one of Jasper in his lacrosse uniform, smiling. There is Daisy, who's just two years younger than Jasper, dressed as an elf, with a fake beard and her tangled hair pulled back. And there is the whole family together, my stepmom, her parents, brother, sister, my dad, my aunt and uncle, my brother, sister, cousins, and, on the far right, me. Walking through the house, I feel dirty – like I'm this charcoal stain polluting everything I touch. I can't even look at the goddamn photographs – it hurts too much. I drink the sake down.

'Let's go take a shower,' I say.

'Yeah. You wanna fix some more first?'

'Definitely.'

We shoot up and take a shower. We have sex in my old bed until my knees are rubbed raw. After that, I smoke cigarettes and look for stuff to steal. I take a guitar and a couple jackets, but nothing bigger than that. Oh, and I need a notebook, so I grab this black thing with Powerpuff Girls stickers on the cover. It turns out to be my sister's diary.

Day 4

We spend the night in some kitschy Art Deco motel off Lombard – the outside all mosaicked with bright-colored tiles. Lauren doesn't actually stay past midnight. Her parents were worried and wondering where she is. I listen to her talking with her father on the phone. Her voice trembles – wanting desperately to sound ... what, innocent? Something like that. Of course, there'd been times when I'd done the same thing – lying about being sober, trying to hide the fact that I'd relapsed. Lauren is able to convince her parents – at least for now. They believe her, I suppose, because they want to. My parents had been that way.

I got thrown into my first treatment center when I was eighteen. I had been doing meth for only about six months, but already my life had begun falling apart. I dropped out of college and ended up having a sort of breakdown – wandering the streets and talking to people who weren't there. I didn't really come out of it until a police car was pulling up beside me. The officer threatened to arrest me but eventually let me go.

My dad helped me get into rehab five days later – a large, Victorian-style, falling-down mansion on Fell and Steiner. I still remember walking in there that first day. It had threadbare red carpeting, a rotted, creaking stairway, and long, misshapen, warped hallways leading to room after room of beds, beds, beds. There must have been around fifty of us in that house – all men. We had groups all day where we were educated about substance abuse, twelve steps, and how to live life sober. Walking through those green-painted wooden doors, my whole body was shaking and I felt like maybe I'd throw up or something. My dad was there beside me, wearing that same old wool sweater he used to shelter me in as a child. His hair was clipped short, black and gray. His square glasses obscured his eyes, which were red from almost crying. Maybe he was shaking too.

'Dad, please,' I begged him. 'I'll stop, I promise. Please, I don't need to do this.'

'You can't come home, Nic.'

'But Dad, I don't belong here.'

I was wrong. I knew it the first group I went to. One of the residents, Johnny, a squat little man with scraggy facial hair and a dyed black Mohawk, told his story. He talked about his descent into crack/cocaine addiction. What struck me wasn't so much the specifics of his story, but rather the feelings he described. He talked about how until he started using, he had always felt like some alien, different from everybody. I think what he said was, 'I felt like everyone else had gotten this instruction manual that explained life to them, but somehow I'd just missed it. They all seemed to know exactly what they were doing while I didn't have a clue. That is, until I found drugs and alcohol. Then it was like my world suddenly went from black-and-white to Technicolor.'

Of course that had been my experience too, but it didn't mean I was willing to change my behavior. I loved drugs. I loved what they did for me. They relieved me of that terrible sense of isolation I had always felt. They gave me the manual to life that Johnny had described. I could not, NOT give that up.

But my parents were so hopeful and the counselors would give you more privileges if you cooperated, so I did. I said what they wanted me to say. I shared about my commitment to repairing the damage I had caused. I talked about being willing to adopt the spiritual principles outlined in the twelve steps. And I suppose part of me meant it. I didn't want to become like some of the other men at Ohlhoff House, grizzled, toothless, having lost everything. But I still had this feeling like it could never happen to me. I had a 4.0 in high school, for Christ's sake. I was a published writer. I came from a good family. Besides, I was too young to really be an addict. I was just experimenting, right?

They released me thirty days later and I moved into a halfway house in the city. I stayed sober three days. Then, one night, I said I was going to a meeting, but drove to hook up crystal instead. The car just seemed to drive itself across the bridge to Oakland. I never came back that night. When my parents found out, I was forced to go into another thirty-day program in Napa. After that I managed to stay clean for over a month, but when I went away to college in Amherst, Massachusetts, I quickly relapsed again. This time, however, I was able to hide it from my parents. As my behavior grew more erratic (stealing credit cards, writing checks to myself) and my lies more improbable (I just wanted to buy presents for Jasper and Daisy), my dad continued to dismiss what was happening – I was wasting away in front of him.

By the time I finished my first year of school, my using had progressed to the point where I could no longer really hide it. At first it was just drinking and smoking pot, a little acid, but then I started asking around to get my hands on some meth. But since there was no crystal I could find in western Massachusetts, I started using heroin. I'd drive my girlfriend's car into the slums of Hollyhock and just walk around till the offers started coming in. There was little doubt as to what a young white kid was doing wandering those streets. But the drug was expensive and snorting the white granulated powder was a waste.

That was my excuse to start sticking myself with needles. Putting the drug straight into the vein allowed me to conserve it a little more. I stole the syringes from the science lab. I taught myself to shoot up by looking at a diagram on the Internet. It was a messy process. I'd miss the vein and pump the drug right into my muscles. It would burn so bad. I didn't realize the veins were just under the skin's surface, so I'd dig way too deep. Before long, my arms were covered in puncture marks and I'd lost a lot of weight.

When I came home for summer vacation, I had my first experience with opiate withdrawals. It was just like in the movies – I was throwing up, shivering, sweating, scratching at my skin like there were termites crawling underneath.

At first I tried lying to my parents, saying I had a stomach flu or something. The first moment I could get away, I went to get some meth from my friends in the city.

Once I started IVing that drug, well, that was pretty much the end. After being off crystal for so long, my tolerance had gone back to nothing. Shooting it, the effect was so powerful, I plunged immediately into a period of about a week where, to this day, I have no idea what I did.

I came to out of this blackout in my bed at my parents' house. I could hear crying from the living room. My little brother's voice was shattered by tears.

'Where is it? Where is it?'

I felt that familiar sickness in my stomach.

'Are you sure it was in there?' my dad asked.

'Yes,' wailed Jasper. 'I had five dollars in there. Daisy, you took it.'

'NO, I DIDN'T!' She was crying too and screaming.

I got out of bed and started to pack. I didn't remember taking the money, but I knew I had.

There was nowhere for me to go, really, but I couldn't stay. I filled my bag with as much as I could carry. I hoisted it on my shoulder, put my eyes on the floor, and started walking out of there.

Out in the living room, my dad and stepmom stood blocking my exit – their faces red and contorted.

'Where are you going?' my father demanded, on the verge of yelling.

'I'm leaving.'

'Nic, we know you're using again.'

'Yeah,' I said – my head down. 'I'm not coming back.'

'This is bullshit,' my stepmom exploded, stomping across the room and slamming a door somewhere.

'You can't just leave,' my dad said, the tears coming now.

'I have to.'

'We'll get you help.'

'No. I need to do this.'

'Nic, no, stop.' He reached out and tried to physically stop me. I pushed him hard.

'What the hell are you doing?' I screamed. 'Jesus Christ, you people suffocate me.'

The truth was, I didn't want to stop. It's not like I enjoyed stealing or hurting my dad, or whatever. I mean, I hated it. But I was so scared of coming off the drugs. It was like this horrible vicious cycle. The more I used, the more I did things I was ashamed of, and the more I had to use so I never had to face that. When I reached a certain point with my drug use, going back just seemed like too far a journey. Accepting responsibility, admitting guilt, making restitution, hell, just saying I'm sorry – it had become too daunting. All I could do was move forward and keep doing everything in my power to forget the past. So I marched out into the hot summer air. I hitchhiked to the bus stop and made my way to my friend Akira's.

After that my parents really stopped believing anything I said. But Lauren obviously hasn't taken things as far as I have. Her parents are still willing to give her the benefit of the doubt or something. So she leaves me alone in that motel room and I write and draw for a while, listen to CDs, then actually sleep a few hours. When I wake up, I'm hungry and almost out of meth. I call Gack and he agrees to meet me at twelve thirty in the TL. I drive to North Beach to get breakfast.

When I was little, maybe six or seven, my dad and I lived at the top of California Street. It was a high-rise apartment that looked out on the cable cars and the gothic towers of Grace Cathedral. It was across the street from a small park with a sandbox, swings, and a wooden play structure. My dad would take me there to play in the mornings, then we'd walk together down to North Beach – the Italian district of San Francisco. We'd go to Caffe Trieste, a rustic coffee shop on the corner of Grant. I would hold his calloused hand and watch the pigeons and the cracks in the sidewalk. Inside the café, my dad would order me hot chocolate and a raspberry pastry ring. We would sit at a corner table – me drawing and my father writing in a notebook. He would drink cappuccinos. Sometimes we wouldn't write or draw at all; we'd just talk. I'd run my fingers over the mosaicked tabletop and smell the coffee and ask my dad questions about things. He would make jokes and tell me stories. Opera would play from the jukebox.

After breakfast maybe we'd walk over to City Lights Books – a damp, earthy-smelling printing house and bookshop. We'd walk past the sex show parlors and strip bars. After dark, women in tight leather costumes would hang around in front of the entrances, luring in passing johns. I remember thinking they were superheroes – Wonder Woman, Catwoman, Supergirl. I would talk with them and they all knew my name.

Driving through North Beach this morning, I look out at the streets of my childhood. I stop my car and walk up to Caffe Trieste. Men and women stand outside talking and smoking. The sky has opened up blue and clear – the wind blowing hard off the bay. I go inside and order some coffee and a sandwich. I sit in the back at the same old table – the same old music coming from the speakers. I shoot up the last of the gram in their bathroom. The place is small and poorly lit. Someone keeps banging on the door 'cause it's taking me so long to find a vein. Once I hit, I start to pump in the mixture, but my hand shakes and I shoot a bunch of it into the muscle of my arm. It burns something terrible and I groan in pain. My whole right arm goes numb and aches. I curse loudly and go to meet Gack. There is blood all over my arm when I walk outta there.

Gack has me meet him in front of the hotel where he lives with his dad. It is named after some saint, but it looks like hell – barred windows, the paint peeling down to nothing, stripped away. He has a teener for me. I ask him if he wants to shoot some up with me right then, since I pretty much wasted the last one. He agrees and we go inside.

The woman who runs the hotel is Indian and wears a traditional sari, with a bindi on her forehead and everything. She makes me give her my driver's license in order to go up. She scowls through her thick, oversize glasses, her hair pulled back tight.

'You stay only one hour. Otherwise you pay.'

I follow Gack up the rotted-out, stained, carpeted stairs, to the third floor. Hollowed-out men and women pace the halls, smoking cigarettes and calling out to us with offers of different crap we can buy.

'Hey, kids,' says a stoned-out-looking black man with a bald, shiny head. 'I gotta get rid of this keyboard. You wanna buy it?' He holds up a small electric piano out for us to see.

'Does it work?' asks Gack.

'Yeah, man, it works good. You wanna try it out?'

'Sure. Nic, you gotta second?'

'Sure, sure, fine, whatever.'

We follow the man back to his room. What it looks like is, well, just trashed. The bed has no sheets or anything and it looks like it is covered in dried blood. The floor is all ash and wrappers and porno mags and beer cans and tinfoil and videotapes. The man introduces himself as Jim. He shakes our hands. He clears off some clothes from the bed. He plugs the piano in, switches it on, and plays a simple chord progression, singing some R & B love song. His voice is deep and moving.

'Right on. How much?' asks Gack.

'Twenty.'

'Twenty?'

'All right, ten. Look, man, I just wanna get high, that's all. Ten bucks'll get me through the night.'

'All right, ten bucks.'

Gack hands him the money. Somehow he manages to pull exactly ten dollars out of his pocket, without exposing the rest of his wad. The man takes the money quickly and stuffs it in his jeans. 'Right on, right on.'

We walk back out into the hallway and into Gack's room.

'This is so great,' says Gack, holding up the keyboard.

'Yeah, that'll be fun to mess around with.'

'No, man, you don't understand. This is a start, a first step in recognizing my dream. I'm gonna start making music.'

I don't know what to say about that.

Gack's room is even more trashed than Jim's was. Gay porn and cigarette butts and ripped paper and wrappers and shoes and jars of peanut butter and boxes of cookies are scattered all over the floor and bed. There is a washbasin in one corner filled with dishes. A computer put together with mismatching parts sits on the dresser. The fluorescent lights shine too bright and buzz overhead. Gack sets about clearing off a space to try out the keyboard.

'Hey, man,' I say. 'You got any more rigs or what?'

'Yeah. There are some cleans in that bag over there.' He points to a brown paper bag on the bedside table.

I reach over and find the needles and set about making us two big-ass shots. Gack asks if I want him to shoot me up. I hold out my arm and he inserts the point effortlessly and efficiently right into my vein. There is something chilling and erotic about the whole thing. He pumps the drug up inside me and I cough and feel the rush and it is so lovely, I mean, really.

Gack shoots himself up and I say, 'Hey, you wanna walk around with me or something?'

'Walk around?'

'Yeah, man, I've been away from the city for, like, over two years.'

'All right, cool.'

We walk back down the stairs. I get my ID back from the Indian woman and then we're out on the street, moving fast down toward the water.

'Was that really your dad the other day?' I ask, just trying to think of something to say.

Gack stuffs his hands in his pockets, his arms jerking convulsively. 'Yeah, man.'

'You live together?'

'Uh, yeah. I never knew him until a year ago. I was adopted when I was, like, two or something.'

'Weird, man. How'd you all hook up again?'

'I guess he just decided he wanted to meet me, so he came and found me at my adopted parents' house.'

'And you just went to go live with him?'

'Yeah. He's pretty cool. Sometimes he'll bring guys back to the room, which is kinda fucked up.'

'Guys?'

'Uh-huh. He's gay.'

We walk on. The clouds are blowing fast overhead and I keep smoking cigarettes and bumming them out to Gack. Gack talks a lot of nonsense about different things – his plans for the future, things like that. I'm not sure where the idea to ask Gack to help me comes from. Suddenly I just trust him completely and I come out with it, walking down Market – toward the shadow of the Bay Bridge.

'Look, man,' I say. 'I'm just puttin' this out there – so hear me out for a second. I've got about twenty-five hundred dollars left, okay. I'd been sober eighteen months, working, and I saved that up. Now, with a habit like I've got, I'm gonna burn through that pretty quick, unless I can figure out some way to make some money. So here's what I was thinking. I don't really know you, right? And you don't know me, but you've been cool to me so far and I have this feeling about you.'

'You felt it too, huh?' he says, stopping to pick up a crumpled bag on the sidewalk. He looks inside, finds nothing, and then throws it down again.

'Yeah,' I say.

'I knew we were gonna be friends.'

'What?'

'Yep, when I saw you that first day.'

'Maybe I did too. Look, you know, I really respect you and all and I was just thinking we could buy, like, some big quantity of meth and then break it down and sell it together.'

'Word. We should cut it.'

'Cut it?'

'Yeah, man. We'll buy a bunch of really good shit, then cut it with, like, Epsom salts or something. I'll sell that shit so fast, man, and we'll be able to use for free, maybe get a place to stay. I could, like, work for you. We could start our own syndicate, man. We'll get walkie-talkies and shit.'

'Well, just think about it, man.'

'Fo'sure.'

'And you know someone that could get us quantity for pretty cheap?'

'I think so. Let me just make some calls. You wanna do this now?'

'Well, uh, all right, sure. And, hey, do you know where I can get some heroin?'

'No doubt. What you want me to work on first?'

'The H, I guess.'

'Cool, brother. Let me see your phone. Bullet'll be able to help us out.'

'Bullet?'

'Yeah. I'll page him.'

'Word.'

'Just let me get another cigarette.'

I give him two.

Bullet is homeless. He is tall and thin, thin, with a carved-up face and greasy hair slicked back. His nose is sort of twisted and broken. There's an off-white scar running down his face and his Adam's apple sticks out dramatically. He wears a backward baseball hat, loose-fitting pants, combat boots, and he smells like stale sweat and urine. His walk is clumsy, with those spindly legs of his and a head that is continuously bobbing back and forth.

'Gack, man, how come you never call me?' He whines when he talks – always.

'Dude, I've been busy.'

'But you guys wanna score some dope, huh?'

'Yeah,' I say.

'Well, I got a number – but maybe we could work out a deal or something before I give it up.'

Gack and I drove to meet Bullet at the Safeway on Church and Market. It is a well-known hangout for street kids and runaways. For one thing, you can go into Safeway and graze out of the dried fruit and nut bins without too much trouble. Plus there is one of those private, self-cleaning toilets out front that is great to shoot up in. It is already getting to be dark and the lights on Twin Peaks are flickering on and off, on and off.

'A deal like what?'

'Like you give me a nice fat shot in exchange for the hookup.'

'No problem.'

'The girl's name is Candy. Here's the number. Don't lose it.' He writes it on the front page of my sister's diary that I've stolen. There is a drawing of a girl with pigtails pointing at blotchy squares on a wall. Underneath it, Daisy'd written: 'We are in L.A. with Nic. We went to a museum. We saw Napoleon things.' That had been this past January, just two months earlier. My family had driven down to see me and we'd all gone to the Museum of Jurassic Technology on Venice Boulevard. Daisy went on to describe the museum and what she ate for lunch. Then she wrote something about seeing me and how I looked sad. She said it made her stomach feel all 'fluddery.'

Reading it, I know just how she felt. My stomach feels fluddery. I wonder if there might be a way to get the diary back to her. It was the last thing I ever wanted to take from her and yet, well, I did it. That's always how it goes for me, isn't it?

Anyway, I call Candy. Her voice is so soft I can barely hear her, but I manage to convince her to meet me at the video store around the corner. She shows up in a yellow Cadillac with a tattered fur coat and dyed black hair that is light at the roots. She wears thick pancake makeup over broken-out skin. She is probably around thirty-something.

'You want two grams, right?'

'Yeah.'

She hands me four tiny balls wrapped in colored wax paper. I give her eighty bucks.

'This is great,' she says. 'Do you always buy this much at one time?'

'I guess.'

'Well, call me any time.'

When I get back to my car, Bullet and Gack are hanging out, laughing and making fun of each other.

'Gack told me your plan,' says Bullet. 'You guys are gonna start your own little dealing syndicate, huh?'

'Sort of.'

'Well,' he says. 'You'll never be able to do it without my help.'

'Why?'

''Cause every crime syndicate needs some muscle.' And with that, he pulls out a giant bowie knife from somewhere and waves it through the air.

I suck in a bunch of breath all at once.

'You got that junk?' he demands.

'Yeah.'

'Well, let's go then.' He puts the knife away and we drive down some side street to shoot up.

Gack doesn't want any heroin, but he sits with us. I melt down half a gram of the sweet-smelling black tar in the jar I took from Lauren's. We suck up the syrupy brown liquid in two needles and push it all home. I wait: one, two, three, four. My head starts to tingle and I feel waves of pulsing calm sweep over me. My body goes slack and I look over at Bullet. He is smiling so big. I drift off somewhere for a minute. It is like everything is infused with this warmth and okayness. I laugh. 'Shit's good.'

'Word.'

'So, Gack,' I say. 'Should we let Bullet in?'

'Hell yeah, man, he's a good kid.'

'That what you want, Bullet?'

'I'm your boy.'

'Awesome.'

'We should come up with a name or something,' says Gack. 'We're gonna start the next big street gang in San Francisco. Before long, we'll have all the kids workin' for us.'

We sit back, talking on like that. I nod in and out, not giving a damn about one goddamn thing – knowing, just knowing, that it is all gonna work out.

addaction

If you've been affected by the issues in this book you can reach out to Addaction for support. Have a friendly, confidential chat with a trained advisor through Addaction's web chat service at www.addaction.org.uk

Addaction is a leading UK charity specialising in supporting people with drug, alcohol and mental health problems. We believe everyone can change and we support them to do it.